PHENOMENOLOGICAL SOCIOLOGY

»»»»»»»»»»»»»»»»»»»»»»»»»»»»«««««««««««««««««««««««

PHENOMENOLOGICAL SOCIOLOGY

Issues and Applications

»»»»»»»»»»»»»»»»»»»»»»»»»»»»»»»«««««««««««««««««««««««««

Edited by

GEORGE PSATHAS

A Wiley-Interscience Publication

JOHN WILEY & SONS, New York · London · Sydney · Toronto

To my father,

MILTON E. PSATHAS

Copyright © 1973, by John Wiley & Sons, Inc.

Library of Congress Cataloging in Publication Data:

Psathas, George.
    Phenomenological sociology.

    "A Wiley-Interscience publication."
    Includes bibliographical references.
    1. Sociology—Addresses, essays, lectures.
2. Phenomenology—Addresses, essays, lectures.
Zaner, Richard M.   II. Title.

HM24.P8   301   73-2805
ISBN 0-471-70152-1

Printed in the United States of America

10 9 8 7 6 5 4 3 2

ACKNOWLEDGMENTS

»»»»»»»»»»»»»»»»»»»»»»» «

The first session on Phenomenological Sociology at the meetings of the American Sociological Association in August 1971, in Denver, Colorado, provided the major impetus for this book. I had written to the President of the ASA, William Sewell, in July, 1970, as follows: My impressions are that phenomenological sociology is growing and considerable writing is beginning to appear. There are many young sociologists who are doing research in what I would call phenomenological sociology though not self-consciously so. A session that would be devoted to the topic itself and to the question of the possibility of a phenomenological sociology might be a good beginning point.

My specific hope was that a paper by a philosopher of the social sciences could introduce the main issues and possibilities for a phenomenological sociology and spark a greater interest among sociologists in this, for many still undiscovered, aspect of themselves. Professor Richard Zaner, whose editing, annotating, and introduction to Schutz' unfinished manuscript, *Reflections on the Problem of Relevance*, I had recently reviewed, came to mind as one who was most qualified for such a presentation. His training in philosophy, his first-hand acquaintance with Alfred Schutz, first as his student and later his editor and translator, and his familiarity with the social sciences provided him with a rare perspective—

v

and one that would be most appropriate for the occasion. His paper, "Solitude and Sociality: The Critical Foundations of the Social Sciences," was presented at that session in Denver and appears as the first paper in this book.

But the presentation by a philosopher should, it seemed to me, be discussed by sociologists who had also studied the same issues from within the sociological tradition. They would be asked to critically comment on and discuss Zaner's paper, preparing their remarks in advance. Kurt Wolff, whose seminars at Brandeis on Alfred Schutz and whose translation and editing of the works of Georg Simmel and Karl Mannheim indicated a thorough familiarity with the phenomenological tradition, was invited to be the first discussant. His remarks, now expanded for publication, appear as the second paper in this volume, "Toward Radicalism in Sociology and Everyday."

Helmut Wagner had recently completed an edition of Alfred Schutz' work for the series by the University of Chicago Press in the Heritage of Sociology in which he carefully selected and organized the writings of Schutz, drawing from his various papers and books. He accepted an invitation to be the second discussant. His comments have been substantially expanded to constitute the third paper in this book, "The Scope of Phenomenological Sociology: Considerations and Suggestions."

Thus three key papers, the latter two inspired by the first, developed from that occasion and formed the nucleus for a book that could introduce the possibilities of phenomenological sociology to an audience larger than the one assembled in the convention meeting on that one day.

At the same ASA meetings I also organized a more informal seminar session on Phenomenological Sociology, a second "first," as it were. At that seminar Roger Jehenson contributed not only informed comments but demonstrations of a grasp of issues in phenomenological sociology. Subsequent to this, I asked him to submit a paper on his research for this volume, "A Phenomenological Approach to the Study of the Formal Organization."

Special mention must be made of Herbert Spiegelberg, whose Workshops on Phenomenology, which I attended at Washington University in St. Louis in 1967, contributed immeasurably to my acquaintance with the philosophical tradition. His paper "On the Right to Say 'We': A Linguistic and Phenomenological Analysis" was first presented as the second Alfred Schutz Memorial Lecture at Boston University in 1972. It was at the Workshop that my own interest in discerning essential features of face-to-face interaction was stimulated. Subsequent discussions and collaboration with Fran Waksler advanced this work.

My acquaintance with Fred Dallmayr began at the meetings of the Society for Phenomenology and Existential Philosophy in 1970, where

I was impressed with the breadth and scope of his scholarship in his paper on "Phenomenology and Social Science." He undertook the paper for this volume, "Phenomenology and Marxism," a major task, in the same spirit of critical scholarship.

Other contributors include persons whose work was already familiar to me. Alex Blumenstiel, whose paper on the "Sociology of Good Times" impressed me immediately with its originality and Simmelian vision; Egon Bittner, whose studies of the police on skid row had first called to my attention how phenomenologically based studies of the everyday world could be done with brilliant clarity and without jargon; John O'Neill with whom I had discussed the need for new approaches in sociology at the ASA meetings in 1969; and Peter Manning and Horacio Fabrega, Jr. who had undertaken collaborative and imaginative ventures relating sociology, anthropology, and medicine in cross-cultural studies of health and illness.

To each of these contributors I am grateful for their interest and willingness to participate in a venture whose birth could not be predicted with certainty and whose life, if born, could not be foretold.

I wish to thank the Boston University Graduate School for support provided and Marian Hughes for editorial and typing assistance. To my wife, Irma, thanks are but a token of all that she knows I feel.

I am especially grateful to Peter Manning for his encouragement and helpfulness, Herbert Spiegelberg for his constant support of the building of bridges between philosophy and sociology, and of course William Sewell and the American Sociological Association who helped us all to get started.

GEORGE PSATHAS

Boston University
Boston, Massachusetts
April 1973

INFORMATION ABOUT THE CONTRIBUTORS

»»»»»»»»»»»»»»»»»»»»»»»»» «« «« «« «« «« «« «« «« «« «« «« «« «« «« ««

RICHARD M. ZANER is Professor of Humanities and Chairman of the Division of Health Sciences and Humanities, the Health Sciences Center, and Professor of Philosophy at the State University of New York at Stony Brook. Prior to this he had served as Chairman of the Department of Philosophy at the University of Texas. He received his Ph.D. from the New School for Social Research and studied with Alfred Schutz. His works include *The Problem of Embodiment*, editing of Alfred Schutz' unfinished manuscript, *Reflections on the Problem of Relevance*, and, most recently, *The Way of Phenomenology: Criticism as a Philosophical Discipline*.

KURT H. WOLFF is Yellen Professor of Social Relations at Brandeis University. He has published papers in numerous professional journals, has edited books on the sociology of Emile Durkheim, Georg Simmel, and Karl Mannheim, is co-editor of *The Critical Spirit: Essays in Honor of Herbert Marcuse*, and author of two books in German and of the forthcoming *Trying Sociology*. His most recent work in phenomenological sociology is *Surrender and Catch: A Palimpsest Story* (a pamphlet).

HELMUT R. WAGNER, now at Hobart and William Smith Colleges, formerly taught sociology at Bucknell University and was a Lecturer for the

Graduate Faculty at the New School for Social Research. He recently edited for the Heritage of Sociology Series, University of Chicago Press, the selected writings of Alfred Schutz, *On Phenomenology and Social Relations*.

JOHN O'NEILL is Professor of Sociology at York University, Toronto, Canada. He has published a book on the social phenomenology of Merleau-Ponty, *Perception, Expression, and History*, and most recently, *Sociology as a Skin Trade: Essays Towards a Reflexive Sociology*. He is an editor of the international quarterly *Philosophy of the Social Sciences*.

EGON BITTNER is Coplan Professor in the Social Sciences at Brandeis University and has taught at the University of California, Riverside, and the University of California Medical School, San Francisco. He worked with Harold Garfinkel and took part in the development of ethnomethodology. He has done research on the everyday routines of police work, formal organizations, radicalism, and, most recently, the phenomenology of blindness.

HERBERT SPIEGELBERG is Professor of Philosophy at Washington University, St. Louis, now emeritus. He studied in Heidelberg, Freiburg, and Munich and wrote his doctoral dissertation under Alexander Pfänder. He has been in the United States since 1938 and has taught at Swarthmore and Lawrence Colleges and at Washington University. He published the comprehensive historical introduction to *The Phenomenological Movement* in 1960. His most recent book is *Phenomenology in Psychology and Psychiatry;* in addition he has written articles of interest to sociologists such as "Some Human Uses of Phenomenology," "Phenomenology Through Vicarious Experience," "Toward a Phenomenology of Imaginative Understanding of Others," and "The Relevance of Phenomenological Philosophy for Psychology."

FRANCES C. WAKSLER, Assistant Professor of Sociology at Wheelock College, recently completed her doctorate at Boston University. In her research studies she has been interested in describing empirical instances as well as analyzing, from a phenomenological perspective, face-to-face interaction.

ALEXANDER D. BLUMENSTIEL received his doctorate in sociology at Washington University, St. Louis. He has taught at the University of Missouri (St. Louis) and Queens College and is currently Assistant Professor of Sociology at Boston University. He is involved in research studies on the sociology of good times as well as the development of audiovisual research methods in sociology.

ROGER JEHENSON majored in industrial sociology at the University of Louvain, Belgium, and industrial social psychology at the University of Montreal. He received his doctorate in the department of administrative sciences at Yale University. He is currently Associate Professor in the School of Business and Administrative Sciences, University of New Mexico, and his research interests include the development of a theory of formal organizations inspired by both phenomenological and ordinary language analysis.

PETER K. MANNING is Associate Professor of Sociology and Psychiatry at Michigan State University. He received his Ph.D. at Duke University and in 1972–1973 is Visiting Scholar at London University Goldsmith's College. His forthcoming book is titled *Explaining Deviance*.

HORACIO FABREGA, JR., is Associate Professor of Psychiatry and Anthopology at Michigan State University. He has collaborated with Manning on several articles and in research. Their most recent work is on cross-cultural studies of the experience of illness.

FRED R. DALLMAYR, Professor of Political Science at the University of Georgia, has his Doctor of Law degree from the University of Munich and his Ph.D. in political science from Duke University. His most recent writings include "Phenomenology and Social Science," "History and Class Consciousness: Georg Lukács' Theory of Social Change," "Reason and Emancipation: Notes on Habermas," and "Toward a Critical Reconstruction of Ethics and Politics."

CONTENTS

»»»»»»»»»»»»»»»»»»»»»»»»»»«««««««««««««««««««««««««

Contents

INTRODUCTION

»»»»»»»»»»»»»»»»»»»»»»»»«««««««««««««««««««««««««

George Psathas

The plan of this book is to present the reader who is not well versed and relatively unsophisticated in phenomenology with an advanced introduction into phenomenological social science and particularly phenomenological sociology. Our concern is to demonstrate the relevance and application of phenomenology to the wide range of problems that have been the traditional concerns of social scientists: communication, interaction, organizations, groups, and society.

 Among the contributors, the social scientists have been actively involved in making such applications, and the philosophers have been contributing studies of considerable theoretical significance. As a function of the current stage of development of a phenomenologically based social science, many of these authors find it necessary to elaborate the theoretical and philosophical underpinnings of their work before proceeding with their studies. Although they may therefore spend considerably more time than they would prefer in arguing for the importance of their approach than in proceeding with applications, their self-consciousness will be instructive to those of us who have yet to go through the struggle of work-

1

ing out and eventually adopting new ways of thought or basing research on different assumptions. Learning to see the social world through different lenses, which I believe a phenomenologically based approach requires, can be facilitated by watching and listening closely to others who have undertaken this intellectual venture. There is value to programmatic statements and overviews of particular theoretical issues since our thinking may be redirected, new paths may be considered, and social support, which even scholars require in the social endeavor of solitary thought, may be provided. Such presentations are opportunities for us to rehearse in our own imagination the idea of a phenomenological approach to the study of social phenomena as different as face-to-face communication and national revolutions and to ask ourselves how research might proceed, what assumptions would have to be made, what kinds of observations would be needed, what interpretative schemas would be applied, and what generalizations would result. Thus programmatic statements can serve the valuable function of orienting, clarifying, and directing our thought.

The reader will find here some discussions of basic theoretical issues and some applications of the phenomenological approach to specific topics of study. It is hoped that this blend of theory and application will expand our vision of what a phenomenologically based social science can contribute to our understanding of man in the social world. These papers span a range of interests found in contemporary sociology and social science and, in this respect, are not exceptional but representative.

HISTORICAL OVERVIEW

Phenomenology is philosophy, method, and approach. As such, phenomenology cannot easily be explicated, particularly when it is still developing and refuses to stand still.

From the days when its major founder, Edmund Husserl, began his contributions to this development, there has been no cessation of phenomenological thought and research (1). The influence of phenomenology on sociology, psychology, and psychiatry—in America more recently than in Europe—has resulted in an increased awareness of this history.

Although not explicitly influenced by phenomenological philosophy, the works of many of the major figures in the development of modern sociology were concerned with theoretical and methodological issues that were also to receive systematic attention and clarification in phenomenology. The work of some may be said to be prephenomenological (Weber) or at best phenomenological in method or spirit (Simmel); others' work is parallel, even converging at times, but more inspiring to the mainstream workers in phenomenology than in the stream themselves (James, Cooley, Mead, Thomas); and the work of others represents a genuine immersion in and contribution to phenomenological social science (Scheler, Schutz).

This overview does not intend to "claim" all these thinkers for phenomenological sociology but rather to show that a rich tradition exists in social theory for the treatment of issues phenomenology has also addressed. The possibility that a phenomenological approach can contribute to the understanding and solution of some of these problems is before us.

Max Weber (1864–1920) (2), one of the leading figures in the development of modern sociology, defined the sociological enterprise as one involving the "interpretative understanding (*verstehen*) of social action." In action he included "all human behavior when and insofar as . . . by virtue of the subjective meaning attached to it by the acting individual, it takes account of the behavior of others and is thereby oriented in its course" (3).

The individual is the important unit in Weber's sociology, and he regards social collectivities as the result and mode of organization of acts by individuals. Concepts that refer to groups or collective activities need to be explained in terms of understandable actions of individuals. In his work, he used the method of ideal types and sought to study typical social action. Weber also proposed methods for determining the adequacy of analyses and explanations that might be developed by the social scientist for subjective meanings. His awareness of and constant effort to understand the subjective aspects of human conduct has provided a powerful influence for directing social scientists' attention to this dimension.

Georg Simmel (1858–1918) (4), in his development of "formal sociology" and his insistence on the study of forms of sociation, showed an approach to the understanding of social phenomena that saw through the particular variations of content and setting to underlying uniformities. In this sense, Simmel's approach was eidetic, the search for forms resembling the phenomenological quest for underlying essential properties or features: ". . . if society is conceived as interaction among individuals, the description of the forms of this interaction is the task of the science of society in its strictest and most essential sense" (5).

Forms, as Simmel sees them, develop in interaction, are influenced by the individual actors, but also influence them. Forms can operate on individuals because they "understand" the situation and the demands placed upon them by its typicalities. The "understanding" of a situation—that is, the grasping of its essential and typical features—is, for Simmel, not restricted to those situations culture has revealed to the actors as typical. Simmel's formal sociology "rests on the assumption that meaningful action can originate in the individuals. It is this assumption which allows for the peculiar understanding of society in which man is at once object and subject, an understanding of society which grasps it in its static and dynamic aspects at the same time" (6).

Max Scheler (1874–1928) (7) was both philosopher and sociologist, and his study of sympathy is the most sociologically relevant phenomenological study. He examined the nature of sympathy to show the variety of experiences that were included under its heading and to distinguish among them. He also contributed clarifying distinctions in the analysis of the "I," the "Me," the Self, and the body in his effort to understand intersubjectivity. He distinguished between the empirical and the cultural in that empirical research was concerned with "real" factors such as drives and impulses, and the study of the cultural was to be concerned with ideas and values at the level of essential structures. His concern with the sociology of knowledge was, in part, an effort to analyze the empirical existent forms of culture.

Karl Mannheim (1893–1947) (8), who had been a student of Husserl, was also acquainted with Weber, Scheler, and Lukács. These influences in his intellectual life led to a blending of the phenomenological with the existential and also with Marxism. His contributions to the sociology of knowledge are profound, and he was instrumental in calling attention not only to the ideas and modes of thinking that may characterize a period or given level of society but also to the social setting and the social factors that affect the acceptance, rejection, or promotion of ideas by groups in society. By focusing on knowledge as an important topic for sociological investigation, Mannheim brought to the forefront the importance of the subjective dimension of social life. Not only are institutions and social structures which support and provide the framework for intellectual life and activity to be studied, but so are the persons, the individuals whose activities are part of and constitute that group, class, or collectively expressed thought. The historical and social formation of the thought of members of society becomes a matter of epistemological importance. In Mannheim's work, the meaningful structure of human activity is ever a subject of study—meanings continually emerge from social interaction and are subject to reinterpretation.

William James (1842–1910) (9), as philosopher and psychologist, contributed many writings dealing with the topics of consciousness, experience, and self. His analysis of the nature of consciousness reveals it to be a flowing "stream" rather than a series of discrete elements. Within each personal consciousness, James saw thought as constantly changing and "no state once gone can recur and be identical with what it was before." Yet thought is felt as continuous, for even where there is a time gap, the self perceives the consciousness as enduring and unbroken. The name for this sensed connectedness and continuity is *myself, I,* or *me.* "Consciousness does not appear to itself chopped up in bits. . . . It is nothing jointed; it flows. A 'river' or a 'stream' are the metaphors by which it is most naturally described. . . . Let us call it the stream of thought, of consciousness, or of subjective life" (10). Consciousness is seen also to be selective with purposive choices being made according to the criteria relevant to the knowing subject. There is considerable room for active attention and will in James' thought.

James' extensive discussions of the self led him to distinguish between various aspects of self and to the clarification of the self's relation to others. He distinguished between the I, the self as knower, and the Me, the self as known. His division of the self into material, social, and spiritual anticipates later social psychological analyses.

James' contributions to psychology and to social science generally are impressive. He ranged over a wide number of topics in general psychology, and his analysis of consciousness contributed even to Husserl's studies. His notions of the unity of consciousness, the distinction between "knowledge about" and "knowledge of acquaintance," his distinctions between the "object" and the "topic" of thought, and his distinction between the "train of thought" and its "conclusion" provide insights that parallel the conceptualizations developed in phenomenological analyses of these same topics. In short, James provides impressive support for some of the results of others' phenomenological analyses.

Charles Cooley (1864–1929), W. I. Thomas (1863–1947), and George Herbert Mead (1863–1931) (11), representatives of the symbolic interactionist school in sociology and social psychology, demonstrated a perspective which is parallel to and compatible with the phenomenological. Each saw society as process, individual and society as closely interrelated, and the subjective aspect of human behavior as a necessary part of the process of formation and dynamic maintenance of the social self and the social group.

Cooley's organic view of society stressed the unity of the whole and the interrelation of individual and society. "A separate individual is an abstraction unknown to experience and so likewise is society when regarded as something apart from individuals. . . . 'Society' and 'individuals' do not denote separable phenomena but are simply the collective and distributive aspects of the same thing." Social reality was conceived of by Cooley as consisting of men's personal ideas of one another and the task of sociology was therefore to study ideas, attitudes, and sentiments as these reflected social relationships.

Thomas proposed that the total situation must be understood in order to explain behavior. The situation includes objective elements such as rules and institutions and subjective elements. The subjective component is represented in what he referred to as "defining the situation," namely, the point of view of the individual when he decides to act. The understanding of behavior requires an understanding of the entire context in which it occurs—both the objective and the subjective—the situation as it exists in a form verifiable by others and as it seems to exist to the individual himself. The latter component is most frequently referred to by Thomas' dictum, "if men define situations as real, they are real in their consequences."

Mead's views of man and society contribute important conceptualizations to the symbolic interactionist perspective (12). Self is seen as process, a reflexive process which provides for self-interaction. Man can make indications to himself and plan and organize his actions with regard to what he has perceived, classified, and evaluated. Rather than being merely a responding creature, man is an active, interpreting, symbol-using, and self-interacting socialized being. Action is constructed by the actor; therefore, to understand how and why men act as they do, their perspective must be understood.

Objects in the world are seen as having meanings constituted by human actors and not simply as entities with an independent existence. The meanings of objects arise from and are integrally a part of the uses made of them by humans. They are social objects in that the process of defining their meaning is a social process. Thus the social world is seen as a social product, a resultant of the dialectical process between individual and society. Different groups can come to develop different social worlds. A task for the observer of such worlds is to understand the meanings objects have for the members of the particular social world being studied.

Human society is seen as a process rather than as established structure. Group life is built up out of social interaction, out of the constructed meanings in action in which individuals jointly engage. Institutions, roles, status positions, organizations, norms, and values develop and reciprocally influence those engaged in their construction and maintenance. "The organization of human society is the framework within which social action takes place and is not the determinant of that action." Acting units, whether individuals or groups, act in relation to defined situations. Included in their definitions are such "objects" as norms, values, organizations, roles, and expectations. To the extent to which culture and social organization "shaped situations in which people act, and to the extent to which (they) supply fixed sets of symbols which people use in interpreting their situations" (13), are they a part of the forces shaping human conduct.

Methodologically, the implication of the symbolic interactionist perspective is that the actor's view of action, objects, and society has to be studied seriously. The situation must be seen as the actor sees it, the meanings of objects and acts must be determined in terms of the actor's meanings, and the organization of a course of action must be understood as the actor organizes it. The role of the actor in the situation would have to be taken by the observer in order to see the social world from his perspective.

Thus symbolic interactionism as a perspective in sociology and social psychology requires the direct and close observation of the empirical world, as it is known to human actors who live in it. "No theorizing, however ingenious, and no observance of scientific protocol, however meticulous, are substitutes for developing a familiarity with what is actually going on in the sphere of life under study" (14). No presuppositions, whether they come from scientific theories or common sense knowledge of social structures, are to influence the observer or cloud his vision. In this sense, symbolic interactionists seek to faithfully represent and describe the social world as it is known to those who live in it. This approach is indeed phenomenological in spirit.

The contribution of Alfred Schutz (1899–1959) (15), however, remains distinctive and monumental, and no modern scholar can ignore his work and consider himself conversant with phenomenological social science. By virtue of his close familiarity with the work of Edmund Husserl, his knowledge of philosophy, and his thorough acquaintance with the sociological tradition, Schutz was able to provide the clearest and most cogent interpretation of the significance of phenomenological philosophy for the social sciences. His *Phenomenology of the Social World*, which expands on Weber's analysis of *verstehen*, and his major writings over many years, now published in three volumes of collected papers, provide the reader with a direct entry into phenomenological sociology. His critical selection, assessment, and use of the phenomenological approach and method has enabled scholars to discover the insights most relevant for social science, without their having to read extensively in original philosophical sources. This is not to say that such inquiry is unimportant or unnecessary; in fact, American-trained social scientists need to read and study extensively in philosophy in order to discover the roots of their own discipline. The ground or origin of any system of thought, such as science, is to be found in philosophical quests and not in social scientific analyses (i.e., the sociology of sociology does not reveal the epistemic and ontological groundings of the discipline itself, what is taken to be knowledge or truth, and what means are to be used to arrive at such knowledge). At the same time, the philosophical quest does not in itself necessarily lead to an understanding of how the results of philosophical investigations can produce a more informed or even modified social science. Schutz' gift is in discerning such implications in philosophy and presenting them to the reader in a manner that clearly reveals the import of phenomenology as philosophy, method, and approach for social science. His most important contributions were concerned with uncovering, describing, and analyzing the essential features of the world of everyday life; with discovering, "in full depth, the presuppositions, structure, and significations of that world"; and with the realization of "a philosophy of mundane reality, or, in more formal language, a phenomenology of the natural attitude" (16).

Rather than attempt a review of the major concepts and analyses of the social world which Schutz developed, I will instead refer the reader to several excellent sources that can perform this function. Natanson's introduction to the *Collected Papers*, Volume I, Gurwitsch's introduction to Volume III (17), and Chapter I of Berger and Luckmann's *The Social Construction of Reality*, titled "The Foundations of Knowledge in Everyday Life" (18), outline and elaborate the major dimensions of Schutz' thought concerning the nature of the everyday world and the concepts that can be used to analyze it. The major theses developed by Schutz in *The Phenomenology of the Social World* are summarized by the translators of that book, Walsh and Lehnert, in the Preface, and are also commented on by Natanson in his essay, "Alfred Schutz on Social Reality and Social Science" (19). Helmut Wagner provides an introduction and also a selection from the various writings and essays of Schutz organized under topical headings that provide a comprehensive survey of his thought (20).

As will be apparent from several of the papers in this book, the indebtedness of social scientists to Alfred Schutz is great indeed. In this brief overview, I specifically refrain from bringing the reader beyond Schutz' work, since the rest of the book is devoted to this task. The work of contemporary phenomenological sociologists is cited extensively by the contributors and, of course, the contributors themselves deserve citation.

I now wish to consider some of the issues and problems that require continued consideration in order for studies of the world of everyday life to be accomplished. Schutz contributed to the clarification of some of these issues; the advance of phenomenological sociology still requires their recognition and solution.

UNDERSTANDING THE WORLD OF EVERYDAY LIFE: ISSUES AND PROBLEMS

The human actor, as a socialized member of society, operates within a life-world that is pregiven and already organized. (See Zaner's paper for a general discussion of the social and the solitary.) The language he learns, the culture he acquires, and the social structures within which he lives provide him with a stockpile of typifications, of recipes for interpreting and acting, and with a stock of knowledge that forms the basis for even his imaginative exploration of courses of action other than those he already knows (21).

The life-world (*Lebenswelt*) is not only prestructured but the meanings of the elements contained within it are also pregiven. The stock of knowledge provides the actor with rules for interpreting interactions, social relationships, organizations, and institutions. And when the unexpected happens or new situations occur and the taken-for-granted is thrown into question, only then is he forced to consider alternative schemes of interpretation. (See Wagner's essay for a discussion of reactions to a disruption of the taken-for-granted.)

Thus, within the standpoint of the natural attitude, the individual is not motivated to question the meaningful structures of his life-world. His interest is a practical one and his task is to *live in* rather than to make a *study of* the life-world. (Bittner discusses the significance of these two perspectives for objectivity.) It remains for the social scientist to adopt the stance of a disinterested observer and to study the life-world of others. Though he may draw on his own experiences, since he is also a human being who may have lived in similar situations, he does not study the life-world from his own perspective. He attempts to transcend the everyday intentionalities in which he is the center of his own existence and adopt another point of reference. Depending on the problem he has chosen for study, as this may be defined within the scientific stock of knowledge, the social scientist selects that which is relevant (22). His concern is not so much with the particular individuals who are subjects of his study, but with the types they represent. His effort is to see through the particulars to that which is essential to the type, those elements without which the type would not be what it is. In this sense, what he does resembles what people do in an ordinary, mundane fashion when perceiving the objects of the world. Objects are concretely empirical as they appear to us. We see a person, living, appearing before us. This corporeal presence is taken as fact. Yet at the same time we "see" the person in the sense of a meaningful object whose various aspects, though not directly seen, are nevertheless known to us. The pregiven type, known to us as "human body," does not refer to any one particular body but to the purely ideal, meaning creation of our human minds (23). (Manning and Fabrega discuss the implications of a phenomenology of body and self specifically for such matters as conceptions of health and illness.) In this realm of the ideal, objectivity can occur in that any one of us can share the identical meaning creation. We can, in the abstract, know the concept of the human body as we share the same language and accept the meanings it provides for us. We need not explicate the fullness of meanings and we are hardly aware of all that we know as we proceed. The meaning structures with which we operate are, for us, real, though we may be only dimly aware that they have a different reality from empirical objects.

The Empirical and the Ideal

The distinction between the empirical and the ideal is important for the social scientist to recognize (24). An "empirical" science may study empirical existential objects and describe these in their particulars or it may form generalizations which refer to and are based on the study of empirical events or occurrences in the everyday world. Generalizations in science do not refer or apply to only a single occurrence but to all occurrences of a type or class. Phenomenological analysis may also start with empirical observations but seek to develop more abstract formulations as in ideal-typical analyses. Eidetic analysis aims at seeing through the particulars (concrete, existential) to discover that which is essential (ideal, typical). Though non-empirical in this sense, ideas, types, or concepts are not fictions that can be arbitrarily created, modified or distorted. Distinctions between their truth or falsity, clarity or vagueness, completeness or incompleteness can be made. The essential structure of the phenomenon under study, whether it be a social organization, social relationship, interaction pattern, or a belief system, refers to those elements which make up the phenomenon and without which it either ceases to be what it is or changes considerably. (See the paper by Psathas and Waksler for an eidetic analysis of "face-to-face interaction.") The essential or necessary structure is derived from a number of empirical observations including imaginative variations of the phenomenon. In an eidetic analysis we analyze the phenomenon, that is, our consciousness of the object, in order to discover its constituent elements and their interrelations. In this way, conceptualizations can be developed which assist us in discerning and understanding the empirical representations of the ideal-typical (25).

However it is not possible to express the "inexact data of perception in an exact manner" (26) and we shall have to rely on ordinary language concepts to describe the social world and social phenomena. Scientific conceptualizations, based on these ordinary language concepts, can be developed with greater rigor and precision than customarily used by members of society but to the extent that first-order conceptualizations are inexact and nonmathematical, second-order conceptualizations will themselves be affected. Thus we cannot expect to quantify and mathematize our descriptions of social phenomena if their nature (essence) is qualitative and nonmathematical. To do so would be to distort or falsify their properties to suit a scientific purpose. However, for certain purposes, such distortion may be perfectly acceptable provided we remember what we have done and why we have done it. One of the critiques of contemporary positivist social science is that it has introduced distortions both knowingly and unknowingly. When known distortions are subsequently forgotten or ignored, the result is self-deception.

The Impossibility of Full Explication

A difficulty that immediately confronts us and poses problems greater than we would at first suppose is that the explication of the activities of human, knowing subjects, acting in the ordinary course of everyday events, requires that we make assumptions about the meanings of their activities which cannot, in themselves, be fully explicated. The same common sense, ordinary, everyday understandings subjects (actors) themselves have and use must also be made and used by the social scientist observer. Not only is such use necessary, but the effort to provide a full explication of such assumptions proves to be a task impossible of completion because as meanings are revealed, the assumptions being made in the analysis must also be explicated, and this further explication, involving additional assumptions, would also need to be explicated, and so on, *ad infinitum* (27). The observer cannot continue indefinitely in this manner. Certainly, the original purpose that motivated his analysis does not require that every assumption be explicated. And so the observer recognizes that he too must operate with some of the same common sense assumptions made by people in the everyday world. The recognition of this fact, however, is a self-conscious one and in this sense the observer is different. He adopts those assumptions on which science is based, including some assumptions similar to those made in the everyday world: things are so, until proven otherwise; the purpose at hand is sufficient to define the range and extent of that analysis, until proven otherwise by new findings, interpretations, and so on; and the accomplishment of understanding is an endless task whose end must nevertheless be provisionally accepted.

All the assumptions the observer must use are there as the background understandings of his work. Their analysis and explication can become the task of the philosopher of social science, but since this is not the task the social scientist has set for himself when operating as a social scientist, he need not undertake it. He must recognize that a philosophical analysis is different from a social scientific one and that he, too, must start with some unexplicated and perhaps inexplicable assumptions concerning knowledge, knowing, objects, and so forth, that he will "take for granted until proven otherwise."

In this sense the observer knows that his scientific findings are themselves provisional truths, contingent upon ways of knowing and modes of understanding which themselves may later be overturned and changed.

The Validity of Studies of the Life-World

The key issue for a sociology of the life-world is whether the results of an inquiry fit, make sense, and are true to the understanding of ordinary actors in the everyday world. (See also Bittner's discussion of objectivity and realism.) One test of the validity of investigations lies in the extent to which the findings are faithful to and consistent with the experiences of those who live in that world. Are the findings faithful representations, descriptions, accounts, or interpretations of what those who ordinarily live those activities would themselves recognize to be true? If second order constructs were translated back into the first order constructs to which they refer, would the observer's report be recognized as a valid and faithful account of "what the activity is really like"?

A second test is whether the descriptions and accounts of the activities would allow others—not directly knowledgeable as to their occurrences but sharing the same cultural stock of knowledge—to recognize the activities if confronted with them in the life-world *after* having only read or seen the account presented by the social scientist analyst. (Such a test may be applied to Blumenstiel's description of courtship, for example.) That is, armed with "only" the knowledge gained from reading the account presented by the observer-scientist, would someone else be able to understand what he was seeing when confronted with the actual life-world reality of the events described (28)?

A third test is more difficult, but perhaps similar to the test made when the rules of a new game one has purchased are read for the first time. The rules provide the recipes for performance, again based on and including many everyday operating assumptions. The "reader" can become a "player" after having "merely" read the rules. Similarly, a social scientist's report on how to find one's way in the city, how to give directions, how to locate objects in space when deprived of a visual sensory mode—based on how ordinary persons in the everyday world actually do these things—can be used as a set of instructions, rules, or operating procedures for performing these same activities (29). Perhaps this is a more stringent test. One risk of adopting such a test is that the observer may restrict his inquiry to those types of activities that can be described by constitutive rules. Instead of studying larger and more complex activities and situations, he engages in microsociological enterprises. An unanticipated result of such an approach is that phenomenological sociology may come to be identified with the study of interaction, of small gatherings, and of events that are not societal in magnitude and scope. (Wagner specifically addresses this issue.) On the other hand, for those activities that can be so described and analyzed, the patterned structure and order of acts can be revealed most fully in formulations of *how* the activities are performed.

The Study of the Subjective Dimension

To conclude that phenomenological sociology is limited to the study of microsociological events is to ignore its relevance for the understanding of larger societal events. (The papers by Wagner and Dallmayr illustrate that phenomenology can be applied to the study of macrosocietal events and even merge with political theory, such as Marxism, to provide explanations of social, political, and economic change.) When social science recognizes that the objective reality of society, groups, community, and formal organizations is subjectively experienced by the individual and that these subjective experiences are intimately related to the subsequent externalization and objectification procedures in which humans engage as they think and act in the social world, then a more informed and reality-based social science will result. There has been a tendency to treat the subjective as "merely" subjective or as so idiosyncratic that social science, concerned with patterns and generalities, cannot seriously study it. This overlooks the possibility of finding patterns in the subjective experiences of individuals and denies the social scientist access to human experiences unless he can, almost in advance of his study, be assured that order and structure will be found. There is a basic misunderstanding among those who adopt positivist and behaviorist approaches that human experience is too subjective, variable, and inaccessible to be studied. Yet at its core, phenomenology represents the effort to describe human experience. How then can the study of the varied, changing, and seemingly inaccessible subjectivity of human experiences be the topic of study?

First, the social scientist must be as faithful to the experiences that are being studied as possible. Rather than starting with those methods and theories that reduce or simplify human experience in order to be parsimonious or rigorous, a phenomenological approach seeks first to remain open to the phenomena themselves. This may mean that one starts by "seeing" rather than by "thinking." One's mind is opened to all the possibilities present—presuppositions about the events or activities being studied are set aside or "bracketed," and assumptions, theories, beliefs, and prejudices themselves do not remain unexamined. There can be no uncritical acceptance of assumptions since assumptions structure the world as we observe it and cloud our vision.

Thus, as some have said, phenomenological inquiry begins in silence. This silence represents a struggle to "see" the phenomena as clearly as possible and as these are given in immediate experience, in one's own *consciousness of* those things. Experience is the experiencing of some consciousness, and, since all experience is first-person experience by a knowing subject, I, as such a subject, although also as a sociological observer, have a chance to examine my experience directly.

My experience has two dimensions, (a) perception (*Schau*) and (b) perception of structural patterns (*Wesensschau*). Perception is sometimes referred to as intuition, but this term carries many distracting connotations and is less preferable. Immediate experience is not a "buzzing confusion" but rather is meaningful and structured. This insight of phenomenology is a basic one.

Phenomenology does not divide or separate the knowing subject from the object of study in order to concentrate on one or the other. The world is not filled with objects that have appearances independent of humans who experience them, nor does subjective experience exist independently of the objects, events, and activities experienced. There is no pure subjective subject or pure objective object. Phenomenology recognizes that all consciousness is consciousness *of* something (where "thing" is not to be taken to literally mean an existential object). Intentionality is the term used to refer to this relation. Phenomenology is an approach that concentrates on the subject-experience (e.g., my perception of the other as a person in a social role), rather than concentrating solely on subjects (e.g., me, the other's subjective experience) or objects (e.g., the social role, the person).

Human experience of the world is that it is a world of *meaningful* objects and relations. The meanings are experienced as being "in the world," not as "in one's head." Perception therefore cannot be limited to what is received through the senses but must include the meaning structures experienced by a knowing subject of that which is being perceived.

Bracketing or Suspending the Assumptions
of the Everyday World

The knowing subject is rooted in the social world as a participant. As a participant he lives in his own acts; but he can also observe since he can reflectively examine his experience. His reflection, however, is from the natural standpoint, from his ordinary, mundane outlook of the taken-for-granted social world involving all the assumptions he makes every day.

For the sociologist, a phenomenological approach to observing the social world requires that he break out of the natural attitude and examine the very assumptions that structure the experience of actors in the world of everyday life. A method that provides assistance in this is "bracketing" the assumptions of everyday life. This does not involve denying the existence of the world or even doubting it (it is not the same as Cartesian doubt). Bracketing changes my attitude toward the world, allowing me to see with clearer vision. I set aside preconceptions and presuppositions, what I already "know" about the social world, in order to discover it with clarity of vision. It is a change of attitude toward the social world and the events and activities of human actors in which I engage. (Cf. footnote 28, Don Juan's teaching Castaneda, the field anthropologist, how to "see." "Seeing" involved setting aside previous assumptions about the meaning of events.) The social world remains there, ready for examination and description as it is experienced. My attitude toward it changes for me, for my purpose at hand is now the examination of my consciousness of it. But I do not deny its existence.

In this manner, all experiences can receive equal attention. The experience of interaction with others who turn out to be illusory or hallucinatory figures (cf. Castaneda) are as "real" as the interaction with existent persons. In the natural attitude, illusions and hallucinations are considered as nonexistent and therefore as not deserving of the same attention given to existent objects, persons, or events. But in a phenomenological approach, a whole range of experiences that would ordinarily be ruled out are instead, as objects of intentional consciousness, entitled to the same serious attention and study. Thus bracketing enables one to expand his view and embrace more aspects of the world for study.

The Description of the Life-World as an Achievement

To describe experience is an achievement and it is in this sense that phenomenological description represents an important method and result. Description, however, must be seen as not limited by or to ordinary sense data. If I describe interaction with another person, I must perceive that interaction as it is given to me in my consciousness, analyze its components and the relations between its components (i.e., its structure). I must avoid the judgment that what I see of the other is only what is physically visible. I see the other as body and object but I also see him as, for example, man, truck driver, white, lower class, tall, physically strong, handsome, uneducated, and so on. All these are meanings (aspects of the intended object) which can be found in the other. The meanings involve the use of interpretative schemes on my part and are part of my perceiving the other. I must continue to examine my perceptions and seek to discover the elements contained in them. This explication or description will involve me in detailed examination of all my experience and I can gradually piece together the component aspects of this experience. Similarly, in studying others, my careful, systematic, and wide-ranging questioning must allow me to discover what *they* are experiencing, how *they* interpret their experiences, and how *they* themselves structure the social world in which they live; but I must not succumb to the naive position (as Bittner hints as being the source of the problem of an abortive phenomenology) of accepting the statements respondents make as the literal and sufficient explanations of their conduct, beliefs, values, or knowledge.

At a more abstract and general level it is also appropriate for me to examine the language system and how it structures experience, the organizational and social structures in which persons live, and the cultural system with its systems of belief, value, and knowledge, all of which provide meaningful structures for those humans who share and live within them.

The Problem of Intersubjectivity

This life-world is experienced as an intersubjective world, known and experienced by others, lived in by other people who understand it and who also experience it as an intersubjective world.

Since the life-world is given to people in the natural attitude as an intersubjective world, one of the tasks of the social scientist is to describe the experience of intersubjectivity. At a more philosophical level, he may ask how intersubjectivity is possible at all—but this quest must be recognized as a different question, the answer to which philosophers themselves have not yet agreed upon. There emerges then the clear necessity to distinguish between the study of the life-world as it is experienced by ordinary human beings living in it and questions about how the life-world is possible, how one can know another's mind, whether society is objectively real, and so forth. This is not to say that these questions cannot or should not be approached by social scientists. Rather, they must be recognized as a different order of question. The solution of these problems is not necessary before proceeding with studies of the life-world. Thus for social scientists, the study of people must take them as they are —people who suspend doubt, live in the natural attitude, and live with the certainty that the social and natural world exist. The serious and careful study of how people live with and renew their assumptions requires close and faithful description. It is to that undertaking that we urge our fellow social scientists to address themselves. The study of how social order is produced by humans in their everyday activities is a study whose value may be as considerable as the more general and theoretical study of how social order is possible at all. (See O'Neill's essay for a discussion of such questions.)

The Phenomenological Approach as a Paradigm

The phenomenological approach does not restrict the observer to a narrow set of methods or perspectives. There is no formula or recipe for procedures which is to be applied ready-made to the problem being studied.

The "steps" described by Spiegelberg (30) in his discussion of the phenomenological method are not sequential stages. One cannot pick up a book of rules on how to do a phenomenological analysis and jump in. The adoption of a new paradigm for research involves the researcher in a major reformulation of his thinking (31).

In adopting a phenomenological perspective, the social scientist must evolve a way of looking that is different from a positivist science approach to data. In fact, he must learn to regard as data some objects, events, and activities he previously did not "see" at all. In this respect, a new paradigm enables him to see "facts that were there all the time."

At this stage of development of sociology, an initial reaction is to try to fit the phenomenological into the paradigm of normal science, to reformulate questions or findings, to show that the data are the same, and to reinterpret or rephrase the resulting accounts to show that the translation renders the "new" results consistent with what is already known or has been done all along. These efforts represent a necessary step, perhaps, in the struggle to understand the significance of a new paradigm, or, for that matter, to understand whether it is a new paradigm at all. Once a paradigm is grasped, understood, and used, then the results of research are presented within such new formulations or conceptualizations as are deemed necessary, and no argumentative or comparative posture which argues that this approach is "better" or "more valid" or "truer to life" than some other is mentioned. The work stands on its own and the reader is expected to understand the paradigm it embodies.

It will be evident, both from the essays in this book and from other works, that this day has not yet arrived in phenomenological sociology. There are still justificatory arguments, programmatic statements and exhortations to the reader, and explanations of why it is important that this approach be used. In contrast, the articles in current issues (1971–1972) of the *American Journal of Sociology* or the *American Sociological Review* spend little if any time arguing the merits of the approaches used. There is a quality of "this is the way sociology is done" about these works, a kind of certainty about method and approach and a lack of self-consciousness or concern about the validity of the paradigm for the study of the problem at hand. The paradigm used is so taken-for-granted that it is hardly likely that the authors of the articles could present an analytic description of it.

What Kuhn refers to as a "paradigm shift" does not occur in an instant as does the *gestalt* switch (e.g., the drawing that appears either as a vase or as two faces). "The transfer of allegiance from paradigm to paradigm is a conversion experience that cannot be forced" (32). Yet the shift from one paradigm to another is possible, as evidenced by the fact that new paradigms are created by those already familiar with the existing ones of normal science. Whether it is fruitful to attempt conversions can be argued. Our view is that the presentation of a variety of problems, each being studied from a phenomenological perspective, can stand as evidence of the possible contributions of a new paradigm. Those who are engaged in research on the same topics from different paradigm perspectives can thereby make more informed decisions about the value of a phenomenological approach to the study of the social world.

» » » » » « « « « «

These papers stand as contributions to a phenomenological social science, particularly to phenomenological sociology. They orient the reader to a field and an approach, they raise theoretical and methodological issues for the social sciences, and they apply phenomenology to specific research problems. The range and breadth of topics covered by these authors and the interests they express are an indication of the vitality and spirit present in phenomenological sociology today.

NOTES

1. For a listing of Husserl's major writings see the bibliography in Wagner's paper in this book, "The Scope of Phenomenological Sociology." Herbert Spiegelberg, *The Phenomenological Movement*, Vols. I and II, 2nd ed., Martinus Nijhoff, The Hague, 1969, provides the most comprehensive survey of the development of phenomenological philosophy. To date no survey of the development of phenomenological social science exists, with the possible exception for psychology and psychiatry of Herbert Spiegelberg, *Phenomenology in Psychology and Psychiatry*, Northwestern University Press, Evanston, Ill., 1972. Briefer treatments of selected aspects of this development are Edward Tiryakian, "Existential Phenomenology and the Sociological Tradition," *American Sociological Review*, 30, 1965, pp. 674–688; Stephen Strasser, "Phenomenological Trends in European Psychology," *Philosophy and Phenomenological Research*, XVIII, 1957, pp. 18–34; Robert B. McLeod, "The Phenomenological Approach in Social Psychology," *Psychological Review*, LIV, 1947, pp. 193–210; Hans P. Neisser, "The Phenomenological Approach in Social Science," *Philosophy and Phenomenological Research*, XX, 1959, pp. 198–212; Stephen Strasser, *Phenomenology and the Human Sciences*, Duquesne University Press, Pittsburgh, 1963; Anna T. Tymieniecka, *Phenomenology and Science in Contemporary European Thought*, Noonday Press, New York, 1962; Amedeo Giorgi, *Psychology as a Human Science: A Phenomenologically Based Approach*, Harper and

Row, New York, 1970; and an essay by Alfred Schutz, "Some Leading Concepts of Phenomenology," in *Collected Papers*, Vol. I, Martinus Nijhoff, The Hague, 1962, pp. 118–139. Phenomenology and sociology are discussed in George Psathas, "Ethnomethods and Phenomenology," *Social Research*, *35*, 1968, pp. 500–520; Jack D. Douglas (ed.), *Understanding Everyday Life*, Aldine, Chicago, 1970; Paul Filmer, Michael Phillipson, David Silverman, and David Walsh, *New Directions in Sociological Theory*, Collier-Macmillan, London, 1972; and all the social sciences in Maurice Natanson (ed.), *Phenomenology and the Social Sciences*, Northwestern University Press, Evanston, Ill., 1973, two volumes.

2. Max Weber, *The Theory of Economic and Social Organization*, translated by A. M. Henderson and Talcott Parsons, Free Press, New York, 1947; from Max Weber, *Essays in Sociology*, translated and edited by H. H. Gerth and C. W. Mills, Oxford University Press, New York, 1946.

3. Weber, *Theory of Economic and Social Organization*, *op. cit.*, p. 85.

4. Georg Simmel, *The Sociology of Georg Simmel*, translated by Kurt Wolff, Free Press, Glencoe, Ill., 1950.

5. *Ibid.*, pp. 21–22.

6. F. H. Tenbruck, "Formal Sociology," in Lewis A. Coser, *Georg Simmel*, Prentice-Hall, Englewood Cliffs, N.J., 1965, p. 95.

7. Max Scheler, *The Nature of Sympathy*, Yale University Press, New Haven, 1954 (originally published 1922); Alfred Schutz, "Scheler's Theory of Intersubjectivity and the General Thesis of the Alter Ego," in *Collected Papers*, Vol. III, Martinus Nijhoff, The Hague, 1966, pp. 133–144; and Alfred Schutz, "Max Scheler's Epistemology and Ethics," *ibid.*, pp. 145–178.

8. Karl Mannheim, *Ideology and Utopia*, Harcourt, Brace, New York, 1936 (originally published 1929), and *Essays on the Sociology of Knowledge*, edited by Paul Kecskemeti, Oxford University Press, New York, 1952.

9. William James, *Principles of Psychology*, 2 vols., Dover Publications, New York, 1950 (first published in 1890); William James, *The Varieties of Religious Experience*, University Books, New Hyde Park, N.Y., 1963 (first published in 1902); Alfred Schutz, "William James' Concept of the Stream of Thought Phenomenologically Interpreted," in *Collected Papers*, Vol. III, pp. 1–14; Robert B. MacLeod (ed.), *William James: Unfinished Business*, American Psychological Association, Washington, D.C., 1969.

10. James, *Principles of Psychology*, *op. cit.*, p. 239.

11. Charles Cooley, *Human Nature and the Social Order*, Schoken Paperback Edition, New York, 1964 (originally published 1902); W. I. Thomas, *On Social Organization and Social Personality: Selected Papers*, edited and with an introduction by Morris Janowitz, University of Chicago Press, Chicago, 1966; Edmund H. Volkart (ed.), *Social Behavior and Personality: Contributions of W. I. Thomas to Social Theory and Social Re-*

search, Social Science Research Council, New York, 1951; George Herbert Mead, *Mind, Self, and Society*, edited and with an introduction by Charles W. Morris, University of Chicago Press, Chicago, 1934; George Herbert Mead, *On Social Psychology: Selected Papers*, edited and with an introduction by Anselm Strauss, University of Chicago Press, Chicago, Phoenix Edition, 1964.

12. Herbert Blumer, *Symbolic Interactionism*, Prentice-Hall, Englewood Cliffs, N.J., 1969, presents the most recent summary and re-conceptualization of this perspective.

13. *Ibid.*, pp. 87–88.

14. *Ibid.*, p. 39.

15. Alfred Schutz, *Collected Papers*, Vols. I, II, and III, Martinus Nijhoff, The Hague, 1962, 1964, 1966; *The Phenomenology of the Social World*, translated by George Walsh and Frederick Lehnert, Northwestern University Press, 1967 (originally published as *Der Sinnhafte Aufbau der Sozialen Welt*, Vienna, Julius Springer, 1932); *Reflections on the Problem of Relevance*, edited, annotated, and with an introduction by Richard Zaner, Yale University Press, New Haven, 1970; with Thomas Luckmann, *The Structures of the Life-World*, translated by Richard Zaner and Tristram Engelhardt, Jr., Northwestern University Press, Evanston, Ill., 1972. The *Festschrift* for Schutz edited by Maurice Natanson, *Phenomenology and Social Reality: Essays in Memory of Alfred Schutz*, Martinus Nijhoff, The Hague, 1970, contains many important and significant discussions of his work.

16. M. Natanson, "Introduction," in Schutz, *Collected Papers*, Vol. I, *op. cit.*, p. xxv.

17. Aaron Gurwitsch, "Introduction," in Schutz, *Collected Papers*, Vol. III, *op. cit.*, pp. xi–xxxi.

18. Peter Berger and Thomas Luckmann, *The Social Construction of Reality: A Treatise in the Sociology of Knowledge*, Doubleday, Anchor, New York, 1967.

19. In Natanson, *Phenomenology and Social Reality: Essays in Memory of Alfred Schutz, op. cit.*, pp. 101–121.

20. Alfred Schutz, *On Phenomenology and Social Relations: Selected Writings*, edited and with an introduction by Helmut R. Wagner, University of Chicago Press, Chicago, 1970.

21. Schutz, *Collected Papers*, Vol. II, *op. cit.* p. 229.

22. Schutz, *Reflections on the Problem of Relevance, op. cit.*

23. Schutz, *Collected Papers*, Vol. I., *op. cit.* p. 28.

24. See Severyn Bruyn, *The Human Perspective in Sociology*, Prentice-Hall, Englewood Cliffs, N.J., 1966, p. 277, for a brief comparison of empirical versus phenomenological observation.

25. I do not wish to imply that all phenomenological studies seek essential insights and are eidetic in intent. But as Spiegelberg notes, "it is not possi-

ble to see (particulars) *as particulars* without seeing the general essence." (Spiegelberg, *The Phenomenological Movement, op. cit.*, p. 678.) One may intuit general essences and not make those essences the topic of investigation.

26. Joseph J. Kockelmans, *Phenomenology*, Doubleday, Anchor, New York, 1967, p. 101.

27. Harold Garfinkel, "Studies of the Routine Grounds of Everyday Activities," in *Studies in Ethnomethodology*, Prentice-Hall, Englewood Cliffs, N.J., 1967, p. 6, makes this point in discussing indexical expressions. ". . . wherever *practical actions are topics of study* the promised distinction and substitutability of objective for indexical expressions remains programmatic in every *particular* case and in every *actual* occasion in which the distinction or substitutability must be demonstrated. In every actual case without exception, conditions will be cited that a competent investigator will be required to recognize, such that in *that* particular case the terms of the demonstration can be relaxed and nevertheless the demonstration be counted an adequate one." This is also referred to as the "infinite regress" feature of accounting by Michael Phillipson, "Phenomenological Philosophy and Sociology" in Filmer *et al., op. cit.*, p. 151.

28. Cf. Carlos Castaneda, *A Separate Reality: Further Conversations with Don Juan*, Simon Schuster, New York, 1971. A test would be whether someone would recognize Don Juan's behavior as that of a sorcerer after having read the account by Castaneda.

29. Cf. Harold Garfinkel, "Some Rules of Correct Decision-Making that Jurors Respect," in *Studies in Ethnomethodology, op. cit.*, pp. 104–115, for a study which presents some rules of decision making used by jurors in daily life.

30. Herbert Spiegelberg, "The Essentials of the Phenomenological Method," in *The Phenomenological Movement, op. cit.*, Chapter 14, pp. 653–701.

31. Thomas Kuhn, "The Structure of Scientific Revolutions," *International Encyclopedia of Unified Science*, Vol. 2, No. 2, 2nd ed., University of Chicago Press, Chicago, 1970. I refer to the broad notion of paradigm described by Kuhn as the "disciplinary matrix," the common possession of symbolic generalizations and shared commitments to beliefs, values, and exemplars (pp. 181–187).

32. *Ibid.*, pp. 150–151.

»»»»»»»»»»»»»»»»»»»»»»»« « « « « « « « « « « « « « « « « « « «

Zaner poses for us the basic dichotomy of social existence, together and apart, social and solitary, society and individual. The role of phenomenological philosophy he proposes is to provide critical inquiry into presuppositions: beginnings, origins, or foundations. As critical inquiry, phenomenology can lead us to an understanding of those basic aspects of self and society that might otherwise remain concealed from our view.

The critical stance, however, does not immediately appear to be as radical as Zaner would have us think. A criticism of phenomenology has been that it is unable to deal with the dynamic and changing aspects of social life, that it presents static and structural analyses, and that, despite the possibility of genetic and constitutive analyses, phenomenological sociology, at least, has not yet succeeded in providing us with examples of such work. These are points to which Wolff and Wagner return in their papers. For Zaner, however, the call to the sociologist is that he first recognize the philosophical presuppositions on which his science rests, that a self-critical or reflexive sociology requires a radical philosophy, and that phenomenology provides a reflexive, critical and radical philosophy of value to social science. It is from this perspective that Zaner can assess Garfinkel's sociology as more radical in that its effort is to discover the invisible, taken-for-granted underpinnings of social life and the reflexive sociology of Gouldner, because it lacks grounding in a radical philosophy, as less so.

SOLITUDE AND SOCIALITY: THE CRITICAL FOUNDATIONS OF THE SOCIAL SCIENCES (1)

» « «

Richard M. Zaner

State University of New York at Stony Brook

There is much talk today of "crisis"—within the various scientific and academic disciplines, in society, and in culture. This sort of talk is, of course, not new nor is it restricted merely to the harbingers of disaster. Such seminal thinkers as Husserl, Heidegger, Cassirer, Scheler, Ortega, and Sorokin have insisted on the presence of a crisis of Western man, and, earlier, Kierkegaard and Nietzsche had already pointed to serious flaws in Western culture.

Some of the more obvious signs of crisis in social science are apparent even with the more casual of glances at the current scene. The many warring factions, the finely developed practice of insult and innuendo, the talent for trying to out-finesse one's fellows and to bewitch students with hypertechnical terminology, deeply entrenched in what Alvin Gouldner calls, doubtless to the distress of many social scientists, "academic sociology," is often matched by a remarkable failure of modesty and self-criticism.

Do not misunderstand me: I am myself in a very fragile glass house. Philosophy, no less than sociology, is in a bad way. If Gouldner is correct in insisting on a "coming crisis in Western sociology," the same is true of philosophy and other disciplines, and perhaps culture generally. If anything, the crisis is not merely "coming," it is already upon us: The "Dreadful," as R. D. Laing says, has already happened—and that is the concrete, living reality we as human beings, much less as pretenders to theoretic thrones, must willy-nilly live with.

If what Laing and others say of such hitherto taken-for-granted categories as "sanity," "madness," "normal," and "abnormal" is true—if these are no longer viable notions for understanding human conduct— the same seems true of such traditionally cherished ideas as "absolute," "relative," "empirical," and "a priori." Indeed, if I read the winds correctly—be they foul or fair—the notions we have long grown accustomed to use as vehicles for understanding ourselves and our world are showing serious signs of cracking and splitting, of not staying still. Yeats' poetic vision of fifty years ago is remarkable:

> Things fall apart; the center cannot hold:
> Mere anarchy is loosed upon the world,
> The blood-dimmed tide is loosed, and everywhere
> The ceremony of innocence is drowned;
> The best lack all conviction, while the worst
> Are full of passionate intensity.

Such notions as "knowledge," "theory," "practice," even "reality" and "nonreality" are no longer as comfortable as once they seemed. One need not look at the so-called "youth culture" to see this "crisis" at the roots of our very lives and our efforts to understand and hence to orient ourselves in our circumstances. One need only visit, say, several different classes in sociology—or several philosophy classes—to see the frequently radical disparity not merely of words, methods, or subject matters but, more basically, of conceptions of the worth, goal, and meaning different scholars place on their own and others' ideas and how these fundamentally conflict. Our very understanding of what it is we are doing, what is proper to it, indeed what we take "understanding" itself to require of us, shows deep-lying conflicts.

One might be tempted, as apparently some have been, to appeal to "ideology" as a way of explaining such disparities. One could also adopt another, more innocuous but frequent tactic and use the lingo of the "strategical gamer": diversity and conflict are merely expressions of different "points of view"—individual, academic, social, economic, or whatever—attempting to strip critical conflict of its sting by conceiving it as a function of the way different people see things and "play the game" of explaining them. Both of these, I am inclined to believe, wind up ultimately as exercises in evasion. The one who accuses others of expressing a mere ideology cannot at the same time exempt himself of precisely the same charge—and thereby cut the ground from beneath his own feet. Similarly, the one who argues for "point-of-viewism" at once presumes himself free from a particular point of view (a point of view on a point of view is not epistemically at the same level as the point of view he claims to be viewing), and in essence has retreated into a self-condemning stance to which he attempts to blind himself.

The point, although superbly simple, is too frequently forgotten: As Plato put it to many Sophists, one cannot sensibly claim that everything is relative (false, meaningless), since then he must claim that his own claim is merely relative (false, meaningless), and thus cannot speak of "everything" at all. Gouldner's charge against academic sociology, as he knows, comes to the same: Much of it, he says, seems but a "symbolic effort to overcome social worlds that have become unpermitted and to readjust the flawed relationship between goodness and potency, restoring them to their 'normal' equilibrium condition, and/or to defend permitted worlds from a threatened disequilibrium between goodness and potency" (2). [A dramatic and forceful illustration of this is found in Carlos Castaneda's "reports," especially his recent *A Separate Reality* (3).] What is sought in such ploys as are found in accusations of ideology and point-of-viewism, I suspect, is not so much understanding but, as Gouldner says, *reassurance* vis-à-vis "permitted worlds"—which can only effectively blind the effort to understand and blunt one's courage and integrity.

» » » » » « « « « «

What is called for in the most urgent way, it seems to me, is the clear recognition of the full dimensions of the "crisis." My hope is that this paper will clarify the task. The way to the required recognition, however, must be somewhat circuitous.

As an opening sally, I refer you to Max Scheler's trenchant remark in 1928 (*The Place of Man in the Cosmos*) to the effect that never before in human history has man become so deeply problematic to himself as in our own times. What is at issue, fundamentally, is what it means *to be human*. The posing of that question, as should become clear as we proceed, inevitably uncovers a veritable nest of further critical questions. Most immediately, to foreshadow some of the ideas I want to develop, it becomes necessary to insist that each of us must *place himself*—whole and entire—into question, that such questioning must be radical—that is, going to the roots, to the ground presuppositions that shape and guide human life—and that this searching for foundations demands that we bring with us none of the usual operative baggage, the epistemological, methodological, metaphysical concepts we typically use in the course of our daily lives, theoretical or practical. Castaneda's bewilderment in trying to comprehend the teachings of Don Juan, his inability to fit them into his suitcase of usual categories, and his resort to "reporting," are quite revealing if we make the effort to understand and counter the crisis. This methodological requirement is by no means new; perhaps the definitive expression of it was given by Husserl in his conception of the phenomenological epoché and reduction. However that may be, one important result of this, I think, is that we necessarily find ourselves impelled to reassess our typical notions of what "social" and "world," "real" and "unreal," "knowledge" and "ignorance" must mean. That in turn will require a very different conception of what social science is all about, and, of equal importance, it will demand that we see that philosophy and social science are intimately tied together.

Showing all this is obviously a heady undertaking. Others have done much to point the way. I am, for instance, very impressed by Gouldner's call for a "reflexive sociology":

> The historical mission of a Reflexive Sociology is to transcend sociology as it now exists. In deepening our understanding of our own sociological selves and of our position in the world, we can, I believe, simultaneously help to produce a new breed of sociologist who can better understand other men and their social worlds. A Reflexive Sociology means that we sociologists must—at the very least—acquire the ingrained *habit* of viewing our own beliefs as we now view those held by others.
>
> . . . [For] Reflexive Sociology . . . implies that sociologists must surrender the assumption, as wrongheaded as it is human, that others believe out of need while we believe—only or primarily—because of the dictates of logic and evidence. (4).

Gouldner's major points are (a) social science is not only a conception of the social world, but is also a *part* of it (5) and (b) this implies that the sociologist must be reflexively cognizant of *himself* as a social being. He must cease treating his "subject-matter" as "alien others or as mere objects" of study. "Awareness of the *self*," Gouldner stresses, "is seen as an indispensable avenue to awareness of the social world. For there is no knowledge of the world that is not a knowledge of our own experience with it and our relation to it" (6). The careful execution of this reflection, for him, leads to a "*transformation*" of the sociologist himself and his relation to what he studies—much as Plato had believed about knowledge and the knower in general.

In its negative thrust, Gouldner's thesis is also twofold: (a) it involves a rejection of the subject/object dichotomy as a viable model for understanding "our social selves"; and (b) it denies the worth and even the possibility of "value-freedom" in social science. It thus encourages what he regards as a radical self-encounter—the direct and candid confrontation of the social theorist with his own subjectivity in all its dimensions—thereby seeking as well the equally candid encounter with the fullness of social reality *as it is*, the "bad news" as well as the "good," much as Peter Berger has argued that we must obtain a precarious vision of social reality in its hidden, "night-time" aspect, as well as in its "day-time" side.

» » » » » « « « « «

All this is well and good, but it remains more programmatic than many would like. After all, who would deny the epistemic and moral worth of the dictum, "Sociologist, know thyself"? But what does this dictum, if I may so put it, really amount to, beyond a kind of general injunction to be more aware of oneself? What does it have to say about the nitty-gritty of actual social scientific work? After the serious charges made against the "business-as-usual" academic sociology, such an appeal would seem a paltry return.

The appeal to the contrary I believe is not only well taken but of profound significance for the understanding of social science, not to say social scientists. Seeing this, however, requires carrying out Gouldner's proposal in a direction he has not himself seen. What, after all, does it mean to be "radically reflexive" or "radically self-critical"? I do not think that Gouldner has adequately grasped this, nor do I agree with all of what he says about so-called academic sociology or about reflexive sociology. It is well and good, for instance, to be extremely cautious about the possibility of "value-freedom," as it is certainly in order to show critically how and where various kinds of bias enter into sociological studies. But a theory that tries to deny even the possibility of maintaining "value-free inquiry" is surely an ultimately self-defeating one, since that very claim itself would then have to be value-committed; that is, it could not possibly be reflexively *critical of itself* in Gouldner's own sense. In such a case, it is difficult indeed to understand what "knowledge" could mean, or even if it is possible.

I freely acknowledge that this issue is terribly difficult. Nevertheless, I submit to you that if the call for a self-critical discipline of sociology is to make any sense at all, if it is to be truly "radical," then it must be acknowledged *in principle* that that "radically self-critical" stance must be able to be adopted, and this requires that the reflexively critical theorist understand what it means to be "value-free," to be able to recognize "values," and that he be able at least to approximate that as a goal of his inquiry. However fashionable it once was to argue for complete value-freedom, and however fashionable it now seems to argue against it, both miss the crucial point—that the critical recognition and radical criticism of "values," if they are cogent possibilities, cannot be *at the same level* as the values criticized. Perhaps that is merely an expression of my own bias as a philosopher. But that admission on my part, as I hope will become clear shortly, cuts another way and has important ramifications for the assessment of the epistemic status and stature of social science.

Let me put that other cutting edge before you bluntly, and then try to elaborate it somewhat. What I find worrisome in Gouldner's and many other social theorists' work is the failure to see that every social scientific theory—along with its methods, techniques, concepts, and so on—rests on *philosophical presuppositions* whose elucidation is absolutely imperative for the understanding and fruitful development of social science. I do not see philosophy's relation to these sciences (as some philosophers have) as that of a kind of janitor in the hall of science, charged merely with the piecemeal task of cleaning up the uses and abuses of language and theory by using what is too often taken to be a sort of universal broom, logic. The philosopher is not a janitor, nor is he a garageman called in at strained moments to straighten out the sundry bent fenders and damaged pistons of the social scientific machinery. His relation to social science is at once far more intimate and yet more distant than such positivistic conceptions can explain.

As a good "reflexive theorist"—although by no means sociologist —it is imperative for me to demand self-criticism of my own beliefs. In a way, this is remarkably easy—for I conceive philosophy to be, in essence, self-criticism. But it is also extraordinarily difficult, for such criticism necessarily requires being *truly* radical, that is, carrying out this critical task "*to the roots,*" to the ultimate foundations or presuppositions, which is much more than the sort of self-awareness Gouldner has called for in his "reflexive sociology."

In somewhat different terms, if philosophy is the quest for truth (love of wisdom), and if one doesn't stop with mere platitudes, then it entails two fundamental exigencies and demands. First, as both Plato and Aristotle saw, it requires that one "be in wonder," that is, that he begin with the admission of his own ignorance; or, in Husserl's phrase, a philosopher must begin by proclaiming his own intellectual poverty. Thus arises the felt necessity to resolve this elemental perplexity: If I would seek knowledge, it must arise as *my own*, coming from a need, an *urgency to understand and acquire*, at every step, insights which are my own and *for which I am at all times able to account from the bottom up*. This implies the second fundamental requirement, an existential commitment by the actually existing individual, his willingness and resolve to comprehend himself and his world with intellectual and moral honesty and courage. Philosophy thus sets itself radically against what Plato calls "misology," Marcel "misosophy," and Yeats "nihilism."

In still different terms, philosophy is the systematic effort to make explicit what is implicit—universally. It seeks to dredge up the hidden, the obscure, the taken-for-granted, the presupposed—to explicate the inobvious lying within the obvious, and to come to an assessment of it in the fullest sense. Or, more restrictedly perhaps, philosophy's fundamental discipline, as I see it, is that of criticism and self-criticism; the explication and assessment just mentioned are the basic meaning of "criticism." In this sense, criticism cannot be an intellectual past-time practiced periodically by this or that person; it is rather, as I conceive it, *a fundamental discipline of knowledge*. This discipline, placed on secure, critically autonomous foundations for the first time by Edmund Husserl, is *the fundamental meaning of "phenomenology."* Hence phenomenology is in no sense merely one more "ism" or "point of view" concocted only to be stored away in the already overstacked closets of history; it is not one more metaphysical view of the nature of things. It is rather the *discipline of philosophical criticism*, a discipline foreshadowed throughout the history of philosophy but brought to fruition only by the remarkable work of Husserl and those following his lead. Philosophy, of course, has other disciplines as well, among them the speculative and the normative, but inasmuch as these seek to know, whatever it may be, they presuppose and continually require criticism. A philosophical theory that is incapable of accounting for its own possibility is a radically mistaken one; similarly, any empirical scientific theory whose philosophical foundations are not thus self-accountable is in serious difficulties.

To say that philosophy's fundamental discipline is phenomenology (radical criticism) is, however, to insist as well that it is necessarily *dialogical and reflexive*. To seek to know is to engage in that vital human activity of questioning; to question is, minimally, to acknowledge one's "not knowing" and "need to know," and thus it is to open oneself up to possible responses, whether from oneself or from another. But to open oneself up is not to become a mere sieve; it is rather to make oneself available to these responses critically—that is, to make oneself ready to "test" all responses, precisely because the act of questioning rests on an admission of "not-knowing" and a "seeking-to-know." Similarly, to respond is to engage oneself in the quest at hand; it is to claim to know (to have the "answer" with some degree of certainty, likelihood, or probability) what the question has put into question. Hence it is to put oneself at the disposal of the *questioner and his quest*, which embodies his "not-knowing" and his "exigency to find out." To respond is to open oneself up to still further questions—of many types, of course.

The act of questioning, with the correlated dialogical act of responding and the further questions emerging from that, then, I see as the fundamental form of *communication*—that is, of sharing what is one's own, or is proper to oneself, with another (even when the "other" is myself). It is, in other words, *dia-logos:* I and thou seeking together, mutually geared into the effort to know and reciprocally open and available to one another in the course of this quest. Hence to question or to respond is necessarily not only dialogical but *reflexive:* To question presupposes having grasped myself in my own not-knowing and wanting to know; to respond presupposes having asked myself the question at hand, having committed myself to searching in order to "find out."

In earlier terms, phenomenology, as dialogical and reflexive criticism, seeks to explicate the foundational presuppositions of every human engagement, including necessarily itself. I must, whatever else concerns me as a philosopher, be continually in an inner reflexive dialogue with myself, at every point criticizing myself—my efforts, my beliefs, conclusions, methods—and similarly criticizing others. And, when focused on whatever problem, my fundamental interest is always to bring out the inobvious, the taken-for-granted, the hidden, in short the foundational presuppositions without which the affairs in question would not be that which they are. In this specific sense, I am concerned to focus on "essences," the invariant in all variations.

What has thus far been said about "radical," that is, philosophical, criticism—phenomenology—is to be sure very sketchy. To be radical in its originary and forceful sense means going to the roots, even, to take the metaphor a bit further, to that which nourishes and sustains the roots or foundations, the soil: Going down to the psychical, mental, or spiritual life-processes and acts through which alone any of us is at all aware of anything whatever. To be radical is thus necessarily to engage in that most difficult and, in many respects, frighteningly personal effort to probe what Ortega calls *"radical solitude,"* that is, "my life" in its deepest dimensions. Hence being radical is in truth being reflexive and critical to the utmost, which means to the inner reaches of radical solitude. That most complex of tasks is what forms the heart of phenomenological inquiry at its deepest, or philosophical, level. Since it moves into "radical solitude" with the aim of critically explicating its fundamental nature and scope, with the aim of understanding what "stands under," makes possible, or constitutes it, the inquiry must be guided by two basic methodological requirements: (a) the inquirer must strive to "map out" the territory with as few preconceptions or presuppositions as possible, and "to lay out" (*auslegen*) its levels and their interconnections; and (b) he must never *forget where he began* in his inquiry, and must not confuse his own *reflexive procedure* with *that on which he reflects*—confuse his own procedures with that which these are designed to make explicit.

Although I cannot enter into that task here, it is important to note the outstanding feature of every actual and possible act and process of consciousness—that mental life is essentially *intentive* or directional in character. Any particular act of consciousness, or concatenation of them, is always a "consciousness of . . ." something or other, whether it be physical things, mathematical items and relations, values, other persons, past events, and so on, and whether these affairs are experienced as clear, confused, vague, distinct, or whatever. The significant result of this insight is that, as Ortega put it, radical solitude is always "circumstantial" in the etymological sense of that term: I find myself always and essentially "in a world," "in the midst of things other than myself." In his famous phrase, which is one way of seeing the basic thrust of Husserl's notion of intentiveness, "I am my life and my circumstances."

What this briefly indicated result shows can be made plainer if we turn to a short example of phenomenological criticism that relates directly to the main problem of social science, namely, the elucidation of the fundamentally implicit beliefs or presuppositions of social life and therefore of social science: *that there is* a "world" and and *that it is* "social," that is, shared, taken for granted by each of us in "common." It is this issue— the nature of social reality, or of sociality—that the rest of this paper is devoted to.

» » » » » « « « « «

In a way, the most remarkable feature of human social life is the apparently most obvious and trivial one: Each of us typically takes it quite for granted that "the world" is not one's own private affair but is a world shared with others. We assume without question that the objects, events, artifacts, ideas, and values and the world in general are common to us all. To be sure, we frequently do bring into question this or that facet of the world: someone deceives us and we question his integrity, something turns out to be otherwise than it seemed at first to be, and we then as it were strike it out as "illusion," "deception," "hallucination." But *that there is* another person, *that there are* objects other than ourselves, *that*, in short, *there is the world* in which we live, breathe, and have our being is the unstated, presupposed, and unquestioned bedrock of our lives. With this in mind, we may well ask: What is that which makes the "social world" be at once "social" and "world"? But, beyond that crucial question is another, even more pressing: How does it happen that we are rarely, if ever, *focally attentive to* either "social" or "world" *as such?* That is, what accounts for the curious fact that the "reality" or "existence" of the social world is so *obvious* for us? These are the principle issues to which Alfred Schutz devoted the major part of his work and what follows here is drawn from his seminal achievements.

The problems are complex because we are ourselves social beings living within the social world; and, as is strikingly clear from such books as Agee's *Let Us Now Praise Famous Men* and Castaneda's two reports (7), have much at stake in the prevailing social world to which we ourselves belong. Just how slippery and precarious the problems are is evident in Gouldner's characterization (I am tempted to say caricature), for instance, of Garfinkel's (8) work as "an attack upon the common sense of *reality*," when it is precisely that "common sense of reality" that is to be placed in question. This point Gouldner seems to miss completely, as when he remarks that "the cry of pain, then, is Garfinkel's triumphal moment," and goes on to assert his belief that Garfinkel is ultimately guilty of deliberately intertwining objectivity and sadism, for Garfinkel's abusing of human beings, Gouldner believes, by stripping away the cloak of invisibility of the cultural matrix, is in fact evidence of his "readiness to use it in cruel ways" (9).

Such a complaint reveals Gouldner's own manifestly moral concern, but it also shows how far he misses the point. For, whatever the peculiarities of Garfinkel's language and techniques, his fundamental point is both clear and important. Admittedly influenced by Schutz, whom Gouldner surprisingly and indicatively mentions but once in passing in his book, Garfinkel seems to me concerned to dis-cover, to make explicit, precisely that "obviousness" which is so fundamental to what makes the social world "tick," as Schutz often put it in classes. Far from being "sadistic," such an effort is strictly "critical" or phenomenological, carried out at a particular level, in concrete situations, for specific sociological purposes. That highly unusual and unorthodox procedures are used to elicit that "cloak of invisibility" is not only not surprising, it is positively necessary if we would understand the structures and dynamics of actual social life. For what constitutes the sociality of the world is not merely "invisible" but is the very cohesiveness without which social life would in truth collapse: *its taken-for-grantedness*, to use Schutz's term. Indeed, I submit that if one were seriously to engage in Gouldner's "reflexive sociology," one would inevitably undergo precisely that wrenching experience which Gouldner faults Garfinkel for bringing about in his "victims." The sorts of reactions he obtains from them are not indicative of an "attack" on their sense of reality but of just how deeply rooted and slippery to apprehend are the "usual," the "commonplace," the "familiar," and the "obvious." The commonplace is the least common of affairs; the familiar is charged with the uncanny and strange; the usual is haunted by the unusual and disorienting. Indeed it is precisely the frequent and dramatic emergence of the hidden, the strange, the unfamiliar in the very midst of our usual daily lives that signals the seriousness of the crisis Gouldner himself, like others, is so anxious to confront and resolve. No one, I venture to say, who lacks a sense for this—for the mysterious, the astonishing, the strange, even (as Karl Jaspers has emphasized) the weird, the alien, and the gripping chill of disorientation—can possibly become that sensitive kind of social scientist Gouldner himself believes is so desperately needed in our times.

How much more chilling and difficult must it therefore be to attempt to make explicit the deepest lying foundations of social life, the presuppositions whose operative functioning makes the social world "tick"? To make them stand out and thus be accessible for understanding, what is needed is not merely the precarious vision undergone, for instance, by Garfinkel's "victims," nor the stunning disorientation Castaneda experiences when confronting the beliefs and acts of Don Juan, but what Maurice Natanson has called a veritable "philosophical upheaval," by which we are alone able to stand in authentic astonishment before what Husserl calls, with deceptive simplicity, the "general thesis of the natural attitude," which undergirds the life-world itself—the unstated, implicit commitment to, or unnoticed "belief" in, the world as "there," existing independently of us in all of its complex and multiform ways. This thesis, which Hume had come across in despairing skepticism as the rudimentary fact of human life ("custom" and "habit") but left completely unanalyzed, and which Santayana suggestively calls "animal faith," can not only be brought to explicit attention but can be studied in depth, as the work of Husserl, Schutz, and others shows.

» » » » » « « « « «

Schutz's work is most directly relevant here. He attempts to defend three fundamental theses concerning sociality: (a) a commonsense, usual knowledge of the world and its items (including other persons) is a system of constructs of their typicality; (b) the world is experienced by each of us as a common, shared, or intersubjective world of objects, events, values, recipes for acting, aims, goals, and so on; (c) perhaps most basic, as I read him, both our typicality-constructs and what we experience and interpret the world to be by means of them are principally characterized by *"taken-for-grantedness"*. We take both our usual typicality-constructs and the world (along with its multiple items) for granted as the unquestioned but always able to be questioned matrix of our thoughts, actions, and being. In brief, what makes the social world "tick"—what constitutes its essence—is a series of implicit beliefs ("theses") which are simply taken for granted "until further notice," as Husserl says, that is, until and if something to the contrary occurs (thus motivating a modification in our system of constructs). In such a case, what occurs, Schutz points out, is not that the fundamental thesis becomes dislodged, but that our experience, action, and knowledge become further differentiated into additional types and subtypes. Hence our lives, as social, are not only *structurally* formed, but are continuously undergoing *modification and change*. Several types of inquiry then become necessary and can be done at many different levels: first, what Husserl calls "static" or structural phenomenology, which focuses on the explication and articulation of the "beliefs" or "theses" prevailing in social life (or, in any particular culture or facet); second, what he calls "genetic" phenomenology, which seeks to unravel the progressive, temporal constitutions of social life, or of what Schutz calls our "stock of knowledge at hand," which is formed and continuously undergoes change in terms of what he calls our "autobiographical situation." Not only is there, then, a kind of "archeological" task ("static" phenomenology) but a "constitutive" one as well ("genetic" phenomenology) which traces out the principal ways in terms of which social life at any level becomes formed in the ways it is. A brief example should clarify these remarks.

Social scientists need no reminders, I know, of the diversity of persons and groups with a particular culture or subculture, much less about the clashes of values, ideas, conduct, and so on, between persons of different cultures. Still, there are several intriguing features of such experiences that are not usually focused upon but can be quite revealing of the sort of fundamental presuppositions which concern the phenomenologist.

Consider a simple case and a variation of it. I come home after work and learn that my wife has made plans to visit Peru; she has not told me of this before, nor have there been any signs indicating this was in her mind. I find such conduct "highly irregular," having known her for years; that part of my stock of knowledge at hand pertaining to her contains no constructs or interpretative schemes that would help me understand this, and consequently I think of the situation as "strange," "peculiar," "calling for discussion," "inquiry," and so on. Maybe she is ill, maybe "something has happened," as we sometimes say. That is, I call on my own prevailing stock of knowledge (including such items as "how to act when one is shocked," the asking of questions, the use of language and various gestures, perhaps also "what one does when one is upset, angry," etc.) in an effort to orient myself with respect to this atypical, unexpected conduct. It may turn out that she has received an urgent communication from a dear friend whom I did not know is in Peru and who now needs her; *that,* I now understand, and I am then able to place it within those sets of typications called "emergency situations concerning friends" and I set about doing other equally typical things such as planning with her and buying airline tickets. The shock becomes somewhat removed; concern and action of other sorts now goes on—I must now plan to see to the children, arrange my work-schedule to handle that, and so on. The atypical conduct becomes interpretable within my prevailing typicality-constructs: I now "understand" what at first I could not understand. However unusual, the situation is now experienced as intelligible. "These things can happen," I say.

Now consider a variation on this. I come home, doing all the usual things, and see my wife. She's sitting in a way which I interpret quite automatically as "despondent." I go up to her, ready to "do what one does" in such situations: show concern, make gentle queries, ask what I can do, and the like. She doesn't respond, but rather continues to hang her head in a "strange" (i.e., atypical) way. I go closer, now more concerned, for "she doesn't usually act this way." As I sit down beside her I notice something quite odd: She appears lifeless, and as I then lean over to her I hear, faintly, a definite "tic-tic-buzz-tic-tic-buzz . . . ," which becomes slower and slower until what I took to be my wife suddenly now appears to be an automaton. This is not only not "my wife," this is not even "a person," for "people just don't go 'tic-tic-buzz-tic-tic-,' and then collapse." Now, obviously, I experience something quite drastic, a veritable upheaval in what I had been taking for granted, and at a really basic level. Briefly, I've glimpsed a rudimentary "presupposition" of human life.

One can imagine many other variations and extensions of such examples. But this is not necessary here. If we focus our attention on the "shock" of the first case (A) and the "upheaval" of the variation (B), we can notice that certain taken-for-granted assumptions were operatively at work, and these are indeed continuously operative in a taken-for-granted way throughout the course of our daily lives. What stands out as still not questioned in A but forced into question in B is one of the rudimentary assumptions of sociality itself. Schutz formulates this as the "general thesis of the alter ego": In our everyday lives, we operatively assume that there are others, that they exist as persons having their own biographies, values, wishes, ideas, desires, plans, and so on—in short, *there are others with whom we share the "world."*

But this "general thesis" shows on closer inspection a number of other facets. We experience, interpret, and act in and on the surrounding world on the taken-for-granted assumption not merely that there are "others" but that these "others" are of *many different types:* strangers, friends, foes; postman, policemen, colleagues, doctors; wives, children, parents, brothers; warm, hostile, odd, crazy, sane; and so on. Moreover, the others who are in our world, are not all *present* before us, for some, although "contemporaries" of ours, we never actually meet face-to-face (as "consociates"); others are *past*, yet they form an intimate part of our world, having helped to shape it as that within which we now must live (our "predecessors"); still others are *future*, yet many of our actions bear directly and indirectly on them, have them "in mind," and hence they, too, form a part of our world (our "successors"). There is, finally, still another class of others (or, perhaps better, "quasi-others") whom we know to be effective in our world in important ways, but who do not "exist" as we usually understand that—fictional and mythical characters, whose actions, deeds, thoughts can influence our own lives in important ways.

To each of these types of "others," moreover, are correlated certain typical "recipes of action" and thought, which are also, for the most part, taken for granted typifications in our daily lives. At every point, however, the "general thesis of the alter ego" is operatively at work. More concretely, this "thesis" reveals, as Schutz emphasizes, at least three further components or subtheses. First, it involves the taken-for-granted assumption Schutz designates as the "reciprocity of perspectives": I assume, and assume that you assume, that the various objects and events in our world are accessible to others as, in general, .they are to me, or they can become so accessible. Thus these affairs "mean" something similar to you and me; for instance, these chairs, or these words I now use. I also take it for granted, however, that these objects mean something different to me and to others, since I am "here" (physically, socially, morally, etc.) and you are "there," and our respective biographically determined situations, with their respective relevancy-systems and other contents, differ. Still, we in our daily lives surmount such differences by means of what Schutz, following Husserl, calls two "idealizations": (a) the idealization of the interchangeability of standpoints; and (b) that of the congruency of systems of relevance. These mean that each of us assumes, and assumes that others assume, (a) that we can change places, within limits, and thereby experience an affair as "the other does"; and (b) that we can, "for all practical purposes" unless counter evidence enters in, ignore the differences in our respective biographical situations. Thus I assume now that the matters I am talking about can also be in some sense viewed by you, under certain conditions, and within certain limits, and also that differences in our respective stocks of knowledge and biographical situations are in general able to be ignored for our specific purposes here. More simply, I assume you can understand me, and can, if you do certain things, "check me out" and confirm for yourselves what I say—despite our various differences. By means of these theses and idealizations, there is formed the "We," the "Us," and correlatively the "They," who do not share our assumptions, ideas, relevance-systems, and so on.

Second, I know and assume you know (and you assume the same about me) that only a small part of my (your) knowledge is unique to me (you). For the most part, what I know is handed down to me by others —such knowledge including not only ideas and values but also how to define and interpret the world, how to find my way in the world, how to think, be, and so on. The medium par excellence for this, Schutz emphasizes, is the common vernacular, a veritable storehouse of the typifications prevailing in any particular group sharing that "common language." A genuine "common language analysis," then, would be highly revealing of the prevailing texture of "definitions of situations" and typifications in any specific "in-group" and would show, indeed, precisely what constitutes that "group" as the "in-group" it is.

Third, I assume (and assume that you assume) that our respective knowledge differs, that our knowledge shows different degrees of clarity, distinctness, precision, vagueness, familiarity, and so on. I am an "expert" in one matter, "know-of" other things less well, and still others not at all. The same, I assume, is true of you, and I continually and implicitly take this for granted, as I assume you do as well.

This very brief venture into phenomenological territory is merely a slight scratch on only one of the surfaces. It does serve, though, to show the kind of thing phenomenological criticism seeks to do. Carried out more fundamentally, one would quickly run into the issue Schutz regarded as the most pressing of philosophical problems, that of the very sense and constitution of intersubjectivity itself—the failure to resolve this he quite correctly regarded as the "scandal of philosophy."

» » » » » « « « « «

I cannot conclude this presentation without some trepidations. Not only has it been a long and somewhat tortuous route, but too many really central issues have been but touched upon only lightly. If I have given something of a "mixed bag," with what may be a blurring of certain traditional lines of distinction between sociology and philosophy, let me only assure you that this has not been altogether without some design. I plead guilty to such charges; for, though I fully realize that many persons do not acknowledge the presence of a fundamental crisis in Western culture and thought, or are inclined to see it as far less serious than others, I for my part cannot but take it as a basic given that estrangement, alienation, disorientation—"crises"—form a central part of our historical, social, and intellectual milieu. Scheler's point, alluded to earlier, that never before in human history has man been so problematic to himself as in our days, that, as he says, we have a theological, a philosophical, and a scientific view of man which know little or nothing of each other—this point does not go far enough. The truth is that we face multiple and often deeply conflicting views within each of these; there are theolo*gies,* philosoph*ies,* and conflicting scientific view*s,* as well as political, artistic, economic, and other ones. And frequently they know little if anything of one another, and are unconcerned about that.

This cluster of systemic rifts, which dramatically underscores the givenness of the "crisis," obviously has had and will continue to have the gravest of implications at the precise point where the human scene is the focal concern: the disciplines concerned with man and the human world. Serious intercultural and intracultural divergencies and splits cannot fail to be mirrored in the sciences studying the human world, for the latter are carried on by persons who themselves are parts of the former, having considerable stake in the outcome and in the structures of social reality. This Gouldner and others recognize, and they draw far-reaching moral and epistemological consequences from it—a main one being to bring into question the very possibility of achieving the sort of objectivity so long cherished as a prime requisite for science.

If I have taken issue with that stance, it is because I am increasingly convinced that a terribly important point is in danger of being obscured; we are in danger of being sucked into the very estrangements and crises we seek to understand and resolve, becoming victims of our own concern. The point I am struggling to make is, I know, a bit elusive. Expressed as a simple dictum, it is this: Precisely because we are ourselves human persons living in the very scene we seek to comprehend, we have a remarkably effective wedge into human reality. The point is one Gouldner clearly appreciates: There is no knowledge of the social world that is not a knowledge of ourselves as social beings. The converse is, however, also true: Knowledge of ourselves is already a knowledge of the social milieu, and that, I take it, is the prime sense of his call for a "reflexive sociology." Only if the social scientist makes that dictum a vital part of his own actual inquiries and life is it at all possible for the social sciences to appreciate—that is, to understand and work within—the human world as comprised of persons having their own dignity, worth, their own "radical solitudes." One forgets this only on pains of systematically distorting the human context, thereby leaving wide the door to dehumanizing and alienating not only the social world but the social scientist as well. In the words of Barbara O'Brien, in her striking autobiography, *Operators and Things*, taking persons as things to be manipulated, dissected, and variously studied as no more than pieces of physicochemical nature invariably forces the hand that holds that knife into the same shape. The corollary to the dictum is equally simple: We see ourselves as we see others, and to the extent that others are taken as mere things, so are we to ourselves. We then become incapable of even seeing, much less scientifically understanding, what Yeats calls the "ceremony of innocence," and thus do we loose anarchy upon the world.

But that dictum, if I may so call it, gives us the very thing sought for by social science. If social science seeks to understand the social world, it is painfully obvious that our own operative taken-for-granted notions of what it means to be "social" and "world" must be the focal issues for social theory. If we would understand the social world, it is to the social world itself that we must turn for instruction, for our clues to develop our hypotheses and theories, as well as our sundry lines of activism and directions for social change. But the latter cannot make sense without the former efforts to understand; and such efforts must on principle begin from the recognition, as Schutz puts it,

that we cannot deal with phenomena in the social world as we do with phenomena belonging to the natural sphere. In the latter, we collect facts and regularities which are not understandable to us, but which we can only refer to certain fundamental assumptions about the world. We shall never understand why the mercury in the thermometer rises if the sun shines on it. We can only interpret this phenomenon as compatible with the laws we have deduced from some basic assumptions about the physical world. We want, on the contrary, to understand social phenomena, and we cannot understand them apart from their placement with the scheme of human motives, human means and ends, human planning—in short—within the categories of human action (10).

It is one thing to "explain" natural phenomena—that is, to place them within an already formed (implicit or explicit) context of assumptions about the physical world. It is quite another matter to "understand" human actions—that is, to determine and appreciate their essential placement within the context of beliefs, values, motives, plans, of the human persons whose actions they are. The dictum mentioned has, in other words, its profound methodological and epistemological ramifications for social scientific labor, specifically, what Schutz calls, following on his critical interpretation of Max Weber, the "postulate of subjective interpretation of meaning," which is but one, although the most significant, of the postulates for social science methodology. To seek to understand the social world *as it is for those whose social world it is* is possible only if one practices the systematic art of listening to them in their own terms and attends to the "social world" they construct for themselves. "Listening" as I intend it here, is no mere fetish, but requires the careful construction of devices—models and ideal types, analysis of common vernaculars, study of the multiple forms of expression (in literature, art, worship, physiognomical phenomena, etc.), and others—by which an attuneful and appreciative "seeing" of social worlds can alone occur, one which is adequate and faithful to the "things themselves" in their own proper settings. It is for this reason that I am persuaded that one of the potent sociological "tools" is precisely the study of the actual "usages," in Ortega's apt term, of a culture—the typified, taken-for-granted ways of doing, speaking, and thinking that find their main expression in the common vernacular and literature of a people. If you will, the sociologist must, in this view, be very much like a creative novelist, and the novelist turns out to be very much of a practicing sociologist.

A final point needs to be made. Gouldner's call for a reflexive sociology, I have said, stops short of being the truly radical affair he thinks it is. If the social world is indeed so proximal to the work of the social scientist, as I believe it is, not only does that fact have serious implications for social science itself, but it also shows the profound connections of any possible social science to phenomenology, the discipline of philosophical criticism. If social scientific knowledge is at the same time knowledge of the self, of the social scientist himself, and, conversely—and this circumstance necessitates making thematic the taken-for-granted typifications (beliefs, values, concepts, etc.) of beings whose typifications they are (the postulate of subjective interpretation of meaning)—then it is clearly evident that this task opens out onto an even more fundamental set of problems. The fact of "taken for grantedness" itself, the fact that typifications even arise in human consciousness, the fact that human beings themselves understand, live in, and act on the social world as the common matrix of their lives in terms of these typifications—all these point to a dimension of issues which undergird those of the social sciences and are systematically presupposed by them. These issues, I have argued, form the prime subject of phenomenological criticism. A truly radical discipline of criticism, then, is one that has that task of explication, and it relates to social science as the soil relates to the tree which is nourished by it, on and through which it can at all thrive.

For the social scientist to achieve knowledge of the social world it is doubtless imperative that he proceed with the full recognition of the dictum mentioned, its corollaries, and its methodological postulates. Not only is "objectivity" not lost or compromised thereby, it is to the contrary only by fully recognizing these that objectivity can be achieved. To the charge, as outmoded as it is irrelevant, that this turns social science into a subjectivism, one can only respond with an unequivocally affirmative answer—provided that one is careful to distinguish "subjectivism" as an errant metaphysical stance from "subjectivity" (solitude and sociality) as a prime arena for inquiry—indeed, as the central focus for social theory and science. And it is the systematic exploration of that territory which occupies phenomenology. I am thus deeply convinced that not only Gouldner's reflexive sociology but Garfinkel's and others' efforts to work out a viable ethnomethodology for social science are properly understandable only as phenomenological efforts, although not at the radically critical level of philosophical phenomenology.

The crisis of Western man is a critical one in both senses: It is critical in that it presents us with an authentic urgency to grapple systematically with the very real and tumultuous issues of the times, and it is critical in that it forces on us the many-leveled tasks of reflexive critical thought. Without that critical and urgent thrust into the reaches of solitude and sociality by the social sciences and philosophy, I very much fear that we shall become mere leaves on the bitter winds of mindless activism and blind belittlers of the ceremonies of innocence which tell of the inner cohesiveness of all things. We must, in short, reclaim the arena of firm conviction, and we can do so only with a passionate intensity for truth at all costs.

NOTES

1. This paper was first presented as a principal talk in the section on Phenomenological Sociology, at the American Sociological Association meetings, Denver, Colorado, 1971.

2. Alvin Gouldner, *The Coming Crisis in Western Sociology*, Basic Books, New York, 1970, p. 486.

3. Carlos Castaneda, *A Separate Reality*, Simon and Schuster, New York, 1971.

4. Gouldner, *op. cit.*, pp. 489–490.

5. *Ibid.*, p. 13.

6. *Ibid.*, p. 493.

7. The first report was Carlos Castaneda, *The Teachings of Don Juan: A Yaqui Way of Knowledge*, Ballantine Books, New York, 1969.

8. Harold Garfinkel, *Studies in Ethnomethodology*, Prentice-Hall, Englewood Cliffs, N.J., 1967.

9. Gouldner, *op. cit.*, pp. 392–394.

10. Alfred Schutz, "The Problem of Rationality in the Social World," *Collected Papers*, Vol. II, Martinus Nijhoff, The Hague, 1964, p. 85.

»»»»»»»»»»»»»»»»»»»»»»»»«‹«‹«‹«‹«‹«‹«‹«‹«‹«‹«‹«‹«‹«‹«

If phenomenology is a radical philosophy involving a criticism of the basic assumptions of the social sciences, sociology among them, then what is its relation to radicalism, the critical examination of society? Wolff comments on the arguments advanced by Zaner with special relevance for developments in sociology. In both senses, sociology is being subjected to critical examination of its own presuppositions and assumptions and political radicalism is subjecting both society and its observers to criticism. Yet the suppositions on which each is based, the characteristics of the subject under study, and the moral issues of the enterprise itself must be considered in both cases.

Can a relation between the two radicalisms be found? Wolff's paper anticipates the relations Dallmayr examines in the work of those who have attempted to blend phenomenology and Marxism.

TOWARD RADICALISM IN SOCIOLOGY AND EVERY DAY

»»»»»»»»»»»»»»»»»»»»»»»«««««««««««««««««««««««

Kurt H. Wolff

Brandeis University

I have come to decide—or, perhaps more accurately, to agree with myself—to write my contribution to this book fundamentally in the form of a commentary on Richard M. Zaner's "Solitude and Sociality: The Critical Foundations of the Social Sciences." I do so, first, because this paper is a concrete and specific occasion, and it recalls a concrete and specific situation. The *occasion* is one which spontaneously makes me not only talk about but *do* phenomenology, that is, show or argue a kind of phenomenological analysis (certainly not an exhaustive or comprehensive one). The *situation* is recalled, and thus better preserved, precisely by this format of the paper, which originated in a session on phenomenological sociology organized and chaired by George Psathas, the first to be sponsored or at least authorized by the American Sociological Association, on August 31, 1971, at its annual meeting in Denver, Colorado. At that session, Professor Zaner presented his paper, and I presented a discussion,

47

now revised for this book. The second reason for casting my contribution in this form is that some if not most of the questions to which my reading of Professor Zaner's paper gives rise are not limited to that paper but are for me raised by phenomenology much more generally, and more specifically also by the exciting work of Alfred Schutz.

Among sociologists, a discussion about and initiated by Professor Zaner's paper might begin thus: Something, sociologists feel—and Professor Zaner appears to share this feeling—something is moving in sociology, even though we don't quite know what it is, or where (if anywhere) it is going, and what thrust it has. But I (for one) find a particular trend in the occurrence of a first session on phenomenological sociology at the annual meeting of a sociological association, a session at which a philosopher introduces his listeners, no doubt most of them sociologists, to "phenomenological sociology" and thus, in a particular sense, to themselves; in the very appearance of the present book; and also in the fact that for several years now there have been radical caucuses at the meetings of the American Sociological Association and its regional affiliates; that *Sociological Abstracts* contains a section on "radical sociology"; and that there have even been sessions and not only caucuses at the official meetings—which I don't think can wholly be disposed of as an effort to coopt the critic; that there seems to be a growing interest in a Marxist approach to sociology, as well as in phenomenology and ethnomethodology; perhaps more specifically, that there have recently appeared several acute self-critiques, if not self-incriminations, of sociology [to one of which Professor Zaner makes repeated reference in his paper (1)]; and likewise related to the moving and groping in that "discipline," that there now exists a reader in English in the so-called sociology of knowledge (2).

Maurice Natanson, a phenomenologist and student and editor of Alfred Schutz, similarly, or at least compatibly with the present writing, thus comments on the contemporary situation in social science more generally:

> The last few years have seen the rise of a bold band of young social scientists who have not only challenged old attitudes but have insisted on locating their professional activity in the midst of mundane reality and on finding clues for their work in whatever quarter seems lively and likely, philosophy included.

He mentions Peter L. Berger, *The Precarious Vision* (1967); Maurice Stein and Arthur Vidich (eds.), *Sociology on Trial* (1963); Harold Garfinkel, *Studies in Ethnomethodology* (1967); Ned Polsky, *Hustlers, Beats, and Others* (1967); Robert Engler, "Social Science and Social Consciousness: The Shame of the Universities" (in Theodore Roszak (ed.), *The Dissenting Academy*, 1967); Christian Bay, "The Cheerful Science of Dismal

Politics" (also in the Roszak volume); and he refers to C. Wright Mills'
The Sociological Imagination (1961) (3).

I am not trying, however, to make a survey of even selected movements in sociology, let alone social science, but only to sketch one of the
backgrounds of Professor Zaner's paper, to which I now turn, although
not in an effort toward anything like an exhaustive or even systematic
treatment. Before I discuss this paper, consider what "discuss" means. It
means to "strike apart." But what does "striking apart" mean? I
conjecture—and this is all it is—that its meaning lies somewhere between "demolishing" and "interpreting." I could try to get acquainted
with the history of discussion, which would presumably lead me into the
history of learned societies, as well as into the history of the semantics of
the word and of what we take as somehow related words, notably, perhaps, the last-named, "interpret," "to be the go-between." Thus, why on
occasions such as this do we use the expression "discussant," and not (for
instance) "interpreter" or perhaps "exegete," expounder, one who leads
out, "educator"—or, for that matter, "commentator"? I don't know.
There is a sense, then, in which I don't know what I am supposed to be
doing and, in fact, am doing; and this hints at one direction in which we
leave, or go beyond, linguistic, or sociolinguistic, analysis.

What is this sense in which I don't know what I am supposed to be
doing and, I repeat, *am* doing? I realize several things. First, I realize that
I don't know what a discussant is, more specifically what he has been historically. Consequently I cannot assess this role and, on the basis of such
an assessment, find and argue my own definition of this role. Second, not
knowing what I am supposed to do or am doing within the frame of reference of the institutional history of which, unbeknownst to myself, I am
yet a part, I realize my discontinuity with that history. And I also recognize, of course, that I have thus far not yet focused on Professor Zaner's
paper but on the word—the word "discussant"—that is supposed to
tell what I am expected to do with that paper; and I have discovered that
if I want to learn the lesson that word can teach me, I have to engage in
inquiries other than into Professor Zaner's paper—indeed, in major inquiries. Should I therefore say that I cannot do my job, at least not before
completing those inquiries into institutional and semantic history?

Clearly, if these inquiries or the knowledge of their results are among
the requirements of my job, I have not got them, and thus cannot do my
job. This, however, tells less, I think, about me as *an individual* than
about me as the *type* (or kind, or sort) *of individual* who is called upon to
do this type (kind, sort) of job; that is, it says something about discussants
in general. For I expect that many if not most discussants—perhaps
more among sociologists than among certain other scholars—are similarly unfamiliar with the history of the word "discuss" and the history of

the type of person called discussant. Probably such ignorance or, as I said earlier, discontinuity, characterizes discussants in most if not all places where the institution of discussion now exists. (Both those "places" and the "now" require specification, which also entails major inquiries.) My incompetence thus is likely not to be idiosyncratic but an instance of a widespread incompetence. But it is obviously general in another sense: it is present on the occasion of papers other than Professor Zaner's. That is, the question of what it means, and has meant, to discuss something is separable from the occasion on which it arises.

Yet there is a thematic connection between this question and Professor Zaner's paper. There are themes connecting the two. These themes are *crisis* and *criticism*. Both terms derive from the Greek *krinein*, to separate, decide, judge (4), sift (5). Thinking about my task, I became aware of the need, and called attention to the need, for "separating" the word "discuss," for teasing apart, inspecting, and judging its history, sifting, that is, merely alerting to the task of sifting, its various "sediments" or "strata"—to use terms from phenomenology. In a kindred spirit, Professor Zaner's paper is concerned, to recall its subtitle, with the "critical foundations" of the social sciences. It undertakes to drive home both the crisis in which we find ourselves and the idea of " 'criticism' " as the *"fundamental meaning of 'phenomenology' "* (Zaner's italics). More specifically, just as I have raised questions about the word "discuss," so Professor Zaner says "that we necessarily find ourselves impelled to reassess our typical notions of what 'social' and 'world,' 'real' and 'unreal,' 'knowledge' and 'ignorance,' must mean" (6); and this list, I am sure, is not exhaustive, and "discuss" might well be one of the many possible additions.

» » » » » « « « « «

The fundamental question I have about Professor Zaner's paper concerns the relation between our crisis and phenomenology understood as criticism (7). Phenomenology is indeed radical criticism. According to Zaner, it engages "in that most difficult and, in many respects, frighteningly personal effort to probe what Ortega calls *'radical solitude,'* that is, 'my life' in its deepest dimensions. Hence being radical is in truth being reflexive and critical to the utmost, which means to the inner reaches of radical solitude."

As to our crisis, Professor Zaner writes: "What is called for in the most urgent way, it seems to me, is the clear recognition of the full dimension of the 'crisis.' " For,

Though I fully realize that many persons do not acknowledge the presence of a fundamental crisis in Western culture and thought, or are inclined to see it as far less serious than others, I for my part cannot but take it as a basic given that estrangement, alienation, disorientation—"crises"—form a central part of our historical, social, and intellectual milieu.

And yet I am not persuaded that Professor Zaner has portrayed "the full dimension" of our crisis. Our crisis appears to be cultural, cognitive, psychic; its limits, his paper implies, coincide with the limits of Western *culture*. But I am not convinced that Professor Zaner has described "the full dimension" even of the crisis in our *culture* (e.g., there is nothing on art or religion). Had he made his diagnosis of our crisis or of his use of the term "culture" and, for that matter, of the term "Western culture," more explicit, he might have argued that what to many observers of our time appear as components of our crisis—to mention only some: nuclear power, the arms race, population problems, pollution—are indeed components of the crisis of Western *culture;* in other words, that technological, political, economic, and demographic problems are most usefully understood as *cultural* problems. Or, instead, he might have justified his limitation to culture in the more common meaning of the term. Perhaps, however, Professor Zaner did not use the word "cultural" in so serious a sense—perhaps he could just as well have spoken of a fundamental crisis in Western *society*. But in this case, his omission of any reference to the kind of processes and events I have just mentioned would have been even less acceptable.

"To be radical," Professor Zaner writes, "in its originary and forceful sense means going to the roots, even, to take the metaphor a bit further, to that which nourishes and sustains the roots or foundations, the soil: Going down to the psychical, mental, or spiritual life-processes and acts through which alone any of us is at all aware of anything whatever." But this is only a particular notion of "roots," against which the recall of other roots—social, political, economic, indeed historical—should be advanced, in order to attain a more comprehensive, a more radical notion of "radical." It appears, then, that Professor Zaner has not practiced the critical analysis he puts forward as well as he undoubtedly could. He thus lays himself open to such questions—he implicitly raises such questions—as how phenomenology, or how greater awareness of the philosophical premises of the social sciences, can liberate us from the Pentagon, or make for a just distribution of wealth, or help prevent nuclear war. He could answer that such questions are absurd, that phenomenology, of course, is not a panacea, that philosophy is not politics or economics, that the phenomenologist is no statesman. Let this pass, and let us ask instead: What *is* the place of the phenomenologist and the phenomenologically sensitive social scientist in our society?

» » » » » « « « «

When we ask this question, we should be aware of at least two senses it may have. Do we mean *where*, in fact, can phenomenologists and phenomenologically sensitive social scientists now be found in this country or in other countries, what do they do, what influence do they have, and so on? Or do we mean where *should* they be, what *should* they be doing, what influence *should* they try for? Should they continue what they are doing? Should they change it and, if so, change it in what sense? Should they do something other than phenomenology? If so, what? Or should they change the meaning of phenomenology, continue what they are doing, and claim it to be phenomenology? On what grounds can any of these or similar options be advocated?

Professor Zaner advocates phenomenology as philosophical criticism and asks social scientists to get acquainted with it because of its relevance to their own enterprise. His grounds, I feel, are mainly two, one of which Professor Zaner states. This is our crisis, a response to which—perhaps Professor Zaner won't object to the expression I am about to use—is a change of consciousness in the direction of a far more radical criticism, precisely as urged and demonstrated by phenomenology. This may be called the historical ground of his advocacy, because it appears embedded in Professor Zaner's diagnosis of our time as it is sketched in his paper. But I also sense an ahistorical ground. It is that the discoveries phenomenologists, and above all, Alfred Schutz, have made concerning "sociality" (8), and especially intersubjectivity, are insights, even if tentative, which had not previously been had; that they are potential or actual truths, which should be more widely known and acted upon. Professor Zaner mentions a number of these insights, notably Schutz's "theses concerning sociality" (9); his "general thesis of the alter ego"; and the "reciprocity of perspectives" and the facts that only a small part of an individual's knowledge is unique to him or her and that this knowledge has "different degrees of clarity, distinctness, precision, vagueness, familiarity, and so on" (10).

If my surmise of the two grounds of Professor Zaner's advocacy of phenomenology as philosophical criticism is even approximately correct, one question it raises concerns the relation between these two grounds, the historical and the ahistorical—a question that may be raised independently of the correctness or incorrectness of my surmise. Another relation that calls for analysis is that between advocating something—in this case, phenomenology—and reporting on it or giving information about it. I am referring not only to the sort of connection that can be developed in the form of a story: I have seen something excellent; I am taken by it; let me tell you about it because I think you too will be persuaded and advocate it as I do. I also mean a minute examination of what actually goes on in oneself as one moves from reporting to advocating, or vice versa; as one moves, possibly, from one of Alfred Schutz' "worlds" into another (11).

» » » » » « « « « «

Here, surely, is a vast area of things we human beings take for granted: "We all know" what happens when the curtain rises on the stage, how our mood changes as we "enter into" a religious service, what it means to wake up or to fall asleep (12), or to "be absorbed by the world" of a painting, a novel, a musical composition, or to move from scientific to philosophical considerations, from walking to driving, from talking with a person of the other sex to making love to that person, from being distracted to focusing attention—but if we ask ourselves whether it is really true that we know, we'll find that we don't know at all, that these and incalculably additional matters of the most ordinary sort, of humdrum everyday life, that the very routine in which we move day-in and day-out remain entirely unpenetrated by us, that we waddle along from birth to death in a quagmire of opacity. Schutz' "typicality" describes this well: We always count on and tell ourselves and others about "sorts of things," "x's like y's," "you knows." Surely, one meaning of Husserl's effort—to get at the things themselves—undeterred by Kant's theory that we cannot know the *Ding an sich*, and inspired by Descartes' doubt to radicalize this doubt, is to illuminate this lava or maelstrom of the trivial.

Zaner advocates a preparatory step: to become aware of this opacity, to study what we students and those we study do take for granted, to draw a map of typicalities and account for the map and what it shows. This is a slightly modified way of indicating what Zaner (and Schutz) mean by social science; phenomenology, then, would (in its relevance for social science) be the illumination, the constitutional and genetic analysis, of the typicalities of the social world. "To the charge," Professor Zaner writes, that such a conception of social science turns it "into a subjectivism, one can only respond with an unequivocally affirmative answer— provided that one is careful to distinguish 'subjectivism' as an errant metaphysical stance from 'subjectivity' (solitude and sociality) as a prime arena for inquiry—indeed, as the central focus for social theory and science."

This is the important passage concerning "solitude and sociality" referred to earlier (in note 8) and now calling for attention. I confess that I find scant instruction in Professor Zaner's paper on how to interpret it; I thus feel free to make what sense of it I can—and this sense I find very important. I neglect " 'subjectivism' as an errant metaphysical stance" and focus on "subjectivity," which for Professor Zaner evidently is composed of solitude and sociality. I cannot read this statement about subjectivity other than as a claim concerning the nature of man, a statement in "philosophical anthropology." The claim concerns the essence of man: Man is essentially both solitary and social. It is a claim regarding not any or all human beings such as we meet them or might meet them or such that as scientists, both natural and social, we might study them, but regarding man as such, namely, such as he must be comprehended if we would have any hope whatever of understanding, comprehending, coming at all close to actually existing human beings, "empirical" human beings. This is what I mean when I say that it is a philosophical in contrast to a scientific claim. It concerns what has by many philosophers, including Husserl, been called the "transcendental subject," in contrast to the "empirical subject." The transcendental subject is one of the many "essences" that may come into view in "phenomenological bracketing," that is, if while thus bracketing myself and the world I focus on it.

Professor Zaner goes some way toward qualifying the subject-object distinction, which is characteristic of everyday life and traditional social science, with reference to social science, above all by reporting on, and supporting, Gouldner's strictures and by emphasizing that knowledge of the social world and self-knowledge of the knower of the social world are inseparable, emerging in one process. In this qualification, he goes as far as Schutz does. I myself would go further toward "the roots": I advocate the suspension of the very distinction between subject and object (in the context of advocating the suspension of "received notions" generally); I plead for the substitution of phenomenological bracketing by what I call "surrender," which is more unconditional, thus more radical, if only because unconditioned by the rule, taken for granted in phenomenology, that its outcome—its "catch"—must be cognitive (13).

» » » » » « « « « «

Obviously, Professor Zaner's paper has raised many important questions for me, although, as I indicated initially, I have been able to undertake only a less than thoroughgoing analysis of it. It should also be clear, as I said at the beginning of this paper, that some of the questions, probably most of them, go beyond his particular view and are raised for me by phenomenology, as I understand it, more generally, especially by Alfred Schutz' version. At this point, I also wish to register my awareness of the fact that, with the notable exception of the last section, most of what I have said consists of questions I found myself asking *about* Professor Zaner's paper, questions of "extrinsic" interpretation (14), such as concern the nature of his paper, rather than about statements contained in it, which would have disregarded or taken for granted its nature, premises, grounds. In so proceeding, I have acted, I think, in the sense of Professor Zaner's and phenomenology's injunction to be critical, "to make explicit what is implicit," without, to repeat again, even thinking that I could be systematic.

I wish to close with a question about the very nature of radical criticism. It is another way of pointing, as I did before, to the relation between phenomenology, *as* radical criticism, and our crisis. I now ask about the relation between such radicalism—philosophical radicalism —and what is more ordinarily meant by "radicalism": political radicalism. In my judgment, both—although the former obviously more programmatically than the latter—must focus more explicitly and thoroughly on what they are doing or, indeed, focusing on: the suspension of received notions. Both philosophical and political radicals must suspend, as far as they can stand it and, in their public roles, can answer for it politically, their received notions—those received notions, that is, which they can imagine in any way to be pertinent to their undertakings. Awareness of this task, of this wide- and deep-ranging change, calls for persuading philosophical radicals, and for philosophical radicals persuading themselves, to recognize the moral inescapability of political responsibility and responsiveness. It calls for persuading political radicals, and for them persuading themselves, to recognize human beings and to understand and treat them as ends. And it calls for persuading both to take seriously and practice the optimal suspension of received notions. I think the two terms of the relation between philosophical radicalism and political radicalism need study and clarification, especially as to the characteristics of their referents in the present and the recent past. The aim of such study and clarification is to attain directives for bringing the two radicalisms, at the very least, to greater mutual awareness (15). Hence the title of this paper, which "fell into place" after I had written it.

NOTES

1. Alvin W. Gouldner, *The Coming Crisis of Western Sociology*, Basic Books, New York and London, 1970. Among others are Robert W.

Friedrichs, *A Sociology of Sociology*, Free Press, New York, 1970, and Larry T. Reynolds and Janice M. Reynolds (eds.), *The Sociology of Sociology*, David McKay, New York, 1970, as well as several readers on "radical," "everyday," and "humanistic" sociology, and periodicals representing these and other relatively new interests.

2. James E. Curtis and John W. Petras (eds.), *The Sociology of Knowledge: A Reader*, Praeger, New York and Washington, 1970. (It may be noted that in some languages, such works are older. Thus: Kurt Lenk (ed.), *Ideologie*, Luchterhand, Neuwied, 1961 [and later revised editions]; Irving Louis Horowitz (ed.), *Historia y elementos de la sociología del conocimiento*, EUDEBA, Buenos Aires, 1964, 2 vols.; Roger Bastide, preface, *Contributions à la sociologie de la connaissance*, Editions Anthropos [Cahiers du Laboratoire de Sociologie de la Connaissance, Vol. I], Paris, 1967 [a symposium rather than a reader]. In 1970, there also appeared the first reader in Italian: Alberto Izzo (ed.), *Il condizionamento sociale del pensiero*, Loescher, Turin. Perhaps there are others.)

3. Maurice Natanson, *The Journeying Self: A Study in Philosophy and Social Role*, Addison-Wesley, Reading, Mass., 1970, pp. 78, 203. *The Dissenting Academy* is one of the "Pantheon Antitextbooks," of which others published thus far (as of January 1973) are Barton J. Bernstein (ed.), *Towards a New Past: Dissenting Essays in American History*, 1969; Philip Green and Sanford Levinson (eds.), *Power and Community: Dissenting Essays in Political Science*, 1970; Edward Friedman and Mark Selden (eds.), *America's Asia: Dissenting Essays on Asian-American Relations*, 1971 (all available as Vintage Books; dates given are the Vintage Book publication dates); Louis Kampf and Paul Lauter (eds.), *The Politics of Literature*, 1972; Dell Hymes (ed.), *Reinventing Anthropology*, 1973.

4. William Morris (ed.), *The American Heritage Dictionary of the English Language*, American Heritage and Houghton Mifflin, Boston, 1969, p. 1540: "skeri-."

5. Eric Partridge, *Origins*, Macmillan, New York, 1958, p. 130: "crisis . . ."

6. As well as of "sanity," "madness," "normal," "abnormal," "relative," "empirical," "a priori," "theory," "practice," and so on. All quotations from Richard M. Zaner are from his paper in this volume, unless otherwise indicated.

7. Also see Richard M. Zaner, *The Way of Phenomenology: Criticism as a Philosophical Discipline*, Pegasus, New York, 1970, where this understanding is worked out more thoroughly.

8. Despite the title of Professor Zaner's paper, it contains surprisingly little on sociality. The advertence to Ortega's solitary thinker has already been quoted. But there is another relevant passage, which needs much development, and to which I shall come.

9. These are, as described in Zaner's paper: everyday knowledge of the world is knowledge of typicalities; the world is experienced as common;

our knowledge of it is taken for granted. For a slightly different version, see Professor Zaner's "Introduction" to Alfred Schutz, *Reflections on the Problem of Relevance*, edited, annotated and with an introduction by Richard M. Zaner, Yale University Press, New Haven and London, 1970, pp. xi–xii.

10. These last three are called by Zaner, following Schutz, respectively, "the structural organization of knowledge," "the genetic socialization of knowledge," and "the social distribution of knowledge." Richard M. Zaner, "Theory of Intersubjectivity: Alfred Schutz," *Social Research, 28,* 1961, pp. 84–86. It need hardly be pointed out that these ideas of Schutz are of systematic relevance for the sociology of knowledge, but they are hardly used in the "treatise in the sociology of knowledge" which is essentially indebted to Schutz: Peter L. Berger and Thomas Luckmann, *The Social Construction of Reality*, Doubleday, Garden City, New York, 1966 ("social distribution of knowledge" is mentioned and acknowledged as derived from Schutz—but not in the above sense; pp. 72 and 182, note 41). One of the most important sources for a sociology of knowledge is to be found in Schutz' own writings in his "The Well-Informed Citizen: An Essay on the Social Distribution of Knowledge" (1946), *Collected Papers,* Vol. II, edited and introduced by Arvid Brodersen, Martinus Nijhoff, The Hague, 1964, pp. 120–134 (to which Berger and Luckmann do not refer).

11. Alfred Schutz, "On Multiple Realities" (1945), *Collected Papers*, Vol. I, edited and introduced by Maurice Natanson, Martinus Nijhoff, The Hague, 1962, pp. 207–259. Schutz does not raise the question, which at this point in the discussion of Professor Zaner's paper also arises, of how many worlds (or realities or finite provinces of meaning) there are or how one might go about seeking to answer this question. It seems promising to entertain beginning with Schutz' six "basic characteristics" of the "cognitive style" of a world: "a specific tension of consciousness," "a specific *epoché*," "a prevalent form of spontaneity," "a specific form of experiencing one's self," "a specific form of sociality," and "a specific time-perspective" (*ibid.*, p. 230). Within limits (to be specified), the "number" of worlds may well depend on the purpose of the discourse or investigation in which they or the question of them figure.

12. Barbara Deck, *Characteristics of Consciousness in Falling Asleep*, unpublished manuscript, Brandeis University, May 1970. (The paper consists of two parts, the transcript of the author's talk into a tape recorder as she was falling asleep, and the analysis of the transcript.) It may be noted that in the beginning of the present paper I found myself *not* taking for granted what in comparable typical situations typically *is:* my understanding of what I was supposed to do (cf. the remarks on "discuss").

13. For a summary, see *Surrender and Catch: A Palimpsest Story*, University of Saskatchewan Press, Saskatoon, 1972 (Sorokin Lectures, No. 3).

14. Cf. Karl Mannheim, "The Ideological and the Sociological Interpretation of Intellectual Phenomena" (1926), trans. Kurt H. Wolff (1963), in *From*

Karl Mannheim, edited and with an introduction by Kurt H. Wolff, Oxford University Press, New York, 1971, pp. 116–131.

15. I have made the beginning of a closely related effort, regarding "humanly radical" and "politically radical" cultural anthropologists, in "This is the Time for Radical Anthropology," in Dell Hymes, ed., *Reinventing Anthropology, op. cit.*, pp. 99–118.

»»»»»»»»»»»»»»»»»»»»»» «« «« «« «« «« «« «« «« «« «« ««

Wagner addresses one of the many criticisms of phenomenological sociology, that it is too narrow in scope and limits itself to studies on the micro level. While phenomenological sociology starts from the subjective experiences of the individual its focus is thereby not restricted. Rather, all social phenomena can be analyzed, both in the structurization of "beliefs" about the social world and in the genetic or constitutive processes by which social life becomes structured and changes.

The dynamic processes of change seem to be most neglected in phenomenological writings. Yet change, as manifested in the minor disruptions of everyday routines and in more significant alterations ranging from disruptions of central routines or relationships such as job or family to crises affecting life styles and belief systems, are ever present and deserve study. Wagner argues that a phenomenological approach to such problems should and can be made and that the past failure of such undertakings is not to be regarded as a basic theoretical or methodological shortcoming of a phenomenological sociology.

THE SCOPE OF PHENOMENOLOGICAL SOCIOLOGY: CONSIDERATIONS AND SUGGESTIONS

» « «

Helmut R. Wagner

Hobart and William Smith Colleges

Husserl's phenomenology came into being as a radically subjective and thus strictly individualistic ("solipsistic") method of inquiry into phenomena and essences of consciousness. The elementary area of his concerns may be described as the observable forms of immediate cognitive experience and reflection.

In exploring this realm, Husserl was able to utilize the work of some outstanding theorists of the late nineteenth century. His teacher, Franz Brentano, established the principle of intentionality: There is no consciousness as such; consciousness is always consciousness of something; it cannot be separated from the "object" it is conscious of. Henri Bergson's conception of *durée* provided the recognition of subjective experience of time in distinction from the mechanical notion of clock time. E. R. Clay

61

offered the idea of the "specious present": the experience of any given "moment" of the present has itself *"durée."* William James, however, made the most important contribution to the understanding of subjective-time experience with his explorations of the stream of consciousness: The specious present itself is not a narrow link in a thin chain of apperceptions, reflections, and so on, but a rather broad floating process with main drifts and additional currents, accompanied by still more fleeting fringe phenomena. (1). Husserl not only drew these notions and discoveries together, he extended them with various devices of his own, such as his conception of expanding cognitive horizons. On this basis, he built his complex theory of the ego which is simultaneously the subject of his consciousness and object of his cognition(2).

If there is a single criterion that allows us to identify a phenomenologist, it is his recognition of this phenomenological anchor ground. From it, he may move in various directions. If he follows the course Husserl's work took from about 1900 to 1930, he will become involved in extremely sophisticated and difficult inquiries concerning several forms of Husserl's famous "reductions," and ultimately concerning the solitary ego in its "pure" or "transcendental" form. But the elaboration of the psychological basis of phenomenology lends itself also to a move in a "social-psychological" direction (3). Such a move leads away from Husserl's attempts at expanding his original "phenomenological method" into a transcendental-idealistic philosophy. After 1930, Husserl himself provided starting points for pursuits in alternate directions. In the studies incorporated in, or written around, his last major work, *The Crisis of European Sciences*, he traced out three paths into his philosophy: the paths from psychology, through history, and across the "life-world." The last of them is significant for sociology.

With it, Husserl offered a means of maintaining a phenomenological position without following the trajectory of his investigations into the solitary ego. Instead of "reducing" the "natural stance" of the "naive" individual to its "eidetic essence," Husserl now accepted the *content* of a "thinking as usual" in everyday-life situations as a legitimate point of departure. His life-world is the world of everyday experiences, accepted as they present themselves to the individual in his "natural stance," that is, a world of experiencing natural objects and other persons, of handling things, and of dealing with people in a purposive and usually practical manner, and of the unquestioning acceptance of socially given "recipes" for practical conduct and of culturally established assumptions and beliefs about the "world" of things, of man, of nature, of society, of God. Two most prominent characteristics of the life-world, as the world of everyday activity and experience, are its thoroughly pragmatic style of thinking, and its robust sense of "reality." What exists and occurs is "taken-for-granted" and accepted as "real"; it remains unquestioned as long as things work out as expected.

Before 1930, Husserl's phenomenology seemed to be radically individualistic and extremely remote from any social-psychological considerations. However, he never had had the intention to create a solipsistic philosophy; he merely had postponed the transition from the subjectivity of the lonely ego to the recognition of the social Other. Yet what he had planned as a straight step forward from the first to the second volume of his *Ideas*, became his most difficult "problem," the "problem of intersubjectivity." After long years, he abandoned the draft of the second volume. Later, he made other efforts to provide an answer, the last one in the fifth of his *Cartesian Meditations*. Today, however, the experts agree that Husserl failed to produce a viable theory of intersubjectivity (4). We suspect that, in fact, the problem is insoluble on the basis of Husserl's point of departure. Fortunately, however, the problem itself does not appear on the level of Husserl's theory of the life-world. In the "natural stance" of everyday experiences, the existence of others is not merely taken for granted, it is one of the very cornerstones of the whole "system" of beliefs and assumptions which makes the world of everyday life as reliable, predictable, and dependable as it is usually experienced.

For a sociology on phenomenological grounds, Husserl's concept of the life-world offers itself as a workable baseline. It would be a mistake to consider it as another "objective" label of the "basic unit" of sociological investigations, such as the term "cultural community." "World," by Husserl, means the world as experienced and made meaningful in consciousness. The term has a subjective connotation that sets it apart from the traditional concepts of sociological positivism, functionalism, and so on. By contrast, it is well suited to serve the purposes of a sociology issuing from a "subjective approach," such as that which was established in Max Weber's theory of meaningful social action. It is also akin to the social-psychological tradition anchored in the work of Charles H. Cooley and of George H. Mead.

» » » » » « « « « «

In 1932, Alfred Schutz synthesized Husserl's phenomenological baseline with Weber's subjective theory of action. Thereby, he mapped out the principal structures of a phenomenological sociology even before Husserl advanced his conception of the life-world. In his later work, Schutz utilized the latter without, however, ignoring its inherent weaknesses due to Husserl's insufficient acquaintance with the social sciences (5). Nevertheless, Schutz was so impressed with the potentialities of this conception that he selected the title *The Structures of the Life-World* for the planned synthesis of his life work (6). He was most concerned with clarifying the fundamental assumptions and presuppositions of a phenomenological sociology, with developing important building blocks for it, and with showing its application to specific problems. These contributions, as yet not sufficiently systematized (7), are indicative of the tremendous scope of problems to which phenomenological sociology may apply itself.

At the base, we find the individual in his dual appearances as a thinking and willing being within the immediate spheres of his experience and as a social actor involved in interchanges with others in face-to-face relations. The stress on the first aspect-configuration, involving cognitive experiences, motivations for conduct, and projects for action, is social-psychological. The second may be called microsociological; it concerns the forms of interaction that exist, for the participants, in "typified" expectations and the recognition of reciprocal motivations, perspectives, and objectives, all of them sufficiently unequivocal for the purposes on hand. But it must be stressed that the distinction of these dual appearances of man-in-his-world is analytical; it does not exist for the actors who experience their life situations as wholes in which subjective-cognitive and cognitive-typifying elements flow into each other.

In contrast to all "small-group" sociologists and some practitioners of symbolic interaction theory, Schutz paid great attention to the larger contexts of concrete interactional situations or the sociological constructs of types of such situations. This applies both to "historical" dimensions and to "structural" contexts of the broader social and cultural configurations within which social situations occur.

Maintaining a subjective position throughout, Schutz saw and interpreted these larger contexts through the medium of an actor's "knowledge" and "understanding" of them. Without using the term, he dealt with the dialectics of the interrelation between subjective cognition and the objective medium of language, on the one hand, and the uncounted "objectified" notions, interpretations, typical labels, type conceptions, and recipes for action under typical conditions, which the individual has "learned" from others and which he "shares" with them. Anthropologists call the totality of such shared orientations the culture of a community. But these cultural elements do not act on the individual with the external power of constraint inherent in Durkheim's "social facts"; they are accepted, interpreted, redefined, modified by the individual who gives collective thoughts his personal note, and who subtly changes, enlarges, or reduces their "meaning for him" in the ongoing accumulation of experiences from situation to situation. Unwittingly, he collects his own "stock of knowledge" in which his experiences are "sedimented," modifying each other or generalizing themselves into personal typifications on top of social typifications without ever acquiring the rigidity functional sociologists ascribe to type concepts, role expectations, or interaction patterns.

The individual, then, is not seen as an actor in isolated situations but as a person living in an ongoing process of experience, a process in which he "gets older" not only by the lapse of biological time, the aging of the organism, but in which he matures in experience. No one, accordingly, can enter twice the "same situation," that is, a later situation similar to an earlier one or, speaking sociologically, a situation of the same type. Aside from the fact that the actual circumstances of no two situations will be exactly alike, the same actors involved are no longer "the same." In the meantime, they have entered other situations apart from each other; but, most significantly, having experienced "the same situation" before, they must now view it differently: they "know" more, their expectations and anticipations of course and outcome of the situation have become more specific and, by this very fact, also more vulnerable to changed conditions or modified "strategies" of their partners.

Thus there is a significant subjective-historical factor involved in the analysis of even the most elementary types of social-interaction constellation. Schutz called this factor, somewhat equivocally, the "biographic situation" of the individual. Any concrete situation in which he finds himself is of course simultaneously his biographic situation in that it represents, next to whatever it socially means, a particular "moment" in his ongoing life. Focusing on the latter, we shall speak of the "biographic process," which is identical with the actual course of the life of an individual, his life history as actually lived and experienced in the succession of his innumerable successive involvements with many kinds of situations and people within many areas of life activities. Since other persons are involved in their own biographic processes, necessarily very different from his own, the chains of long-lasting interactional involvements of a number of specific persons, be they labeled family life, friendship, or employment, are subject to possible subtle but efficient change over longer periods. Even if no technological changes or shifts in personal positions to each other occurred, no durable social relationship can be called entirely stable. The stability of the "social system" of the structural functionalists is a theoretical myth which bestows upon rigid definitions and propositions the dignity of reality they do not possess. Since "social systems" of every kind and description, realistically appraised, are nothing but intricate "networks" of concretely interlinked interactional situations, all such systems are subject to internal changes. These changes, of course, are only more accentuated when such a system involves individuals of different age groups. In the long run, it suffers the effects of the succession of generations.

With these considerations we highlighted Schutz' idea of the fluidity that is of the essence of all social relations. Its recognition followed from his decision to view social matters from the subjective angle, that is, from the pivot of the experiences of the actors involved. To accept this instability, in turn, is a basic condition for dealing with social phenomena on the level of a subjective approach.

The same fluidity is implied in Schutz's dealings with the ways in which the individual is linked to a social world transcending the spheres of his own activities and his direct acquaintance with others. This social world is presented to the individual in the form of the objectified system of the conglomerate of shared designations and expressive forms which is called the vernacular of a collectivity. This language in itself is a kind of objective interpretation of "the world" and a preestablished combination of innumerable foci of attention toward innumerable specific points within and aspects of the spheres of reality with which a person deals in active everyday life. With its help, the individual grasps the existence of remoter horizons of nature and social life which stretch far beyond the reach of his immediate view, his direct experience, and his active involvements. He cannot doubt the existence of these realms, because they impinge upon his own spheres. The typifications included in his language enable him to deal with them meaningfully. In various degrees of vagueness, he "knows" areas he has never seen, persons he has never met, agencies he has never visited, and so forth. In extreme cases, he knows hardly more than names and labels. Beyond this, he is left with the "empty" conviction that spheres "must" exist of which he knows nothing.

The recognition of the "horizonal" character of man's knowledge has to be credited to Husserl. Schutz utilized it in his analysis of the social world: many degrees of acquaintance with social spheres and persons can be discerned, reaching from nearness and familiarity to remoteness and unspecific notions. His language, a collective stock of abstracted and objectified knowledge, provides man with a chance of ascribing semantically meanings to the objects of his cognitive attention. In addition, he has "learned," and is "learning," traditionally or otherwise accepted interpretational "theories" about aspects, regions of "reality" beyond his personal horizons. If language enabled him originally to name and thus cope with the objects and persons in his immediate sphere of life, it later conveyed to him a second-hand knowledge of the "world beyond his reach." His own experiences thus combine with the collective meaning complexes embodied in his language and the culturally ready-made interpretations handed down to him by educators, informants, or indoctrinators. He gains a cognitive image of the "structures" of the natural and social worlds of which he is a subjective-experiental center. Much of the work of Schutz is concerned with and refers to exactly these structures, and most of all those of the life-world.

Within the confines of this essay, it will not be possible to do justice to the pioneering work Schutz did in this respect. We merely point out that, on the one hand, he analyzed the workings of subjective cognition within all areas of human experiences, thus contributing to our knowledge of the basic facts of social phenomena themselves. On the other hand, he generalized the processes of subjective experience and widened them to sociological interpretations of the general aspects of social life. Outstanding among these contributions are, first, his analysis of the processes of typification and of the conversion of typifications of everyday life into "typifications of typifications," which make up an essential part of sociological knowledge; and, second, his expositions of the forms of direct and indirect interaction, including those among anonymous contemporaries which secure social cohesion on the large scale and, in fact, make up all social structures, the term taken not as a fixed scheme but as a going concern.

This conception of social structure is rooted in an awareness of its subjective base. As such, it is an antidote against the fallacy of reification, a characteristic of "objective" theories of social structure. Representatives of such theories have uncritically accepted the type concepts of everyday language, which abounds with social abstractions such as society, government, culture, institution. These constructs are endowed with volitional and executive qualities that inhere only in humans. The "scientific sociologists," here, unthinkingly share the most common prejudices and mystifications of the "unscientific" man in the street. By contrast, phenomenologists, having taken for a starting point the world of this same man in the street, are aware of the fallacies of "common sense" and have developed a "realistic" conception of the phenomena of social life. They insist on the reduction of abstractions such as "society" to their concrete social core. With Max Weber, they hold that: "In sociology, concepts like 'state,' 'cooperative,' 'feudalism,' and similar ones, in general designate categories of specific kinds of human interaction; thus, it is its task to reduce them to 'understandable' action, and this means without exception: to the actions of specific single individuals." Behind the terms mentioned "stands nothing but a course of human actions of a specific kind" (8).

In principle, Schutz' design of sociology on a phenomenological basis provides for the analysis of social phenomena from small-scale situations to large-scale structures. In its execution, Schutz had to confine himself to elaborating the cognitive foundations and to indicating the lines of their extension into the large-scale realms of language as well as those of the interactive and cognitive structures of large collectivities. As impressive as these outlines are, they are in need of substantive elaboration. And as large as their range is, they do as yet not cover the whole realm of sociological concerns. Schutz was aware of the unfinished character of his work. He left to his successors not merely the heritage of his challenging thoughts and suggestions, but also a series of formidable tasks.

Since Schutz' untimely death, a number of philosophers and sociologists have been actively involved in work along the lines of a phenomenological approach to the study of social phenomena. They have made sure that the approach, which had found only scanty attention during Schutz' lifetime, was kept alive and gained in influence. A number of encouraging contributions have been made to its further theoretical and empirical development (9). Yet much remains to be done.

The remainder of the present essay will be devoted to a discussion of some areas of sociological concern that must be considered of major importance but which, so far, have not been sufficiently explored by proponents of phenomenological sociology.

» » » » » « « « « «

One of the most persistent limitations of observing, analyzing, and exposing consciousness through self-observation is embodied in man's inability to apperceive, discern, and represent complex units simultaneously in all their aspects. Intentionality is tantamount to the volitional limitation of attention to selected areas; analytical description is the perceptional and mental dismantling of units which are one in their complexity. The mind cannot cope with complexes of simultaneous impressions but can only present them as separate items in a quasi-time series: "one thing at a time." A significant part of this cognitive limitation is the dualization of all objects of thought that appear as "objects in motion." Western thought, insofar as it is dominated by its rational-analytical style of thinking, operates in time-honored juxtapositions of time and space, matter and motion, morphology and genetics, statics and dynamics, structure and function, system and process.

Such dichotomies played a prominent role in the development of sociological theory. They are also found in the body of Husserl's work. His earlier phenomenology, best presented in the first volume of his *Ideas*, has become known as static or structural phenomenology. His later expositions, for instance, those of his *Formal and Transcendental Logic*, are labeled "genetic." In his structural conceptions, Husserl dealt with apperceived objects as grasped intuitively in their wholeness and perfection. His genetic reasoning, on the other hand, was concerned with the processes of the construction and sedimentation of various conceptions which form the structural content of a mature individual's consciousness. According to Richard Zaner, a phenomenological sociology would have to be concerned both with the structural problems of, for example, the explication and articulation of "beliefs" prevailing in social life, and with the lines of investigations seeking "genetically" to "unravel the progressive, temporal constitution of social life . . . which is formed and continuously undergoes change" (10).

Accepting this distinction, we will turn to a number of topics that illustrate the possibilities of phenomenological-sociological work along either structural or genetic and dynamic lines.

» » » » » « « « « «

Phenomenological sociology is relatively most advanced in areas of structural inquiries. Schutz' contributions, in this respect, are basic. What he did, for instance, in the areas of the study of the typifications of everyday life and of the role of the vernacular in "gearing" the individual into a larger social mesh is genuine phenomenological sociology. It should be accepted as a wide-range framework for further research. Peter Berger and Thomas Luckmann's inquiry into *The Social Construction of Reality* transcends Schutz' work in several ways. It preserves and accentuates the fluidity of Schutz' starting point and is concerned with the dialectic interweaving of subjective and objective factors in the formation of cognitive structures in which the "objective reality" of "society" is confronted with the "subjective reality" of the individual's acquisition of his knowledge about society. In the latter respect, the book fits Zaner's category of genetics; with regard to the former, it may be viewed as a contribution to exploration of structural problems on the large scale.

Both the original work of Schutz and the contributions by Berger and Luckmann offer starting points for the one central topic of structural character which we will introduce here: the problem of Weltanschauung.

Schutz kept his consideration of an individual's stock of knowledge at hand closely to the baseline, stressing its apparently unconnected sections whose consistency with one another usually is of no concern for people in the natural stance and its pragmatic bent. But it should not be forgotten that the orientations of people within the life-world display a second dimension or, better, a superstructure which contains whatever general principles and orientations are held concerning the *meaning* of a life not exhausted by its practical concerns. Into this realm belong, among other things, the moral principles assumed to hold beyond all exigencies (the "golden rule," etc.). These elements are culturally fixed in a tradition-guided community; they are institutionally imposed in large societies in the form of religious beliefs, interpretations, and moral impositions of religious and patriotic connotation. However, a phenomenological sociologist would not focus on the official belief systems for their own sake, as is prescribed by Durkheim's conception of the collective consciousness or Parsons' theory of the cultural system. Rather, he would deal with an individual's "construction" of such a belief system made up according to his understanding of these aspects of the "official" system he encounters in the small sector of the society within which he lives, and by the reinterpretation if not modification of the institutional tenets as presented to him in the process of his enculturation. Berger and Luckmann's work moves well into this direction. Subcultural groupings play an important intermediate and differentiating role. But they also will have to be studied as the social background to the formation of an individual's actual outlook on his social surroundings, which, in every individual case, is a flexible combination of the elements "taught" to him with the experience of their being-taught-to-him by specific persons in particular situations and their absorption, application, adaptation, and reinterpretation in the course of his ongoing life-experiences.

"World view" becomes an important phenomenological-sociological theme in a dual sense. On the one hand, there is the collection of "information" about aspects of Nature, ranging from plants to the stars, and offered in the form of "objective" knowledge with the prefix of science and the affix of truth. In its immediate form, such information is pragmatic and discrete; but the pieces are combined to a mosaic of a loosely comprehensive picture of Nature and given the accent of reality in detail and as a whole. On the other hand, there is the effort to fit social realities into the picture, to impose sense-giving meanings on the totality of the social and natural features of one's world and to transcend its pragmatic discreteness by "higher meanings" which unify the pieces into a whole of moral-esthetic-ontological significance. The pragmatic stock of knowledge, then, is overlaid by what Max Scheler called the relative-natural view of the world. This becomes a relevant topic for sociological investigation. We need both a broad theory and the detailed investigation of world views in this sense, and should attempt on the phenomenological level what Wilhelm Dilthey, 75 years ago, did from his general humanistic perspective.

» » » » » « « « « «

Next to structural concerns, Zaner placed genetic considerations. Upon closer inspection, these genetic considerations hide three different topics.

The first is individual-cognitive. In Husserl's sense, it focuses on the processes in which a person's manifold notions and conceptions of the realms of his social preoccupations, activities, and social partners are gradually sedimented and "constructed," each of them taken as a unit in itself. By contrast, the second and third topics are social. They differ from each other in that one centers on the longitudinal biographical process of the individual, and the other on the broader social effects of the interaction of this individual with his social environment, including the broader conditions of this environment's existence. If the second deals with the growth processes of the individual, the third is concerned with the processes of an ongoing, developing, and changing social life in its ramifications on all levels. With some arbitrariness, we shall refer to the second as genetic and the third as dynamic.

The genetic concern touches one of the weak points of Husserl's phenomenology. His interest was restricted to the consciousness of the "normal" adult, that is, of the mature ego capable not only of rational reflection but of self-reflection. The whole eidetic-transcendental phenomenology of Husserl is built upon this presupposition. In accepting it, the later exponents of the presuppositionless philosophy *par excellence*, phenomenology, have saved themselves the occupation with a set of tricky problems, all of them issuing from one fundamental question: How does consciousness appear and mature in the human organism which, at birth, displays no trace of it, and which needs long years of development to acquire the capacity to reflect, and still more years to gain the ability of self-reflection?

Schutz drove a wedge into the phenomenological presupposition of adult consciousness when he developed the foundation for the thesis of the biographic process unique to each individual. This thesis means, first, that the assumption of an equal effect of situational elements and conditions upon any individual exposed to a given situation—the basic assumption of any rigidly situational approach from Kurt Lewin to George Homans—does not hold: The unique past experiences of an individual are brought into any new situation and may become important factors in his definition of this situation as well as in his decision to adopt a certain course of action and response in the unfolding process circumscribed by "the situation." Second, by implication, Schutz' original term, biographic situation, refers to *one* passing phase of the ongoing process of the course of the life of an individual. It is only a momentary phase in what we called the biographic process, the process of an ongoing life-story. Schutz, in stressing the importance of past experiences for present behavior, opened a path for the inquiry into the growth process of the consciousness of growing individuals. But he never found time and occasion to follow it up systematically. Like many younger phenomenologists, he praised Piaget's challenging investigations of the mental growth of children, and he paid his respect to George H. Mead's explorations of the emergence of consciousness in the early growth of the human organism. Mead's conceptions, from the "conversation of gestures" to the "generalized other," are most fascinating because they emphasize the primacy of the social factor in the emergence of consciousness and its primary development. Mead offers a genetic answer to the problem of intersubjectivity which demands most serious consideration in spite of—or maybe because of—Mead's behaviorist starting point.

When Schutz spoke of the "scandal of philosophy," manifested in the failure to solve the problem of intersubjectivity according to the terms posed by Husserl, he seemed to be unaware that he himself had pointed toward different paths to its solution, first by insisting that the point of departure for a phenomenological sociology is the life-world, and second by introjecting the conception of the biographic situation or process into the picture. If there is a "scandal of phenomenology," it consists of the failure to develop a consistent theory of the subjective-individual genesis of consciousness in the social setting of the individual's growth process. Recently, though, promising beginnings have been made in this direction. For instance, Berger and Luckmann treated the "internalization of reality" in the context of "primary socialization" in some detail and thus set the framework for further explorations (11). The field has been opened up; yet the main tasks of comprehensive as well as specific investigations still lie ahead.

» » » » » « « « « «

With regard to dynamic concerns, phenomenological sociology seems to be wanting most. This lag in areas of most timely concern may explain why, to many outsiders, the whole approach seems to be still in its formative stage. Although the progress in the areas of structural concerns, due to prevalent theoretical interests of the authors in question, has been impressive, it has not been impressive enough to offset this suspicion of aloofness. The points at issue in phenomenological writings treating social-psychological, sociological, or historical themes may be found too esoteric to be brought to test in serious social research. The interpretation of basic conceptions may be taken as a redundant elaboration of the obvious; and the more extended bodies of theory may be considered too abstract and general for empirical application. Most of all, a younger generation of sociologists, pushing toward a sociology relevant to the issues of the day, may conclude that the phenomenological approach has nothing to offer that could be relevant to their concerns.

Such judgments and conclusions are understandable but erroneous. In order to rectify them, it is desirable, first, to show that phenomenological sociology is equipped to deal with the dynamic aspects of social life on the larger scale, and, second, to indicate that it is relevant to present-day problems such as the "generation gap" or alienation. The following examples will serve both of these purposes. Under most circumstances, one's everyday life is seen and experienced as "life as usual"; however, the assumptions, ideas, and recipes of everyday life are taken for granted only "until further notice." If things do not go as expected, "life as usual" is interrupted, and the taken-for-granted assumptions become "thematic." What was unquestionably accepted has become a "problem," and the deviation from the expected has to be dealt with mentally if not practically. At first glance, this seems indeed stating the obvious (12). However, this impression is deceptive. In real life, the circumstances and consequences of the necessity of making thematic what had been taken for granted vary tremendously. Three basic types of responses may be recognized, each of them representing a different type of "social dynamics."

The first deals with correction of minor disruptions of limited areas of a life of everyday routine; its long-range effects are slight. The second refers to overcoming more drastic changes which necessitate significant and multiple alterations in various complexes of daily life; the basic outlooks and beliefs of the person in question, however, are not affected. The third concerns experiences of the chain-effects of extreme upsets of routine and orientation which precipitate severe personality crisis; if overcome, they result in drastically changed styles of life and radically altered belief system.

Illustrations of responses to the first type of disruptions of life routine can be easily located in the phenomenological literature. Phenomenologists, like logicians, love to illustrate their conceptions by examples of disarming simplicity. Thus they prefer common everyday situations for discussing the occurrence of the unexpected in a familiar setting. For instance, a husband comes home and is told by his wife that she has decided to go abroad. He is upset because sudden solitary trips do not occur in his typified picture of her. After receiving a satisfactory explanation of her decision, however, he not only approves of it but also enriches his private stereotype of her by some "new" features (13). Actually, they are old features within his stock of knowledge on hand; yet they had not been connected with his image of his own wife. Forthwith, they will belong to the things taken for granted, or at least to be expected, in her conduct.

There is nothing dramatic in such an example. After it has been told, everybody remembers that something of that sort happened many times in his life. So why the fuss? But this is just the beauty of it, a phenomenologist will answer: If you have become aware of this, you have made a first step in the direction of a phenomenological understanding of the affairs of everyday life. What is common is not necessarily trite. When M. Jourdain learned to his astonishment that he had talked prose all his life, he seemed to have a highly exaggerated idea of the importance of this discovery, but he had learned something nevertheless. A "social scientist" who takes for granted the common explanatory schemes of matters social of his own discipline may emphatically reject any suggestions to scrutinize their hidden presuppositions. If he does so, he may also discard the suggestion to inquire into the nature of things taken for granted in everyday life. Insisting on the obviousness of the obvious, he learns nothing. Yet the simplest case of spelling out the obvious may gain significance, if not for its own sake, then as an innocuous beginning of considerations leading to more complex cases, cases either less common or of heavier consequences for the individual.

In the "trite" example mentioned earlier, the deviation from the course of things taken for granted was settled by a slight rearrangement of known factors. In other cases, new elements have to be constituted and added to existing typifications. So, if the philosopher's wife reveals to him that her doctor informed her of an unusual condition of her metabolism demanding long-lasting changes in her diet and her daily living habits, the husband, having been ignorant of the existence of such a condition, will have to cope with this piece of consequential information, first by adding "having this condition" to his personal stereotype of his wife, and second by further changing it in terms of new "things she has to do" and "things she cannot do."

Subjectively, this is one variation of the process of "learning by experience"; objectively, it is one illustration of a phenomenologist's idea of the "expansion of the stock of knowledge" of an individual. In this way, as well as in many others, the typifications of everyday life grow and change in minute and imperceptible as well as in small yet noticeable increments, even though all the disturbances that give rise to them may be minor. A slow process of growth and change takes place in the ongoing life of every individual. Yet his prevailing impression may be that of stability. Given sufficient time, however, the accumulated changes become noticeable. The subjective feeling of immutability stands corrected if the retrospective glance is directed upon episodes experienced and notions held in one's remoter past: The "same" situation, remembered as having been experienced 20 years ago, turns out not to be the same situation at all; the ideas remembered as having been formed then in its interpretation may not hold water now and may even appear as rather "naive" and inadequate for the explanation of a long past situation as seen from the standpoint of a person "matured" by 20 years (14).

The second form of response to changed conditions of life occurs when sudden shifts in one's immediate environment cannot be managed with the help of minor adjustments or redefinitions that would allow a person to continue "life as usual." Deviations from the familiar may occur which cannot be reconciled with the given stock of knowledge on hand. Let's say that an employee of long years of service, who had reasons to expect the continuation of his employment till retirement age, is suddenly laid off. Due to his advanced age, he cannot find another job in a tight labor market and becomes permanently unemployed. A significant part of his stock of knowledge has become problematic; parts of his beliefs in the reliability of the world are destroyed. He will experience a partial shock and live through a period of crisis. Eventually, however, he will accustom himself to the sizable changes he has to make in the immediate concerned areas of his life-orientations. He may manage this by drastic reformulations of some of the pragmatic aspects of his life-world without putting into question the superstructural beliefs that have given meaning to his life up to now: God's will is still not to be questioned; the American economic system is still the best in the world. This may be called adaptation to drastically changed conditions, bringing redefinitions of various aspects of one's daily life and leading to different daily routines. Numerous items in the stock of knowledge of the person under consideration will have to be discarded, and numerous new ones will have to be added in a new learning process of an intensity which may be reminiscent of the man's first ventures into the world of work and business. A crisis has taken place, but it has been confined to partial areas of life; thus it could be overcome within the framework of the old world view.

The man who had enjoyed a long period of steady employment had been well protected against the vicissitudes of the modern economic system. The constant acceleration of technological change adversely affects stability in all areas of life. Most of all, it brings frequent redeployment of personnel and displacement of workers, and it makes the skills of whole occupational groups obsolescent. Modern Society is the very antithesis of the closed human community of the cultural anthropologists, the ideal-typical functional unity of stable life conditions, style of life, customs, world interpretation, and belief system. It is a fundamental paradox of Modern Society that it demands a maximum of flexibility and adaptability from the individual yet holds him to the immutability and sanctity of traditional articles of faith. The practical areas of modern life are sharply separated from the spheres of world view and belief. 'Modern Man' would not be modern if he refused to accept insecurity as a virtue of socioeconomic life, and he would not be man if he sacrificed the psychic security of immutable beliefs.

The recipe for dealing with these contradictory impositions is simple: Let thy left hand not know what thy right hand is doing. But since both hands belong to the same conscious individual, this pretense cannot prevent traditional beliefs from being deeply affected by unprincipled practice. The "successful" individual will achieve two things: he will develop adaptation techniques in order to cope practically with all exigencies as they arise, and he will bifurcate his overall "systems" of orientation. Not allowing basic principles to be undermined, he will maintain them. Religious values are to be served by the sundaily drive to Church; the American Way of Life is to be upheld at solemn patriotic occasions; and the immutable morality of the Puritan heritage is to be stressed in exhortation of the young and in judgment of transgressors. This stable set of fundamentals, however, is addended by a second set of principles and orientations: The "pillar of the Church" does not let religion interfere with business; the "solid citizen" becomes a "dynamic personality"; the "sacred heritage of our forefathers" is paired with the positive acceptance of change which, in turn, becomes virtue by being called "progress." Similarly, the "sanctity of home and family" is stressed, but "my wife doesn't understand me" becomes both excuse and opening line for a transgression of the most moral of all moral middle-class principles.

This duality of values, principles, and orientations is a most convenient arrangement; with its help, a modern man can have his cake and eat it too. Since eclecticism and opportunism are most useful bases for all practical adaptation techniques, the "old" and "timeless" values and principles can be pressed into the service of any momentary exigencies, or else they can be ignored. The "world view" of a man living in the climate of adaptability and opportunity thus becomes a conglomerate of disconnected bits and pieces, and the coherence of the whole is never tested. The "old" moral and other principles, in this conglomerate, have undergone a basic change of function. Originally, they had been meant to be prescriptions by which the members of the community were to live. Now they have become principles which are privately accepted not with a grain but a chunk of salt but which, simultaneously, are publicly utilized to exhort and judge others if this be found convenient. At best, they serve as so many magical-word covers. In the extreme case, their mere repetition, combined with the assertion of one's "belief" in them, helps the individual to hide from himself the pragmatic nihilism of his actual existence. To discerning outsiders, not in the least his own children, the glaring discrepancies between his articles of faith and his practical conduct appear to be so many signs of complete insincerity.

» » » » » « « « « «

By far the most challenging of our three cases of responses to change is the third one. Its complexity calls for a more extended discussion. Like "organization man," our "man in modern society" is only one "advanced" ideal type among others. The socioeconomic "system" of present-day America represents a most complex interweaving of many kinds of enterprises, occupations, communities, subcultures, social-class groupings, and so forth, which exert the most diversified demands on the individual exposed to them. They inspire a great variety of concrete life styles, and they call for many kinds of adaptation techniques. Consequently, the "socioregional" conditions of human existence are greatly varied and, among other things, suggest many kinds of mixtures of immutable traditional and modern adaptive values and principles, and many degrees of importance for each of them. Anyone in a modern society is but a "member" of a "subculture" or, as we prefer to say more loosely, a socioregional subdivision. If such "membership" were permanent for the individuals concerned, and if such regions were not subject to differential change, growth, or decline, greater chances for at least temporarily stable stretches of "life as usual" would exist for more people. But the "dynamic" character of modern society produces two effects that drastically reduce these chances for many. One is the fact that particular social regions may have no room for particular individuals, especially young ones, and thus eject them, forcing them to move into regions of makeup rather different from that of their origin (15). The other is the occurrence of excessively rapid changes and/or processes of deterioration, which make it impossible for all but the most astute and most cynical individuals to work out adaptation techniques. These two sets of conditions provide the background for many of the cases of an individual's inability to find a toehold for conducting his life with a minimum of an at least temporary stability and to acquire a maximum of methods to cope with the unforeseen. Of course, any particular individual's failure is a combination of the severity of the condition he encounters and the adaptive abilities he had a chance to acquire in the preceding stages of his life. What breaks one person may be another's sphere of individual survival and even success.

In any case, the individual becomes an "extreme case" when the deviations from established expectations become either too numerous or too drastic to be handled adaptively by him; or when they pile up on top of each other in short periods and thus dislodge his life orientations by their combined weight and destroy all adaptative efforts by making them obsolete before they could become effective; or when the life conditions in his social environment become more or less permanently chaotic so that the very idea of adaptation becomes meaningless. On the other hand, changes, insecure conditions, and dislodgings may be encountered by persons inexperienced in the techniques of swift, pragmatic adaptations in easily making value compromises, or in maintaining beliefs that are irrelevant for, if not contrary to, their significant practical conduct. In consequence, an essential part, if not the basic structure of one's stock of knowledge, may become useless and thereby meaningless, and the world view lending it cohesion may collapse.

If this occurs as the individual experiences of a person who is, or feels himself to be, isolated from the mainstream of life as lived by others, various reactions may occur: flight into an autistic world of fantasy or reality distortion which is socially described as mental illness; removal of oneself from the spheres of a senseless existence by suicide; acceptance of a world devoid of meaning by adapting cynical outlooks and practices; "conversion" to a creed or world view securely removed from that which failed the individual in the hour of crisis; flight into spheres of artificially induced fantasy-experiences that represent an "ultimate reality" in place of the negated realities of everyday life; retreat from the main spheres of modern life either into complete isolation or into most marginal social regions; sudden assumption of the aggressive role of the "rebel" and "revolutionary."

The first of these reactions is the concern of psychiatrists of phenomenological orientation. Men like Harry Stack Sullivan have discovered that the "field of psychiatry is the field of interpersonal relations" (16) and identified the manifestations of most mental derangements as results of a construction or reconstruction of the individual's social reality so that a part, if not all of it, is blocked from intersubjective confirmation; thus no reciprocity of perspectives is achieved in interaction with others, or the other's motivations are no longer grasped in empathy but defined in hostility. In all cases, all or some of the definitions of given social situations on the part of the disturbed person are unacceptable to others and make reciprocal understanding and thus effective interaction mutually impossible.

The second type of reaction falls under the category of anomic suicide. A person removes himself radically from the social scene by ending his life because it has become completely meaningless to him. In contrast to Durkheim, we do not consider such an act a statistical tribute to societal pressures and conditions. Anomie is not an objective factor of societal structures under stress; it is a form of response of individuals to these stresses. The stresses themselves consist of the individual's experience that none of the essential things he took for granted can be taken for granted, and his inability to counteract the concomitant collapse of his view of the world. He then defines his overall situation as unbearable and thus his life as impossible: What is defined as unbearable becomes unbearable, and what is defined as impossible becomes impossible.

The third response may be rooted in objective conditions similar to those that are conducive to suicide, but it points in an opposite direction. One's social experiences are seen not as the negation of all realities, but as a refutation of the moral guidelines for the conduct of one's social affairs, which heretofore had been taken for granted. The meaninglessness of the socio-moral world is compensated for by concentrating all meaning of life on one's own ego. The utter self-affirmation of this ego occurs in a "real world" to whom he "owes nothing" and toward whom he has no obligation whatever; it exists for the sole purpose of serving and profiting himself. Such an individual invariably is "highly successful." He may be the man who ruthlessly competes on the market and destroys his competitors by any means available to him, who flaunts the law and bribes legislators if it is to his material advantage, and who may be seen as "economic man" of classical economy in the flesh. He acts out the extreme consequences of the principles of an acquisitive and competitive society, that is, of the central elements of a modern world view which have been attached to the prior immutable values and prescriptions of traditional Western Christianity. In other than economic and especially in personal spheres, the active egotist resorts to forcing or maneuvering others into the service for his selfish purposes. He may bully and intimidate others, but he is likely to be most successful if he develops the art of manipulating others. In any case, the secret of his success is a keen grasp of the economic and social realities of his spheres of activities. He exploits the "rules of the game" accepted by others in order to circumvent them; he utilizes empathy to invite others to trust him in order to make them do what is against their, but very much in his own, interests. The "con man" is only an extreme type of the psychological manipulator. Similarly, the criminal offender who steals, burglarizes, robs, and mugs is an extreme case of the exploitative competitor. He differs from the ruthless businessman in that he does not give the appearance of staying within the letter of the law; in ignoring it, he is free to use direct methods of robbery. For him, crime has become a way of life as exploitative competition has for others.

Examples of the fourth form of reaction include the unsuccessful businessman who gives up the struggle and becomes a witness for Jehovah and the disenchanted intellectual who seriously turns to Zen Buddhism. In both cases, material defeats or intellectual disenchantments have corroded the belief systems above the actual spheres of life that could no longer be taken for granted. But the need for reliable belief systems persisted and was satisfied in a conversion to systems which, by their spiritual nature as well as their location in the spectrum of religions, are absolutely unconnected with one's sociocultural spheres and thus untouchable by the disappointing realities of these spheres. Thus the whole modern world view is negated in favor of orientations guided by religious values that have their roots in the simplicity of social conditions of existence long lost in the Western world, or in the similarly obsolete conditions of non-Western civilizations. In Max Weber's terms, an "other-worldly" stance is adopted, utterly devaluating "this world" in which one's presence is an accidental matter. This-worldly life thereby maintains no significance other than that of a nuisance, a nuisance which in itself does not matter in the face of the satisfactions and promises of the new creed.

The fifth form of reaction is that of a partial or practically total retreat from the realities of one's involvement in preestablished social arrangements, notably occupational or educational settings. The impositions of the "systems" in which he is enmeshed are experienced as coercive without the benefit of worthwhile compensations. Here experiences suggest the collapse of not only whole sets of prescribed values but also of set goals. If goals are no longer taken for granted, and, in fact, rejected with hostile feelings, subjection to the disciplines of work and/or education becomes meaningless. Where the egotistic realist exploits the setting of his social activities for his own pursuit of socially accepted goals, the negators of these goals want to negate the setting without being able or willing to actually move out of it. Realities of life settings are externally tolerated but internally devaluated, and meaning is only to be found in spheres of dream, fantasy, or meditation. The "spiritual" rejection of external realities and its impositions leads to turning away from, and hostility toward, rationality in thought and action. The definition of life along these lines is embedded in a feeling tone that greatly fosters the use of drugs, reaching from the occasional enhancement of sociability through the collective smoking of marijuana to the individualistic forms of LSD tripping and the intake of other "mind-expanding" drugs which black out the consciousness of one's waking life and produce psychedelic and similar dream-worlds, which the user and/or addict craves to reach again and again. Where the flight into drug-induced worlds of fantasy becomes central to a person's concern, he may move into the "drug culture" with like-minded individuals; it provides a social setting for a life-style rotating around drug use. The most severe self-isolation, however, is of necessity created by the addicts of heroin and other "hard drugs."

The sixth form of reaction, like the sociability forms of the "drug-culture" and in fact often related to them, is best illustrated by the new-styled "communes," permissive heirs of the disciplined utopian communes of past centuries. The founders of the new communes are usually displaced city-dwellers of middle-class background. They too experienced the life styles of their upbringing and the imposed obligations of modern educational and economic life as meaningless: The values and goals with which they had been indoctrinated failed to work for them. The devaluation of the world view, a feature shared with other types of sociocultural dissenters, leads here to the decision to remove oneself physically as well as spiritually and socially from the urban-suburban settings of the modern life of their upbringing. They are willing to pay a material price for their exodus without sacrificing the rational pursuit of a livelihood altogether.

Thus they settle down in ramshackle farm houses, try themselves in "organic farming," and, with the possible exception of an old jalopy, forgo the technical luxuries of the modern world (electricity, telephone, flush toilets). In Vermont, they may produce maple syrup. Elsewhere, they may take up simple crafts, like sandal making, and cut into the tourist trade of the summer resorts. Relative inaccessibility and isolation, combined with "closeness to nature," is the trademark of these communes.

Other communes form in an urban environment of tenements and slum dwellings, financing a precarious existence by the occasional or permanent work of some members, the unemployment insurance payments or welfare subsidies of others, benefiting from food-stamp programs, replenishing food supplies by pilfering in supermarkets, and possibly with the help of an occasional parental check. Since both the rural and the urban communards have forgone the principles of affluence, the requirements of neatness in dress and appearance, the technical comfort in living accommodations, and other expensive habits characteristic of the class from which they come, they have not too many difficulties in securing their material and in part parasitic existence (17). The affluent society affords their survival as much as that of its genuine slum dwellers. The common characteristic of these types of communes is their establishment as possible unstable enclaves in that societal system into which they refuse to functionally incorporate themselves.

Finally, the seventh form of reaction is presented by two types: one transforms his frustrations and ill-feelings into a "radical" rhetoric through which he reanimates ancestral morality patterns of the world struggle between Good and Evil in reversed order; the other acts them out in the "direct action" of the bombing of banks and laboratories or department stores. The experience of drastic discrepancies between experienced realities and beliefs here brings about resentment which is translated into active hostility against those considered responsible, and notably against the "system," the "establishment" (18).

» » » » » « « « « «

If the experience of drastic discrepancies between accepted beliefs, taken-for-granted expectations, and the changing "realities" of social life is made by those who have had no occasion to develop their personal defense and adaptation strategies through long years of practice, the consequences will be aggravated. The age groups of adolescents and postadolescents certainly have their full share of mentally disturbed persons, suicides, cynics and delinquents, apostates, drug addicts, dropouts, and "radicals."

However, the picture changes considerably when the shock of dislocation itself is experienced not as one's individual fate but as an experience shared by many; the reactions become collective and gain social importance as they are positively sanctioned by "significant others." In this sense, the American institutes of higher learning function as social centers for the development of a deviant culture of the young. In particular, the undergraduate colleges foster this process by concentrating sizable numbers of young people in settings that comprise all relevant aspects of their life. However, due to the educational nature of the college setting, the crucial aspect of serious economic and occupational involvement is missing. Higher education keeps large numbers of the young far beyond the years of adolescence from joining the country's labor force and thus shields them from the concomitant experiences and responsibilities of the adult "world of work." The young individual thus finds himself in the company of many others; he lives in a relatively sheltered world which serves as the ready-made social ground for converting disenchantment, shock, and despair into the mass phenomena of generational culture discontent, escape, and collective reorientation. The dislocating experiences of the individuals involved are essentially not those of the failure of the learned definitions of the situations of practical life—which they had hardly the occasion to test—but the failure of the interpretations, values, and goal orientations which their parents and teachers urged upon them.

Still observers of an adult world they are supposed to enter, students discover the discrepancies between the lofty moral principles and the actual conduct of economic, social, and political affairs by their elders. Responding in genuine moral indignation, they point to the breach that runs through modern culture, which the established generation has failed to conceal from them: the fateful dualism of social practice and confessed principles. All the cant, doubletalk, and newspeak which has saved the world view of the majority of the older generations does not work for many members of the young generation, and they respond to it in open distrust. What has been put in question for them is primarily not "life as usual" but rather the culturally established middle-class values and principles as usual. As a consequence, all meaning has been taken out of the traditional educational conception of a preparation for adult life as usual. Thus the practical academic process is viewed with a mixture of defiance and despair, or at least in indifference as a matter of senseless routine.

In themselves, these reactions may be registered as manifestations of the alienation of individuals. On the college scene, however, they are converted into a collective force. Through this force, socially positive— that is, group and culture-forming—tendencies are created within the campus setting. Many features of a "youth culture" occur there which cannot be adequately explained as subcultural elements, like the "rating and dating" complex of past college generations; they tend to become countercultural elements. Out of the negation of the "established" society comes the establishment of a different life-style; out of the rejection of "official" beliefs and values come the counterbeliefs and values of the deviators: the work ethic is replaced by the fun ethic, the purpose of preparation for the distant future by the striving for immediate gratification, the Puritan sex morality by unrestricted permissiveness, and so on. The protest against the "cold rationality" of a technological and business world tends to bring a negation of all rationality. Rational orientations are largely replaced by abstruse cults, astrology, witchcraft, drug euphoria, rock music blasted at highest intensity. Rational learning in the classroom is resented and attacked as meaningless drudgery set up by the establishment for the express purpose of suppressing "individuality" and "creativity."

All this is permeated by a kind of generation solidarity in the face of the rules, laws, and authority-claims of the adult world. This generation morality runs from flaunting the principles of private property to the protection of drug pushers in their midst. But it also has brought a spirit of mutual aid and comradeship which stands in sharp contrast to the naked self-interest orientations of our business society. While having its admirable aspects, this solidarity is often blind. The stranger, if he wears the uniform and the insignia of the youth culture and acts the part, is welcomed, sheltered, and protected against the college administration; an ideal situation for the undercovermen of federal, state, and local police agencies and for their *agents provocateurs*, like Tommy the Traveler of Hobart College fame.

This short characterization of some of the salient aspects of present-day campus life leads to the following general considerations: Subjective experiences have put into question what had been, and was supposed to be, taken for granted. These experiences are intense and make the ensuing problems urgent, and the directions in which answers may be sought are largely imposed by the dominant influence of peer group orientations and even pressures. Negatively, the collective setting helps the individual to "clear the deck," that is, get rid of essential elements and areas of the world view and interpretation of the larger culture of their elders. Personal experiences within the collective climate of opinion of the college student world thus bring drastic changes in a person's view of the world and significantly alter his relative-natural world view as a whole. Positively, tendencies toward the formation of a deviating culture appear, even though to a degree the "situation" remains chaotic and the collective life process directionless.

The realization of the existence of these processes should significantly contribute to the study of large-scale social change by bringing into focus crucial factors that hitherto have been all but completely ignored in theory and investigation of social change.

» » » » « « « « «

Rudimentary as they are, the considerations embodied in this essay indicate the potentialities of phenomenological sociology. It can make contributions to the understanding of problems beyond the intricate psycho-phenomenological analysis of individual experience and cognition, including some of large sociological scope and great timeliness. This has been shown here merely by dealing with one simple point of departure: experiences serving notice that things can no longer be taken for granted and that the pursuit of life as usual has become problematic.

Phenomenological sociology, we submit, can operate on all levels of sociological concerns and can cover the scope of sociological problem areas. It fills the requirements of a study of the subjective aspects of the subtle changes in a person's outlook and conduct in quasi-static settings. It promises to make contributions to the recognition of the processes of primary cognitive growth in children, of cognitive changes in adolescents and young adults, and of cognitive adaptations in mature persons. Beyond this, it is equipped to deal with the more drastic dynamics of flexible individuals, maneuvering within the realms continuous, sometimes quick and sizable changes, which characterize a precariously functioning modern society. Most of all, however, it can deal with the subjective problems of modern society in crisis, that is, a society in which the number of things that can no longer be taken for granted by many people multiplies, where more and more persons are unable to perform the "dynamic" adaptations and reinterpretations characteristic of the previous era.

Phenomenologists have made their best contributions to the recognition of phenomena of the first category, but it is the other categories which, for a sociologist, are the urgent ones. They lend themselves ideally to a sociological treatment of the topic of Solitude and Sociality, as suggested by Zaner (19): the solitude of the alienated individual against the sociality of those who persist in thinking as usual in spite of social disturbances and who manage to absorb the shifts and changes of their social world without allowing their views of the world to be deranged; and the sociality of the alienated against the sociality of the unalienated, the control structures of the "established" groups, strata, and professions of a society in permanent disequilibrium.

It is our conviction that phenomenological sociology will make a relevant contribution to our knowledge of the whole range of social phenomena to exactly the degree to which it will manage to make inquiries not only into the certainly basic areas of social-psychological concerns but also into those of the broader, socially crucial aspects of modern society in perpetual change, upheaval, and crisis.

NOTES

1. Franz Brentano, *Psychologie vom empirischen Standpunkte*, 1874. Henri Bergson, *Essay sur les donnés immédiates de la conscience*, 1889. (*Time and Free Will*, Harper and Row, New York, 1960) E. R. Clay, "The Alternative," quoted by William James, *The Principles of Psychology*, Vol. I, Holt, New York, 1890, p. 609. James, *op. cit.*, pp. 224–290. Of significance here is also George Herbert Mead, *The Philosophy of the Present*, Open Court, Chicago, 1932, pp. 1–31. It would be too cumbersome to cite all the writings of Edmund Husserl which have been consulted. Main titles are: *Ideen zu einer Phaenomenologie und phaenomenologischen Philosophie*, Vol. I, 1913 (*Ideas: General Introduction to Pure Phenomenology*, Collier Books, New York, 1962); *Vorlesungen zu einer Phaenomenologie des inneren Zeitbewusstseins*, 1928 (*The Phenomenology of Internal Time Consciousness*, Indiana University Press, Bloomington, 1964); *Formale und transzendentale Logik*, 1929 (*Formal and Transcendental Logic*, Martinus Nijhoff, The Hague, 1969). Also "Phenomenology," in *The Encyclopedia Britannica*, 14th ed., Vol. 17, col. 699–702, 1929; *Meditations cartesiennes*, 1931 (*Cartesian Meditations*, Martinus Nijhoff, The Hague, 1960); *Die Krisis der europaeischen Wissenschaften und die transzendentale Phaenomenologie* Pt. I, 1936 (*The Crisis of European Sciences and Transcendental Phenomenology*, Northwestern University Press, Evanston, Ill. 1970).

2. This, of course, is not a summary of Husserl's intricate phenomenology.

3. Alfred Schutz, "Some Leading Concepts of Phenomenology," *Social Research*, Vol. 12 (1), 1945, pp. 77–97.

4. Consult Alfred Schutz' thorough critique, "The Problem of Transcendental Intersubjectivity in Husserl," in *Collected Papers*, Vol. III: *Studies in Phenomenological Philosophy*, Martinus Nijhoff, The Hague, 1966, pp. 51–84.

5. Compare Schutz' critical remarks at the end of his review of the second volume of Husserl's *Ideas* in *Philosophy and Phenomenological Research*, Vol. 13, No. 3, 1953, pp. 412–413.

6. Thomas Luckmann has accepted the task of transferring the notes and outline sketches for this book, on which Schutz worked during the last years of his life, into a full-fledged representation. A two-volume work is

in preparation with the first volume now having appeared. Alfred Schutz with Thomas Luckmann, *The Structures of the Life-World*, translated by Richard Zaner and Tristram Engelhardt, Jr., Northwestern University Press, Evanston, Ill., 1973.

7. The interested reader may consult the volume *Alfred Schutz on Phenomenology and Social Relations*, which the present author edited for The University of Chicago Press, 1970 (paperback edition, 1972).

8. Max Weber, "Ueber einige Kategorien der verstehenden Soziologie," reprinted in Max Weber, *Gesammelte Aufsaetze zur Wissenschaftslehre*, 2nd ed., Mohr, Tuebingen, 1951, pp. 439, 440. The quotation has been translated by the present author.

9. I refer to the work of such philosophers as Maurice Natanson and Richard Zaner; such sociologists as Peter Berger and Thomas Luckmann; the ethnomethodologists, notably Harold Garfinkel and Aaron Cicourel; to George Psathas and various other authors.

10. Richard Zaner, "Solitude and Sociality: The Critical Foundations of the Social Sciences," in this volume.

11. Berger and Luckmann, *op. cit.*, pp. 119–127.

12. See Harold Garfinkel's ingenious experiments challenging commonplace assumptions, thereby revealing the significance of the obvious. See his *Studies in Ethnomethodology*, Prentice-Hall, Englewoods Cliff, N.J., 1967.

13. Zaner, *op. cit.*

14. We are using the term "mature" in the sense in which Schutz spoke of "growing older," that is, constantly moving through experiences in time which of necessity change one's "stock of knowledge at hand" in general and his conceptions of all things remembered in particular.

15. The present author lived for long years in a small Central Pennsylvanian town, where nineteenth-century socioeconomic conditions combined with a formal educational system of the early and the mass media trimmings of the later twentieth century. Year after year, 85 percent of the graduating high school classes had to leave town in search of a livelihood in urban regions.

16. Harry Stack Sullivan, *Conceptions of Modern Psychiatry*, Norton, New York, 1940, p. 10.

17. If the communes are greatly involved in the drug culture, they will have to reckon with heavier expenses. Both internally and externally, then, their chances for survival are considerably reduced.

18. All of these "forms of reaction" had to be sketched out in a highly condensed manner. This, possibly, is most distressing with regard to the last form. The present author is well aware that he could do no more than state the topics whose adequate treatment must be reserved for another occasion.

19. The title of Zaner's paper, of course, reflects the age-old problem of "Individual and Society." This has persisted in philosophy as a dilemma which either remained unanswered or lead into absurdities. Phenomenology allows us to pose the problems anew on a different level. Whether it can provide the answer remains to be seen.

»»»»»»»»»»»»»»»»»»»»»»»«««««««««««««««««««««

The phenomenologically oriented approach in the sociology of knowledge, particularly as recently developed by Berger and Luckmann, provides O'Neill with a new question about the problem of society: How is
society made possible? That humans interacting in society proceed in
their everyday lives with typifications, that they know others exist as they
themselves do, that selves are not merely the performances found in roles,
and that society is both outside of and internal to us—all of these are
relevant to answer the questions posed by Simmel. The sociologist cannot, argues O'Neill, fail to apprehend the everyday assumptions people
make in their everyday lives if he wishes to find the answer of how society is "made."

Simmel's question concerning society is seen also to concern the
limits of sociology in its effort to study and conceptualize social reality
systematically. A reflexive sociology cannot ignore the "fundamental
metaphysics of everyday life."

ON SIMMEL'S
"SOCIOLOGICAL APRIORITIES"

»» »» »» »» »» »» »» »» »» »» »» »» »» »» »» »» »» »» «« «« «« «« «« «« «« «« «« «« «« «« «« «« «« «« «« ««

John O'Neill

York University

Before any consideration of the question "How is Society Possible?" (1), we should note that this is not merely a problem sociologists raise when haunted by the ghosts of philosophy. Thus those who dismiss the question as "philosophical," because of its kinship with Kant's speculations on the a priori constitution of nature, might be reminded that the same question concerned both the practical Hobbes and Machiavelli. These two for all their toughmindedness, answered the question in terms of a theory of human nature which still left the preconditions of order, or the intersubjective bases of recognition and virtue, undetermined by the protocols of violence and divine fiat on which they rested the social order (2).

The problem of order is, of course, as much a question about the subjective nature of social reality or its meaningfulness and value as an inquiry into the nature of the moral and political order. These questions in turn involve us in a conception of knowledge and rationality that implicitly determines the theory of conduct and congruent social order. Thus the question of the possibility of society poses simultaneously a problem in the sociology of knowledge. It raises questions concerning the ultimate legitimacy of the formal and substantive modes of rationality as well as questions concerning the institutionalization of the sentimental bases of rationality, contract and order.

It is no longer obvious how we should relate the moral claim of everyday conceptions of identity and order to the sociological reconstruction of these phenomena determined by the standards of scientific rationality and its own organizational claims. The problem here is not simply that the paradigm of natural science observation and theory construction does not answer to the interference problem produced by the interaction between the social scientist and his object of study, for similar effects can be found in experimental science. The essential distinction between the natural and social sciences which makes the standard of rationality fostered by the social sciences intrinsically a problem of the sociology, if not the politics, of knowledge is that human relationships, customs, and institutions are not merely "orders" produced by scientific reconstruction. The human order is initially a pretheoretical conduct resting on the unarticulated "commonsense" knowledge of others as "kindred" when they experience dependable needs and wants expressed in the "relevances" of the human body, time, and place. The nature of this order cannot be settled through a dogmatic rationalism which subordinates commonsense knowledge of individual and social life to the standards of realism and objectivism which are maxims of scientific conduct but not obviously normative for all social praxes. Indeed, a fundamental task of the sociology of knowledge must be its reflexive concern with the grounds of *communication* between everyday commonsense reason and scientific rationality. Such a concern would answer the problem of the possibility of a democratic society in the modern world.

We may perhaps contribute to this task by an analysis of the fundamental grounds of social life as the unalienable competence of individuals exhibited in their everyday lives together. Although this might involve us in much of the theoretical literature in sociology, I propose to concentrate my attention upon Simmel's question, "How is society possible?," and to interpret it in the light of recent phenomenological sociology which I believe recovers its sense in the less Kantian formulation "How is society *made* possible?" In other words, I want to show that by shifting Simmel's question away from the search for invariant categories or forms of social reality the real nature of the question may be proposed as an inquiry into the subjective constitution of social reality, which has been the concern of so much sociological theory and upon which we shall then be able to make comment.

Before proceeding, I should clarify briefly the relationship between this proposal and the traditional concerns of the sociology of knowledge. Recently the foundations of the sociology of knowledge have been strengthened by phenomenological and ethnomethodological analyses that take the classical sources in Marx, Nietzsche, Durkheim, Weber, and Mannheim beyond the first steps in which they have become frozen. Although the new tradition has its own classics in Dilthey and Scheler, both of whom raised the question of the nature of the existential truths underlying the natural and social sciences, in general it refers more to the exploration of Husserl as developed by Schutz (3). The study of Schutz' writings on the phenomenology of the social world and commonsense knowledge of social institutions, courses of action, and motivation has led to a sociology of practical reasoning and relevances which contributes fresh theoretical and empirical dimensions to the concerns of the sociology of knowledge (4).

Berger and Luckmann have argued that the sociology of knowledge must now be concerned with the basic processes of the social construction of reality in order to correct its classical intellectualist bias:

> The theoretical foundations of reality, whether they be scientific or philosophical or even mythological, do not exhaust what is "real" for the members of a society. Since this is so, the sociology of knowledge must first of all concern itself with what people "know" in their everyday, non or pretheoretical lives. In other words, common-sense "knowledge" rather than "ideas" must be the central focus for the sociology of knowledge. It is precisely this "knowledge" that constitutes the fabric of meanings without which no society could exist (5).

I propose, then, to follow out this prescription by taking Simmel's apparently intellectualist formulation of the "apriorities" in the constitution of social reality and showing how they can be understood as an everyday practical accomplishment which continuously resolves its own contingencies in ways that do not invite existential absurdities. I shall expand upon Simmel's three "sociological apriorities," drawing on Schutz' account of the phenomenon of typification (6) and Goffman's concept of "face" (7). In this manner I hope to connect the cognitive and expressive "motivations" of "knowing" through which individuals organize their standing as expectable members in any common enterprise. These processes are fundamental to any empirical pattern of motives or ideology that usually furnishes the subject of analysis in the sociology of knowledge.

FIRST A PRIORI

Each of Simmel's three sociological apriorities is intended to elucidate the fundamental axiom that we inhabit a common world in which the presence of the other is not simply an alien perspective whose relation to myself is always problematic. In this enterprise Simmel adopts as his starting point the axiom that the transcendental ego is equally and indubitably consciousness of self and the other. This "naive" starting point represents the massive everyday assumption we make that there is a world which, despite the variety of viewpoint and circumstance, we nevertheless have in common. Indeed, it is to this "common" world and its platitudes that we refer our differences in order to settle them within its limits. We do not ordinarily question our world and thus even the alienated and sectarians find their place within the fold of the society they seek to renew. Hence the assumption of intersubjectivity may be regarded as an ideal in the sense of the truth of sociological knowledge (8) or it may be analyzed as a process which is a constitutive as well as regulative principle of sociation. In turn, each of three "sociological apriorities" or antinomies upon which the synthesis of individual and social conduct rests may be understood as an alternation with constitutive biographical consequences as well as heuristic results. In other words, according to which side of the antinomies of social life we are attracted, we may produce conceptions of the self and social order which are Machiavellian in the practical and theoretical sense, that is, an exploitation of the distance between individual and public life, or else Durkheimian ironies of their congruency. Thus our conception of sociological theory is simultaneously open to the options of morality and determinism which it appears otherwise to produce experimentally and to offer as scientific recommendations.

In his first a priori Simmel undertakes the clarification of my relation to the other *as an exemplar of the same social system* (9). The wider context of Simmel's question is the relationship between the generalized other and the philosophical problem of universals and particulars. In *Mind, Self, and Society*, Mead raises the problem of universals in terms of a theory of abstraction based upon taking the roles of the generalized other and the "specific other." Apart from the generalized other there could be no universality in human experience and consequently nothing to correspond to the emergence of a self, which is properly a social and not an individual status. Alternatively, where the individual is adopted as a starting point, as in *The Philosophy of the Act*, then the status of the generalized other, that is to say, its constitution by the individual, is a problem that cannot be solved within the framework of methodological individualism (10).

It is important to stress the interplay between cognitive and expressive behavior in the reflexive process whereby the self is able to present itself as an object to itself. Mead's formulation of the generalized other is especially valuable for its precision with regard to the place of the abstract attitude within the structure of the social self:

In abstract thought the individual takes the attitude of the generalized other toward himself, without reference to its expression in any particular other individuals; and in concrete thought he takes that attitude insofar as it is expressed in the attitudes towards his behaviour of those other individuals with whom he is involved in the given social situation or act. But only by taking the attitude of the generalized other toward himself, in one or other of these ways, can he think at all; for only thus can thinking—or the internalized conversation of gestures which constitutes thinking—occur. And only through the taking by individuals of the attitude or attitudes of the generalized other toward themselves is the existence of a universe of discourse, as that system of common or social meanings which thinking presupposes as its context, rendered possible (11).

Like Mead, Simmel rejects any notion of the construction of a common social world as the production of scientific abstraction and synthesis: "the unity of society needs no observer. It is directly realized by its own elements because these elements are themselves conscious and synthesizing units." Nor does Simmel see the synthesis of social life as the direct focus of individual action but as the by-product of innumerable specific relations governed by "the feeling and knowledge of determining others and being determined by them." This is not to say that the sociologist for his own specific purposes may not elaborate an "additional" synthesis. But the problem here is that the synthesis of external observation which takes as its paradigm the observation of nature is not analogous to human unity, "which is grounded in understanding, love, or common work." The unity of social life lives somewhere in the range of the unities of "décor," which is the unification of our domestic surroundings, and "landscape," which is the unity of river, meadow, trees, and house.

The social synthesis is the work of individuals for whom others have the same reality as their own egological consciousness and are not reducible simply to the contents of individual conscious but function to orient language, thought, and conduct toward the social world. We *think* the other but at the same time we are so "affected" by him that sociation is better regarded as a "knowing" than a "cognizing," says Simmel. But neither is sociation simply an empathic projection of psychological similarities. "We see the other person generalized, in some measure."

Simmel's account of the generalized other proceeds in terms of a remarkable anticipation of the existential basis of the notion of typification with respect to the structure of self, other, and specific world relations:

We see the other not simply as an individual but as a colleague or comrade or fellow party member—in short, as a cohabitant of the same specific world. And this inevitable, quite automatic assumption is one of the means by which one's personality and reality assume, in the imagination of the other, the quality and form required by sociability (12).

At the same time, Simmel argues as though the need to employ self-typifications, as well as role and course-of-action typifications, was not the constitutive foundation of social reality but arises from our inability to ever penetrate to the ideal core either of ourselves or of others. Thus typification is merely a compensation for the inadequacy of our knowledge and imagination in respect of one another. It is at best a veil we throw over our mutual ignorance:

> The distortions derive from all these a priori, operative categories: from the individual's type as a man, from the idea of his perfection, and from the general society to which he belongs. Beyond all of these, there is, as a heuristic principle of knowledge, the idea of his real, unconditionally individual nature (13).

It is not my purpose merely to point out Simmel's equivocal conception of the constitutive role of typifications in the construction of social reality. Here in this first antinomy of the particularity-generalization of the other I think it is quite possible to express Simmel's argument in terms of a range of typifications from face-to-face to increasingly anonymous situations in which the repertoire of tasks, relevances, gestures, language, and context varies as something that can be assumed in common but does so *without any radical break between what can be taken for granted and what becomes problematic.* This is not to say that we cannot be mistaken about one another or in ourselves. But it means that we do not presume ourselves in error and that we encounter error and deceit only in the same world we rely on to correct for them. Thus ordinary vision is not simply a compensation for the blind spot in our field of vision, and no one would think of arguing that perfect vision can never be achieved unless this blind spot were removed. Similarly, the phenomenon of typification rather than being a substitute for knowledge of particulars is the only way they can be given to us at all:

> The practice of life urges us to make the picture of a man only from the real pieces that we empirically know of him, but it is precisely the practice of life which is based on those modifications and supplementations, on the transformation of the given fragments into the generality of a type and into the completeness of the ideal personality (14).

At this point it would be necessary to undertake a constitutive phenomenology of meaning and understanding to clarify the foundations of Simmel's first a priori. It would then be possible to show that the phenomenon of typification provides the objective meaning context which is presupposed by the antinomy of subjective and objective understanding. As Schutz has shown in *The Phenomonology of the Social World*, this requires an analysis of the problem of subjective and objective meaning as problems of temporal institution (15). Here, in view of other essays in this volume (16), it may suffice to indicate the place of such an analysis and its natural fit with the structure of Simmel's sociological apriorities.

SECOND A PRIORI

Each of Simmel's sociological antinomies may be related to the expressive as well as the cognitive dimensions of the self and social reality. Schutz' analysis of subjective meaning in face-to-face and increasingly anonymous social situations may be referred to in respect of the first a priori. In the case of the second a priori or antinomy of social commitment and social withdrawal, as we shall call it, what we can know of the self and the other is a question of the "presentation" (17) of the self to others who support the self in a certain "face." Simmel's emphasis is not so much on the "reality" problem suggested by the stage metaphor of the *persona*. Again, though he sometimes suggests the contrary, Simmel's argument is directed against the notion that the individual is not really present in his social roles or that he can literally enter or exit from the social scene:

Rather, the fact that in certain respects the individual is not an element of society constitutes the positive condition for the possibility that in other respects he is: the way in which he is sociated is determined or codetermined by the way in which he is not (18).

Our experience of social reality would be something quite different from what it is if we were to assume that those we encounter are neither more nor less than what they find scope for in a specific social role. We are not to suppose that people lead double lives, far less many lives. Rather, people lead their various lives, in a manner that may be expressed in terms of a social continuum ranging from the maximal degree of commitment, as evinced, by the bureaucrat or priest, to a minimal degree of such commitment or a maximal degree of social withdrawal, as in the case of the lover or hermit (19). This, of course, does not mean that the *same person* cannot be both a bureaucrat and a lover. But in this he counts upon the *discretion* (20) through which he and others mutually adjust the congruity and incongruity of life's postures. Discretion involves not just a respect for persons and their property but a mutual limit to the use that we make of each other's inadvertent revelations. Thus none of us is made of such solid stuff as we pretend, none so hard, so efficient, none so dreaming and without any practicality.

Simmel very carefully distinguishes the sense in which certain types such as the stranger, the enemy, and the pauper may be said to be outside of society. This use depends on the degree to which individuals are deprived of typical chances to operate the normal stock of knowledge, symbolic means, and resources available to the average member of the society in question (21). Simmel points out that the postures of loneliness, solipsism, rebellion, and alienation require social support from others who must adapt their behavior accordingly to respect the boundaries of subculture and milieu, locale, or scene in which these attitudes are cultivated:

> The essence and deepest significance of the specific sociological a priori which is founded on this phenomenon is this: The "within" and the "without" between individual and society are not two unrelated definitions but define together the fully homogeneous position of man as a social animal (22).

Simmel's second a priori focuses the options of what I have called transcendental sociology in reference to the work of Berger and Goffman (23). The contemporary concerns of transcendental sociology are not simply a problem of fallen epistemologies but lie deep in the sociological conception of the self and its institutional settings. The truth is that sociology is an indoor sport, more at home in the classroom, or in prisons, hospitals, and other large bureaucracies that invent our vicarious experience of life. Sociology has now to pay the price of its theoretical demonstrations of the socially determined self in ways that it could not foresee. Thus Goffman appears as the sociological counterpart of Dostoyevsky's underground man or Camus' Clemence in *The Fall*, while Berger elucidates Musil's "man without qualities," an amalgam of role-distance and the sociology of knowledge. In both cases sociological knowledge is the remedy of a wounded omnipotence, the last alternation of the critical ratio of self and social space and the pitiful props on which the self relies in its obsessive concern with the basic questions of identity, position, and relation.

KNOWLEDGE, TRUTH, AND FALSEHOOD
IN HUMAN RELATIONS (24)

> Yet, just as our apprehension of external nature, along with elusions and inadequacies, nevertheless attains the truth required for the life and progress of our species, so everybody knows, by and large correctly, the other person with whom he has to deal, so that interaction and relation become possible (25).

Before taking up Simmel's third a priori, or antinomy of vocation and symbiosis, it may be useful to try to convey more of the sense of the cognitive and expressive bases of intersubjectivity contained in Simmel's first two apriorities of typification and presentation. The value of this may be to counter the likely objection that Simmel's social phenomenology is based upon a naive realism that confounds the subjective and objective approaches to conduct. At the same time, it is necessary to give some account of error and deception which does not open the door to the misanthropy and scientism that govern even humanistic sociology. For the latter gives no place to human folly in mending appearances (26).

It is the starting assumption of every social relationship that each of us knows with whom he is interacting. This involves the typification of each partner's actions, motives, and situation. What is required is that each person be able to observe the rules of *self-respect* and *considerateness* that sustain the ritual of social interaction:

> A person's performance of face-work, extended by his tacit agreement to help others perform theirs, represents his willingness to abide by the ground rules of social interaction. Here is the hallmark of his socialization as an interactant. If he and the others were not socialized in this way, interaction in most societies and most situations would be a much more hazardous thing for feelings and faces. The person would find it impractical to be oriented to symbolically conveyed appraisals of social worth, or to be possessed of feelings—that is, it would be impractical for him to be a ritually delicate object (27).

It is not necessary that the typifications of respect and consideration be accessible in a perfectly reciprocal way in order to sustain social interaction. Person and action typifications are corrigible through experience and interaction. But what is not true is that we withhold our trust in others until we have absolutely certain grounds for it. Socially speaking, seduction precedes both deduction and induction as the basis of our experience with others. Thus in the ordinary course of life we take others at face-value and expect to be sustained in the face that we ourselves project. In these exchanges the primary focus of social interaction is the expressive communication between self and other. We must then regard language, gesture, task, motive, and situation as resources for expressive social bonding, which is itself the precontractual basis of all other covenants, even those in which we deceive one another:

> With an instinct automatically preventing us from doing otherwise, we show nobody the course of our psychic processes in their purely causal reality and—from the standpoints of logic, objectivity, and meaningfulness—complete incoherence and irrationality. Always, we show only a section of them, stylized by selection and arrangement. We simply cannot imagine any interaction or social relation or society which are *not* based on this teleologically determined non-knowledge of one another. This intrinsic, *a priori*, and (as it were) absolute presupposition includes all relative differences which are familiar to us under the concepts of sincere revelations and mendacious concealments (28).

From the standpoint of sociability, truth and falsehood or knowledge and ignorance are practicalities in which any member of a social group may ordinarily be expected to be versed under pain of risking his status as a fellow. Where a commonsense awareness of the practical typifications and self-presentations is lacking, either on occasion or in some more serious way, a member's sense of social reality may be questioned, apologies, excuses, or explanations demanded, which in turn touch upon the member's continued identity in the group. Simmel's fundamental insight into the nature of social interaction lies in his demonstration that ordinary social interaction presupposes the a prioris of knowledge and ignorance as practicalities that any social agent can articulate without explicit rule and according to the needs of specific social enterprises. In other words, the way in which society is possible is never anything other than a practical task which commonsense rationality and sentiment solves continuously (29), or, as Simmel would say, "teleologically."

THIRD A PRIORI

The a priori of the individual's social existence is the fundamental correlation between his life and the society that surrounds him, the integrative function and necessity of his specific character, as it is determined by his personal life, to the life of the whole (30).

Simmel's third a priori or antinomy of vocation and symbiosis, as I call it, is concerned with society experienced alternately as a deterministic environment or force (milieu) and as our very element or beneficent shell (ambiance) (31). This alternation is essential to the dialectic of individual and social consciousness which are not separate entities but simply vital dimensions of our human awareness and biography (32). As Mead puts it, the "I" is the response of the self which arises through taking the attitudes of others—the "me"—and together these responses constitute our social experience of freedom and determinism:

Over against the "me" is the "I." The individual not only has rights, but he has duties; he is not only a citizen, a member of the community, but he is one who reacts to this community and in his reaction to it, as we have seen in the conversation of gestures, changes it. The "I" is the response of the individual to the attitude of the community as this appears in his own experience. His response to that organized attitude in turn changes it. . . . The adjustment to that organized world which is present in our own nature is one that represents the "me" and is constantly there. But if the response to it is a response which is of the nature of the conversation of gestures, if it creates a situation which is in some sense novel, if one puts up his side of the case, asserts himself over against others and insists that they take a different attitude toward himself, then there is something important occurring that is not previously present in experience (33).

There are times when we experience ourselves as the simplest element in the vast swarm of social life. This experience of the transcendence of society is not fundamentally an experience of alienation, even though the metaphors of organicism and machinery used to convey the experience may be given this interpretation. But there is a common-sense experience of the world and society as that which precedes us and survives us and in which the simple sense of tradition and posterity is cultivated. So far from being an alien experience, social transcendence provides us with a sense of the social world as somehow fashioned to our wants and needs, shaped to the scheme of our practices and relevances. If the social world is larger than us, it is in the way that a child finds his home richer than himself in meeting all his needs. In this sense we experience social transcendence in the daily borrowings of our lives and in the symbiosis of gift and exigency which is the presupposition of all exchange and organization.

Yet it is also the case that we experience the great anonymity of society and the social division of labor as something in which we are called to find a place through our own peculiar vocation. Indeed, as Durkheim has shown, it is the modern development of the social division of labor that creates the moral space in which vocation and personality flourish. Simmel, as well as Durkheim and Weber, remarks on the crisis of trust which arises with the volume of exchange and abstract communication in a modern society. Yet here again we may remark that the sense of individual vocation is not necessarily anomic. It may, for example, be perfectly synchronous with the symbiosis of social life. This may be seen from the original Christian conception of charisma (34) in which the varieties of gifts, of tongues, of healing, of liberality, and of teaching are conceived as operations of the same spirit and the same God in us and exercised within the same unity as the temporal and Christian body-politic.

Human experience and vision accumulate only in the circle of social relations and institutions which enlarge and deepen the sense of our sentiments and deeds and work through the symbiosis of solidarity and personality. Social action is essentially the unfolding of a personal and cultural space through a constant dialogue with others that involves a recovery of the past and the projection of breaks that are never complete. But this is not the source of an irremediable alienation; it is precisely the feature of our experience that calls for a collectivity and history in which there is past and future. Such a collectivity or *institution* is never wholly reified; it is made and unmade, with a particular grain in each of us who lives and alters the surroundings from which he draws his life. This is a feature not only of social institutions, but also of human thoughts, emotions, and, above all, of human talk (35). Understood in this way, human institutions are the sole means that we have of keeping faith with one another while being true to ourselves.

Each of Simmel's antinomies, or, as we may call them, the *a prioris of typification, presentation, and symbiosis,* are constituent features of individual and social existence. They circumscribe the cognitive and expressive operations of social bonding but are prior to all empirical patterns of motivation. However, these sociological a prioris taken as practical antinomies may also provide the sociological imagination with a critical or "experimental intentionality" in which the constituent practices of individual and social reality may be revealed, as in the classical works of Erving Goffman and Harold Garfinkel's studies in ethnomethodology.

The deep sense of the incongruity procedures of Goffman and Garfinkel, if not of Berger, is to show that the sense of social possibility and its techniques of face and impression management is false to the unarticulated structure of our everyday trust and social competence with one another. They may be understood to challenge manipulative and expert knowledge through an appeal to our mundane experience of the self and its definition of the social situation which is given to us through the same set of typifications and motives that are the convenience of anyone. Thus it is only by some incongruity of experience, some outrage or manipulation, that I discover that my self is not synonymous with selves in general, or that what I take to be the perceivedly normal and typical features of my situation are not in fact shared or available to anyone like me.

We have tried to expand upon Simmel's question concerning the possibility of society. To some this is a metaphysical question with which sociology need not concern itself. Indeed, it might even be pointed out by sociologists that this question, known to philosophers as the problem of intersubjectivity or other minds, is one that presents the greatest difficulty, which is not escaped even by phenomenology (36). But the reflexive nature of social reality makes it impossible to choose between philosophy and sociology in the analysis of social reality. Scientific sociology is presently having to adjust its limits to the great platitude that its topic is the everyday resource of social life:

Now experience in anthropology is our insertion as social subjects into a whole, in which, the synthesis our intelligence laboriously looks for has already been effected, since we live in the unity of one single life all the systems our culture is composed of. We gain some knowledge from the synthesis which is ourselves. Furthermore, the equipment of our social being can be dismantled and reconstructed through the voyage as we are able to learn to speak other languages. This provides a second way to the universal: no longer the overarching universal of a strictly objective method, but a sort of lateral universal which we acquire through ethnological experience and its incessant testing of the self through the other person and the other person through the self. It is a question of constructing a general system of reference in which the point of view of the native, the point of view of the civilized man, and the mistaken views each has of the other can all find a place—that is, of constituting a more comprehensive experience which becomes in principle accessible to men of a different time and country (37).

Thus Simmel's question concerning the possibility of social life is simultaneously a question concerning the limits of scientific sociology as a form of theoretical life and its pretension to order the everyday constructions of conduct, motive, relevance, and order. Where exponents of the task of reflexive sociology ignore these fundamental metaphysics of everyday life, as does Gouldner, the options of sociological theorizing are reduced to either biographical or political sentiments (38). In either case, the want of an adequate ground in philosophical anthropology is evident. Moreover, its consequences are apparent at the empirical level where the task of sociological research is in turn impossible without reliance upon common interpretative procedures for the production and evaluation of appropriate courses of action and conceptions of constitutional norms and structure (39). In the past, sociological theory has resolved this problem through a variety of cognitivist accounts of the deduction of everyday social life from normative institutional structures (40). In practice, these accounts have relied on a conception of rationality which is itself the construct of a long historical process that is presupposed by the very form of sociological reasoning seeking to furnish an analysis of the social order in which it is embedded. Thus the limits of sociological theory reappear as the limits of the tradition of reason to which sociology adheres.

Finally, whether or not Simmel's question touches upon the everyday practice of sociology (although there can be no doubt that it does), there is no need to appeal for converts between sociology and philosophy. Simmel's question need no more disturb these two armies than the notions of night and day are upset by the phenomenon of dawn. For the dawn keeps its own watch and there are always workers about.

NOTES

1. Georg Simmel, "How is Society Possible?," in *Essays on Sociology, Philosophy and Aesthetics*, translated and edited by Kurt H. Wolff, Harper and Row, New York, 1965, pp. 335–356. The present essay is a revised version of an earlier effort, "How is Society Possible?," in John O'Neill, *Sociology as a Skin Trade: Essays Towards a Reflexive Sociology*, Heinemann Educational Books, London, (and Harper and Row, New York), 1972. Unless otherwise cited, all references to other essays of mine may be found in this volume.

2. O'Neill, "The Hobbesian Problem in Marx and Parsons," *op. cit.*, Chap. 13.

3. Alfred Schutz, *The Phenomenology of the Social World*, translated by George Walsh and Frederick Lehnert, Northwestern University Press, Evanston, Ill., 1967; *Collected Papers*, Vol. I: *The Problem of Social Reality*, edited by Maurice Natanson, Martinus Nijhoff, The Hague, 1962; *Collected Papers*, Vol. II: *Studies in Social Theory*, edited by Arvid Broderson, Martinus Nijhoff, The Hague, 1964; *Collected Papers*, Vol. III: *Studies in Phenomenological Philosophy*, edited by Ilse Schutz, Martinus Nijhoff, The Hague, 1966; *Reflections on the Problem of Relevance*, edited, annotated, and with an Introduction by Richard M. Zaner, Yale University Press, New Haven and London, 1970.

4. Harold Garfinkel, *Studies in Ethnomethodology*, Prentice-Hall, Englewood Cliffs, N.J., 1967; Aaron V. Cicourel, *The Social Organization of Juvenile Justice*, John Wiley and Sons, New York, 1968; Burkhart Holzner, *Reality Construction in Society*, Schenkman Publishing Company, Cambridge, Mass., 1968; Peter L. Berger and Thomas Luckmann, *The Social Construction of Reality: A Treatise in the Sociology of Knowledge*, Doubleday and Company, New York, 1967.

5. Berger and Luckmann, *op. cit.*, p. 15.

6. Schutz, *Collected Papers*, Vol. II, pp. 229–238.

7. Erving Goffman, *Interaction Ritual: Essays on Face-to-Face Behaviour*, Doubleday Anchor Books, New York, 1967.

8. Simmel *op. cit.*, p. 349. On the problem of the existential truth underlying the sociology of knowledge and sociological theory, see Kurt H. Wolff, "The Sociology of Knowledge and Sociological Theory," *Symposium on Sociological Theory*, edited by Llewellyn Gross, Harper and Row, New York, 1959, pp. 567–602.

9. Maurice Natanson, *The Social Dynamics of George H. Mead*, Public Affairs Press, Washington, D.C., 1956, pp. 64–68.

10. George H. Mead, *The Philosophy of the Act*, edited by Charles W. Morris in collaboration with John M. Brewster, Albert M. Dunham, and David L. Milher, University of Chicago Press, Chicago, 1938, pp. 152–153. John O'Neill (ed.), *Modes of Individualism and Collectivism*, Heinemann Educational Books, London, 1972.

11. George H. Mead, *Mind, Self, and Society*, edited and with an introduction by Charles W. Morris, The University of Chicago Press, Chicago and London, 1967, pp. 155–156. Nevertheless, Mead's position is a more "cognitivist" one than we are advancing.

12. Simmel, *op. cit.*, p. 344.

13. *Ibid.*, p. 345.

14. *Ibid.*, p. 344.

15. Schutz, *The Phenomenology of the Social World*, *op. cit.*, p. 8.

16. See papers by Zaner and by Psathas and Waksler in this volume.

17. Erving Goffman, *The Presentation of Self in Everyday Life*, Doubleday Anchor Books, New York, 1959.

18. Simmel, *op. cit.*, p. 345.

19. Philip E. Slater, "On Social Regression," *American Sociological Review*, *28* (3), June 1963, pp. 339–364.

20. *The Sociology of Georg Simmel*, translated, edited and with an introduction by Kurt H. Wolff, The Free Press, Glencoe, 1950, pp. 320–324.

21. Schutz, "The Stranger," *Collected Papers*, Vol. II, pp. 91–105.

22. Simmel, *op. cit.*, p. 350.

23. O'Neill, "Self-Prescription and Social Machiavellianism," *op. cit.*, Chap. 2.

24. *The Sociology of Georg Simmel*, *op. cit.*, Part IV.

25. *Ibid.*, p. 307.

26. Desiderius Erasmus, *The Praise of Folly*, translated from the Latin, with an essay and commentary by Hoyt Hopewell Hudson, Princeton University Press, Princeton, N.J., 1970, pp. 37–38.

27. Goffman, *Interaction Ritual*, *op. cit.*, p. 31.

28. *The Sociology of Georg Simmel*, *op. cit.*, p. 312.

29. For an experimental confirmation of this basic postulate of constitutive social phenomenology, see Harold Garfinkel, "Studies of the Routine Grounds of Everyday Activities," *Social Problems*, 2 (3), Winter 1964, pp. 225–250.

30. Simmel, *op. cit.*, pp. 353–354.

31. Leo Spitzer, "Milieu and Ambiance: An Essay in Historical Semantics," *Philosophy and Phenomenological Research*, *3*, 1942–1943, pp. 1–42, 169–218.

32. For the concepts of alternation and biography see Peter Berger, *Invitation to Sociology*, Doubleday and Company, New York, 1963, Chap. 3.

33. Mead, *Mind, Self, and Society*, *op. cit.*, p. 196.

34. *I Corinthians*, ii, 4–31.

35. Michael Oakeshott, "The Voice of Poetry in the Conversation of Mankind," in his *Rationalism in Politics* and other essays, Methuen and Co. Ltd., London, 1962; John O'Neill, "Institution, Language and Historicity," in *Perception, Expression and History: The Social Phenomenology of Maurice Merleau-Ponty*, Northwestern University Press, Evanston, Ill., 1970, pp. 46–64.

36. Schutz, "The Problem of Transcendental Intersubjectivity in Husserl," *Collected Papers*, Vol. III, pp. 51–91.

37. Maurice Merleau-Ponty, "From Mauss to Claude Lévi-Strauss," *Signs*, translated with an introduction by Richard C. McCleary, Northwestern University Press, Evanston, Ill., 1964, pp. 119–120.

38. O'Neill, "Reflexive Sociology or the Advent of Alvin W. Gouldner," *op. cit.*, Chap. 14.

39. Aaron V. Cicourel, "Basic and Normative Rules in the Negotiation of Status and Role," *Recent Sociology No. 2: Patterns of Communicative Behavior*, edited by Hans Peter Dreitzel, Macmillan, New York, 1970, pp. 4–45.

40. For a critique of cognitivist mechanist approaches and an account of the function of the "corporeal schema" and the "specular image" in the socialization of the child, see John O'Neill, "Embodiment and Child Development: A Phenomenological Approach," *Recent Sociology No. 5: Childhood and Socialization*, edited by Hans Peter Dreitzel, Macmillan, New York, 1973.

» » » » » » » » » » » » » ·» » » » » » » » » «

The positivist approach in science, when applied to the social sciences, has recently been subjected to a most devastating critique by the work of Harold Garfinkel and ethnomethodologists. Advancing the argument, and raising the theoretical issues that underlie the methodological objections to a positivist approach, Bittner notes that the ideal of objectivity, as proposed in positivism, is unattainable in sociology because "it fails to do justice to cultural reality."

Yet the rebirth of the "Chicago school" of realism in sociology, the new urban ethnographies, and other such developments promise a less than satisfactory solution to the problem of objectivity to the extent that they uncritically accept the perspective of the subject as reality. It is not enough to describe empirically the lives and beliefs of those whom one observes, nor to regard one's acceptance into the everyday circumstances and lives of one's informants as a sign of objectivity. The difference between the actor or member's perspective and that of the observer remains.

Phenomenology may appear to provide the observer with a solution to the problem of objectivity, but the uncritical interpretation of phenomenology as a justification for the "description of unanalyzed impressions" will not provide the answer. The phenomenology of cultural relativism is thus to be seen as an abortive effort at phenomenological sociology inconsistent with the critical orientation of phenomenology which Zaner, Wolff, and Wagner call to our attention. (Later in this book we shall see efforts by Blumenstiel, Jehensen, and Manning and Fabrega to apply the phenomenological approach in actual field studies.)

OBJECTIVITY AND REALISM
IN SOCIOLOGY

»»»»»»»»»»»»»»»»»»»»»»»» «««««««««««««««««««««««««

Egon Bittner

Brandeis University

For many years, until recently, sociologists used the word "objective" with reference to their research procedures and findings to imply that what they did was altogether true, important, interesting, rigorous, lucid, useful, elegant, and whatever else could conceivably matter in their favor. By the same token, the characterization of some endeavor as "subjective" had the inevitable import of a general condemnation. The use was no mere linguistic affectation. In the then prevailing opinion, strict compliance with certain canons of objectivity alone guaranteed the attainment of all the objectives of rational inquiry (1). Clearly this is no longer the prevailing view, at least not for the discipline as a whole. Quite the contrary, in some quarters objectivity has fallen into ill repute and is explicitly denounced; in many parts of the discipline the problem of objectivity is treated as insignificant and uninteresting; and even where the criteria of objectivity are adhered to in the inherited sense much less is made of it than used to be the case. But neither contempt nor neglect will make the problem of objectivity disappear and sociologists cannot—must not!—divest themselves of the responsibility for rendering an accounting of the way in which they try to do justice to the realities they study.

What has been forsaken, or lost, as the case may be, in this change? What could induce an avowedly empirical discipline to retreat from a position of more stringent objectivity to a position of lesser stringency? And, finally, how is the taking of leave from inherited understandings of objectivity connected, or connectable, with influences emanating from phenomenology, in view of phenomenologists' self-conscious interest in subjectivity? This paper attempts to suggest an answer to these questions.

The past dominance of certain criteria of objectivity was closely related to the past dominance of a positivistic philosophy of science in sociology, whose two most prominent features were an extraordinarily high level of deliberate preoccupation with questions of research technique and a theory of knowledge sometimes referred to as naive realism. The latter entails the belief that the knowledge normally competent, wide awake adults have of the world around them, about the society in the midst of which they live, and concerning human affairs *is*, despite its ambiguity, uncertainty, and incompleteness, an adequate beginning point for more systematic study aimed at the removal of these inadequacies. That the commonsense knowledge people share about the nature of their circumstances and about themselves is to them a matter of decidedly practical import, and that therefore the structure and the content of this knowledge must be assumed to be determined by this interest, was not, according to the perspectives of naive realism, deemed relevant for deciding questions of validity. Although it may well be true that the proverbial man on the street has motives in seeking information that differ substantially from the motives that move scientific curiosity, answers and findings are subject to assessment of their truth value without regard for the position from which the question might have been framed. In sum, "naive" in naive realism, in relation to positivist sociology, meant the unexamined acceptance of the reality of the world of everyday experience as a heuristic fact, in preference to alternatives, especially in preference to a variety of conceptions drawn from, or formulated in connection with, inherited forms of philosophical reflection.

Lest too much is made of the positivist "naiveté," it should be remembered that it was, *mutatis mutandis*, on a philosophical foundation like that upon which the magnificent edifice of modern science was built. That is, even though positivism—the doctrine designated by this name —is a product of the second half of the nineteenth century, it would have been an entirely adequate philosophy for the growth of science since

Galileo. To be sure, this is a philosophy *for* science, not *of* science (2).

The sciences, especially the physical sciences, have, of course, lost all the outward signs of adhering to a naive realist theory of knowledge and have tended to acquire arcane bodies of technique and information in which a person of average talent can partake only after an arduous and protracted preparation of the kind ordinarily associated with making a life commitment to a vocation. It would lead far afield to discuss in detail the process by which the sciences originating in the outlook of quotidian experience of ordinary persons have been transformed into fully emancipated, self-contained intellectual entities (3). Suffice it to say that in the course of their development, from time to time certain monumental achievements of inquisitive spirits appear and serve "implicitly to define the legitimate problems and methods of a research field for succeeding generations of practitioners" (4).

For example, the achievement of Copernicus served as a *paradigm* determining the normal conduct of inquiry in astronomy for centuries. And the thus normalized conduct of inquiry gave rise to an enormously rich complex of professional interest, of standardized technique, and of accepted information, all of which is frequently quite unbelievable and incomprehensible, and some of which is literally not sensible in commonsense terms. Indeed, contrary to the sensibilities of commonsense, the "organ" through which scientific realities are "sensed" is the scientific method. As part of this method, efforts to do justice to realities-as-they-are, that is, efforts to be objective, are controlled by explicit procedural norms, whose aim is to permit the formulation of assertions that would be as far as can be controlled free of implications arising out of the actual circumstances under which they were formulated and free of implications that arise out of the particular interest and limitations of him who makes them.

The norms that control objectivity in science are (a) the operational definition of meaning, and (b) strict formalization of rules of inference. In accordance with the first "we mean by any concept nothing more than a set of operations" (5). Accordingly, the notion of length can be said to have its meaning fixed by fixed procedures of measuring and be exhaustively coincident with it. The objective sense of a statement gains in clarity and determinateness in proportion to the degree to which procedures of observation that underlie its formulation can be made explicit. The norm of formalization of rules of inference, on the other hand, provides that in statements involving conclusions of any kind, objectivity is commensurate with the degree to which reaching them can be mathematicized. It is easy to see that with both, the procedures of observation and the procedures of inference regulated by general norm, there is nothing left to the unruly factor of subjectivity—or so it would seem, in any case. And it is no doubt true that in fields like astronomy or bacteriology such conceptions of control of objectivity are indispensable (whether they are sufficient is another matter) to talk sensibly about the realities with which these disciplines purportedly deal. That is, it appears that in the physical sciences the just described canons of objectivity are attuned to the object they are intended to do justice.

But if these concepts serve well and make sense in the most advanced of the sciences, does it not stand to reason that they ought to be made use of in those sciences that have thus far only aspired to advancement? Is it not worth an attempt to treat the notion of, let us say, prestige in the way scientists treat matters like velocity? As is well known, attempts along these lines have been made and there exists a small library of reports of studies in which the concept of prestige has been operationalized and dealt with by means of mathematical modes of analysis. Despite these *bona fide* attempts, we have not achieved a normalization of usage and procedure around the concept of prestige that might be considered— even when considered with the most favorable bias—to be remotely analogous to the normalization achieved around the concept of velocity by means of the differential calculus and, more important, although there are occasionally poignant flarings of optimism on this score, there exist no grounds for realistic hope that such a normalization might be forthcoming about the concept of prestige or any other concept of this kind in the foreseeable future. This is not to say that sociologists cannot devise instruments and procedures to measure, nor even that the measurements thereby achieved cannot be used for the attainment of some practical, manipulative objectives. It only forebodes that these successes contain no promise of contributing anything to our understanding of society in the manner in which such achievements in the physical sciences did contribute to the understanding of the physical cosmos.

If it is correct to say that the principle of objectivity that has dominated sociology during the years past has failed to contribute to the development of sociology in a manner anywhere commensurate to the contribution it made to the development of the natural sciences, where it originates, then it is fair to say that forsaking it, or at least taking a highly skeptical view of its merits, creates no loss at all. To be sure, it could be argued that several decades of trial do not yet constitute a fully adequate test. But the decline in the faith that upheld the spirits of the positivists during lean years is not wholly due to disappointing performance. There are, in fact, at least three other reasons for the growing ascendance of the view that positivist objectivity represented a gratuitous exercise in intellectual discipline that had, most outward appearances aside, nothing to do with science. For in all the technicality, precision, and formalism that attached to positivist methodology, the object of its objectivity vanished.

That is, the suspicion is stirring that it is not only far-fetched to expect that a prestige scale might measure prestige in the way the notion is actually conceived theoretically, but it seems likely that it does not measure anything at all!

Of the three positive reasons for the abandonment of the positivist idea of objectivity, the first consists of a version of the inherited views about the methodological contrast between the natural and the social sciences; the second advances the consideration that far from being practiced in the interest of building a science of society, positivist objectivity was partly a deliberate and partly an unwitting way of *not* facing the tasks of studying social reality; and the third—the most radical of the three—urges that efforts to impose positivistic objectivity on sociological inquiry involve a contradiction in terms inasmuch as the discipline is programmatically oriented to the study of matters that are inherently devoid of objective meaning.

The modern distinction between the theories of knowledge applicable to the social and the physical reality, respectively, goes back at least to the anti-Cartesian polemics of Giambatista Vico. Its best known and most influential form is in the arguments of Heinrich Rickert concerning the difference between the nomothetic *Naturwissenschaften* and the idiographic *Geisteswissenschaften*. But the strongest statement is contained in the unjustly neglected *Cultural Reality* by Florian Znaniecki (6). In brief, Znaniecki argued that all efforts to study and render accounts of sociocultural matters in a manner that accords with the procedures of natural-scientific objectivity must inevitably face an insoluble paradox. Objective scientific explanation means, essentially, explanation in terms of lawfully linked chains or complexes of antecedents and consequences. Even when the object of the researcher's interest is the analysis of a structure—for example, the structure of a molecule—the attempt involves throughout references to causal ties between the elements of the structure and within the structure as a whole, and therefore every *why* and every *how* in the sciences searches for answers and explanations of a causal nature.

It is claimed that the introduction of canons of objectivity into science had as its result laying bare material structures purged of extraneous relevances and stabilized wholly by causal ties (7). There is no offhand reason why this approach should not be applied to explanations of human behavior and appearance, and to the structure of human relations. Surely, there can be no objection to someone's holding that the ability to rotate matrices stands in a relation of causal dependence to having studied algebra, *ceteris paribus* of course. This explanation is not very powerful, as every mathematics teacher will readily attest, but it is an explanation as far as it goes, and its demonstration could probably be accomplished by methods that do not do excessive violence to principles of scientific objectivity. But if this approach is followed one step further, a peculiar difficulty comes to the fore. If a sociologist used what he learned in algebra to rotate matrices, as he well might if he were to resort to factor analysis, could it be said that what he discovered in this process, his findings, are also caused? Surely no scientist in his right mind can concede that the findings he reports and, by extension, scientific knowledge as a whole, is itself merely a contingent fact, and that it be accorded the same consideration as the facts it bespeaks.

Learning how to do something may be said to fit into a causal texture of explanations, but it does not seem fitting to say that the knowledge that obtains from doing something is caused thereby. Whereas knowing and believing may be said to be contingent fact, the known and the believed are not. The molecule is merely there actually, but that which is known about it is not merely known actually, it is by definition subject to assessment with respect to its truth value. Thereby, however, is created a wholly new domain of realities, of cultural realities, about which assertions formulated in accordance with canons of scientific objectivity reveal remarkably little. Encompassed in it are things like the kinetic theory of gasses, but also the musical score of "Stars and Stripes Forever," pocket-watches, criminals, bridge tournaments, french-fried potatoes, credit, Indian arrowheads, and so on. About all these and such things it must be said that they are not merely actually existent, if they are existent, but that it inheres in the nature of their existence that what they truly are is inextricably connected with some human interest in them, and this makes them subject to normative assessment according to the specific nature of their value.

In sum, it is the case of science itself, taken precisely in the sense in which scientists themselves understand it and engage in it—more specifically, it is the recognition of science as a fact transcendent to the facts it is about—which presents the cardinal demonstration that methods of scientific objectivity are not the appropriate methods to be used in sociology. This is so because what holds true for science must also hold true for all other kinds of culturally controlled activity without any exceptions whatever and, accordingly, it is clear that canons of positivist objectivity cannot be trusted to do justice to the objects of sociological interest.

The view that compliance with ideals of objectivity in the positivist style is merely a way of avoiding having to face the study of society, and the related view that society cannot be studied seriously from a position that is deliberately uninvolved, often invokes Karl Marx as its main protagonist. According to this view all efforts to come up with an impartially objective depiction and analysis of the actually existing state of affairs as a functioning social order is in effect nothing else but a defense of this order together with the injustices and inequities that inhere in it. When one disregards the import of political bias of positivist objectivism (or if one happens to share its political biases), one cannot help but find that its products are bland, uninteresting, and insignificant. Far from being adequate to the professed topics of their interest, positivist sociologists spend their time and imagination on generally vacuous scholastic analyses of the shadows of reality.

One of the most outspoken critics of modern objectivism finds two kinds of quite unflattering traits in scholars who turn to it. They tend to be people who seek compensation when "their capacity to love has been crippled." Alternatively, and more on the level of practical expedience, they are those "whose resentment is shackled by their timidity and privilege" (8). It is difficult to think of a more complete condemnation; objectivists are not merely mistaken or misguided, they are persons who either have nothing to give or persons who will only sell what they have. In either case the endeavor and its products are a banality, a pastime, the sole possible value of which is that it can be—like virtually everything else in the "right" hand—an instrument of exploitation and oppression. In the most charitable view it merely perpetuates the idle conceits of philosophers who have "only interpreted the world . . . (while) the point is to change it" (9). Positivists cannot understand that the realities of society and culture are a function of passion and of judgment, and that without passion and judgment they cannot be apprehended in their true nature. It is of the greatest importance that dealing with human matters from a distance and by means of instruments is no mere innocent mistake, it is artful deception (even when the individual practitioner is not himself personally deceitful), the ultimate effect of which cannot be anything but the further spiritual deracination of man and the increase of the sum total of alienation in society. The only kind of true objectivity that can be attributed to positivistic sociology is that insofar as its teachings become incorporated into the ruling ideology they become embodiments of its intentions.

The third denial of the possibility of objectivism in sociology comes from an extraordinarily rigorous program of empirical research known as ethnomethodology. It is in the nature of this approach that it should seek to yield evidence in favor of the presumption against objectivity, rather than either proof or exhortation. The demonstration could be briefly stated as follows (10). All "accounts" (i.e., all manner of describing, analyzing, questioning, criticizing, believing, doubting, idealizing, schematizing, denigrating, and so on) are unavoidably and irremediably tied to the social settings that occasion them or within which they are situated. This condition of *reflexivity* that exists between accounts and settings does not refer to the phenomenon of ideology in Mannheim's sense. That is, it is not said that situational reality intrudes upon the content of belief through the impact of nonadventitious interest, a mechanism that causes all social knowledge to be existentially grounded. Instead, the point made is that factual realities of socially organized settings are throughout permeated by the ways-in-which-they-are-known, and derive, keep, and change their meanings with it. Moreover, the tie of accounts to settings is unavoidable and irremediable because the accounts derive their sensibility and warrant from it. The absence of this feature—the feature of dependence of accounts, and incidentally of all expressions and of all practical action, on the natural habitat of their occurrence for recognizable meaning, a feature known as "indexicality"—tends to give representations of social settings the aspect of confabulation or fiction, an ever-present risk in narrative historiography which Wilhelm Dilthey attempted to overcome through strictly period-bound hermeneutics of cultural contents (11).

Although many might accept as demonstrated the fact of indexicality of naturally occurring accounts, they could still hold out for an explanation as to why privileged status should not be claimed for the scientific character of accounts attempted by sociologists. It is important to make clear what this involves at a minimum. Note first that sociologists always attempt to render accounts of matters about which accounts already exist. For example, to be analyzed, kinship structure is always already known to those who constitute it. Furthermore, the sociologist is required to draw the terms of his analysis from what is known from the perspective of the actor. Consequently, to gratify the hope for a scientifically objective sociological account the sociologist would have to substitute objective for indexical expressions. Harold Garfinkel writes about this, "In every actual case without exception, conditions will be cited that a competent investigator will be required to recognize, such that in *that* particular case the terms of the demonstration can be relaxed and nevertheless the demonstration be counted an adequate one" (Garfinkel's italics) (12). According to this statement, no one has ever succeeded in the objective study of society without relaxing canons of objectivity, and therefore it is not unreasonable to argue that this relaxation is indispensable, thereby defeating the conceit of privilege. It is important to emphasize that this is not at all due to lack of sophistication, care, or effort—quite the contrary. It appears that the more disciplined, the more rigorous the effort to apply the standard of scientific objectivity in sociological research becomes, the more tenuous grows the connection between the theoretical ideas and interest that motivate the research, and its execution. Thus, paradoxically, it is the violation of outward stringencies of formalized research technique, not compliance with them, that betrays the researcher who feels a sense of responsibility for doing justice to the object of his inquiry.

The central point of the foregoing arguments is that the ideal of objectivity embodied in the joint norms of *operational definition* and *for-*

malization of inference is unattainable in sociology because it fails to do justice to cultural reality. In fact, they suggest that it still remains to be made clear what objectivity in sociology might consist of, if it were to take full account of the objects of social science inquiry in their actually given nature, and if it were to refrain from the mechanical acceptance of methods of research developed with other aims in mind.

What then is left for a new start? Granted that the bright promise of a science of society built on a foundation of formalistically regulated observation and inference was not to be, what are the prospects of having a science of society at all? A brief summary stock-taking might be helpful in looking over the brink of that question.

It is worth taking note of the fact that although the attacks on positivist objectivism were mounted from positions that involved strong commitments to philosophically well-grounded and rigorous scholarship, the arguments of the attack were often invoked as the aegis for studies of a loose, impressionistic, and personal nature. Thus the attack was harnessed to advance the emancipation from a discipline which, aside from leading nowhere itself, prevented the movement forward of scholars who forever complained that no sooner did they conceive of a good idea when pressures to operationalize and to measure turned their efforts into busywork from which the ghost of the initial interest quickly departed. At the same time the taking of leave from objectivism was heralded as a genuine return to what is generally accepted to be the fundamental percept of all social science inquiry, the recognition of the relevance of the perspective of the actor. Above all, however, the newly liberated research stood for the revival, or the reinstatement into its rightful place, of *realism* in sociology of the kind associated with the celebrated achievements of the Chicago School in the 1920s (13). The claim to realism—of faithfulness to reality—is important because its consideration makes available for analysis the manner in which objects come into view and are seen as objects of research interest, and realism can therefore be considered as the methodological equivalent of positivist objectivity.

The work to which the foregoing remarks allude consists mainly of a number of urban ethnographies (14). Characteristically, to carry out their studies the researchers rely exclusively on those competences and resources they possess as members of society. To be sure, experience and a tutored subtlety of perception are highly valued, but the only thing that might be considered to be a required intellectual posture in this sort of field work is total immersion in the life studied. Accordingly, field workers find putting themselves into the picture they are drawing not only unavoidable but also a welcome obligation. The obligation to make clear who is talking draws its validity from the highest authority. "There is no absolutely 'objective' analysis of culture—or perhaps more narrowly but certainly not essentially different for our purposes—of 'social phenomena' independent of special and 'one-sided' viewpoints according to which—expressly or tacitly, consciously or subconsciously—they are selected, analyzed and organized for expository purposes." And later from the same source, "All knowledge of cultural reality, as may be seen, is always knowledge from *particular points of view*" (Weber's italics) (15).

It follows necessarily from these percepts that if anything said about social reality is to make sense, especially if it is to make unambiguous sense, it must be said in ways such that the point of view is either implicitly obvious or explicitly explained. The question is, of course, whether the researcher's immersion in the reality he studies and his emergence into the description he renders satisfied the requirement of making his point of view explicit. The question has not been studied with the care it deserves. Indeed it is not too difficult to sense in reading the urban ethnographies mentioned that the practice of writing in the "as-I-see-it" manner is more plucky than considered. Pluck is a virtue, especially in this case, but it does not set all things right.

The truth is that there attaches a spirit of adventure to field work such that questions concerning realism of perception and description are decided by how one feels about it. This personal aspect of field work is ill-concealed by referring to it as a method of research on par with, let us say, survey analysis or laboratory experimentation, a reference that is probably best understood by treating it as an expression of a live and let live attitude. Unfortunately the combination of personal enthusiasm and compromise, taken together with the ethnographer's notorious disdain for hypercomplicated, metacritical hair-splitting, are not very hospitable to analysis. Yet if the field worker's claim to realism and to respect for the perspective of the actor are to be given serious credence, then it will have to be made clear what form they assume when they are a function not of a natural attitude of the actor but of a deliberately appropriated "natural attitude" of the observer. That is, if it is true that the quality of an object or event—its meaning—does not attach to them objectively but is instead discernible only within the frameworks of socially organized settings, and there only from a perspective of specially oriented interest (for instance, the meaning of the remark "you old son-of-a-bitch" is something to which those between whom it passes have, on the occasion of its passage, a uniquely privileged access) then a field worker must somehow *contrive* an appreciation for these objects and events, since they do not constitute the actual circumstances of *his* life and therefore do not matter to *him* in ways he must nevertheless recognize them as mattering, regardless how participating a participant-observer he might succeed in being. In other words, the field worker re-turns to seeing things as they appear to those who live their lives in their midst, and thereby appears to take re-course to an objectiveness that rests on directly intuited facticity for its warrant. Whereas this turn to reality does not call for an argued defense when it occurs in the natural course, *choosing* it as a preferred way of seeing things does require justification.

Field workers are, of course, not unaware of the need to *contrive* access to information and explanation, but they tend to view it as a matter of maintaining trustful relations with people whose activities and lives they study and of cultivating open-mindedness and perceptual subtlety on their own part. In fact, how to achieve these objectives is a matter of very considerable concern among field workers and is usually treated in connection with ethical questions; there is a good deal of practical lore available on these matters. The concentration on how to do field work well and how to get it done, laudable as it is, not only fails to cast light on the epistemological problem underlying realism but actually obscures it. The greater the effort to enhance the adequacy of observation on counts such as acceptance, transfer of trust, subtlety, perspicacity, open-mindedness, patience, and scope, the less likely that serious, searching questions will be asked about that which has come to view by means of all this loving care. That is, the more satisfied the field worker is about having done all in his power to solve procedural research problems, the less likely he is to note, and if noted attribute significance to, the fact that the reality he has seen and is describing is of a special kind, no matter how closely it resembles the "real" reality. The aim of contrivance is the approximation of authenticity, thus the more successful the outcome, the less likely that it will be remembered as contrived. In fact, however, the nature of reality the field worker attends to and, by extension, the realism embodied in his observations have nothing at all to do with the particulars of research technique. It is not whether he observes well or poorly that matters but the circumstance of his being an outside observer with all the consequences issuing from it.

Perhaps the best way to capture and render the actual reality in field work is to consider the reality it *seeks* to capture, namely, the reality of everyday life. It is important to emphasize that the term "world of everyday life" refers to a zone of reality that is not limited, as the terms might be mistakenly taken to imply, to the ordinary, routine, broadly common aspects of existence from which the rare, the celebrated, the dramatic have been excluded. The feature that defines the world of everyday life is not its familiarity—familiar though it surely is!—but that it is the zone in which "*my* life takes place," the zone in which "*my* existence is actually located." There exist certain other "realities" (finite provinces of meaning), as we all know, but "*this one is my home*" (16). Here is where I dream about being elsewhere, here is where I play being Hamlet, here is where I expect to cash in on promises made to me, and here is where I will have to live up to promises I made. It is impossible to overestimate the *centrality of the subject* for the phenomenal constitution of the world of everyday life. *But* while I am undeniably the center, the "null-point," toward which the world of everyday life is structured, I recognize within this world, through the office of the *general thesis of the alter ego*, you, him, them, all "null-points" in their own rights (17). And so the world of everyday life is above all *our* home in which we live, in some ways identically, similarly, jointly, reciprocally, according to arrangements some of which we claim to have authored whereas others appear to belong to preexisting realities.

Although this is not the place to go into details concerning the constitution of the world of everyday life, stopping the discussion at this point leaves open the possibility of a most serious misunderstanding (which actually exists in the minds of many people who profess a phenomenological outlook). To say that the world of everyday life is organized relative to the perceiving subject seems to imply that its meaning structures are freely determined at this "null-point." To counteract this possible implication it will be worthwhile to draw attention to the ways in which the factual reality of the world actually impresses its hold on the subject.

First, I, the perceiving subject who faces the world knowingly, know that as an object among objects I enjoy no special privilege. I come into being, endure, and perish as a thing among things and even if I have it within me to look forward to redemption, it will not be in this world. However much I may have taken charge of my own life, the bare fact of my existence is just that, a fact over which I have no control. Moreover, a great many of the features of my existence are also given in just the same way as the fact of existence itself. And all of this is prior to either stoic calm or *Angst* about it.

Second, despite the fact that I have (together with the rest of mankind, of course) an enormous span of control over the world surrounding me and can arrange my life so as to avoid, evade, master, or harness whatever I will not abide in its natural form, it remains a melancholy truth that the world as a whole will always have its way with me, in the long run. What the length of my tether and the scope of my options might turn out to be will undoubtedly depend to a large degree on my own initiative. But wisdom in the exercise of freedom—or simply reasonableness—consists of aligning one's will with the immutable urgencies that inhere in the realities of circumstance. What else is folly if not the neglect of or oblivion to the intractabilities of the world?

Third, and finally, the preceding two points could be viewed as expressions of someone's personal philosophy of life. But they were recounted here as also describing the outlook of people whose professed beliefs run counter to them. We are not now interested in professed beliefs, however, but in that outlook which takes over when something must be done, for example, when someone must do what needs doing to successfully take a plane across the country. The point here is that when someone has business with the world, or any part of it, he must be prepared to deal on the world's terms. What these terms are is not reliably taken from what the timid have to say. Instead, the terms are, from case to case, in what even the most radical of the radical comes to see when he sees that sometimes some things *have* to be done, and sometimes there is no getting around certain things, no matter what, in spite of all rational considerations.

Now, into this setting moves the field worker, a visitor whose main interest in things is to *see* them, and to whom, accordingly, all things are primarily *exhibits*. His orientation to the setting of his study is one of unrelieved and undifferentiated curiosity, and if he is good at it he will soon be able to see things appropriately to their situated meanings. But he will only be able to learn *that* they are this or that, not to recognize them *as* themselves. Thus, for example, he might learn to recognize the amusing without being amused by it; and even if he permits himself the joy of amusement, either indulgently or in remorseless exploitation of his own responses, he cannot appreciate it in its natural sense while remaining faithful to his aims as a field worker. For he must never relax the guard of skepticism about his own responses. After all, *his* sense of humor is not a guide to be trusted!

The paramount fact about the reality bounded by an ethnographic field work project is that it is not the field worker's own, actual life situation. This is so not because he might disdain accepting it as his own world, nor because he somehow fails in his attempts to make it his world, but because he *cedes* it as not being his world. He has deliberately undertaken to view it as the world of others. He is the only person in the setting who is solely and specifically interested in what things are for "them," and who controls his own feelings and judgment lest they interfere with his project. Of course, a good field worker learns quickly to recognize things according to the sense assigned to them within the field of his study. And he could probably impersonate a native well enough to get away with it. But even at the very height of his field competence, perhaps especially then, he cannot yield and be responsive to the sense things naturally importune. In other words, for the field worker things are never naturally themselves but only *specimens* of themselves. Specimens, because he sees them subsisting outside the natural subject-object relation within which alone they have founded meaning.

Since the field worker, as field worker of course, always sees things from a freely chosen vantage point—chosen, to be sure, from among actually taken vantage points—he tends to experience reality as being of subjective origin to a far greater extent than is typical in the natural attitude. Slipping in and out of points of view, he cannot avoid appreciating meanings of objects as more or less freely conjured. Thus he will read signs of the future from entrails of animals, believe that the distance objects fall is a function of the square of time, accept money in return for valuables, and do almost anything else along this line; but the perceived reality of it will be that it is so because someone is so seeing it, and it could be and probably is altogether different for someone else, because whatever necessity there is in a thing being what it seems to be is wholly contained in the mind of the perceiving subject. Hence, without it ever becoming entirely clear, the accent of the field worker's interest shifts from the object to the subject.

It is in this shift of interest that the field worker encounters phenomenology, which he correctly identifies as the major school of thought dedicated to the systematic study of subjectivity in a descriptive, although not empirical sense. But it appears that the availability of phenomenology at this point is somewhat of a mixed blessing. On the one hand, phenomenology, especially in the version contained in the writings of the late Alfred Schutz, offers an enormously fruitful theory of social reality. On the other hand, there is the risk that phenomenological teaching could be mistaken as encouraging descriptions consisting of unanalyzed impressions.

The promise contained in the work of Schutz is well known: Phenomenological sociology builds on an understanding of the constitution of meaning in the solitary ego, moves to the exploration of conditions that account for interpersonally shared meaning, and leads to a full-fledged study of the phenomena of objective culture like law, language, and above all that "ideal of community life which has the power to sustain itself through time in the minds of members" (18), society. Though these meaning structures have their locus in consciousness and are in this sense "subjective objects" (19), they are phenomenally outside the perceiving subject and confronted by him. The retention of this sense of "objectiveness" of social reality—the retention of an unbiased interest in *things as they actually present themselves* to the perceiving subject—is the foundation of *realism in field work*. For this, however, the field worker needs not only a good grasp of the perspectives of those he studies but also a good understanding of the distortive tendencies his own special perspective tends to introduce.

The risk alluded to as the second alternative is commonly neglected. It involves a self-indulgent concentration on what in theology is called *fides qua creditur* (subjective faith) to the exclusion of interest in *fides quae creditur* (the object of faith) (20). That is, one takes phenomenology to be the study of the actual appearing of reality in consciousness. Now, there is a certain ordinary reasonableness in thinking that all phenomenology calls for is describing what this or that thing seems to him who does the relating.

The risk that the teachings of phenomenology on the topic of subjectivity will be taken to urge the uncritical acceptance of variously occasioned impressions as the last word concerning the meaning structures of the social world is probably no greater in the case of field workers than any others, but it is more serious. For the field worker, as noted earlier, forever confronts "someone's social reality." And even when he dwells on the fact that this reality is to "them" incontrovertibly real in just the way "they" perceive it, he knows that to some "others" it may seem altogether different, and that, in fact, the most impressive feature of "the" social world is its colorful plurality. Indeed, the more seriously he takes this observation, the more he relies on his sensitivity as an observer who has seen firsthand how variously things can be perceived, the less likely he is to perceive those traits of depth, stability, and necessity that people recognize as actually inherent in the circumstances of their existence. Moreover, since he finds the perceived features of social reality to be perceived as they are because of certain psychological dispositions people acquire as members of their cultures, he renders them in ways that far from being realistic are actually heavily intellectualized constructions that partake more of the character of theoretical formulation than of realistic description (21).

The risk of an abortive phenomenology has another aspect worth mentioning. Not only does it constitute a failure of realism and thus become, in effect, a factor in the estrangement between man and the world, but it also signals a retreat from unity among men. For this unity depends in part on the sharing of circumstances of existence constituted as a meaningful environment. And to the extent that the abortive phenomenology of social reality seeps into modern consciousness, taking the form of a pallid ideology of cultural relativism, it attenuates the natural bonds of human community.

By the same token, however, it is only by means of a genuine phenomenological analysis that the special epoché of the observer of social reality can be understood in all its ramifications. And it is only within the framework of this understanding that the field workers' observations can be assigned their proper relevance.

NOTES

1. This view is taken virtually without exception in the textbooks of sociological research methods published in the 1950s. Cf., e.g., W. J. Goode and P. K. Hatt, *Methods in Social Research*, McGraw-Hill, New York,

124 *Phenomenological Sociology: Issues and Applications*

1952; L. Festinger and D. Katz, (eds.), *Research Methods in the Behavioral Sciences*, Holt, Rinehart and Winston, New York, 1953.

2. That is, a philosophy that would constitute an adequate *vademecum* for the conduct of research but not necessarily the best philosophical interpretation of the endeavor. Cf. Michael Polanyi, *Personal Knowledge*, University of Chicago Press, Chicago, 1958; N. R. Hanson, *Patterns of Discovery*, Cambridge University Press, Cambridge, 1958.

3. Concerning the rootedness of scientific thought in commonsense knowledge the principal authority must be found in Edmund Husserl, *The Crisis of European Sciences and Transcendental Phenomenology*, translated by D. Carr, Northwestern University Press, Evanston, Ill., 1970; cf. also, Jacob Klein, "Phenomenology and the History of Science," in M. Farber, (ed.), *Philosophical Essays in Memory of Edmund Husserl*, Harvard University Press, Cambridge, 1940, pp. 143–163.

4. Reference is made to Thomas S. Kuhn, *The Structure of Scientific Revolutions*, Phoenix Books, Chicago, 1964, p. 10.

5. P. W. Bridgeman, *The Logic of Modern Physics*, Macmillan, New York, 1927, p. 5; the work is, of course, the well-known source of the operational definition of meaning.

6. The principal works referred to are Giambatista Vico, *The New Science*, translated by T. G. Bergin and M. H. Fisch, Anchor Books, Garden City, N.Y., 1961 (the translation is from the third edition, originally published in 1744); Heinrich Rickert, *Kulturwissenschaft und Naturwissenschaft*, 6th ed., Mohr, Tuebingen, Germany, 1926; Florian Znaniecki, *Cultural Reality*, University of Chicago Press, Chicago, 1919.

7. For example, older notions of affinity among chemical elements were replaced with dynamic conceptions of causally linked events within a field of forces; cf. J. R. Partington, *A Short History of Chemistry*, 3rd ed., Harper Torchbooks, New York, 1960, *passim*.

8. The quotes are from Alvin W. Gouldner, *The Coming Crisis of Western Sociology*, Basic Books, New York, 1970, pp. 103 and 440, respectively.

9. The phrase is taken from the thirteenth Thesis on Feuerbach; more generally, the Marxian text that would seem the most relevant to the point is the book authored jointly with Engels, *The German Ideology*, International Publishers, New York, 1960.

10. The most recent comprehensive statement of the ethnomethodological perspective in print is Harold Garfinkel and Harvey Sacks, "On Formal Structures of Practical Actions," in J. C. McKinney and E. A. Tiryakian, (eds.), *Theoretical Sociology*, Appleton-Century-Crofts, New York, 1970, pp. 338–366.

11. Cf. William Kluback, *Wilhelm Dilthey's Philosophy of History*, Columbia University Press, New York, 1956.

12. Harold Garfinkel, *Studies in Ethnomethodology*, Prentice-Hall, Englewood Cliffs, N.J., 1967, p. 6.

13. I use the term "realism" to refer to the field workers' efforts to discover and describe the full complexity and actual import of the features of settings as they are appreciated by persons to whom these settings are the circumstances of their lives. The use is not intended to contain any implications linking it with the old nominalist-realist controversy.

14. A very large number of studies would qualify for inclusion here; some are Sherri Cavan, *Liquor License*, Aldine, Chicago, 1966; Laud Humphreys, *Tearoom Trade*, Aldine, Chicago, 1970; Ned Polsky, *Hustlers, Beats and Others*, Aldine, Chicago, 1967; Marvin B. Scott, *The Racing Game*, Aldine, Chicago, 1968; and a collection of shorter studies, Jack D. Douglas, (ed.), *Observation of Deviance*, Random House, New York, 1970.

15. The high authority is Max Weber, *The Methodology of the Social Sciences*, translated by E. A. Shils and H. A. Finch, The Free Press, Glencoe, Ill., 1949, pp. 72 and 81, respectively.

16. The following discussion draws to the extent required by the present argument on the "constitutive phenomenology of the natural standpoint," as taught by Alfred Schutz; cf. his *The Phenomenology of the Social World*, translated by G. Walsh and F. Lehnert, Northwestern University Press, Evanston, Ill., 1967, p. 44, where the sentence in which the phrase occurs is unfortunately somewhat garbled.

17. Concerning the matter of the subject's "null-point" position in the world of everyday life see Alfred Schutz, "Phenomenology and the Social Sciences," in M. Farber, (ed.), *Philosophical Essays in Memory of Edmund Husserl*, Harvard University Press, Cambridge, 1940, p. 180; on the "general thesis of the alter ego" cf. Schutz, *The Phenomenology of the Social World*, *op. cit.*, Chap. 3.

18. These remarks are an attempt to state the teachings of Schutz in a few words. The remarkable quote is from Dwight van de Vate, "The Problem of Robot Consciousness," *Philosophy and Phenomenological Research*, 32, 1971, p. 149.

19. Cf. Aron Gurwitsch, "On the Object of Thought," in his *Studies in Phenomenology and Psychology*, Northwestern University Press, Evanston, Ill., 1966, pp. 141–147.

20. Cf. Walter Lindstrom, "The Problem of Objectivity in Kierkegaard," in H. A. Johnson and N. Thulstrup, (eds.), *A Kierkegaard Critique*, Henry Regnery, Chicago, 1967, pp. 228–243.

21. Concerning constructive analysis and the process of formulating cf. Garfinkel and Sacks, *op. cit.*

»»»»»»»»»»»»»»»»»»»»»»»» «««««««««««««««««««««««««

One might hope that a cooperative relation between linguistic and phenomenological analysis would lead to promising and fruitful mutual benefits. Yet the links between these approaches are not established nor are there sufficient examples of how such collaboration might contribute to the understanding of social phenomena. Spiegelberg breaks new ground in this effort by dealing with the use of the first person plural pronoun "we," examining its uses and meanings by way of linguistic analysis and then considering the experience of "we" phenomenologically: what is meant (phenomenological ontology) and what is given (phenomenology of appearances).

The significance of such work for phenomenological sociology is apparent in that basic social relationships are referred to in talk and yet the analysis of the talk alone is not sufficient to understand the experiences to which such talk refers. Much work remains for sociologists to explore the varieties of social relationships, as meant and as given. The tools of both linguistic and phenomenological analysis may, collaboratively used, add to such explorations. However, the problem of objective determinations of subjective meanings remains—the question of whether the observer can legitimately claim to know what others are about is in some ways similar to the right of any one of us to refer to what "we" believe to be known in common.

ON THE RIGHT TO SAY "WE": A LINGUISTIC AND PHENOMENOLOGICAL ANALYSIS (1)

»»»»»»»»»»»»»»»»»»»»»»»«««««««««««««««««««««««

Herbert Spiegelberg

Washington University

> *We felt that the right to say "we" required so much more than the simple "revolution" that was to resolve everything.*
>
> *Richard Zorza*, The Right to Say "We" (*Praeger, New York, 1970, p. 21*)

> *Monday*
> *Cloudy today, wind in the east, think we shall have rain.... We? Where did I get that word? ...I remember now—the new creature uses it.*
>
> *Mark Twain*, Extracts from Adam's Diary (*Harper and Bros., New York, 1904, p. 3*)

This essay has three major objectives. The first is to me the most urgent one. I believe that it is time to challenge the social arrogance expressed in the universal tendency to say "we," "us," and "our" when one has no business talking for anyone but oneself. This tendency is part of the "arrogance of power" behind the patronizing usurpation of the right to speak for the "free" people of the world, when they have never been asked, or the arrogant claim to speak for the "old" or the "new" generation, for "we philosophers," and even for "we phenomenologists." It is time to check on the credentials for such imposture.

My second objective is more esoteric. I wish to show in a concrete instance that the seeming antagonism between analytic, and especially linguistic, philosophy and phenomenology is based on misunderstandings. Both have legitimate tasks. I would like to show how they can even cooperate and contribute to a cumulative answer to the specific issue I am raising.

My third objective is to initiate the exploration of a basic concept in the social sciences which, to the best of my knowledge, has not yet been tackled: the linguistic meaning of the personal pronoun "we" and the structure of the phenomenon that corresponds to it.

Obviously I shall be unable to reach all, if any, of these objectives. It is difficult enough to kill two birds with one stone. Three are bound to escape unhurt. This I won't mind. The important thing to me is to stir them up, or, to change the metaphor, to bell three cats.

Social philosophy, sociology, and even phenomenological sociology talk a great deal about "we," about "we-ness," "we-hood" and the "we-relation." But I am not aware of more than passing remarks about the language and the meanings of "we"-saying. For such purposes one would have to turn to the new philosophy of ordinary language. But even here I have not come across any general discussion of the pronoun "we" and its "grammar" (2). Pronouns are usually lumped together as "indexical signs," with no significant structural differences among them. This lack of differentiation is indicated by their symmetrical grammatical numbering. The chief example is the "I," with occasional references to the other persons of the singular. Only comparative linguistics offers observations such as the distinction between the inclusive and the exclusive "we."

Thus the linguistic analysis of we-talk in general is apparently unbroken ground. I enter it with some trepidation, but in the hope that what I can offer here will at least stimulate others to cultivate it in more definitive fashion than can I, for whom this example is largely a test case for possible cooperation between linguistic analysis and phenomenology. In making such a raid I have tried to utilize some of the new tools forged by its pioneer master, John L. Austin, in *How to Do Things with Words*.

I propose to begin with a linguistic analysis of ordinary we-talk. I shall then undertake in two stages a phenomenological analysis of what corresponds to it in our experience, first determining the essential structure of the phenomenon meant and then of the ways and degree in which it is given subjectively. Finally, I intend to make some first recommendations on the right to say "we" in the light of these analyses.

A LINGUISTIC ANALYSIS OF WE-TALK

First Distinctions

In beginning with the we-talk of ordinary language I shall mention merely in passing such clearly secondary uses of the pronoun as the editorial "we" and the plurals of majesty and of modesty. Even if grammatically defensible, all of them seem to me morally questionable. The best case one could make for them is that in special cases they seem to deemphasize the self-important single ego or to express a generous identification with "fellow sinners." But mostly they are devices of evasion of personal responsibility and of false pretense. Some of them, such as the plural of majesty, have interesting historical roots originating in the period of double emperorship in the early Roman empire, leading later to an inflation of the single sovereign into a many-headed superman. As to the plural of modesty there is something cowardly, if not funny, in surrounding oneself with imaginary others, as if it were not much more pretentious to speak in the name of others as well as of one's seemingly self-effacing little I.

The situation is much more serious in the case of the editorial we, used all too often even in philosophical writing. I believe that only in very rare cases has an author any business speaking for his listeners or readers—only when he has good reasons to believe that they have already had a chance to share his own experience. Otherwise the editorial we is nothing but an underhanded attempt to overwhelm one's audience by persuasion, not giving it even a chance to test, accept, or reject one's opinions. I consider such seeming selflessness as a sheer usurpation. Unless the editor speaks at least for a board or with special authorization, this is simply intellectual dishonesty and self-importance in disguise. Yet I know how hard it is to suppress it—and that in spite of strenuous efforts I myself am likely to provide additional examples of this bad habit (3).

I now turn to the use of the "we" in everyday discourse. Here I discern two basically different situations where use of the pronoun in its original sense occurs, depending on the presence or absence of those whom the speaker includes as his partners.

1. The "*we of copresence*," as I shall call it, includes only people with whom the speaker stands in the kind of direct face-to-face relation-

ship for which Alfred Schutz coined the term "consociates," as distinguished from mere "contemporaries." However, "copresents" need not be a small group of persons knowing one another personally. Even participants in a mass demonstration are copresent, although they know one another only "face to back." But they are at least in direct audiovisual contact with the speaker, to whom they can respond (4).

2. The we in the absence of the we-partners I shall call the *absentee-we*. It occurs chiefly where the speaker talks to outsiders as a representative of contemporaries who are not only absent but whom he, at least usually, does not know in person; thus in the absence of any St. Louisians in the audience I can tell you Bostonians: "We in St. Louis are fond of your Boston Symphony broadcasts."

The We of Copresence

I shall focus first on the we of copresence. The word "we" like all personal pronouns is grammatically a substitute for a noun, such as a proper name or several names. As such it has at least indirectly objective reference and gives a certain amount of information about these referents, especially when it differentiates between the sexes. A pronoun differs from the represented nouns by not having a stable reference to one and only one referent. What name and object it refers to depends on the concrete occasion in which it is uttered and by whom. In this relativity to a variable point of reference pronouns are what is usually called "indexical signs" or "occasional expressions" (Husserl). However, personal pronouns do more than convey information about the nouns for which they stand. As uttered in a special situation they not only have "informative" meaning but perform certain functions that have not yet been sufficiently distinguished and described, particularly in the case of the "we" of copresence. I shall call these "formative" or, better, "transformative" meanings.

I shall begin with some informative meanings of the word "we":

1. "We" refers to more than one person, thus requiring multiple rays of meaning. It may mean these persons collectively, as in "we are together a part of humanity," or distributively, as in "we are all humans." "We" may refer to only two such beings, for which case a language like Samoan has a special form of the pronoun, the dual "we" (5); but it may also include any number of referents; only in the case of the we in copresence (consociates) it has to be a finite number.

2. "We" in this case refers to each and every member of this plurality in whatever is predicated of them. In this sense it makes a claim to unanimity. Majority, however qualified, is not enough.

3. "We" points at a collection of referents standing in polar relationship: the speaking "I" as the focal pole and the "we-partners" as

counterpoles, as it were. And whereas the pronoun "I" is a self-referential sign referring back to the speaker himself, this is only partially true for "we," namely for its speaking I-pole. The situation may be different when all members respond to a challenge in unison by shouting "we," but even then the self-referential nature of the "we" is distributed over the contributory shouters.

4. The referents of "we" must be personal beings who the speaking "I" believes to be human beings. "We" is inapplicable to nonspeaking beings, inanimate and animate, below the human level except in animal fables. Any attempt by an owner to include his domestic pets in a "we" can at best be a playful fiction.

5. "We" is basically equalitarian. Normally it can be applied only to personal beings of the same social standing or class. Especially in a nondemocratic or in a hierarchical organization such as an army a superior will hardly be included in we-talk in his presence by his inferiors, even if the superior may do this condescendingly with his subordinates.

6. We-talk makes sense only with regard to people capable of understanding the speaker acoustically or by some other language. It is senseless in the presence of a sleeping "audience" or one ignorant of the English language. In other words, "we" has a place only among mutually understanding partners.

7. "We" as used in English and many, if not most, other languages does not make it clear whether all those within reach are included, or some, in particular one or many persons to whom one is speaking, are excluded, either as individuals or as members of an "out-group." It is therefore not without interest that some languages distinguish between an inclusive and exclusive "we"—inclusive if addressing an in-group only, or exclusive if addressing an out-group, addressed of course as "you" (6).

I now turn to the formative or transforming functions of the we pronoun of copresence. When Austin claimed that one can do "things" with a phrase like "I promise," he referred only to utterances in the form of whole sentences. What I would like to show is that even single words such as pronouns have such power, much as this power has to be seen in the context of the total situation described by the surrounding sentences (7).

The first of these transforming functions is that of social address. The we of copresence, whether inclusive or exclusive, is not merely informative, it also tries to do something to one's we-partners, to "tackle" them. It tries to make them (a) listen and (b) realize that they are appealed to as partners. But in what sense can such addressing be considered as a transformation of the situation? In itself the mere address does not lead to any change in the person addressed. However, such change does occur as soon as he pays attention to this appeal. It is his turning of face, his focusing on the speaker as his spokesman, which the address aims to bring about. Yet properly speaking addressing by itself is merely an attempt to make others "tune in," as it were. It merely exerts a certain social pressure or has "illocutionary force" (Austin). But only if such pressure is effective, and brings about a real change in the interpersonal field in the sense of Austin's "perlocutionary force," does it make sense to talk about an actual transformation of the social field. Strictly, we must distinguish therefore between the transforming intent and the transforming force or effect of words.

The primary example of this addressing function is the second person singular and plural pronoun "you" in English and its modifications in other languages such as the intimate "tu" in French and "du" in German, the more solemn or religious "thou" and the vocative case in Greek and Latin. Here the individual listener is tackled frontally, as it were. No wonder that so many languages try to camouflage this attack either by putting it in plural form, thus distributing the "shock," or by using the third person singular (Italian, Spanish) or plural (German) to divert the blow, as it were.

But the addressing function operates also, though in a less frontal manner, in the we of copresence with consociates, when the speaker expects the we-partners to be aware of the fact that he is speaking for them, that is, to listen and realize what he is saying to others. I do not mean to assert that always before saying "we" there has to be an explicit you-contact with these we-partners. It may be desirable to be on you-terms with a person before one includes him in one's we-talk, and some people might actually feel offended by it prior to having been formally introduced to the speaker (8). In informal context the you-address may very well be implicit in the we-address. The main point is that the we of copresence, while uttered within the other's earshot, also addresses him. True, one does not address him "face-to-face." But there is also such a thing as an oblique addressing by implication, "face-by-face," as it were, appealing to him while at the same time inviting him to participate in some outward-bound action. "We protest" implies "You are my partner."

The addressing function of we-talk becomes even more explicit in the case of the exclusive "we." For here, in telling an outsider what "we others" think or feel, we still try to make him realize that he is being addressed.

But addressing and thus orienting one's consociates toward the speaker is not the only and the most characteristic "thing" done by we-talk. It is an attempt not only to attract his attention but to pull him over completely to the speaker's side, to claim him as an associate, or to "align" him. What is this function of alignment?

Perhaps the best way to exhibit this function is to compare it with those of other personal pronouns. At first sight one might think that there is a perfect parallel in their linguistic functions. But here one must not be misled by the categories of the grammarians as evidence of linguistic structure. This is not the place for analyzing all the functions of all the personal pronouns. Some of their peculiarities will serve as a foil for the analysis of the new we-function.

1. In saying "I," as in "I am talking," I am merely self-referentially pointing to myself; nothing else is "done" about and to the referent of my talking. Only by implication am I suggesting to my listener to transpose this "I" into the proper "you" or "he" if he wants to respond to me.

2. You-talk presents a very different picture, namely, the pure type of the addressing function as described previously.

3. The function of the third person singular is in this regard the very opposite of that of the second person. It not only leaves the referent untouched, normally it is used only "behind his back," and if used within his earshot, it has almost an insulting connotation, treating him as if absent. The third person pronoun has no social function in relation to its referent, since he is not even supposed to hear it. Its social function is restricted to describing to a second person someone not in present contact with either one of the speakers.

4. It needs little reflection to realize that the functions of the pronouns in the plural are more complex, since more than one person is referred to. The differences from the singular pronouns are perhaps easy to grasp in the case of the second and third person plural. For what is involved is simply the multiplication of the functions of the singular pronouns. In the case of the "you" in the plural, several persons are addressed at the same time. The only new feature is that they are addressed collectively, in this sense lumped together, with the understanding that they are in mutual social contact, not separate, and are on the same social level, not superiors and inferiors such as God, man and animal, master and slave. In the case of the third person "they" no such "lumping" is implied: "They" may be single or in a group. In fact, the "they" in English also has the function of the notorious "*man*" in German, the anonymous other or others, faceless and no longer individualized as to singular or plural.

In the case of the "we" of copresence the situation is very different. Here the speaker, in referring to himself and to others whom he wants to include, tries two things: (a) As to himself, he describes his own part and also commits himself to whatever the we-sentence predicates about him, at least in the case of an action; this implies doing it together with the we-partners. (b) As to the others, the speaker claims them *as partners* taking the same position as he himself does. This claim is, at least on the surface, mostly a factual one, asserting that the others already share his position. But it also implies the intent to make them acknowledge their alignment with him, the speaker. This involves a transformational function, especially in fluid situations. Here the use of the "we" may be an attempt of the speaker, more or less underhanded, to swing others over to his position and to make them join him. In both cases the use of the "we" uttered in the copresence of others involves an attempt to influence and transform one's consociates and transform them into associates.

"We" as Used in the Absence of We-Partners: The Absentee We

The situation is basically changed when the "we" is used in the absence of those for whom one claims to speak. Not only is this "we" essentially an exclusive we, excluding all those addressed, there are also other important differences in both the informative and the transformative function with regard to the absent we-partners included.

The number of fellow-beings for whom the speaker claims to speak need not be known even to himself. Perhaps no one knows it. However, in this case, where the we-fellows are not delimited by presence within earshot, it is essential that "we" be specified as a certain class of persons such as "we sociologists" or "we phenomenologists." However, it does not seem necessary to restrict the range of absentee we's to contemporaries, although the right to speak for one's predecessors and successors is more than problematic. But as far as predecessors are concerned, a statement like "We Americans have always stood for self-determination" not only makes linguistic good sense but may, on the basis of the historical record, be even more justified than with regard to our contemporaries. However, a sentence like "We Americans will always stand for self-determination," which tries to commit even our unborn successors, is not only risky but unwarranted in principle, since we can have no evidence for their future actions. To that extent such a statement is sheer arrogance.

Even more important is the difference in the transforming functions of the absentee we. First, this is not the situation of a speaker addressing we-partners, since by definition the absentees are beyond the range of his direct address. Whatever addressing occurs is directed at the listeners in front of the speaker and this address will take the form of the second person.

Moreover, the aligning function by which the speaker tried to enlist copresent we-partners is obviously impossible in any literal sense. Yet the speaker who talks in the name of his absent we-partners clearly means to commit them in some manner and degree. How is this possible? Clearly it presupposes some prior authorization or subsequent ratification. In this sense all we-talk in the absence of the committed is on credit, as it were. The decisive question is whether or not the speaker has some kind of a proxy for them. Without it all we-talk in the absence of the we-partners is clearly false pretense. Hence the speaker's credentials have to be based on such explicit authorization as an election or a vote. This is perhaps not always possible and necessary. But unless he can produce good reasons as to why he need not bother about possible protests from his we-partners, he had better be on his guard—and so had his listeners.

(Note: An interesting case of the use of "we" occurs in philosophical writings as discussed in M. B. Foster's pioneer article mentioned in footnote 2. These writings address only potential readers, who are not copresent unless the papers were read to a live audience. Either they speak in the name of "we modern philosophers," who are likewise absent, or sometimes of "all of us," meaning the users of the King's English.

What is also interesting is that Foster points out that in using "we,"

the philosopher is not reporting a usage which he has observed in himself and among his associates. The utterance seems more like those which Professor Austin has taught us to call "performatory." In using the first person plural I am not merely describing a usage but I am subscribing to it, or expressing my own adhesion to it (9).

However, Foster is concerned only with the "performance" of the commitment by the speaker to the use of a certain language. The aspect of claiming the we-partners for this use and one's right to claim them is never questioned or even mentioned. The fact that Foster is concerned merely with the absentee we case also makes it of particular importance to him to determine what is the group or society of persons to which the "we" refers. It turns out to be "we men.")

Strengths and Weaknesses of Linguistic Analysis

Thus far I have attempted merely a sample of linguistic analysis. By studying the use of the pronoun "we" in various settings I have tried to determine its functions, attending to the phenomena meant by these uses only insofar as they are needed to understand these utterances. Beyond that I have made no attempt to analyze the structure of the phenomena referred to in themselves and for their own sakes.

Nevertheless, I submit that this analysis has yielded some important results even for phenomenology. Some of these may be merely negative in the sense that they can break up certain stereotypes that have interfered with the unprejudiced approach to the phenomena. Thus the linguistic study of the ordinary use of personal pronouns can help us to get rid of the type of thing-like entities that go with the substantivization of the live pronouns into "the I" (*das Ich*), or "the we," or we-hood, all terms that do not occur in our everyday speech (10). Such linguistic monsters have invaded even the language of phenomenologists. There may be good reasons for introducing technical terms (even linguistic analysis has found it necessary to invent a metalanguage); but it is more important to pay attention first to the concrete occasions in which the ordinary words occur, and what they refer to here.

Also by immediately introducing such highpower terminology one may very well conceal the basic phenomena underneath a scientific superstructure. I maintain that this is exactly what has happened in social philosophy in the case of "the we." I hope that the previous examples have shown that the study of the concrete uses of the personal pronouns in actual situations has shown that "we" can mean very different phenomena. An embargo on all reifying substantivization could very well at the same time unclutter and enrich social phenomenology.

But this does not mean that linguistic analysis and even linguistic phenomenology can take the place of phenomenology. Even Austin knew and stated explicitly that linguistic analysis can supply only the "first word" (11) in the exploration of the phenomena. But he did not state who is to say the last word. He himself certainly never tried to go beyond the first word. Linguistic analysis can tell us what we actually do with words, for example, that certain utterances can make changes in the world, and, if I am right, then certain pronouns direct or even align people. But it fails to describe what exactly is taking place on the side of the phenomena, for instance, in the case of such performatory transformations. What is the structure of these changes? Linguistic analysis, after having distinguished different uses of these utterances, simply stops, as if, once the phenomena are properly distinguished, one knows all about them. That this is not the case is what I would like to show for the two main uses of "we" which I have distinguished.

Furthermore, it is not enough to establish the finer shades of meaning in present ordinary language. Language is no ultimate fact, it has developed historically. Hence it is important to understand why distinctions have developed, and, more specifically, what features in the phenomena are responsible for such differentiations. Such understanding requires insight into the phenomena themselves. To provide it is one of the objectives of phenomenological analysis proper. True, linguistic analysis supplies a grammar of ordinary language more differentiated and sophisticated than the grammar of the grammarians. In fact, for Wittgenstein the final goal of philosophy seems to have coincided with the discovery of a philosophical grammar (which at one time he oddly identified with "phenomenology") (12). Now grammar can tell the correct way of talking, for instance, in the case of the "we" and distinguish between "proper use" and solecisms. But no attempt is made to account for the rules of this grammar, leaving them as nothing but arbitrary brute facts of history.

Finally, in the case of performative expressions, all the reader is told is that certain utterances for example, promises, have the "force" to bring about such changes in the world as obligations. This sounds like word magic as practiced by sorcerers. At best such expressions can be understood metaphorically. What do the metaphors stand for? What is really going on when a word makes a difference in the world of facts? And how is such "word magic" possible? This calls, even clamors, for a description of the actual happenings in our experience—for a concrete phenomenology.

TOWARD A PHENOMENOLOGY OF THE WE-CONSCIOUSNESS

What I intend to do here is to give at least a first idea of how phenomenology can further enrich the study of the we-phenomena with a view to determining the right to say "we." I shall not waste time by a lengthy explanation of what is meant or rather what I mean by the still mystifying label "phenomenology." I hope this will become sufficiently apparent from "doing it," leaving it to further reflections what it is or was that I have been doing. But I still have to state what specific task I want to attack. From now on I shall focus no longer on what it is proper to *say* in a certain situation—which is the primary concern of linguistic philosophy —but on what it is that we *see* in it, describing the seen as fully and as faithfully as I can, and on exploring the ways in which it is given me, regardless of whether what I thus experience is ultimately real or merely a phenomenon. I shall try to demonstrate this kind of phenomenology (13) in two stages.

1. Clarification of the Phenomenon as Meant (Phenomenological Ontology). A phenomenological investigation as here conceived presupposes a clear understanding of one's beliefs about such phenomena as life, social relations, or values before looking for them in actual experience. This stage begins with the elimination of vague and distorting interpretations of the phenomena. But it has also to determine positively the typical or essential structure of the phenomena meant. In this sense it is a (nonmetaphysical) ontology. This enterprise has been cultivated particularly by the early Göttingen-Munich branch of phenomenology.

2. Exploration of the Phenomena as Given (Phenomenology of Appearances). Clarity of meaning with regard to the phenomenon as meant is no guarantee that it is actually given. To establish this fact, one has to explore how far it is present in our experience. To many phenomena as meant nothing may correspond at all. Or they may be given only indirectly and partially, as they are presented in various perspectives. The study of these modes of givenness is clearly of crucial importance for the answer to the question of whether one can claim real knowledge about the phenomena meant. Adequate knowledge as conceived by Husserl implies that the phenomenon meant is given in such a way that all meanings are fulfilled and that no new perspectives can upset one's anticipations. Since, for instance, in the case of three-dimensional visual perceptions there can be infinite perspectives, adequate knowledge is impossible in principle. Even without such adequacy knowledge can still be direct and reach the thing itself or "in person" as it were; but knowledge of such objects lacks complete certainty. In any case, the knowledge claim has to be measured against *what* is actually given and *how* it is given. This is why the analysis of the phenomena as meant has to be followed by a critical investigation of the phenomena as given or of what appears.

Clarification of the We-Phenomenon as Meant (*Phenomenological Ontology*)

We-consciousness means consciousness of "we" or, better, of being we or us, and thus implies a distinction between the object of consciousness (Husserl's "intentional object") and the condition or state of being conscious (his "intentional act"). Although both would have to be examined in parallel manner, I shall in the present context concentrate on the object or content of the we-consciousness. What are its essential constituents? One particularly helpful way of determining them is by imaginative variation, adding or leaving off some, one at a time. I shall begin by leaving off such factors with a view to pointing out certain prestages of the full we-phenomenon.

I would like to focus on a specific case of we-consciousness, namely, the situation which my readers could experience in listening to a live lecture.

Prestages of the We-Phenomenon. Suppose each of you as listeners were to hear a lecture alone on your private television set. Suppose you also did not know whether anyone else was listening to it. Obviously in such a situation there could be no we-consciousness. Even if there should be parallel listeners on other sets, as long as they do not know of one another, the essential precondition for the formation of we-consciousness is missing.

Suppose now that you are in the same room as a member of the audience who knows that he has neighbors undergoing the same kind of auditory, if not intellectual and emotional, experience as he is. But assume also—and this is probably true for most of you—that you have not yet had a chance, and probably never will have, to make contact among each other, as it happens usually in the movies in contrast to theaters and concert halls. Now is mere awareness of parallel experiences enough to establish a social bond among you? I submit that this situation is conducive to developing we-consciousness, but that thus far your social relationship remains unchanged. Two witnesses to the same event, even if they know of one another, are not necessarily co-witnesses. In fact, the value of their testimonies will to no small extent depend on their not yet having taken up contact.

Suppose now you not only know about your fellow listener's experiences but also are in personal contact with him, either before these experiences or subsequently by talking with him. Is this a sufficient condition for developing a we-consciousness and the use of we-language? By itself such contact means only a "you" relation, in which each one sees his partner face-to-face at a certain (social) distance. At this stage, in discussing the shared experience, one might say: "You seem to have had the same experience I had" and even "you and I seem to see eye to eye on this issue." But there is an experiential difference once one substitutes for "you and I" and even for 'I and thou" the single pronoun "we." There is more than verbal economy involved in a switch from one expression to the other. The two may be equivalent, and the former may be a stage on the way to the other. But phenomenologically they do not coincide. What is the difference?

Stages of the We-Union. At this stage on the scale of variations I shall introduce a substantially new factor. Thus far the partners in the social relation I have described have maintained their separate stations in getting to know and making contact with each other. But these positions themselves can be subjected to variation. They may be increased and decreased. Finally, instead of confronting one another across a social distance the partners in you-contact may perform a peculiar shift: they "turn their faces" and "move together," as it were. By "turning faces" I do not mean that they abandon their face-to-face relationship. But now they no longer confront one another, but face outward from a new common station. By "moving together" I mean an attempt to move from one's prior separate station to one single position, no longer separated by a social distance. Obviously all such characterizations are metaphorical and require translation into more direct phenomenological description. But such a description would require the framework of a phenomenological social psychology as outlined for instance by Alexander Pfänder.

It is enough if in the present context they can be suggestive of phenomena still to be explored in greater depth.

But what is even more important here is to focus on what goes on after this shift: the link-up of the joiners in a new union. Here each abandons his separateness (though not his individuality) and enters an embracing whole, whose parts dovetail. In this whole each claims the other as belonging to him and is claimed by the other in return. In this sense and to this extent they might be said to identify and become "solidaric" through a kind of "soldering" which imbeds them into a "solid" unit, as the etymology of the word "solidaric" suggests. This change could and should be described even more concretely by attending to the experiences in each partner, such as their feeling no longer separate and alone, but of being "together," "united," "at one," or "merged." But all these descriptions must ultimately be understood as invitations to enter and live through vicarious experiences all too easily ignored and made trivial.

What I have characterized thus far is clearly an ideal case. Few if any situations where one uses "we" in ordinary discourse attain this kind of solidarity. Yet I maintain that they all contain some degree of it. Nevertheless, it is important to distinguish between the following different types of we-unions:

1. We-unions may be *strong* or *weak* according to how much their partners have "invested" in them. The casual and unemphatic way in which we use the "we" in ordinary conversation certainly does not express the kind of solidarity that would resist questioning or pressure.

2. The union may be *permanent* or merely *temporary* and even limited to a single occasion, to be disbanded immediately after it has passed. Only a few we-unions are meant to establish lasting associations.

3. The union may be *superficial* or *deep*. Especially in their emotions partners may remain completely uninvolved.

These dimensions of strength, duration, and depth can and must be explored by a phenomenological sociology.

Thus the we-union implies more than an external link-up, comparable to the riveting of beams into a steel frame, or to the jamming of passengers into a public conveyance, where actually physical closeness makes social closeness next to impossible. Union is not merely a matter of removing distance, physical or social, but the establishment of a new positive relationship within the union. It means that its partners not only "touch," but "embrace" one another in a nonliteral sense. By these terms I mean to suggest that each partner tries to include the other and his experience within his own parallel experience ("I experience you as experiencing happiness"), to participate or share in it. This need not mean that he experiences the other's experience exactly like his own. But whenever they hear or sing the same song together as "we," and not only as "he, she, or they," or as "you and I," each partner in his experience is conscious of the other's experiencing, coexperiences it, and identifies with it. Thus the other partner's experience is part of the prime partner's own. Of course it does not form a real but merely an "intentional" part of it, is mentally included in it. Such coexperiencing may mean anything from mere awareness to full empathy. It is at best vicarious. Nevertheless, it is an integral element of the primary experiences. In this sense each partner enters the experience of the other. Their experiences interpenetrate. Obviously here even more than in the case of the personal union the interpenetration may vary in extent and intensity.

Among additional features essential to a fully developed and strong we-union are the following:

1. The union, being based on the reciprocity of the independent contributions of several partners, needs reinforcements to keep it viable. One of these is the belief, implicit or explicit, that one's own contribution is reciprocated, and that the union is not merely one-sided, as it happens only too often in friendship and love. One could speak here of trust in the reciprocity of the we-acts contributed by each partner.

2. But even this trust may not be enough. For if I cannot trust your reciprocating trust in me (and vice versa, you cannot do so), my primary trust will be misplaced. In other words, without a secondary trust in the other's primary trust in me and vice versa, the first trust and the union lose strength.

3. At this point there is clearly room for an infinite regress. Although theoretically possible, such iteration has diminishing phenomenological and practical returns. Only in rare cases may it be important to spell out and check on these higher-order trusts in reciprocity; usually they lack significance.

Other complementary features of a strong we-union are connected with the fact that we-acts and the coexperiences based on them essentially stand in a wider context. Thus the experiences of each we-partner are part of the setting of his personal world as their *background horizon*. The we-acts performed by a socialite mean something quite different from those of a person in a less socially crowded world. Now in coexperiencing his fellow partner's world each partner will see it only in more or less adequate perspective. Yet a full understanding of the other's world will include at least some perspective of it. In order to understand actions including the we-acts of a Chinese I have to have a picture of the world he lives in (as he needs one of ours).

Again, this is not the end of the story. For the other's social world as I see it in perspective includes his picture of my world as he sees mine, that is, very probably a caricature of it. This perspective of the other's perspective is what R. D. Laing calls a "metaperspective." Such meta-perspectives of the other's perspective can of course again be reflected in endless iteration. My perspective of the caricature of the psychotic's picture of the "normal" world will be mirrored and probably again distorted in a possible psychotic view of the normal perspective on him. In principle there is no end to such iterations of perspectives. But their importance drops with each iteration. What is practically important for better understanding is to work on a correction of the distorting metaperspectives toward a gradual assimilation of the primary perspectives as the basis for a possible better we-union.

The main result of the preceding analysis of the ontological meaning of the we-phenomenon may be summed up in the following statements:

1. The phenomenon meant by the we-pronoun is a union of several persons into a whole of which they experience themselves as solidaric partners.

2. These partners embrace and interpenetrate each other's experiences vicariously in their coexperiences.

3. They trust in each other's reciprocal acts.

4. These acts are imbedded in one another's worlds.

In the preceding direct approach to the phenomena I have thus far avoided most of the terms applied to the we-phenomena in the past. Thus I have not used the term "we-relationship" (Schutz' most frequent term) not because I deny that there are characteristic relations between the partners of a we-union, but because what seems even more important to me is the encompassing unions based on such relations of which the we-partners form integral members.

Defective We-Unions. Normally one might pay attention only to situations where all members of the we-group use we-language among each other and, perhaps more frequently, in talking to outsiders. But this should not make one overlook the case when there is no perfect reciprocity. In a nation torn by class struggle or an international organization torn by power groups some of these may cease to use we-talk in relation to the other members of whom they think only as "they" or "you." Such a we-group is certainly incomplete, if not "sick." If this sickness is incurable, the we-union has become an illusion or a fiction. Meanwhile it is important to realize that the we-phenomenon is not only dependent on one partner's perspective but interdependent on that of several, though not always of all of them. Such defects can occur both in the copresence and in the absence of the we-partners. In their copresence they are perhaps more likely to come to the surface, especially in a free, democratic atmosphere that does not suppress dissent. In the absence of the we-partners their reciprocating acts are not only likely to become marginal and potential, but finally to vanish, leaving the we-speaker unsupported in midair, as it were.

Exploration of the We-Phenomenon as Given (Phenomenology of Appearances)

The preceding attempt to describe the structure of the we-phenomenon as really meant in one's everyday beliefs provides no assurance that such meaning is fulfilled in actual experiences and hence epistemologically justified. This can be established only by that branch of phenomenology which examines how and how far this phenomenon appears in intuitive experience (*Anschauung*). I shall therefore try to examine next some of the appearances of the we-phenomenon.

The Perspectives of the We-Phenomenon. Like all other social phenomena the we-phenomenon is given not only to one but to several subjects distributively. There is no phenomenological evidence for the existence of a we-subject to which the we-phenomenon could appear all at once. Consequently the we-phenomenon, as distinguished, for instance, from the you-phenomenon, can be given fully only in the composite experiences of the several partners making up the we-union. Here one has to distinguish between the viewing partner or I-pole and the viewed partners or counterpoles joined with him. Both are given only in the perspectives of each I-pole. What does this asymmetry mean for the givenness of the symmetrical we-union?

Obviously such perspectives are lopsided as compared with the balanced perspective one may have of an outside object of which one is not a part. One partner of the we-union, the viewing I, can be given only obliquely in acts of reflection, whereas the other partners are given straightforwardly and frontally, as it were. This situation is comparable only to that of the givenness of one's own body to vision from within the body, where one's head and the eyes cannot be seen directly. Thus it seems appropriate to consider the givenness of these two aspects of the composite we-union separately.

Beginning with the appearance of the other we-partners as the counterpoles of the we-union, one has to face up to the general problem of knowledge of other persons and their experiences. Settling this vexing problem is clearly beyond the scope and control of this essay. All that can and need be done is to proceed on the assumption that (a) such knowledge is possible, and (b) other bodies and other "minds" and their acts are given more or less directly. True, such knowledge is always inadequate: one can never exhaust all aspects of other minds in all conceivable perspectives and one is therefore always in for surprises for one's anticipating beliefs concerning new perspectives, at least in principle. Some of these inadequacies in the perception of persons, for example, those affecting one's perception of other people's bodies with regard to their backs or their insides, may be irrelevant for our knowledge of their minds and mental acts. But even so there remains enough ambiguity, for instance, in their bodily expressions, to make other-mind knowledge ambiguous and precarious. This general situation is modified by the specific factors entering the we-perception. Thus the other's abandoning of his separateness by joining a solidaric union may be given quite vividly through speech and gesture.

But, quite apart from ambiguous cases, one is never safe from deceitful pretense. As far as the second feature of we-unions is concerned, the interpenetration of the partners through vicarious coexperience, one is clearly on even more treacherous ground. True, one is not without clues for such an extension of direct experience beyond the immediately given. Furthermore, the others may bear us out in the case of more responsive partners. But they may also be merely trying to please us and lull us into overconfidence. This is particularly true of the trust in the union which one would like to find in others. There are perfectly valid tokens of their trust, but even so we cannot assess their trust directly. This is of course multiply true of the iteration of their trust (e.g., their trust in our trust of their trust) which can never be adequately given in principle but at best nonintuitively in the "etc."-consciousness of infinite series.

All this applies even more fully to our knowledge of their encompassing social world as horizon for the unionizing acts. At best we can construct and imagine parts of this world and depend for the rest on volunteered information communicated at our request. Thus the other half (in a dual union) and an even larger proportion (in a plural union) is given directly only in part, and never adequately beyond the possibility of error or deception.

What then about the self-knowledge of the I-pole of the we-union and his own unionizing experiences? One may hope to achieve all the self-evidence of the Cartesian *ego-cogito* for this facet of the we-union. But here too one has to be on one's guard against Cartesian oversimplifications. Self-knowledge, especially adequate self-knowledge in reflection, is anything but self-evident, once one becomes aware of the possibilities of self-deception, for which psychopathology and psychoanalysis have supplied unsettling evidence. Moreover, the general epistemology of self-knowledge poses serious problems, especially in the light of phenomenology of the temporal appearances of the self. Thus full thematic self-perception is possible only in retrospect, that is, in the retentive phase of memory, whereas instant self-knowledge is possible at best in the form of unthematic awareness, which does not allow for clear and distinct presentation. Although such circumstances do not invalidate the claims of self-knowledge, they certainly weaken claims to its absolute certainty. For some aspects they may be stronger than the claims to knowledge of one's partners in the we-union, for example, in the case of knowledge of one's own existence and of belief in it. But precisely in the area of one's unionizing acts one may be mistaken about one's ability to perform an effective union rather than a mere semblance of it, and to experience vicariously one's partners' experiences. Also, my trust in the others, and even more my trust in their trust in my primary trust, may be a mere semblance of real trust. Furthermore, my picturing of their social world may be mere projection of what I would like to see in them, not allowing for alternative interpretations. Thus there are special pitfalls in our reflective and nonreflective knowledge of our own we-perspective, but hardly differences in principle.

On the strength of this phenomenological examination of the two kinds of perspectives on the partners of the we-union there is reason to question the adequacy of direct we-knowledge. Even if one should claim a privileged status for the *ego-cogito* as the best possible case for reliable adequate knowledge, there is no convincing basis for an equal or even superior epistemological claim for a "*nos cogitamus*," as it has been asserted. The claim for any certainty in this area can be assessed only on the basis of the previous findings about the two perspectives, the straightforward one on the other's part in the we-union and the reflective one on one's own.

Implications for Other Phenomenological Theories. At first sight it may seem that the results of the preceding analyses of the we-phenomenon conflict with most of the phenomenological literature on the subject. Thus Scheler boldly claimed that "we" had priority over the I and you, and to some extent Schutz seems to have backed him up on this claim. Certainly to Schutz the we-relation was a basic fact of the social lifeworld, which even Husserl's transcendental or "egological" phenomenology of intersubjectivity cannot account for. And to Binswanger and many advocates of "dialogical" philosophy the priority of the "we" seems to be nearly axiomatic.

What I have been doing thus far does not contradict such claims, especially if taken in a historical or evolutionary sense. It may very well be the case that we-consciousness preceded the development of an explicit individualized I- and you-consciousness. But the evidence presented for such vast claims seems to me anything but sufficient and certainly not phenomenological in a critical sense. What I wanted to show is that in one's personal experience the "we" has no privileged status. Linguistically, the pronoun "we" has a very limited place and function. Phenomenologically, what is really meant by "we" and given in experience is a certain union of individual persons supported by conscious special acts that require the support of I's and you's as partners, and these are given only in rather indirect and inadequate perspectives. In this sense the we-phenomenon is secondary compared with the I- and you-phenomena and "founded" upon them.

All this is a matter of a "static" phenomenology, describing how the we-phenomenon appears in consciousness. It does not yet raise the question posed in Husserl's transcendental phenomenology as to how this phenomenon is constituted in consciousness "genetically." Once one raises this question there seems to me no escape from claiming some kind of priority to the individual consciousness in which the we-phenomenon takes shape, if only in the form of "passive constitution." This does not require the adoption of Husserl's transcendental idealism. The previous studies seem to me to have produced important evidence for the view that the we-phenomenon owes its genesis and support to the we-acts of its members. In this light any sweeping claims for the priority of the we over the I appear to be unwarranted and certainly need phenomenological underpinning by showing how the we-phenomenon is given as something independent of the supporting acts of the we-partners. It is one thing to show that the I in its structure is essentially oriented toward the we, which is often attempted with considerable evidence. It is a very different matter to claim that the we is a more basic entity than the I.

Contributions of Phenomenological to Linguistic Analysis of the We-Phenomenon. Austin conceived of linguistic analysis as a means to "sharpen our perception of the phenomena" and to "direct our attention to the multiplicity and the richness of our experiences." In fact, an analysis of the meaning of linguistic expression cannot fail to describe to some extent the phenomena meant. To what extent? Linguistic analysis as such goes only far enough to distinguish meanings, not to analyze the phenomena for their own sake. As far as the we-phenomena not yet tackled by linguistic analysis proper are concerned, all that would be needed is to distinguish we-talk from you-and-I-talk by pointing out the different ways of grouping these phenomena. But such analysis need not explore the structure of the we-union and its varieties. This should be the primary contribution of phenomenological analysis in its concentration on the phenomena for their own sake.

Furthermore, most linguistic analysis seems to be satisfied with the discovery of the rules of grammar for the proper use of words such as pronouns, without trying to understand their reasons, if any. I submit that a direct study of the phenomena may supply such understanding, at least to some extent. Thus the rule that we-talk can apply only to personal beings can be understood when it is seen that only persons can perform the kind of we-acts that are essential to a we-union. Similarly the rule that the we of copresence, in contrast to the absentee we, must address the we-partners with the intent of aligning them with the speaker becomes intelligible in the light of the fact that their direct cooperation is needed for the constitution and maintenance of the we-union, something that is not the case in the absentee union.

Implications of the Phenomenological Analysis of the We-Phenomenon for Social Science. Social science, like all science, aspires to "objectivity," at least in the sense of knowledge that does not depend on the so-called subjective factors in the observer's personality, such as likes, moods, or bias. It requires knowledge that can be checked by other observers on the basis of evidence publicly displayed. This does not prevent science from dealing with facts that take place within a subject and even with this subject's views, provided they can be established in a way that can be shared by several observers.

It is agreed, at least among followers of the Max Weber tradition, that the subject matter of social science is subjective in this second sense. But this is only part of the situation. If the present analysis is correct, then social facts are given only in the subjective perspectives of the social partners. The immediate implication of this situation is that the social scientist has to study in each case all the perspectives of all the participants and to correlate them in parallel columns, as it were. In a sense this is what opinion research is doing. But this perspectival research must also include the study of metaperspectives—the partners' perspectives of one another's perspectives—a task attacked explicitly by R. D. Laing and his collaborators.

It may seem possible to overcome this complication by such idealizations as Schutz' principle of the "reciprocity of perspectives" to the effect that standpoints are interchangeable and that differences in perspectives are "congruent" or irrelevant for the purpose at hand (14). To Schutz these are assumptions "taken for granted," and they may be workable in most cases and pragmatically justified. But for a critical science and especially for a phenomenological approach it is a grave question whether these assumptions identified by Schutz are justified. Critical science and especially a critical philosophy like phenomenology can never take anything for granted. Beside, in the area of social tensions and conflicts it is a fact that the perspectives fail to be reciprocal and congruent. In all such cases there is then clearly no escape from such multiperspectival research.

This situation may suggest that the only objectivity social science can hope for is to put these subjective perspectives side by side and report about them. If this were universally true, something which has been asserted about certain regions of the world, namely that they contain no facts but only opinions, then indeed all that objective science could do is collect opinions and possibly examine them for consistencies and inconsistencies. But fortunately this need not always be the last word. The superperspective of the scientist, to be sure itself a metaperspective, allows him to some extent to relativize the relativity of the original perspectives, to de-center them and to construct a new perspective in which the lopsidedness of the original observers' perspectives have been neutralized. In this process the scientist's direct perspectives based at times also upon documents or other objective evidence can help. But this does not nullify the basic fact that the objectivity of social science is based on the raw material of subjective perspectives, reciprocal and nonreciprocal, which have to be explored conscientiously. This fact should also serve as a reminder that social science is usually at first remove from the facts. Such indirectness calls for epistemological modesty and humility. On this basis it can proceed with a critical selection from the direct perspectives of the firsthand witnesses, especially when they contradict one another.

SOME CONDITIONS FOR THE RIGHT TO SAY "WE"

I did not promise that this paper would result in a definite answer to the question of the right to say "we." This was one reason why I entitled it "*On* the Right" not "*The* Right," which could have been understood as a promise to tell "all about it." To me the most important thing was to raise the question and to find ways of approaching an answer, but not of serving it up ready-made. Yet I owe at least a preliminary answer.

But first it is in order to clarify finally what kind of right I am questioning. Obviously I do not mean the *legal* right to use a particular personal pronoun in any way one wants, including lying. One might consider here the conception of a *logical* right, or *epistemological* right, depending on whether there are valid reasons for asserting that some people stand in a we-relationship rather than that they think about each other merely as "you and I." Also one may conceive of a *linguistic* right, under the rules of good grammar, including philosophical grammar, to say "we." Thus linguistically there is nothing wrong about using the pronoun "we" to include one's defenseless dead predecessors or unborn successors. All the more questionable is whether one has a *moral* right to do so. It is indeed this moral right to say "we" in the name of others which I would like to test. For there is indeed such a thing as an ethics of language and speech, little though it has been discussed thus far. The ethics of pronouns might well be one of its major fields. There are, for instance, also questions of ethics involved in addressing others by use of the second person singular, especially in languages which distinguish between the intimate address of friendship and the less intimate general form of the pronoun as does French and German. But the moral right to say "we," which not only addresses but tries to align the other with the speaker, is a much more serious issue. Whenever I claim to speak in your name as well as in my own without your consent and especially over your protest, I have violated your moral right to the respect I owe you as a person.

However, such a blunt statement would have to be backed up not only by a clarification of the concept of moral right but also by a general theory of its foundations and its limits. If only for the sake of the argument I have to take it for granted that this concept makes sense and that there are definite good reasons justifying the claim to such rights. Nevertheless, I would like to point out what seems to me some of the most relevant considerations for an attempt to answer the question about the right to say "we."

The Case Against the Right

A remarkable book about "the adventures of a young Englishman at Harvard and in the Youth Movement" by Richard Zorza, from which I took part of my title and the first motto of this article, contains in the only chapter which resumes the title (*The Right to Say "We"*) and in the one paragraph speaking about it explicitly, the following continuation of my motto:

> No, that something [required for the right to say "we"] had to be the response of the whole youth movement, that whole new consciousness that we had seen developing, that we had responded to, that we had felt growing in ourselves as it grew in others . . . (15).

There is obviously something odd about such a statement made in the name of "we," which at the same time denies the right to say "we" until certain conditions can be fulfilled in the future. But more important is the question whether these conditions can ever be met. For in asking for the response of the entire youth movement the author practically calls for the unanimous support of all those to whom he appeals. How far is such a demand realizable, not only in the particular case but in general?

As the linguistic analysis of we-talk earlier in this essay tried to show, "we" indeed makes a claim to unanimity among all the we-partners. Majority, simple or qualified, won't do and one dissenter can wreck the pretense of speaking in the name of a group. Now in the case of the we of copresence such unanimity can be established, at least in principle and certainly in small face-to-face groups. But in the case of the absentee we with its indefinite class membership, the establishment of unanimity by securing everyone's consent seems to be more than impracticable. At least in this case the right to say "we" for others seems to be indefensible in principle.

But there may be an even more general objection to the right to say "we" even in the case of copresents. If it should be true that no one can speak for another person without his consent, then he should always be given a chance to give or withhold it. Now, there is practically no possibility of ever consulting every copresent we-partner beforehand. In fact, the very idea of asking them in each case, "May I speak for you too and say 'we' in your name?" would seem to be almost absurdly unrealistic. Seen in this light all we-talk is necessarily usurpation. At worst using it means speaking under false pretense, if not lying. At best it is a belated attempt to persuade others to acquiesce with this pretense.

Even more important, the preceding investigations have shown that the we-phenomenon can never be given adequately to any we-partner, neither with regard to his own share of unionizing acts nor to those of the others. At best we can have incomplete evidence for the presence of these acts. Under these circumstances the right to say we is certainly essentially precarious and never absolute.

In Defense of a Limited Right

But this does not mean that this right is nonexistent. Although I would like to be much more sparing and scrupulous in the use of we-language (I have certainly tried hard to do so in this paper), I am not advocating its total abolition.

To begin with, is it really necessary to give the we-talk this strong and forbidding sense? Could it be the case that in saying "we" I do not yet assert that you are behind me unconditionally? The very fact that I say so in your presence puts my claim to the test and gives you a chance to protest, thus giving me the lie. The "we" is then merely an invitation to accept my "we" formulation and an attempt to simplify matters for you by way of a rejectable offer. Your very presence at my speaking constitutes your protection against my usurpation. Thus it seems at least possible to describe the aligning function of the "we" as an attempt to enlist others as free associates on approval, by tacit assent, or on disapproval, by open dissent and protest. The main need for justifying we-talk is then good, if not conclusive, evidence that one's partner reciprocates one's we-consciousness. In the case of dual union this is comparatively easy.

But the larger the group, the more problematic such evidence becomes and thus the weaker is one's right to say "we."

This does not contradict the sad truth that the "we" is only too frequently misused as a persuasive device for capitalizing on the other's reluctance to protest and speak up. It may serve to shame him into accepting the speaker's judgment, perhaps even by flattery, as being credited with his views. I submit that this is the real threat of the usual we-talk, particularly when used in authoritarian situations, in teaching or in politics. "We" is one of the most insidious weapons in the arsenal of demagogues and dictators posing as democrats.

Nevertheless, I am prepared to defend a limited right to say "we" even without previous consultation of the prospective we-partners. To start with a rather obvious example: I would feel perfectly safe in making in a lecture the statement, "We have now spent 50 minutes together in this room," without fear of being contradicted except by some latecomers. What this signifies is that in cases where the we-statement refers merely to external circumstances and behavior, the evidence for sharing them is practically foolproof and the willingness of other we-partners to be included in a we-statement can be assumed notwithstanding the possibility that in cases of disorientation or absent-mindedness they may not be aware of such external facts or they may see them very differently.

But the situation is clearly very different in the case of "mental acts" such as seeing, believing, feeling, or wanting, which are certainly not as plainly and fully given to the we-speaker as are external circumstances. Suppose I had said, "We have now seen and know that all we-statements are precarious." How dare I say that about you as I may about myself? Such a we-statement would be not only an unwarranted claim to knowledge about you but an interference with your intellectual independence, your right to give or withhold assent. For my own part I confess that I always feel put upon, if not antagonistic, when a speaker or writer, under the guise of chummy fraternizing, includes me in his we-talk without giving me a chance to dissociate myself from him. Does he want to flatter me or to shame me into acquiescence with what is actually patronizing condescension?

The situation differs considerably in the case of the absentee we, where only one of the "we" is present in talking to an audience. Here any immediate assent or protest or subsequent approval is essentially out of the question. Hence one may well wonder whether it is at all defensible to speak for absent we-partners. But the absence is so obvious that no one can be misled. To this extent the use of the absentee we should be harmless. Nevertheless, the temptation to take advantage of the absence of possible protesters occurs too frequently. Thus there is a need for specifying the conditions when the use of this "we" is legitimate.

The major question would seem to be what reasons the we-speaker has for assuming that the absent we-partners would support him in saying "we" if present. For now he speaks not only in their joint names, but as their isolated representative. The clearest title is that of an actual proxy. Here the we-speaker, if he himself is ready to join with those he represents, may be considered authorized not only to cast the absentees' vote but, by adding his own, speak in the name of a new "we." In other cases, such as elections, the we-speaker may have legitimate ground for thinking that at least the majority of his voters would authorize inclusion in the "we," and the outvoted minority consent to it, if they have really freely adopted the rules of the majority game. Yet here too the absent we-partners must have at least some chance of dissenting and dissociating from their spokesman if he no longer keeps in touch with them. To say "we, the people" and even more so "we, the United Nations" is a bold claim indeed, which can all too easily turn out to be a rhetorical fiction invalidated by the fact that none of the we-partners even knew that he was included by his representatives. (More honest, if less impressive, is the formulation "We, the Assembly of the United Nations" used in the "Universal Declaration of Human Rights.") In short, in the case of the absentee we one's right depends on the existence of live credentials testifying to the support of the absentees. Ultimately even the absentee we points back to the conditions for the legitimate use of the we of copresence. But even with antecedent proxies and subsequent ratifications of his we-talk the absentee we-speaker must be aware that he is not in actual touch with those for whom he speaks and whose very number he usually does not know. Under such circumstances the right to say "we" is at best precarious.

It should also be realized that there is no clear-cut division between the two we's. It may well happen that part of the audience of a speech is within earshot, whereas others are only within the earshot of a one-way public address system and thus are not strictly copresent. Hence the justification of the right to speak for those only within one-way reach will differ from those within two-way reach.

These considerations do not add up to a neat formula specifying the terms for the right to say "we." But they suggest at least a maxim: Limit we-talk to occasions where you honestly believe that your we-partners want you to speak for them. Without good evidence for such an honest belief one had better speak only for oneself. This is a matter of social humility for humans who cannot know one another's hearts. It is a matter of respect for their dignity. It is also a matter of intellectual honesty and moral courage.

NOTES

1. Read in part as Alfred Schutz Memorial Lecture at Boston University, April 13, 1972. The quotation from Mark Twain was contributed by my friend Charles Courtney.

2. Since I gave the Schutz lecture Professor Joel Feinberg has drawn my attention to an essay by M. B. Foster, " 'We' in Modern Philosophy," in B. Mitchell, ed., *Faith and Logic*, Allen & Unwin, London, 1957, pp. 194–200. However, in this article Foster is concerned only with the way in which such analytic philosophers as G. E. Moore use the pronoun in their writings addressed to possible readers with whom they are not in direct contact. The most original but narrow treatment of the we-phenomenon by a "phenomenological ontologist" can be found in Jean-Paul Sartre, *L'Être et le néant*, Part III, Chapter 3, Section 3.

3. Even substituting the impersonal "one" for "we," as I am often doing, may be merely a partial remedy suggesting that I am speaking by way of generalization for everyone else—a generalization not to be taken lightly.

4. The situation is different when the audience is addressed by transmission to another room, by radio, or by television, even though the listeners may have a chance to reach the speaker subsequently by telephonic questions. These are clearly transitional situations. Telephonic conversation, with or without visual screen, can establish copresence. And correspondents, though separated in time as well as in space, may use the we of copresence.

5. "ita-us"=for we two; see C. Bloomfield, *Language*, Holt, New York, 1961, p. 257.

6. Bloomfield, *op. cit.*, p. 256 f. gives examples from the Algonquian language in which the inclusive and the exclusive "we" are distinguished by the prefixes "ke" and "ne," respectively; the same is true of Samoan. The Spanish *"nosotros"* was originally exclusive like French *"nous autres"* but is now used also for inclusive purposes. See José Ortega y Gasset, *El Hombre y la gente*, Revista de Occidente, pp. 139–140 (English translation *Man and People*, W. W. Norton, New York, 1957, p. 111).

7. That even single words have linguistic force is already suggested by W. Alston, *Philosophy of Language*, Prentice-Hall, Englewood Cliffs, N.J., 1964, p. 36.

8. In the following story from old-time northern Germany, a patriotic gentleman addresses an unknown elderly spinster: "Isn't it wonderful that we have won another victory?" Spinster: "Sir, you have not yet been introduced to me."

9. Foster, *op. cit.*, pp. 196–197.

10. A particularly striking example of such hypostatization can be found in Fritz Künkel's *Das Wir, Die Grundbegriffe der Wir-psychologie,* Darnstadt, Wissenschaftliche Buchgesellschaft, 1972. His "we-experiences" (*Wirerlebnisse*) need not be denied by questioning his uncritical interpretation without prior linguisitic and phenomenological analysis.

11. "A Plea for Excuses" in *Philosophical Papers,* Clarendon, Oxford, 1961, p. 133.

12. Herbert Spiegelberg, "The Puzzle of *Wittgenstein's Phaenomenologie* 1929–?" *American Philosophical Quarterly,* V, 1968, pp. 244–256.

13. This version is a slight simplification of the phenomenological approach advocated by Alexander Pfänder, which in turn is a development of certain key ideas in Husserl's pre-idealistic phenomenology. See my *The Phenomenological Movement,* Martinus Nijhoff, The Hague, 1965, pp. 180–185; and Alexander Pfänder, *Phenomenology of Willing and Motivation and Other Phaenomenologica,* Northwestern University Press, Evanston, Ill., 1967. Many of the substantive ideas in the subsequent section are parallel to those of Gerda Walther, who developed Pfänder's phenomenological psychology in "Zur Ontologie der sozialen Gemeinschaften," *Jahrbuch für Philosophie and phänomenologische Forschung,* VI, 1923, 1–158. However, my conception of "union" and "unionizing acts" does not coincide with their conception of "*Einigung*."

14. Alfred Schutz, *Collected Papers,* Vol. I, Martinus Nijhoff, The Hague, 1962, pp. 1–13.

15. Richard Zorza, *The Right to Say "We"*, Praeger, New York, 1970, p. 21.

»»»»»»»»»»»»»»»»»»»»»»»«««««««««««««««««««««

One of the most frequently used concepts in social psychology is here subjected to a phenomenological analysis in order to determine its essential structure. The value of such eidetic analyses lies in more than the initial conceptual clarification that may be achieved. A possible refocusing of research may be attained by the analysis of the several elements of the phenomenon and the discovery of their interrelationships. Goffman's work represents a rich mine of observations concerning face-to-face interaction in everyday life situations, yet the conceptual analysis he presents is shown not to be sufficiently precise nor sensitive to the distinctions between essentially necessary elements and those that are contingent. Ethnography is again shown to need more than descriptive detail to provide essential insights.

Together with Spiegelberg's, this paper contributes to the clarification of the we-phenomenon by analyzing the preconditions of social interaction in the face-to-face situation.

ESSENTIAL FEATURES OF
FACE-TO-FACE INTERACTION (1)

»»»»»»»»»»»»»»»»»»»»»»»»»«««««««««««««««««««««««««

George Psathas
Frances C. Waksler

Boston University
Wheelock College

> *All the other manifold social relationships are derived from*
> *the originary experiencing of the totality of the Other's self*
> *in the community of time and space. Any theoretical analysis*
> *of the notion of environment . . . would have to start from the face*
> *to face relations as a basic structure of the world of daily life (2).*

Alfred Schutz in *The Phenomenology of the Social World* presents one
of the most comprehensive analyses of the phenomena of social action, social relationship, and social interaction starting from a thorough critical
analysis of Max Weber's work. Social action, according to Schutz, involves "intentional conscious experiences directed toward the other
self" where the other is a conscious living being; when such experiences are formed into a project of action, social action is the result. The

attitude one adopts based on positing the other as an other self (the general thesis of the other self) he refers to as "Other-orientation" and the acts directed to an other "which have as an in-order-to motive the bringing about of a certain conscious experience in the other person" he calls social action of the "affecting-the-Other" type (*Fremdwirken*). This is to be distinguished from actions affected by another (*fremdbewirktes Handeln*).

When two people become reciprocally oriented toward each other, a social relationship, in Weber's terms, exists, but the existence of such a relationship may be from either the actor's or the observer's perspective and the two are not necessarily in agreement. For the external observer, the *objective probability* of the existence of a social relationship involves him in judgments concerning the correspondence between conscious processes and the outward indications of those processes. He assumes that each has an Other-orientation and seeks to discover with greater certainty whether in fact they are in a social relationship and what effect they are having on each other.

It is easier for him to judge that they are affecting each other by their social actions—their engaging in "social interaction" (*Wirkensbeziehung*)—than it is to judge whether they are in a social relationship in which they are merely taking each other into account, that is, in an Other-orientation or "orientation relationship" (*Einstellungsbeziehung*). However, it is not clear whether Schutz means that two persons must mutually affect one another in social interaction or whether an unreciprocated social action in the presence of the other is sufficient for social interaction to be said to occur. He seems to conclude that social interaction can be one-sided when he notes:

> An interaction exists if one person acts upon another with the expectation that the latter will respond, or at least notice. It is not necessary that the partner reciprocally affect the actor or act himself. All that is required is that the partner be aware of the actor and interpret what he does or says as evidence for what is going on in his mind. All the partner's subjective experiences will, naturally, be modified by his attention to the actor.
>
> Every interaction is, therefore, based on an action of affecting another within a social situation. The *object* of the action is to lead the partner to have conscious experiences of a desired sort. The *necessary condition* of the action is that the partner be paying attention to the actor. But not every act of affecting-the-Other is carried out within a relationship of interaction, indeed within any social relationship whatever; not every act of affecting-the-Other presupposes that the Other is oriented toward me (p. 158).

A few sentences later he introduces the notion that one may have as part of his project the intention that the other will know that he is being affected:

. . . But whenever in affecting another I intend him to know that I am affecting him, then we have the relationship of interaction. His attentional attitude toward me has now entered into the very project of my act. It has become my in-order-to motive. It has become the "for-sake-of-which" of my affecting him in the sense that it is either my final goal or my intermediate goal. Every time I establish a meaning, therefore I will be looking forward to its interpretation by my partner. This expectation of mine will enter into the broader goal-content within which the meaning-establishment takes place. *Social interaction is, accordingly, a motivational context and, in fact, an intersubjective motivational context.* It is essential to the constitution of interaction that each act of affecting the partner be undertaken in order to bring about a certain reciprocal Other-orientation on his part (p. 159).

The other may become very aware of the action and a reciprocal Other-orientation may exist but this does not necessarily mean that the other will in fact produce action of an affecting-the-Other type. Thus reciprocal acts of affecting-the-Other (*Akte wechselseitigen Fremdwirkens*) may or may not be involved in what Schutz has called social interaction.

Social interaction can occur even though the two actors are not in a situation of copresence. They can be physically separated yet in communication with one another. However, if social interaction occurs, according to Schutz, it is essential that

the person who is interacting with another should anticipate the in-order-to motives of his own action as the genuine because-motives of the expected behavior of his partner and, conversely, that he should be prepared to regard the in-order-to motives of his partner as the genuine because-motives of his own behavior (p. 162).

This is the important element in a social relationship that makes it one of social interaction. Schutz goes on to note that it is not necessary that the other be aware of it: The motivational context of the interaction is most visible in the "living intentionality of the *direct social relationship*" (our italics) (p. 162).

The *direct social relationship* involves persons sharing space and time, aware of each other, as persons, as particular individuals, and of each other's body as the field of expression of inner processes of consciousness. When these conditions exist, Schutz speaks of the partners as being in a "face-to-face situation." As the partners live in this situation, each is intentionally conscious of the other person and assumes an Other-orientation toward him (which, in this situation, Schutz refers to as a "Thou-orientation"). If each is aware of the other in this way and also aware that the other is aware of him, then they are in a "we-relation" (3). As lived, the we-relation is experienced as concrete, a relationship with a specific person for whom one knows specifically how he is being regarded: "only here do our glances actually meet, only here can one actually note how the other is looking at him" (p. 168). Concrete we-relations vary in terms of the degrees of intimacy, intensity, and immediacy with which the partners experience each other, and they differ in degrees of directness.

Schutz then proceeds to examine different types of face-to-face relationships and it is in this discussion that a number of elements are added which appear to be related to the continuity of acts and actions which the two partners are assumed to engage in if they are in a we-relation.

However, though Schutz does not do this, it is possible to analytically distinguish between the conditions that are necessary for the we-relation to begin from those involved in its continuation, and, similarly, to distinguish between the essential requirements for social interaction in the face-to-face situation and the consequences or results of the continuity of the action.

Schutz's discussion includes reference to some properties of the situation whose status as essential necessities cannot be discerned. For example, "in the face-to-face situation I literally see my partner in front of me" (p. 169). Is sight essential for both parties in order for them to be in a face-to-face situation? Or, "to this encounter, I bring a whole stock of previously constituted knowledge" (p. 169); but what knowledge is necessary for the face-to-face situation to develop?

In addition, the distinction between characteristics of the persons, the situation, and the relationship are not made sharply. And, since much of his discussion is presented from the standpoint of a partner in the interaction, an "I" who is interacting and who, as observer, then stands back to reflect on his experience, it is not clear what an observer of two persons must know in order for him to judge whether, from his observer's perspective, they are interacting. It appears fairly obvious that Schutz intended his analysis to enable us to specify what an observer must know, but without such an elaboration it is not possible to discern what elements are essential from the observer's point of view.

Of those sociologists who have looked closely and systematically at the face-to-face situation from an observer's perspective, Erving Goffman's work stands out as most brilliant and perceptive (4). His descriptions and analyses, particularly of relationships of brief temporal duration, as in behavior in public places, have provided some of the most valuable concepts in sociology for understanding such settings and their social occasions. We turn to his work to discover what elements he has identified as essential for face-to-face interaction.

Although his stated aim is to "develop the study of face-to-face interaction as a naturally bounded, analytically coherent field—a sub-area of sociology" (5), there is no single place in his writings where one may find an analysis of those elements which he would regard as minimum essentials for "face-to-face interaction." He himself is aware of the importance of such an analysis when he states:

> Since it is individual actors who contribute the ultimate materials, it will always be reasonable to ask what general properties they must have if this sort of contribution is to be expected of them. What minimal model of the actor is needed if we are to wind him up, stick him in amongst his fellows, and have an orderly traffic of behavior emerge? What minimal model is required if the student is to anticipate the lines along which an individual, *qua* interactant, can be effective or break down? (6).

His approach is to seek the recurrent features of the "natural units of interaction," the "normative order prevailing within and between these units," and presumably also the features of the actors, through "serious ethnography (which will enable the identification of) the countless patterns and natural sequences of behavior occurring whenever persons come into one another's immediate presence."

In advancing his aim, Goffman has not only offered rich ethnographic accounts of particular social occasions, social gatherings, and the natural units of interaction, but has also attempted to isolate, by means of definitions, the phenomena he observes and analyses.

His most comprehensive discussion appears in the chapter "Introductory Definitions" in *Behavior in Public Places*. Here he enumerates "two distinctive features of face-to-face interaction: richness of information flow and facilitation of feedback." By the first he refers to "experiencing someone else with one's naked senses" and receiving "embodied messages," that is, messages that are linked to the immediate present and are conveyed by one's own current bodily activity. Under this condition, as Goffman notes, "any message that an individual sends is likely to be qualified and modified by much additional information that the other can glean from him simultaneously, often unbeknownst to him; further, a very large number of brief messages may be sent" (7).

The second condition is due to the fact that the parties in the interaction are available to each other by virtue of their co-presence i.e. they share time and space: "not only are they receiving and conveying (messages) of the naked and embodied kind, but each giver is himself a receiver, and each receiver a giver" (8).

He then proceeds to discuss some of the implications of this second feature and notes that sight takes on a special role in that each person "can *see* that he is being experienced in some way, and he will guide at least some of his conduct according to the perceived identity and initial response of his audience. Further, he can be seen to be seeing this, and can see that he has been seen seeing this" (9).

It is not clear from Goffman's discussion whether these consequences follow merely from the two features delineated, nor is it apparent whether he assumes that the features of the persons and their relations include those elements which Schutz has carefully analyzed. It would seem from Goffman's discussion and from the rich variety of observations he presents in this and other works that he is aware of many more features of the phenomenon of face-to-face interaction.

But, more critically, Goffman does not distinguish among the characteristics of the person engaged in interaction, the contents of that person's consciousness, and what he, as actor, must attribute to the other with whom he is copresent. He is not attentive to the distinction between the behaviors of the actors and the assumptions they make about themselves and one another before they can interact at all. The fact that interaction is known to occur, and can be intersubjectively verified by independent observers, does not mean that the preconditions of interaction are understood by either the actors or the observers.

In *Encounters* Goffman comes closest to presenting a full listing of what he considers face-to-face interaction to include. He defines encounters as:

a type of social arrangement that occurs when persons are in one another's physical presence. (For participants, this seems to involve a single visual and cognitive focus of attention; a mutual and preferential openness to verbal communication; a heightened mutual relevance of acts; an eye-to-eye ecological huddle that maximizes each participant's monitoring of him. Given these communication arrangements, their presence tends to be acknowledged or ratified through expressive signs, and a "we rationale" is likely to emerge, that is, a sense of the single thing that *we* are doing together at the time. Ceremonies of entrance and departure are also likely to be employed, as are signs acknowledging the initiation and termination of the encounter or focused gathering as a unit . . . Encounters provide the communication base for a circular flow of feeling among the participants as well as corrective compensation for deviant acts (10).

Elsewhere, Goffman defines face-to-face interaction as "the reciprocal influence of individuals upon one another's action when in one another's immediate physical presence" (11). And in *Behavior in Public Places* he refers to a *face engagement* or an *encounter* as "instances of two or more participants in a situation joining each other openly in maintaining a single focus of cognitive and visual attention—what is sensed as a single *mutual activity*, entailing preferential communication rights" (12).

He briefly analyses how encounters are initiated when he says:

An encounter is initiated by someone making an opening move, typically by means of a special expression of the eyes but sometimes by a statement or special tone of voice at the beginning of a statement. The engagement proper beings when this overture is acknowledged by the other, who signals back with his eyes, voice, or stance that he has placed himself at the disposal of the other for purposes of a mutual eye-to-eye activity (13).

Goffman also proposes that face-to-face interaction includes experiencing the other with one's naked senses, that receiving and conveying involve "naked senses and embodied messages with the giver a receiver and each receiver a giver." However, he does not extend the analysis to include the conscious awareness persons have of one another. Thus, in saying that copresence involves persons sensing "that they are close enough to be perceived in whatever they are doing including their experiencing of others, and close enough to be perceived in this sensing of being perceived," (14) he comes closest, as in *Encounters*, to explicitly including conscious awareness of the other's consciousness of oneself as a necessary feature of face-to-face interaction. But he does not make it clear whether this conscious awareness of being perceived is necessary in all instances that are classified as face-to-face.

From these discussions it is apparent that for Goffman face-to-face interaction is most likely to be characterized by the copresence of two or more actors who are aware of and communicate with one another in ways that indicate that each takes the other into account, and that each is aware that the other is so doing.

Throughout his discussions and analyses, Goffman fails to specify what elements are a necessary part of the phenomenon being studied, which are contingent or possible, and which, by virtue of their presence or absence, affect the "normal" character of the situation and of interaction but do not change it completely.

Thus it seems that (a) a single focus of attention is not essential but when it does occur and only two actors are present, a *fully focused gathering* emerges; (b) visual monitoring is not essential but when it occurs actors are able to glean rich amounts of information from one another; (c) a sense of "we" may emerge from the interaction, but this is a possible result rather than an essential precondition for interaction; and (d) the mere presence of others in a social situation involves normatively guided conduct on the part of both parties. It is increasingly clear, as Goffman's work is read, that the force of his analyses of social situations and interaction derives from the perceptive classifications and observations of particular behaviors in particular situations, in short, ethnographic descriptions which, when analyzed and classified, allow him to discover naturally occurring behavior patterns.

One of the distinctions between Schutz and Goffman is that Schutz uses a phenomenological analysis to clarify and reveal the dimensions of interaction as it is experienced by the actor, whereas Goffman starts with and retains commonsense understandings of everyday situations, classifies these from an observer's perspective, and uses definitions as a means of orienting the reader to these same commonsense understandings. The assumptions underlying these commonsense understandings are not themselves analyzed by Goffman, except in his brief efforts to set forth "definitions."

It is precisely at this level of analysis, understanding the essential features that characterize social interaction occurring among persons in a face-to-face situation and determining what an observer of interaction is assuming, that we believe a close analysis is still needed. The work of Goffman continues to call our attention to this need since he impresses us with the richness of his descriptions of face-to-face interactions in everyday life and assumes we can understand these phenomena in the same way that he can. In sending us to observe, however, it is necessary to provide a more detailed guide to the subject of study so that we will not only be able to recognize it when we see it but also know what assumptions we are making when we in fact grasp it.

In the present paper, we will follow Schutz most closely and develop a framework based on the conceptual clarifications he provided. We will indicate how Goffman's insights may be further enhanced by this analysis. Our effort is to determine what features are essential to the phenomenon without which face-to-face interaction would not be assessed as occurring.

Our analysis takes the perspective of the observer and we are asking: What must an observer know in order to interpret the behavior of two actors as an instance of face-to-face interaction?

We recognize that the perspective of the actor and the observer differ. The observation carried on by someone not engaged in the actual ongoing social relationship involves interpretations that cannot be subjected to direct verification except perhaps by entering the relationship itself and interacting with the partners. We are aware of the importance of the difference between the two perspectives but do not wish to analyze these differences at this time. Rather, we are concerned with the ordinary situation in which one person knows that two others are interacting with each other and we ask what is it that this observer must know in order to make the interpretation that two others are interacting.

The observer we refer to is not necessarily a social scientist; rather he is any "normal" person making a judgment about the behavior of others, that is, whether they are or are not engaged in face-to-face interaction. We do not consider how the observer interprets the content of their interaction, their because- and in-order-to motives, their schemes of interpretation, or the stock of knowledge they use. These issues are more complex. The prior question that must be answered is, it seems to us: What does the observer know or take to be fact in making the judgment that interaction is occurring?

In this respect we adopt Berger and Luckmann's notion of knowledge as "the certainty that phenomena are real, that they possess certain characteristics" and that knowledge consists, for members of society in the world of everyday life, of whatever passes for knowledge in society" (15). Rather than put the terms "reality" and "knowledge" into quotation marks each time they are used, it should be clear that we are considering what the observer of an everyday life situation knows, what facts he accepts about the persons and the situation which enable him to say that the two persons he observes are in "face-to-face interaction."

Our analysis will be presented as a listing of those facts, that is, what the observer knows. We are not studying *how* the observer comes to know what he knows but only *what* he knows. Nor do we imply that the observer is consciously considering the features analyzed here; he may simply grasp them in immediate experiences. However, we do propose that if he encounters discrepancies or if essential aspects of his knowledge are called into question, he may be confronted, in a conscious and direct manner, with those facts that were unquestioned and taken for granted. However, even in such instances, he may be able to resolve his confusion or disturbance by normalizing events, reinterpreting their meanings, and not have his grasp of the structure of social reality remain questioned. If this analysis of essential aspects of his knowledge is correct, then even his efforts to restore the normal appearance of events will presumably involve him in reestablishing his assumptions about these same aspects of his knowledge.

We have selected the perspective of the observer for this analysis because, unlike one of the participants, whose knowledge of himself is greater than and different from his knowledge of the other, the observer has the same knowledge of each of the partners. Whereas one actor knows himself and his own projects and must make assumptions only about the other, the observer knows neither one better or more intimately than the other and must make the same assumptions about both.

We wish to discover the absolute essential necessities, those features without which the phenomenon is not possible (16). No omission or substitution of these features is possible without destroying the phenomenon. For example, the phenomenon would no longer be face-to-face interaction if only one person were present. But we cannot tell before an analysis whether they must in fact face each other, share the same language, or have the capacity to use language, and so forth. Using the method of free imaginative variation and also including instances of empirical observations, we shall examine all instances in order to discover the essential elements.

We may discover that some elements, when present or absent, change the fundamental structure of the phenomenon but do not destroy it. Such elements may be said to be relatively necessary as long as the specific phenomenon is to be kept as it is. For example, face-to-face interaction may still be seen as occurring but in a very different form when the senses of sight, hearing, and touch are lacking for both partners, who must then rely on tasting, smelling, or third-party reports to sense each other even though they are copresent.

The analysis of any complex phenomenon will elicit features that are absolutely essential, relatively essential, and unessential. (The latter category will include those elements that are possible and whose omission or substitution does not affect the fundamental structure of the phenomenon, the essential possibilities). When the phenomenon under investigation is as complex as that of face-to-face interaction, the task of discovering the absolute or the relatively essential features is difficult. Each feature or element discovered may in itself be complex and deserving of further phenomenological analysis. It will be apparent that the many comparisons and contrasts that were necessary before we could arrive at the list of these features are not presented herein.

ESSENTIAL FEATURES OF FACE-TO-FACE INTERACTION

The features that the observer must find before he can judge an occurrence to be one of face-to-face interaction can be divided into three categories: features of the actors (17) features of the relation between the actors, and features of their action. We will discuss each of these separately, detailing the knowledge that the observer must have or come to have. These points are outlined in Table 1. When we describe an actor as having some characteristic it should be clear that we mean that this is what the observer knows of the actor. However he goes about it, he must conclude that all of the following features are present if he is to identify the situation as one of face-to-face interaction.

I. FEATURES OF THE ACTORS
A. 1.   *Ego* (18) *is conscious and is aware of that consciousness.*
    2.   *Other is conscious and is aware of that consciousness.*

All consciousness is consciousness *of* something, whether that something is real or ideal, existent or imaginary (19). A conscious person is one who has subjective experiences and is conscious *of* these experiences. An actor can be said to be conscious when he can be said to have experiences and to reflect on those experiences. His consciousness is constituted in part by taken-for-granted knowledge, in part by information of which he is explicitly aware. An observer must judge that Ego and Other are conscious and see themselves as conscious if they are to be capable of face-to-face interaction.

B. 1. *Ego has constituted a self.*
   2. *Other has constituted a self.*

The observer must judge that both Ego and Other see themselves as unitary beings, acted upon by and acting on the world. Each must view himself as having a past, present, and future. Each must be capable of reacting to the other and eliciting reactions in him. The observer must judge that each is at least potentially effective in his world.

C. 1. *Ego has acquired and is able to use a stock of knowledge and a system of relevance.*
   2. *Other has acquired and is able to use a stock of knowledge and a system of relevance.*

Both actors have had socialization experiences which have provided them with a stock of knowledge and a system of relevances. It is on the basis of these that each can interpret his own and the other's experiences. Such knowledge includes learned interpretive schemes, background knowledge, foreground knowledge (20) and whatever passes for knowledge among members of society.

That stock of knowledge can include what Schutz has called "common sense knowledge" (21) and what we will elaborate in Part II of this outline: Features of the Relation between Actors and Part III: Features of Action. It is necessary that they are judged able to understand or have knowledge of these features in order for them to be considered able to interact. As in the case of background understandings or background knowledge ["routine grounds" or "background features" (22)] what they know is part of their shared stock of commonsense knowledge: it is practical, prescientific knowledge the individual has *at hand*. The observer must also judge that Ego and Other share at least some of this stock of knowledge, the amount depending upon their purpose at hand.

D. 1. *Ego is able to communicate and to use a symbolic system of meaning.*
   2. *Other is able to communicate and to use a symbolic system of meaning.*

Each is able to communicate using signs or symbols. Signs involve the use of nonarbitrary indicators whose meaning is tied to the context of the situation, for example, a gesture indicating to the other the location of an object. Communication with either signs or symbols is necessary in order for Ego and Other to be able to intentionally affect one another (see Part III, Features of Action).

Although a symbolic system of meaning need not be used to communicate, it must be available to each actor to be used. It is this that makes possible (a) the formulation of a project of action (see Part IIIA below), (b) the interpretation of the other's acts (see Part IIID below), (c) the interpretation of the other's bodily expressions as indications of his subjective experiences (see Part IF below), and (d) the verification of the presence or absence of the essential features of face-to-face interaction which allow him to know that he is engaged in such interaction. A symbolic system of meaning makes possible that internal conversation by means of which the person interprets the meaning of his experiences.

E.　1.　*Ego is motivated to act.*
　　2.　*Other is motivated to act.*

Each actor is motivated to act. Each is able to project actions which are intentional (23).

F.　1.　*Ego views his body as a field of experience.*
　　2.　*Other views his body as a field of experience.*

Goffman speaks of Ego's emitting expressive messages that Other can glean. Further, he states that these expressive messages are expected to be unintended. Without getting into the issue of intention, we are adopting, in a somewhat extended form, Goffman's concept of expressive messages. We do not wish to minimize the potential importance of linguistic messages as indicators of the other's subjectivity, but we are focusing here on the interpretation of the actor's body in the understanding of his responses and his projects of action, as well as indications of the presence or absence of those features essential in face-to-face interaction. That the actor may encounter difficulty in utilizing such bodily signs does not minimize the importance of his holding the assumption that his body is "readable."

The observer must then judge that both Ego and Other realize or are in some way conscious of this potential of their own body, that it can be "read" for indications of internal states, intentions, retentions, and so forth.

II. FEATURES OF THE RELATION BETWEEN ACTORS

A.　1.　*Ego is present.*
　　2.　*Other is present.*

When two actors are present in the same time and space we can speak of copresence. In this sharing of time and space the actors are "close enough" to (a) become aware of one another's bodily presence and (b) monitor the other's body as an indicator of his experience or, as Goffman would state it, "close enough: to send expressive messages and read those emitted by the other (24). Copresence does not assure that the two actors will become aware of each other, only that *each is within reach of the other's direct experience* (25). For present purposes we have restricted ourselves to the judgment of copresence based on the use of the *naked senses*. We omit any discussion of interaction aided by mechanical devices such as radio, telegraph, or telephone which allow persons to augment their sensory reception or transmission. As long as the observer determines that the actors are "close enough" to use their naked senses to interact, he can judge them to be copresent (26).

B. 1. *Ego is aware of Other's bodily presence.*
   2. *Other is aware of Ego's bodily presence.*

To be aware of another is to direct one's consciousness toward that person. Ego may become aware of Other's bodily presence without Other being reciprocally aware; this is one-sided bodily awareness. If the observer judges that each is aware of the other, then a reciprocal or mutual bodily awareness may be said to occur (27). But this awareness does not yet include the awareness *that* the other is aware. Each may be aware of the other but not be aware *that* the other is so aware.

Awareness of the other as body does not necessarily include awareness of his consciousness. For example, one can perceive a form and shape which experience would indicate is another body. It is perceived as the body of a person with whom one is copresent. One does not expect it to act or to be aware of one's intended actions. It exists as the form within which a consciousness may exist but all that one experiences of it is its shape, mass, weight, or other physical features.

C. 1. *Ego constitutes Other as an actor, with features of an actor.*
   2. *Other constitutes Ego as an actor, with features of an actor.*

Just as the observer must constitute both Ego and Other as actors, attributing to each the foregoing six features, so also must he judge that Ego makes such attributions to Other and that Other makes such attributions to Ego. Thus, if the observer constitutes both Ego and Other as actors but believes, for example, that Ego does not attribute the feature of ability to communicate to Other, then the observer will judge that face-to-face interaction cannot take place even though he, the observer, disagrees with Ego's judgment.

If only one person constitutes the other as an actor, then a "thou-orientation" exists (28): the relation is one-sided. If each constitutes the other as an actor, then a reciprocal thou-orientation or "we-relation" exists. The thou-orientation is a prepredicative experience in which one simply grasps the pure being-there (*Dasein*) of the other as a live conscious human being. It presupposes Ego's perception of the other. A we-relation, on the other hand, could be called a reciprocal, or mutual, consciousness awareness.

D. 1. *Ego is aware that Other is conscious of Ego's bodily presence.*
    2. *Other is aware that Ego is conscious of Other's bodily presence.*

This refers to awareness of certain aspects of the other's consciousness. Again, this can be one-sided awareness when only one person is aware or mutual when both are aware. When both parties are aware we can speak of a mutual awareness of Other's awareness of oneself as body (29).

E. 1. *Ego is aware that Other constitutes him as an actor.*
    2. *Other is aware that Ego constitutes him as an actor.*

Here the observer attributes to each actor that he is aware that the other attributes to him the features of an actor. Each is aware of the other's awareness of his awareness.

This reciprocality is well presented in Westlake's statement: "I know this, and he knew that I knew it, and I knew he knew I knew it, and so on through an infinity of facing mirrors, each of us aware of the receding levels of the other's knowledge . . ." (30).

Since Ego and Other share these assumptions and since they share time and space, Ego may say of Other (and vice versa), "his experience is flowing side by side with mine when I can at any moment look over and grasp his thoughts as they come into being, i.e., when we are growing old together" (31). Each actor is able to receive information about the other's subjective experiences *as these are occurring*.

III. FEATURES OF ACTION

A. 1. *Ego projects action of the affecting-the-Other type.*
    2. *Other projects action of the affecting-the-Other type.*

Here we wish to follow the terminology and distinctions by Schutz in which a *project of action* refers to the formulated plan of acts which are imagined as performed but which are not yet performed; and *act* refers to the completed, performed action arising out of a previously formulated project. Each person can project action which is intentionally related to the other as an other self. When such projects "have as their in-order-to motive to bring about a certain conscious experience in the other person," they can be called "affecting-the-Other" types of projects (32).

B. 1. *Ego develops an act on the basis of his project of action.*
    2. *Other develops an act on the basis of his project of action*

Social action, according to Schutz, consists of conscious experiences related to another self which may emerge in the form of spontaneous activity and which are previously projected. Each is involved in developing an act on the basis of his previously formulated project.

In the formulation of a project of action and of acts, each actor is involved in the use of a symbolic system of meaning. He interprets his experiences, interprets the behavior of the Other, and continually attempts to "make sense" out of the events that are occurring.

C. 1. *Ego acts.*

Ego performs an act with the intention that Other will interpret it as an act, that is, as meaningful behavior arising out of a project. This can be regarded as the initial act in face-to-face interaction, but up to this point interaction has not yet occurred. Two additional features are necessary.

D. 1. *Other is aware of Ego's act as arising from his project of action.*

Other interprets Ego's behavior as meaningful and arising out of some project. He is not necessarily accurate in his interpretation of the project. He must see the behavior as an act involving, at the least, an affecting-the-Other project of action even if that project is limited to making Other aware of Ego's body and consciousness.

C. 2. *Other acts.*

Other now may act on the basis of his project formulated prior to Ego's act or he may act on the basis of a newly formulated project based on the preceding performed act by Ego. That is, Other can include the act performed by Ego in the formulation of his project. In either case, it is possible for Ego to perceive Other's act as a *response*.

D. 2. *Ego is aware of Other's act as arising from his project of action.*

When Ego perceives Other's act as arising from a project of action *and* views this project as including Ego's presence and his (Ego's) previously performed act, then a situation in which the in-order-to motives of one become the genuine because-motives of the other has emerged. Each can now be seen as looking forward to the other's interpretation of the meaning of his acts and as then developing his project of action in the light of this understanding. Each is also looking backward to the previously performed acts to ascertain the meaning they may provide concerning the underlying project of action (33). A progressive emergence of meaning, constructed out of the actions and acts of both partners, is a newly added element created by their joint endeavor.

Table 1   Outline of the Essential Features of Face-To-Face Interaction

I. *Features of the Actors*
  A. 1. Ego is conscious and is aware of that consciousness.
      2. Other is conscious and is aware of that consciousness.
  B. 1. Ego has constituted a self.
      2. Other has constituted a self.
  C. 1. Ego has acquired and is able to use a stock of knowledge and a system of relevance.
      2. Other has acquired and is able to use a stock of knowledge and a system of relevance.
  D. 1. Ego is able to communicate and to use a symbolic system of meaning.
      2. Other is able to communicate and to use a symbolic system of meaning.
  E. 1. Ego is motivated to act.
      2. Other is motivated to act.
  F. 1. Ego views his body as a field of experience.
      2. Other views his body as a field of experience.

II. *Features of the Relation between Actors*
  A. 1. Ego is present.
      2. Other is present.
  B. 1. Ego is aware of Other's bodily presence.
      2. Other is aware of Ego's bodily presence.
  C. 1. Ego constitutes Other as an actor, with features of an actor.
      2. Other constitutes Ego as an actor, with features of an actor.
  D. 1. Ego is aware that Other is conscious of Ego's bodily presence.
      2. Other is aware that Ego is conscious of Other's bodily presence.
  E. 1. Ego is aware that Other constitutes him as an actor.
      2. Other is aware that Ego constitutes him as an actor.

III. *Features of Action*
  A. 1. Ego projects action of the affecting-the-Other type.
      2. Other projects action of the affecting-the-Other type.
  B. 1. Ego develops an act on the basis of his project of action.
      2. Other develops an act on the basis of his project of action.
  C. 1. Ego acts.   C. 2. Other acts.
  D. 1. Other is aware of   D. 2. Ego is aware of
          Ego's act as arising   Other's act as aris-
          from his project   ing from his project
          of action.   of action.

In the living intentionality of the direct social relationship, the two partners are face-to-face, their streams of consciousness are synchronized and geared into each other, each immediately affects the other, and the in-order-to motives of the one become the because-motive of the other, the two motives complementing and validating each other as objects of reciprocal attention (34).

THE EMERGENCE OF FACE-TO-FACE INTERACTION

It is at this point that the observer can say that the two parties are *in* face-to-face interaction. Determining the *actual* beginning of such interaction in an empirical case is difficult, however. The observer cannot know which of the essential elements each of the persons has already established and which he is still seeking to verify. Only when an act is generated by each can he judge more accurately that they are aware of each other, and so forth. Since many of the elements involve the person's making assumptions "until further notice," and the contents of each person's consciousness are not directly observable, the observer may have to "wait and see." Once a judgment is made that interaction is occurring, a retrospective judgment can be made about its beginning point, how it began or even that it began.

For face-to-face interaction to continue, all the required features must remain present and be continually validated. It is possible for disturbances in these assumptions to occur, either deliberately or not, if either or both actors are behaving in such a way as to call into question whether they are maintaining their assumptions. For example, if one appears not to be aware of the other's presence, he may be ignoring him and so communicating a snub, indicating civil inattention, or actually have no awareness of the other.

One may deliberately act to disturb the other, as in the case of Garfinkel's "nasty surprise," which calls into question the other's taken-for-granted assumptions. If the other is unable or not permitted to reestablish those features that are necessary to interact, then the relationship may be terminated.

As face-to-face interaction continues, there are a variety of techniques which persons may use to indicate to each other and which may be similarly interpreted by an observer, that they are continuing to maintain their assumptions. For example, each may give explicit signs, and the other may reciprocate, which can be interpreted as indicators of attention, interest, and awareness: the nod of a head, the meeting of a glance, or a vocal grunt. Yet the fragile quality of this relation is ever-present and the absence of such indicators may lead the observer to wonder whether "something is wrong" (35).

The interaction between the persons is not necessarily continual. It may be interrupted, broken off, resumed after a pause, and even be repeatedly broken and reestablished. The complexities of everyday situations, particularly in public places, are such that two persons are not in uninterrupted contact with each other. The observer judges that an occurrence of face-to-face interaction has terminated when one or more of the essential features is no longer present. If interaction is reestablished, then his judgment of its reestablishment involves his assumption that all elements are present. In such cases, the expectations which actors are presumed to have for each other, based on their previous experiences, make it easier for them to be seen as reestablishing their assumptions—this may occur in a flash, whereas the judgment as to whether their first act occurred may have been more difficult to make.

In everyday situations, as Goffman notes, "ceremonies of entrance and departure are often employed as are signs acknowledging the initiation or termination of the encounter," which, to the extent that the observer shares the same stock of knowledge and system of relevances, enable him to more easily judge the beginnings and endings of an encounter.

It should be emphasized that to the degree that the observer and the actors share a common cultural perspective, their judgments about the presence or absence of face-to-face interaction are likely to be identical. However, it cannot be *assumed* that this is the case. There is a possibility that from their different perspectives, different judgments will result. For example, the observer may determine that Ego and Other are close enough to be aware of each other, although Ego, hampered by a vision problem, may not yet be aware of Other.

As they remain together and generate a series of acts, they are able to develop the richness of information flow and feedback to which Goffman refers, and enter the concrete we-relation which has been characterized by Schutz as follows:

. . . in the face-to-face situation you and I grow older together, and I can add to my expectation of what you are going to do, the actual sight of you making up your mind, and then of your action itself in all its constituent phases. During all this time we are aware of each other's stream of consciousness as contemporaneous with our own; we share a rich, concrete we-relation without any need to reflect on it. In a flash I see your whole plan and its execution in action. The episode of my biography is full of continuous lived experiences of you grasped within the we-relation; meanwhile, you are experiencing me in the same way, and I am aware of the fact (p. 172).

Schutz is correct in his analysis that the two partners must be involved in social interaction in a face-to-face situation in order for a we-relation to develop, but it does not follow that all such instances result in a we-relation characterized by the richness he describes. It appears from our analysis that additional requirements for the we-relation are a temporal continuity or repeated reoccurrence of the face-to-face situation for the same partners and the initiation and receipt of a multiplicity of acts by each to and from the other. Similar to Goffman's notions concerning richness of information flow and facilitation of feedback, these characteristics are *made possible* by the copresence of the parties in face-to-face interaction but are not inevitably or invariably produced by mere copresence or single acts. Goffman is aware of this difference when he distinguishes between the situation of "sheer and mere copresence" which he says "involves the kind of communication that occurs when one gleans information about another person by glancing at him, if only momentarily, as he passes into and then out of one's view" (36). He called this "unfocused interaction" as opposed to "focused interaction," wherein persons openly cooperate to sustain a single focus of attention and presumably are mutually aware of one another.

Schutz expands on this and quite distinctly adds the elements of temporal duration and recurrence of acts when he notes:

. . . and when I am face-to-face with someone, my knowledge of him is increasing from moment to moment. My ideas of him undergo continuous revision as the concrete experience unfolds. For no direct social relationship is one isolated intentional act. Rather it consists of a continuous series of such acts. The orientation relationship, for instance, consists of a continuous series of intentional acts of Other-orientation, while social interaction consists in a continuous series of acts of meaning-establishment and meaning-interpretation (p. 169).

It is now apparent that the distinctions between orientation, situation, and relation are clearer in Schutz than in Goffman. For Schutz, orientation refers to an attitude on the part of the actor (e.g., an Other-orientation); situation refers to the presence or absence of others in particular ways; social interaction refers to the formulation of a project of action (e.g., an affecting-the-Other type); and relation refers to the unreflective living in the other's subjective meaning-contexts which, when reciprocated, becomes a we-relation rather than a one-sided thou-relation.

For Goffman, no concept such as orientation is explicit, though he assumes that Other is there for Ego, who, in turn, constitutes an Other for Other. His descriptions of the varieties of social situations are richer in their particulars than Schutz'; they include sheer and mere copresence, encounter, gatherings (focused and unfocused), face engagements. However, he does not use consistent terminology in referring to and distinguishing these from one another. His discussion of social interaction does not involve him in any detailed analysis of its constituent elements and he does not provide analytic distinctions between such constructs as act, social action, project-of-action, or action of affecting-the-Other type. Instead, he takes for granted that interaction is understood in its common-sense meaning.

Goffman does not elaborate on the concept of relation when referring to such matters as a single visual and cognitive focus of attention; "a mutual and preferential openness to communication"; an "eye-to-eye ecological huddle that maximizes each participant's monitoring of him"; and "a we-rationale . . . that is, a sense of the single thing that *we* are doing together at the time" (37). However, it is apparent from these quotations that he mixes characteristics of the relation (a "we-rationale") with the preconditions for interaction ("openness to communication") and with the particular modality through which conscious perception of the other may be mediated ("eye-to-eye"). The concept of consciousness is implicit in his use of terms such as "attention," "openness," "heightened mutual relevance of acts," and "monitoring," but the variety of terms which are used indicate that concepts such as intentionality and consciousness from phenomenology could provide valuable clarifications for his conceptualizations.

CONCLUSION

We can point to a number of insights that now appear to us, which may illuminate some of the concerns students of face-to-face interaction, such as Goffman, have expressed.

Face-to-face interaction may be judged to occur without the actor's using language for the purpose of communication of content or for communicating to the other an awareness of his presence. But in order for mutual awareness to occur, the *internal* use of a symbolic system of meaning, such as language, by both parties, is an absolute essential necessity.

Face-to-face interaction is seen as possible only between socialized human beings who are spatially and temporally present to one another, who are mutually aware of one another, and who make continual indications of that awareness.

They need not see, hear, or touch one another as long as at least one of their naked senses is operating and they are considered to be within sensory range of one another. This is the reason why it is not possible to specify what actual distance is necessary before interaction can occur. The range varies with the naked sense (or senses) being used, and if these senses are supplemented by mechanical or electronic aids, the physical distance can be increased greatly.

They need not be *literally* face-to-face but each must be able to orient a project of action to the other as a consciously experiencing person who is also making the same assumptions about his partner. In fact, actually being able to see the other's face or even being close enough to discern it is not an absolute essential necessity, as, for example, when one's eyes are closed. In this respect Goffman appears to have misled us by emphasizing the visual mode. The lack of vision on the part of one or both does affect the character of their interaction, but substitutions can be made for the visual, and therefore vision appears to be relatively essential but not absolutely essential.

The face-to-faceness of face-to-face interaction is thus seen to be a metaphor rather than a literal description of an essentially necessary condition. Face-to-face interaction can occur even though both parties are "faceless," not visible to each other, or turned away from each other just as they may interact in the dark without being able to clearly see one another. The probable reason for the continued use of the term "face" in the discussion of this type of interaction by so many social scientists is that it is a convenient commonsense metaphor for conveying a number of understood and taken-for-granted essentially necessary elements. That is, if two persons are face-to-face they will tend to be close enough to be mutually aware, able to interpret each other's expressive signs as indications of awareness, able to use all naked senses to full advantage, able to communicate, and able to engage in social interaction of an affecting-the-Other type. "Face-to-face" appears to be a convenient shorthand term for conveying much of what has been intuitively grasped as necessary but only a closer analysis can reveal all the features that are absolute essential necessities.

An implication of this analysis is that the study of variations produced by the presence or absence of each of these elements can lead to a better description and understanding of the variety of face-to-face interaction possibilities. In this respect, Goffman's studies already lead in this direction and it will require considerable work to elaborate the dimensions of those situations he has delineated.

In conclusion, from the observer's perspective, social interaction in the face-to-face situation, or *face-to-face interaction*, is possible only between socialized human beings who may or may not communicate with the same language but who necessarily have language and who use some sign or symbol system to communicate with each other; who are spatially and temporally present to one another; and who are mutually aware of one another and make continual indication of that awareness. They need not see one another so long as they are within sensory range of each other and can use their naked senses. They need not be literally face-to-face, but each must be able to orient a project of action to the other as a conscious, experiencing other, like himself, who is also making the same assumptions about his partner in the relation and situation.

NOTES

1. Support for this study was provided by a research grant from the U.S. Public Health Service, MH 18127-01, and by the Center for Applied Social Science, the Graduate School, Boston University.

2. Alfred Schutz, *Collected Papers* Vol. I, Martinus Nijhoff, The Hague, 1962, p. 221. The most extensive discussion of this issue is to be found in Alfred Schutz, *The Phenomenology of the Social World* translated by George Walsh and Frederick Lehnert, Northwestern University Press, Evanston, Ill., 1967, pp. 139–214. (Originally published in German as *Der sinnhafte Aurfbau der sozialen Welt*, Springer-verlag, Vienna, 1932.) Unless otherwise indicated all succeeding page references to Schutz are from this latter source.

3. Walsh and Lehnert translate *wirbeziehung* as "we-relationship" while Luckmann (in Alfred Schutz, *Collected Papers*, Vol. II, Martinus Nijhoff, The Hague, 1964) translates it as "we-relation." We prefer the Luckmann translation and will use this consistently throughout.

4. Goffman's works which have been examined for this purpose are: *Behavior in Public Places: Notes on the Social Organization of Gatherings*, Free Press of Glencoe, Macmillan, New York, 1963; *Encounters: Two Studies in the Sociology of Interaction*, Bobbs-Merrill, Indianapolis, 1961; *Interaction Ritual: Essays on Face-to-Face Behavior*, Doubleday and Co., Garden City, N.Y., 1967; *Strategic Interaction*, University of Pennsylvania Press, Philadelphia, 1969; and *Relations in Public: Microstudies of the Public Order*, Basic Books, New York, 1971.

5. Goffman, *Strategic Interaction, op. cit.*, p. ix.

6. Goffman, *Interaction Ritual, op. cit.*, p. 3.

7. Goffman, *Behavior in Public Places, op. cit.*, p. 15, 17.

8. *Ibid*, p. 16.

9. *Ibid*.

10. Goffman, *Encounters, op. cit.*, pp. 17–18.

11. Goffman, *The Presentation of Self in Everyday Life*, Doubleday, Garden City, N.Y., 1959, p. 15. Here he states that the term "encounter" would do as well for referring to face-to-face interaction occurring "when a given set of individuals are in one another's continuous presence."

12. Goffman, *Behavior in Public Places, op. cit.*, p. 89.

13. *Ibid*, p. 91.

14. *Ibid*, p. 16, 17.

15. Peter Berger and Thomas Luckmann, *The Social Construction of Reality*, Doubleday Anchor, Garden City, N.Y., 1967, p. 1.

16. Herbert Spiegelberg, "The Essentials of the Phenomenological Method," in *The Phenomenological Movement*, Martinus Nijhoff, The Hague, 1965, pp. 676 ff.

17. For present purposes, we have restricted our analysis to two actors. Although the addition of others may affect whether all or only some of the persons must show the features analyzed, we do not expect that the features themselves will be changed. Waksler has considered the problem of the actor's perspective more extensively in her dissertation, *The Essential Structure of Face-to-Face Interaction: A Phenomenological Analysis*, Boston University, 1973.

18. As used here, Ego is the impersonal "one" and does not refer to any psychological aspects of self.

19. Edmund Husserl, *Ideas: General Introduction to Pure Phenomenology*, translated by W. R. Boyce Gibson, Collier-Macmillan, New York, 1962. (First published in German, 1913.)

20. Rolf Kjolseth, "Making Sense: Natural Language and Shared Knowledge," in J. Fishman, *Advances in the Sociology of Language*, Vol. 2, Mouton, The Hague, 1972.

21. Alfred Schutz, *Collected Papers*, Vol. I, Martinus Nijhoff, The Hague, 1962, p. 208.

22. Harold Garfinkel, *Studies in Ethnomethodology*, Prentice-Hall, Englewood Cliffs, N.J., 1967, pp. 35–36.

23. Schutz, *The Phenomenology of the Social World, op. cit.*, pp. 144–145.

24. Goffman, *Behavior in Public Places, op. cit.*, p. 17.

25. Schutz, *op. cit.*, p. 163.

26. There is no physical distance which can be specified as an upper limit for copresence to occur other than that the observer must believe the persons to be within sensory range of each other. One or more of the "naked" senses must be capable of keeping the participants within the field, which is the range within which those senses that are being used nakedly can operate. The naked senses each have a different range, the visual extending further than the auditory, tactile, olfactory, or gustatory.

If we examine each sense separately, and here we speak of the ability to both send and receive information via that sensory modality, we find at least five senses, each with different characteristics that can affect interaction in the face-to-face situation. Addressing ourselves first to the matter of awareness of the other through the senses (sensory awareness), we find that mutual awareness of the other's bodily presence is possible with any one of the naked senses used separately.

These five senses could occur in various combinations of two, three, or four at a time as well as the "normal" circumstances of all at a time. Various possible combinations present relative essential necessities since the character of interaction can be fundamentally altered. Insofar as mutual awareness is concerned, the use of those senses whose spatial range is restricted, for example, olfactory, gustatory, and tactile, requires a reduction in the physical distance separating the two persons to bring them to "arm's length" for the tactile sense, "tongue's length" for the gustatory sense, and some unspecified "nose range" for the olfactory sense. A phenomenology of the senses as well as ethnographic descriptions would provide much needed data here.

27. It is only when Ego becomes aware of Other that copresence exists for him. And similarly for Other. Thus Ego and Other may be judged by an observer to be copresent when, from their perspectives, they are not yet aware of each other's body. This discrepancy indicates the importance of distinguishing between the observer's and the actor's perspective.

28. Schutz, *op. cit.*, p. 163.

29. Goffman comes close to making a similar analysis of mutual awareness when he defines the "full conditions of co-presence" as: "persons must sense that they are close enough to be perceived in whatever they are doing, including their experiencing of others, and close enough to be perceived in this sensing of being perceived" (*Behavior in Public Places, op. cit.*, p. 17). The matter of how close is close enough for copresence to occur is also left open by Goffman as we ourselves have done since it depends on (a) the sense modality being utilized, (b) the presence of obstructions, and (c) the assumptions made by the observer. Since these factors cannot all be specified in advance in any empirical instance, we prefer to say that the range of physical distance within which awareness can occur is that within which it is essentially possible for it to occur given the operation of the naked senses for both persons and the assumptions they make about such operations.

30. Donald Westlake, *The Spy in the Ointment*, Random House, New York, 1966, p. 131.

31. Schutz, *op. cit.*, p. 163.

32. *Ibid.*, p. 147.

33. It is quite possible, as in strategic interaction, that one actor has not intended an act but his expressions are interpreted as being intended. As should be apparent in this analysis, if one assigns such a meaning, he has attributed to the other some of those features which are necessary for him to judge that the other is interacting with him; thus the possibility of misjudged slights and affronts as well as judgments of concealment, deception, or intended ignoring.

34. Schutz, *op. cit.*, p. 162.

35. Further discussion is needed of those instances where there is delayed feedback, that is, where Other's return message is delayed sufficiently long such that Ego is not certain whether his first message was received or not. Ego may continue to transmit messages (as in a ship's continued signaling SOS without knowledge of the receipt of the message by any-

one). If Ego waits to hear from Other before transmitting another message, then he may be said to be in a state of "waiting" rather than "interacting." This does not preclude the possibility that Ego will assign meaning to Other's nonresponse (e.g., "he's waiting for more information" or "he's really thinking about what I said") and continue. Ego may proceed to interpret total silence as meaningful and even respond to what he thinks Other's nonresponse means, that is, treat it as an intentional communication. (Cf. Peter McHugh, *Defining the Situation*, Bobbs-Merrill, Indianapolis, 1968.)

36. Goffman, *Behavior in Public Places, op. cit.*, p. 24.
37. Goffman, *Encounters, op. cit.*, pp. 17–18.

»»»»»»»»»»»»»»»»»»»»»»« « «« «« «« «« «« «« «« «« «« «« «« «« «« ««

In this paper, the analysis of interaction is carried into a study of court-ship as a good time. The theoretical significance of courtship is shown to be considerable when good times are opposed to bad times or social problems. The members themselves define what a good time is and this is not necessarily the same as leisure time.

From such a perspective the phenomenological approach can be seen to illuminate the study of work, leisure, social problems, and good times, revealing each to be different and each showing facets of the social dimension of man.

Blumenstiel is not concerned with analyzing the experience of "we" (Spiegelberg) or the features of the face-to-face relationship (Psathas and Waksler) that are necessary to good times. His analysis shows how the phenomenological approach can be applied to the larger social issues which Wagner argues is possible, such as those of social problems and good times. The conceptualization of good times proposes to add a major theoretical area of study to sociology—a much needed relief perhaps from the preoccupation with problems.

THE SOCIOLOGY OF GOOD TIMES (1)

»» »» »» »» »» »» »» »» »» »» »» »» »» »» «

Alexander D. Blumenstiel

Boston University

During the course of Western civilization there has long been a tendency to describe things dichotomously. We are familiar with this both as a mode of intellectual reflection on life and as a general organization of consciousness which structures many levels of reality. For example, the Bible, of enormous significance as a theological, intellectual, moral, and popular document, one of the central literary artifacts of our society, presents basic dichotomies as fundamental realities: good and evil, for instance. People do not have to have scholarly and intellectual interest in learning these and other dichotomies. They are beliefs that are socially pervasive ways of thinking, of structuring the reality of life, and particularly of human interaction. Thus good and evil are deeply imbedded in Western consciousness as alternative interpretations of acts, of personalities, of groups, and of nations.

Today, many like to think that dichotomies such as good and evil have been replaced by more enlightened ways of thinking; that at least the social scientifically informed have a more relativistic point of view. However, as I intend to show in the following pages, there is no getting away from dichotomies. In fact, the relativistic viewpoint is itself dependent on them. For example, in my own field of sociology, the dichotomous evaluation of human behavior is a pervasive theme. Examples appear in the anomie theory of deviance and the labeling theory of deviance, supposedly one of the more sophisticated.

It seems to me, in fact, that the dichotomous foundation of our consciousness is a rather enlightened way of thinking in any case. And I question the need to get away from it and to become supposedly more "liberal." Every liberalism, in the final analysis, turns out to be dichotomously based. For the liberal, the conservative is the evil. It is simply hard to get away from good and evil.

The Questions

The sociology of good times asks: How is the consciousness of everyday life constructed in such a way that Good, as well as Evil, is a possibility? And it also asks: What are the intellectual, ethical, and sociological foundations of good as an interpretation of everyday acts? However, by addressing itself to the question of good, it necessarily must confront evil. The one, so it seems, does not make sense without the other. Of course, were the meanings of these terms clear and their relationship to each other obvious there would be no need for most of literature.

Approaches

In my efforts to answer these questions I have taken two approaches. I have analyzed the meanings of concepts in Classical Greek and Hebrew writings toward the end of formulating an intellectual basis for what I call a *general suggestive definition* of good times, which I see as the product of work not yet completed and as a suggestive basis for a discipline of the sociology of good times. In this essay I present materials prepared by way of a second kind of approach. Specifically, these are empirical treatments of particular contemporary good times—here courtship.

My work on the analysis of concepts found in ancient writings has influenced this essay, however. It led me to explicate the ways in which some of the theories of social problems offer a sociological perspective in which human behavior is dominantly interpreted in terms of evil. I suggest that the sociology of good times interprets human behavior dominantly in terms of good and offer the example of an analysis of courtship from this perspective.

The Goal

The goal of any disciplinary effort in the sociology of good times, and my purpose in writing this essay, is not the achievement of scientific explanation. Rather, work in this area should be evaluated in terms of the extent to which it provides for a clearer understanding of our daily lives and the structure of our social consciousness as members of this society. Because of this, my method is not "scientific" but phenomenological.

What is Phenomenology?

Phenomenology is, essentially, the trick of making things whose meanings seem clear meaningless and then discovering what they mean. By doing this we reveal meanings that are not actually apparent to the uncritical mind but which nonetheless are present at some other level of consciousness. The goal of a phenomenological analysis is to describe what the total, systematic meanings of social events are to people who participate in them. Thus it describes the "reality" of events in terms of the frames of mind of participants.

Phenomenological methods are becoming respectable in sociology and, for the purposes of this study, I think that they serve better than others. Good times are, at any rate, frames of mind. Applied to the study of historical materials, phenomenology reveals general suggestive definitions. Applied to contemporary situations, it describes the meanings of those situations in terms of how participants see them.

Although phenomenological analysis is the method used in studies, the presentations of actual good times will frequently not include the details of that analysis. Rather than detailing all of the particulars of what sometimes seem rather picayune points, they are put together in more general form for purposes of presentation.

Which Contemporary Situations

Contemporary situations I have studied include zoos, parks, resorts, playgrounds, movie theaters, marijuana smoking, courtship, and sensitivity training. These are situations which I and my students have researched. Although for the most part they were selected as researchable situations of good times before any historical study was done toward the end of formulating a general suggestive definition, they were and remain situations which we, as members of this society, intuitively selected as situations of good times for ourselves and assumed that they are for other members as well. For instance, I personally selected courtship and zoos as researchable situations of good times. I personally enjoy going to zoos. So does my wife. So do millions of other people. The same with parks. There have been resorts that I have enjoyed going to. My daughter, now four years old, certainly has good times at playgrounds. When I was single, I really liked courtship. Some games I enjoy, some I don't. I like going to the movies—any movie. Marijuana smoking, well, . . . Sensitivity training: I spent a lot of time doing research on sensitivity training and have published the results. I do not regard sensitivity training as a particularly good time for me, but it is a good time for many other people.

The same kind of list can be compiled for everyone. Except perhaps for the dyed-in-the-wool pessimist, there are some good times for everyone. I assume that even the good times just listed are appreciated by more people than myself and my family and students. In any case, since we are asking theoretical questions and performing phenomenological analysis, in a strict sense it does not matter just how many people regard any one situation as a good time. If one person regards one situation as a good time, and we can find out why, that is a study. Of course, the more people who consider any one situation a good time, the more people will find a study of that situation interesting.

Identifying Situations by Observing Labeling

To identify empirical instances of such good times, we listened for people to apply certain labels before, during, and/or after they participated in a situation. Situations of good times are those, operationally defined, which we heard being talked about as good times. We heard people say, for example, that they were, "Having a good time." Or they bid each other to "Have a good time." They said that they "Had a good time." Of course, there were other labels as well. "Isn't this great!" would serve if accompanied by gestures which indicated it was being offered as a label for the situation. The jovial *"bon voyage"* is another example. In fact, such utterances upon a departure may have injunctive implications. It may be felt that, after hearing the label, the vacationers will be more likely to construct in actuality the good time that they then know they are supposed to have.

SOCIAL PROBLEMS, ANOMIE, AND EVIL

Social Problems

Because of Adam's violation of the prohibition against eating the fruit of the tree of knowledge of good and evil, he is cast out of the Garden of

Eden and forced to live a life of travail. This is the prototypical story of the end of innocence. It is an awakening of man into social consciousness, in which good and evil become interpretations of his actions.

It is similar to a current sociological notion that men may be cast out of society into a condition of deviance. That deviants are sometimes called "wise" indicates a view of deviance as a type of knowledge: The deviant, knowing both good and evil, has chosen the latter. The rubric of intentionality in our juridical philosophy is supposed to insure that only the *guilty* are punished and that the *innocent* go free. "Knowledge of right and wrong" (good and evil) and some awareness of the consequences of acts are two criteria.

The general range of issues relating to this kind of casting out are, in the discipline of sociology, called "social problems." The concept of social problems implies that society is a Garden of Eden from which deviants have been cast. Research on social problems has come to dominate a significant scope of current sociological inquiry. An ameliorative pathos helps to sell studies of social problems to those institutions and agencies that fund sociological research. If only they could be solved, society and the quality of life would be better. A common view of progress is that the final solution of all social problems would herald the utopian age. On the other hand, with this ameliorative pathos, deviance and other social problems have also long been considered inevitable and even necessary evils. One explanation is that they are necessary in order to support those institutions, agencies, and people whose function it is to study and to attempt to ameliorate them.

In this section, we will briefly review some of the major theories in the field of the study of social problems. The review has two purposes: first, to present some of the major theoretical currents in an area of sociological study which seems to be the opposite of the one offered; and second, to reveal some of the implied definitions of good and evil in these theories and thus in current thinking on social problems. It also happens that these theories have general implications for doing general sociology which have influenced my thoughts on good times. The implications will be noted.

I think that the study of social problems has generally been conducive to a rather pessimistic mood in sociology. That funding is largely confined to that area seems to have the effect of making the pessimists optimistic. There has been heavy support of studies of deviance, alcoholism, drug addiction, unwed motherhood, poverty, and all of the other nasty facts of life. Recently, in fact, there was a rush on drug monies. People who thought their respectability as professionals rested upon the size of their budgets got the word that "Washington" was interested in that area. Prisons are another popular institution today for the money seekers. I do not think that the research performed on these problems has much, if any ameliorative effect. I welcome any attempt to prove otherwise. And, if anything, perhaps the intensification of concern with these issues, the legitimation of them as facts of life, might be conducive to their permanence as troubles which so many suffer.

Anomie

The term *anomie* was introduced into popular sociology by Emile Durkheim. Durkheim, a French professor of education, is considered a "classical" sociologist. According to him, anomie is a condition in which the norms of society do not have a controlling effect upon the individual. For example, when there is a high incidence of divorce, the control of the family on the individual is weakened. Durkheim considered this to be a fairly intolerable condition. Because of it, he claimed, there was a likely increase in the suicide rate. Durkheim also thought that the social and psychological integrity of the individual depend upon integration into society and everyday acceptance of its dictates. Anomie, since it disrupts social solidarity, is an evil. He also thought it to be more prevalent in the more industrially advanced societies.

While Durkheim defines anomie as "normlessness" (the usual translation of the term), as a gap in the force of society over the individual, there is another significant meaning. By outside of the norms the term implies that the individual is detached and, in fact, in an objective position vis-à-vis social controls. The rules become objective knowledge, rather than internal constraints to which he reacts automatically. He cannot simply follow the habits of his normal life. He becomes aware that society exists outside of himself. He sees himself as an independent actor who must make choices between objectively equivalent alternatives. He is, in other words, in a situation of "knowledge."

A slightly different definition of anomie is offered in the anomie theory of deviance presented by Robert K. Merton. In that theory, anomie is a condition in which the goals and the norms of a society are discrepant. This means, essentially, that an individual with socially conditioned needs cannot satisfy them if he conforms to the prescribed ways of behaving. Anomie is here also a situation of tension in which the individual must make a choice. According to Merton, there are seven possible resolutions of anomie: deviance, ritualism, rebellion, revolution, conformity, suppression, and innovation. All of these in one way or another are social problems. A resolution of anomie that does not entail a social problem does not seem to exist, as far as the theory is concerned.

For both Durkheim and Merton, anomie is an underlying condition, resolved in a number of ways, all of them involving some form of social problem. Since they see anomie as inevitable in a complex society, social problems are inevitable as well. In any case, it is because of anomie that men do evil.

The dichotomous implication of the anomie theory of deviance is that there is a condition of anomie or there is a condition of social solidarity. Social solidarity is considered good and anomie and its consequent social problems are considered evil, regardless of whatever functional necessities they are seen as fulfilling.

Labeling Theory

There is another theory of deviance. Its author, Howard S. Becker, a leader in the field of the study of social problems, is one of the more brilliant and original contributors to contemporary sociological theory. Essentially, labeling theory holds that deviance and other social problems are produced through a process of designating who is deviant and who is not. Adjudication, for example, is seen as a system of labeling the deviant and thus as "causing" deviance. It is saying that the punishment creates the crime. Becker's best known work on deviance is his book *Outsiders* (2). There he reports on two studies: one of jazz musicians and the other of marijuana use. Jazz musicians are also heavy marijuana users. From the perspective of jazz musicians the public is an aggregate of naive outsiders, while the musicians regard themselves as insiders "in the know." However, as far as the public is concerned, the musicians are the outsiders and, in fact, are considered somewhat shady characters, either deviant or on the borderline of deviance. This reciprocity of labeling creates the categories of deviant and normal and constructs the reality of these as types of persons. The "deviant" is a result of such designations by both insiders and outsiders.

On the surface, Becker's labeling theory essentially defines social problems as political phenomena. It dismisses the concept of anomie as describing an underlying cause. Labeling theory presents both deviants and normals as members of society. They are merely members of different groups within the society. From the perspective of each, the other is an outsider. Normals may be ignorant about the life style and social solidarity of some group of deviants and of the support given the individual by his fellows. They may be ignorant about the process whereby the deviant has learned to be deviant and has come to achieve the acceptance of others like himself. Because of their ignorance, normals may believe deviants to be anomic when, in fact, the deviant is not anomic at all. Since they are mostly middle-class normals, it follows that sociologists also wrongly see deviants as anomic. Of course, deviants may believe so-called "normals" to be anomic members of mass society. Each sees the other as being an outsider.

One implication of Becker's work is that should insiders and outsiders come to understand each other, social problems would be no more. Whether he thinks so or not, there is this utopian implication to labeling theory. But, I am sure, Becker would agree that this might be all right when dealing with jazz musicians and marijuana users, who are rather harmless for the most part. I doubt the efficacy of the approach as the sole method for dealing with violent crimes against persons. In fact the utopian implication of labeling theory somewhat weakens one of the criticisms of Becker. Alvin W. Gouldner claims that Becker works for the Establishment because he writes about deviants (3). The Establishment supposedly uses his work to formulate policies that punish the deviants. Gouldner also criticizes Becker for making gain from others' misfortunes. Becker, according to Gouldner, exploits the miserable and the lowly. However, if Becker is pleading for understanding of the dynamics of the labeling process and for the legitimacy of different life styles, the criticism is unjust.

In one respect labeling theory is remarkably reminiscent of the anomie theory which it supposedly dismisses. Both the labeling of insiders by outsiders and of outsiders by insiders, and their mutual misunderstanding of the validity of each other's life styles and in-group legitimacy, result in social problems. It is the labeling that places each group outside as far as the other is concerned. In other words, social detachment is inherent in the very term "outsider." Outsiders are detached from membership in the so-labeled group of insiders. As I said earlier, detachment is the essence of anomie. Thus any member of any group is anomic as far as his membership in some other group is concerned. Following labeling theory, labeling creates detachment (or anomie), which is then sustained by intergroup misunderstandings. Further, the creation by deviants of their own groups and subsocieties is a solution to their anomie in facing groups to which they do not belong—such as the Establishment. And labeling —which is knowledge of both the name of the other group and of methods to identify people as being outsiders (members of the other group) —creates anomie much as do the discrepancies of Merton's theory.

The implicit notion of good in labeling theory is membership, understanding, tolerance, and variety. The evil is labeling, misunderstanding, violence, intolerance, and suppression. Another dichotomy is the distinction between outsiders and insiders, which sometimes seems to be the good guys versus the bad guys, and which is which depends on whose side you are on. Moreover, regardless of *Outsiders* usually being advertised as a social problems book, I think that Becker is a scholar with good times at heart (marijuana and jazz!).

Differential Association

Edwin Sutherland's theory of differential association explains that people become deviant because they associate with deviants. It is a matter of socialization. Sutherland does not explicate a connection between association, anomie, and labeling. However, a relationship can be claimed to exist.

Socialization means the training of individuals to be members of a society. Differential association means that some persons receive more training to be members of deviant subsocieties than they do to be members of the society of the upright. The result of socialization is membership, which is the antithesis of anomie. Furthermore, to be socialized into becoming a member of a deviant group means that one is considered an outsider by normals.

Differential association theory stresses that people learn how to be deviant. Deviance is a matter of association and of knowledge, with the latter dependent upon the former. It is clear that Sutherland considers deviance an evil and that to learn how to be deviant by associating with deviants is equally evil. Stopping social problems, according to this theory, simply entails insuring that children do not associate with evil men and that they do receive a good upbringing.

Drift

In his fascinating book *Delinquincy and Drift* (4), David Matza formulates one of the more learned theories of deviance. According to Matza, boys become delinquent by participating in situations in which delinquency is a possible outcome of will. The situation provides the "mood" for the act. They "drift" into delinquency by becoming involved in such situations. A complex combination of labeling, legal definitions, individual motivations, group expectations, pressures, and support comprise each situation of drift.

Unlike the other theories, Matza's shows how a total set of social circumstances make up a situation in which individuals decide to commit delinquent acts. He claims that delinquent boys are not consistently delinquent, in the sense that they are committed to and engage in delinquent careers, for the most part. Thus, although delinquency is often committed in "company" with others, the delinquent has not become a member of a delinquent subsociety rather than of the wider society, as Sutherland's and other "delinquent subculture" theories would lead us to believe. Neither does Matza claim that deviance is the result of an underlying anomie. And, although labeling is one aspect of the situation, the delinquent boy himself considers the alternatives and does commit a delinquent act. The act is a reality.

To understand deviance one has to analyze the complex of events that provide conditions for people to commit legally reprehensible acts and under which they do, indeed, commit and may be apprehended and prosecuted for committing those acts. Deviance is "willful" in the sense that the act itself is the result of a decision. That decision has moral implications both before and after the act is committed, for the deviant as well as for others involved.

One of the conditions that create the mood for a drift into delinquency is peer group pressure—when, for example, boys in a group taunt and dare members of the group to commit an act. Regardless of the lack of seriousness of such talk, the act may result. None of the boys may be serious in proposing that one or more of them actually do something illegal, yet such an act may result from their talk. Typically, the delinquency may occur when one of them feels his status threatened or, in need of accepting a dare, attempts to prove himself. That act may be considered illegal by the boys and, if they are caught, by members of the community, including police, courts, parents, and school officials. Then the boys achieve a "record" and are labeled delinquents.

The delinquent act is subject to moral interpretation, like other action. Unlike other action, perhaps, it is performed as the result of an unintentionally created and fatalistic situation of drift. It resolves the drift by stopping the talk. It ends fatalism by being an adventure. Action is tension-resolving, usually bold and exciting. It is not routine behavior, but a special episode. It throws the individual into spontaneity and makes him seem psychologically penultimately real to himself.

Through action, the individual becomes truly alive. And acts which are risky enhance this. In fact, we can consider the fatalistic situation of drift anomic in the sense that in it the individual is seemingly drifting to the point at which he exercises his will by acting. The exercise of will ends the drift. The act, being willful and risky, forces the individual into total involvement in its course.

I find Matza's theory most appealing. By describing the act in a context of mood he shows that action is volitional within a context. And the other theories do not take into account the juridical literature, with its profound philosophies of ethics, morality, and intentionality, and its insights into the relationship between law, society, and action. Other types of deviance, and other social problems, could be similarly described. Perhaps this theory, with its broad existentialist implications, can serve as an analytic perspective for all human actions. For one thing, since law seems to apply as a moral framework for so many kinds of acts and since the concept of intentionality is a keystone of law, all voluntary behavior may be seen as the result of some situation of drift.

Evil, here, is one interpretation of the willful act. We can speculate that good is another plausible interpretation. It is the definition of the situation and particularly of its mood which comprises the context for such interpretations of actions. The mood of the judgment of the act after it has occurred also provides a context. Matza's theory has elements transcending delinquency, extending beyond delinquency, encompassing social problems, and going further to provide part of the basis for a general sociology, particularly a sociology of good times.

Mood, Anomie, and Evil

All of the foregoing theories describe a relationship between anomie and evil. Anomie is a situation of moral tension, in which the person is between opposites. For this reason, we speak of the anomic man as being *outside* of society. He suffers from a condition of *drift*. His eventual decision to act is willful. The act itself is the resolution of *anomie*, the ending of drift, a bursting out of the tension and the creation of reality. Another way of putting this is that the actor, through his act, creates a social fact. The prelude to his creative act is a mood of drift, anomie, and detachment. The social fact (the existential reality of his action as first a future and then an historical event) is either a good or an evil within the total context of its moral evaluation.

All of the preceding theories, essentially theories of deviance, are biased. They predict that the anomie is inevitably resolved in the commission of a deviant act. In other words, they predict that the end of anomie is evil. I cannot accept this as a general definitive framework for sociology or as an appropriate evaluation of all of social behavior. Rather, anomie is one of the factors in the development of social problems, and perhaps a major factor in the production of social action. For instance, some good times may be seen as dependent variables, with anomie as the independent variable. Anomie, in other words, might generate good times as well as social problems.

GOOD TIMES AND SOCIAL PROBLEMS

The Social Problems Pathos

For the sake of argument, let us assume that anomie can be resolved by either a good or an evil act. The act itself, described "objectively," might *be* neither good nor evil. However, the interpretation of the act by those committing it, affected by it, studying it, or attempting to promote or eliminate it is in terms of good and evil. The sociology of social problems defines most acts that resolve *anomie* as evil.

Let us further assume that the label "normal" is not usually applied to acts evaluated as evil. One reason is a consistent and staunch effort on the part of most of us to refrain from making damning general judgments of humanity. Not making such judgments, we escape anomie by making our own membership possible without intolerable moral stress. If we assume these things, it follows that normal behavior is believed to be good and abnormal behavior is believed to be evil. (The currently popular term "pathological" synthesizes the abnormal and the evil.) *This assumption underlies most studies of social problems, most social problems theories, and all efforts to ameliorate social problems.*

Assuming this, many people in the social problems trade forget that there are other possible interpretations. Since they are currently popularized by the media, the one-sidedness of their assumption has become a widespread opinion. I call it the "social problems pathos." The social problems pathos is evident where the following terms are used to describe forms of social behavior: sick, abnormal, deviant, pathological. The pathos is also evident in the scientific approach to social welfare and in all of the programs eventuating from welfarism. It is evident in the politics of rehabilitation and other ideologies that claim that by manipulating people— justified on the basis of their past behavior—society will be bettered. The pathos is particularly evident in psychiatric adjudication—as the result of which deviants are labeled "sick" and shut up in mental "hospitals."

Good Times

The metaphysic of the sociology of good times is opposite the social problems pathos. In fact, dialectically speaking, the social problems pathos is a thesis, the sociology of good times an antithesis. By offering studies of good times I intend to complete contemporary sociology, to provide the "other half" of the dialectic. I don't yet know what the synthesis is other than life.

Of course others have studied good times. Georg Simmel's essays on sociability, coquetry, and even his basic concept of formal sociology were essentially a sociology of good times. I think that in all fairness Simmel might be considered the founder of the field.

The sociology of good times refuses to accept the social problems pathos as an accurate, complete, and sufficient position. But this does not mean that the sociology of good times is polemically opposed to the sociology of social problems. True, while doing a sociology of good times we want little to do with unhappiness. That is not our problem. Any interest in misery that we might have is either for comparative purposes or because misery provides boundaries for some situations of good times, or because for some good times some participants must be miserable if the others are to have fun. But we should still recognize the validity of the study of social problems in itself. Misery is an existential reality apart from situations of good times. I do not think that the development of either type of study replaces the other. The main difference is that whereas the sociology of social problems sees anomie and its resolutions as evils, the sociology of good times sees them as good times. Although our studies do not encompass the same range of situations as do typical studies of social problems (except for marijuana use, which we treat as a good time), I do think that, following Matza, a number of the events that comprise so-called social problems probably at least in part constitute good times for participants. In fact, there might be some propensity to generally consider good times to be evil, from the puritanical point of view of the social problems pathos.

Whereas the mood of the social problems pathos (except for Becker and Matza) is pessimistic in its evaluation of the behavior encompassed by its field of study, the mood of the sociology of good times is optimistic. On the other hand, the mood of the social problems pathos is ameliorative and utopian, while the sociology of good times has neither an ameliorative nor an utopian orientation. The way I look at it, the sociology of good times does not promise to "make the world a better place to live." It is not a natural gas commercial, promoting plastic people in plastic packages run on clean fuel, never getting upset.

The purpose of the sociology of good times is to find some understanding of how good times are made by those having them and, in the process, to establish a more optimistic mood. It will enter into the consciousness, much as the miniaturized submarine in *Fantastic Voyage* (5), seeking out the *joie de vie* and plotting its course. To understand joy, to delight in the description and analysis of good times—who benefits? Well, who benefits from life?

In summary, events and situations may be seen in terms of good or evil. Both good and evil are modes of interpretation applied to events and situations. Similarly, situations may be either social problems or good times, depending on the interpretation employed and thus on the mood of the observer and the analyst. Social life in general can be seen in terms of the good times or the bad. The sociology of good times is addressed to the question of the maintenance of the reality of situations of good times, as the sociology of social problems is addressed to the question of the construction of the bad.

GOOD TIMES AND LEISURE

Good times and leisure seem compatible enough. But are they the same? Students in my classes seem to agree that you can have a good time while not being at leisure. They have said that leisure may not be a good time, or that, on the other hand, there are occasions where leisure is a good time and where a good time is also leisure.

These assertions by students led me to think of good times and leisure as different concepts. They may be two historically different points of view which stem from different philosophies and interpretations of the meaning of human happiness. It seems to me the case can be made that within the context of major philosophical and ethical systems the notion of good times is more directly connected to Judeo-Christian perspectives, whereas the notion of leisure has more to do with some basic ideas from Classical Greece. In the latter case the concept of human happiness from leisure is a Platonic idea.

Leisure and the Greek Ideal

I believe the major book to date on the sociology of leisure is Sebastian De Grazia's *Of Time, Work and Leisure* (6). Although there are many interesting lessons to be learned from this work, one has particular bearing upon this attempt to clarify the differences between leisure and good times. According to De Grazia, the major basis of the contemporary concept of leisure is the Greek term *scholis*. For the Greeks, *scholis* (the root of school, scholar, etc.) connoted a range of activities value-biased toward intellectual and artistic endeavors. These were considered the main activities and goals of the superior style of life. These aristocratically ideal activities, available to people like Plato and to other comparatively wealthy men from good families, required the participant to free himself from the mundane, bothersome routines of everyday life. Freedom of thought, talent, and the ability to create, the cultivating of intellect and understanding, were considered dependent upon time off from tedious physical labor. Unlike physical labor, athletics were considered art forms since the various exercises could be perfected in their own right.

In Plato's *Republic* (7) (the first utopian social theory), a description of the ideal social stratification system elevates those gifted in "philosophy" to purely leisure status. Their civic responsibilities rest upon their philosophical capacities and they were to devote themselves to the development of understanding of the ideal, the good, the true, and the beautiful. These philosophers were to be provided all of the basic necessities of life by a lowly hoi polloi. The latter would benefit from the relationship since the philosophers insure a higher degree of happiness for the entire population of the city by making it approximate the ideal of a city to a higher degree than it otherwise would. The application of philosophical wisdom to everyday life was to bring everyday life into closer relationship with the ideal, which is not spelled out in particularly concrete terms—except that it is the model of the republic itself. Quoting from De Grazia's book:

A man of leisure, according to Aristotle and Plato, was a man who devoted the best of himself to the state, and who believed that cultivating the mind, so important for the state, was the brightest of all activities. The single one in which man was revealed as related to the gods, and in the exercise of which he celebrated the gods. Politics and religion were at the heart of leisure. *Fun never dominated the picture.* This element, which some writers today maintain is a characteristic of leisure or free time—its mood of the anticipation of pleasure, its having-a-good-time-ness—is not a necessary part of leisure. What a man does when he does not have to do anything he does for its own sake, but he does not think of it as fun or having a good time. It may be difficult or easy, pleasant or unpleasant, and look suspiciously like hard work, but it is something he wants to do. That is all (8). (Italics mine.)

There is no necessary correspondence between good times and leisure in general, if thought of in this way. But there is a relation between the two within a specific context: within the academy. And, within that context, leisure time activities might be good times that "look suspiciously like hard work," or, at any rate, are called "hard work" by those engaged, perhaps in part to legitimate their participation in such a life. On the other hand, admittedly, such activities might actually be hard work for many.

As a matter of fact, it can be argued that considering leisure to be a higher kind of life of the mind provides the excuse for withdrawing from the daily grind and being intensely involved in what is, after all, quite an egocentric pursuit. Plato's *Republic* serves as a rhetorical legitimation of the philosopher as a man who essentially does nothing but engage in intense philosophical conversations. He is released from the tedium of daily life and permitted to enjoy an almost uninterrupted leisure life.

When, upon occasion, I have presented some of my ideas on good times to scholarly gatherings, inevitably someone says, "Well, this is a good time right now, isn't it?" The operational definition of good times forces us to take such a remark seriously and to include that situation as one of the type. For those academics intellectual discussion might very well be a good time. Also, by philosophy Plato meant intellectual dialogue—conversation. He founded the Academy as the site of such conversations. In short, leisure defined in terms of "cultivation of the mind" corresponds to good times within the context of academic life.

COURTSHIP

Courtship need not be a good time as far as everyone is concerned in order for it to qualify as a proper subject for the sociology of good times. And I didn't do surveys to find out precisely or approximately how many people do consider courtship to be a good time. I think that such surveys would, in fact, violate the basic operational definition of good times by basing them on numbers rather than on utterances.

It is undeniable that courtship is a good time in the sense of the operational definition. People refer to it as a good time. In general, it is supposed to be a good time. Realistically, of course, that may be more true of the young and the passionate than of the elderly and enervated. Woody Allen's movie "Play it Again, Sam" presents the ultimately excruciating in courting. For some people (the lucky ones perhaps), courting remains fascinating at any age. For others it is always a terrible trial.

Courtship is sometimes regarded as a kind of social problem. In a puritanically oriented milieu, the sexual proprieties—when to do what and how far to go—have provided for decades of tedious issues which advice columnists make a going trade out of. And many are the parents of adolescents turning grey over a variety of bewildering related problems.

Courtship may require a good deal of time and energy. It is most intensely engaged in by those who have little else to do: adolescents and wealthy voluptuaries. They can enjoy obsessional delight and adventure. The *bon vivant*, however, might enjoy it as a simple pastime, as a time off from other activities. In any case, it can be a source of great leisure time amusement (doing violence to the academic definition of leisure). In pornography and philosophy, leisure time and courting have been considered to go hand in hand. Søren Kierkegaard, in "The Diary of a Seducer" (9), as well as the anonymous author of "A Man with a Maid" (10) both remark on the benefits of having unlimited time to spend insuring that courting is a true "event." The voluptuary should make sure that the game, as well as the act of sex itself, can be savored to the fullest.

Why is courtship a good time? There are two hypothetical answers to this question. First, courting is a good time, perhaps, because it is a way of intensifying one's sense of involvement in life. To the degree to which it is considered an extraordinary event by those participating, it is an escape from tedium and from anomie. Second, courtship entails many interactional events which are good times. Basically, it is a relationship in which the participants often take pains to insure that it is good times. They strategically and tactically direct their interaction toward that end, though there may be other ends as well. I next describe some of the ways in which this is done.

During courtship, the courter should be devoted body and soul to the management of the affair. All of the moods, incredible joys and devastating tragedies, moments of fantastic rapport and inexplicable misunderstandings, are included in its context. As long as the final tactic in any strategy does not signal the absolute end of the relationship, the lovers are never "outsiders." Of course, as Simmel noted, the affair is the prototype of all dyads. Its very intensity is matched by ultimate fragility. Should one of the parties become disinterested, and the other be incapable of attracting him back, there is no saving grace. Then insiders become outsiders. Although the problems they had with each other were encompassed within their affair and within its context could be sources of entertainment, afterward they are left with anomie and life becomes tasteless. Until the next time.

Conceptualizing Courting as a Game

Developing a courtship entails intentional production of tensions, mysteries, and drama toward the end of participants inducing involvement. People talk about courting as a game in reference to the process of inducement. As a game, courtship is considered a relationship in which behavior can properly be rationally used; events can be directed toward a number of goals. All of them, as far as we are concerned here, involve the participants in a "good time."

Gaming

People who are gaming or, to use another expression, "making game" (a term which is synonymous with "gaming" but which emphasizes the total concept of the action as a manipulative sequence to a greater extent, which I heard in lower-class circles), often do not consider it necessary for the other to be aware that that is what they are doing. In fact, they may take pains to conceal their sophistication. The other is treated as an object which, usually with a good deal of arrogance, the gamester considers to have been created for his own pleasure. The melodramatic villain is the ideal type of this kind of character. I will refer to the characterological model of this type of involvement in courting as "the gamester."

Playing the Game

There are cases when the skilled player wishes to court someone equally skilled. Much like chess, the more equitable the capacities of the players, the more alluring the challenge. When participants are aware of each other's sophistication, they may more likely consider the strategic exchange of moves the chief source of delight. For the true sophisticate, playing with a novice can be a bore.

Playing the game, unlike gaming or making game, implies a definitely cooperative endeavor in which some respect for the other as a player of equal status, if not equal skill, is accorded. I refer to the characterological model of participants in the game as players, implying this mutuality of regard. When truly playing the game, the good time is dependent upon the awareness of both that they are so engaged with each other. Players may praise each other's skills. They may grant each other "time out." They are anything but crude. It is both an art and a science.

It frequently seems that the terminology of the game makes it out to be a zero-sum situation, in which one person wins only what the other loses. To me, the zero-sum terminology does express one stance that can be taken. By taking it, players can keep up the spirit of competition without which some of the excitement would be lost. But it seems more the expression of the gaming attitude than of playing. In zero-sum terminology we hear that the gamester wins when he believes that the other has been captivated "body and soul," or that the other is "crazy in love with" the gamester and "will do anything for him." It should be apparent, I think, that this terminology indicates at least momentary apprehension of the role of the player(s) as gamester(s) rather than as a true "player." Zero-sum politics do have this kind of depersonalizing effect, often enough. Thus to hear zero-sum terms being used, as in a stag discussion about women, might place the discussants in the position of brave and bold adventurers who are totally in command of themselves and winners at the game. But, as players, that might not be at all how they act and feel when on the field.

The Logic of Losing

We can follow through with the logic of the zero-sum terminology, just to see what a situation of courtship which eventuates in a bad time might be like. First, it can entail one of the participants coming to believe that he has kept his cool, while his partner has not—that he is now in a position of being able to "hustle" the other and that the other cannot avoid being taken advantage of. The loser might sense himself to be so involved that he cannot avoid being taken advantage of, that he is no longer an actor with a will of his own. He feels the future of the relationship and his personal destiny isomorphic, and it is bad for him. He believes he is being exploited or may be exploited or he is being exploited without really knowing in what way. Exploitation can be defined as the sense that one is subject to the will of the other in an immediately inescapable way and will comply with demands though the cost is great. Being so subjected, those who think they are losing the game also believe that they are losing their dignity.

In this situation, the so-called winner, believing the other completely in his control, can become bored. The relationship is no longer a challenge; the game is over. It is not intellectually interesting and may be physically a drag as well. At that point, it is usually said the other "gets hurt." If this situation is a phase in the relationship, however, which changes when the tables are turned, or when some fortuitous occurrence alters their feelings about each other, then the future may see its redefinition. And courting remains the good time that it is supposed to be. If the relationship ends on this note, sad to say, the whole thing, particularly the final despair, typically is remembered with remorse.

STRATEGIES AND TACTICS: HOW TO DO IT

In the sections that follow I describe strategies, tactics, and moves in the game of courtship which are inducements of involvement and thus create conditions for participants experiencing their affair as good times. This is, of course, not a complete compendium. It consists of descriptions of some of those behaviors that came to my attention during the course of doing ethnographic research on courtship and on other relational activities, through my association with the Pruitt-Igoe Project Studies in Saint Louis in 1964 when Lee Rainwater was directing that going concern, as a college student (unmarried, free, and I thought swinging those years ago), and during the course of my graduate studies and my years as a college instructor. Many of my students contributed observations and I greatly enjoyed some of the discussions during my undergraduate classes.

Admittedly, the descriptions are somewhat abstract and the particulars of physical acts are left unmentioned. This is to make some concession to academic scholarship.

The Introduction

A good courtship strategy for meeting someone is, in middle-class society, to obtain an introduction from a mutual acquaintance. Particularly when that person is a friend of both those introduced, a first-name introduction implies that they should regard each other in terms of some of the rules of friendship. They are supposed at least to grant each other a pleasant encounter in the immediate situation.

According each other respect, courtesy, and consideration whether or not it is felt to be warranted saves the mutual friend the embarrassment of having the soundness of his choice of friends blatantly considered doubtful.

It also saves him from the unpleasant duty of later defending the conduct of one to the other and from suffering humiliation by association. By greeting each other kindly, their relationships with him are protected. It is a matter of tact.

People who are cognizant of this, naturally enough, when the occasion arises can request an introduction to someone whom they wish to court, and expect at least courteous treatment which, they hope, lasts long enough for attraction to be produced.

Unlike impersonal forms of introduction, when someone introduces two of his good friends he demonstrates that he approves of both of them and this may enhance each in the eyes of the other. Such an introduction, according to Erving Goffman, "even more than acquaintance that develops informally, ought, it is felt, to have a permanent effect, placing the introduced persons forever after in a special position with regards to each other" (11).

If a friend introduces two of his friends he in part sanctions a relationship that may develop between them. People may assume that, when introduced by a mutual friend, the latter wishes they would get along well together. A person who realizes this may be reluctant to introduce those who could foreseeably court each other, particularly if he doesn't really trust one or the other of them. Should either find himself badly taken advantage of, the friend could be held in part accountable and be "badmouthed" as an associate of rascals.

Of course, a friend may find it difficult to disregard a direct request. And the consolation for taking the risk is that there is some delight in introducing people who eventually have a great romance. The mutual friend can claim some credit. And, even if not, it is interesting to watch the affair develop and to be able to gossip about it with others.

The Approach

Players can also make contact in situations where it is proper to approach others without introductions. Church socials, mixers, youth clubs, political campaign headquarters, crowded lunch counters, singles and dating bars, and, for the student, the right seat in a classroom may serve. At resorts a typical move is to sit at the same diningroom table and as close as possible to the one courted. Some people are skilled and ambitious enough to make practically any place do.

The approach typically is an intentional personal engagement of the other. It usually involves moving toward that other in such a way that he or she is made aware that an engagement is intended. This can be done by the use of flirtatious glances and/or quick smiles. These may serve as preludes to walking toward the other. Or if physical proximity has already been achieved, the same kinds of expressive behavior may serve to indicate that a symbolic proximity, if not immediate physical intimacy, is desired as well.

Casual remarks also serve. The "line" used for an approach frequently combines both verbal and gestural commentaries on the possibilities inherent in the situation being constructed. Of course, mistakes can be made. When a player "comes on too strong," he can elicit a feeling of imposition and fail to create an obligation. The other then sees him as a gamester, and forewarned is forearmed.

The approach thus entails the management of body movements and verbal responses so that the other is affected in the ways typically desired. It usually has either manifest or latent but obvious sexual implications for those concerned. A successful approach is defined as a situation in which the other is obligated to enter into and to continue interaction on this basis.

Toward the end of successfully managing the approach, persons may prepare themselves beforehand. For example, my friend and colleague Boone Hammond reported the following when he asked some lower-class Black men why they drink:

> They do not drink so much because they enjoy the taste of the alcoholic beverages, but rather for the effect that the alcohol gives . . . it made them "right," "mellow," "ready," "in shape" . . . the use of alcohol made them "high" and by virtue of being "high" made them less inhibited in their behaviors . . . increased their ability to communicate—"rap"—especially in those situations where influence and manipulative techniques are required (12).

There are several effects of the skillful approach which can establish a *quid pro quo*. The approach entails greeting the other first. In sociable gatherings some reply to a greeting is called for if one is to avoid appearing surly and boorish. The person making the approach indicates that he desires an acquaintance with the other. He is "obvious in his intentions," as it is put in ultrapolite circles. By so being, he risks the affront and embarrassment of having his approach ignored and himself rejected. He risks being at the least a momentary social outcast. The one approached may be expected to repay the approacher for taking such a risk by at least being polite to him. Also, of course, since an approach is flattering, the one so flattered owes something to the other for the compliment. Repayment, in all cases, entails being drawn into a conversation with specific developmental possibilities.

Enticement

Enticement is the art of inducing an approach. The enticer induces the other to make an approach by making herself attractive. By her (his) dress, her facial expressions, her body movements and the modulation of her voice she conveys the impression that she has a lot to give to those that approach her.

For the sophisticate enticement is not straightforward. Involved is communication of the fact that it is risky to attempt to make her acquaintance. She indicates by her manner that in spite of outward appearances there is a reservation in her mind and thus that it is possible for her to reject those who approach her. This is an element of coquetry. It is being coy.

By being promising and yet not a "sure thing" the enticer (a) enhances her value by presenting herself as available only to those who fulfill the conditions which she indicates she may have in mind, and (b) produces a situation in which those who approach her interpret their own possibilities in terms of a success or failure that is contingent upon her decision to accept them. By her manner she intimates that he who approaches her will suffer disappointment and possibly embarrassment or some other form of degradation unless she chooses to verify by her conduct that he is acceptable as a possible recipient of that which her appearance indicates he can aspire to.

If the enticement is sophisticated, the approacher enters a situation in which he knows that he could be cut or rejected—he takes a chance.

It can be argued that this is always the case. Empirically speaking, however, it is not. Those who make an approach to an unsophisticated enticer can enter a situation in which they believe that the outcome is entirely up to them.

Being enticed by a sophisticated person, one enters into a situation in which it is mutually known (he knows that she knows that he knows and so forth), that her company is a gift to be conferred only upon those whom she considers worthy. Then, if the approach is successful, the fact that he receives company and conversation when these gifts are hers to give obligates him. In effect she gives him something that he has asked for and which both consider valuable; he is then obligated to continue the conversation, momentarily overlooking inanities on her part and at least seeming to strive to overcome any difficulties she places in the path of his successfully completing the seduction that they both have in mind.

The Creation of Reciprocal Obligations

For those playing the game of courtship, enticement and the approach are, of course, complementary activities. Even more, they are activities that establish a system of reciprocity between the players. They do so by creating rights and obligations which are apparent and yet ill defined in terms of their limitations (13).

The approach creates an obligation on the part of the one approached. Enticement creates an obligation on the part of the one enticed into approaching. Since both of these are obligations to interact, given the potentially infinite boundaries of interaction, they are not easy to satisfy. After all, how does one know when enough has been done? Or, more to the point, when the last sexual encounter has occurred? The last can always be followed by another, and another, until death. And even then there may be obligations to continue a relationship.

The approach and enticement are starting mechanisms, in the sense that Ruth Leeds uses the term (14). They can be interpreted as gifts to others which initiate obligations and returns and form the basis for a relationship.

On the other hand, simply establishing such obligations is no insurance that the interaction will continue. That depends upon other inducements which the people involved offer to each other.

Impressions: The Hostile Front

One inducement that would seem more reasonably to promote just the opposite of attraction—avoidance—and hardly be the basis of a situation of good times is what I call the hostile front. This entails facial, verbal, metacommunicative, and body behavior during initial encounters which convey a generalized personality attitude of apprehensive hostility to others. The hostile front may be used to create interest, excitement, and attraction. For this reason, its forms and effects interest me.

A hostile person may think that his presentation indicates to others that he is a "person with a past," unapproachable, fascinating, and mysterious. As Saul Bellow put it in *Mr. Sammler's Planet*, "women used sometimes to act insolent to get his attention and say stinging things imagining that it made them fascinating" (15). The hostile person may have a past that he thinks actually gives him reasons for displaying hostile sentiments toward mere acquaintances. He may also think that they will consider him interesting by virtue of the story he tells when called upon to reveal whatever his reasons for being hostile are.

Those on the receiving end of a hostile front can have complementary expectations. At least, they may think, it would be interesting to discover the other's reasons for being so obviously hostile. The risk of making an approach can pay off in terms of satisfying this curiosity.

Given hostility, the risks in attempting to strike up an acquaintance may seem greater. At least those who are outwardly genial present some evidence of welcoming the attentions of others. Those who are hostile do not. Presenting hostility and expecting others to overcome the apparently intensified risk of being cut, the hostile person may also expect them to be more committed when they do make an approach. It may require a momentary greater show of nerve and output of anxious energy to approach a hostile person and the initial investment made in the relationship can thus be greater than in other cases.

On the other hand, this is certainly not necessary. Those who approach the hostile person can do so with the attitude that, in the event of a cut, there is nothing gained, but nothing lost either—given the minimal chances of success connoted by the front. Or it can be thought that the hostile person owes it to those who approach him to drop the hostility. It is they who have given him the gift. One interpretation is that the hostility is a "cover-up" for "deeper feelings" of nervousness, shyness, rejection, or whatever, and that those who approach are bothering to find out. He owes them for that.

If those who approach a hostile person interpret him as being "interesting"—if, in other words, his hostility has aroused their curiosity—any initial investment they may make in the approach they might later think paid off when he reveals reasons for hostility, thereby proving that his initial front was justified. Since he started out being hostile and this led the other to believe him interesting, he may turn out to be as interesting as was thought; first because that frame of reference is already established and second because the other would not later want to have to think that he wasted his time. The latter then considers himself indebted for having been accorded the trust and recognition of such a gem of a person.

Those players who believe a hostile front a practical strategy for courting and who, having attracted attention in this way, grant the other the favor of explaining the hostility (e.g., through some confession about a past affair which left him embittered), may consider that other obligated by virtue of this special favor. And one to whom reasons for hostility are revealed may act the part of someone who has received a valuable gift, admitting that the risk he has taken has paid off and that the other is really a worthwhile person. In fact, both the play of hostility and the revelation of reasons for it can form a little sequence of scenes which gives them both a bit of amusement.

Announcing Controlled Disclosure

Sometimes people who are courting tell each other that they have things that they are not telling each other about. I call this kind of talk announcing controlled disclosure. It means that, when suitable, the player may announce that he is controlling what he is revealing.

Consider this selection of announcements of controlled disclosure: "If I could only tell you." "Someday maybe we'll really talk." "I really can't say now." "Well . . . let me think about it for a while and then maybe I'll tell you." Frequently statements like these intimate that revelation of some kind is a distinct possibility, but that important things are not immediately apparent and are being reserved for later issue.

They may also connote that the announcer is more complex than he might appear to be, and that he can document his complexity when he chooses. He may be thought "interesting" because of this, or think he appears as such. However, he risks being considered phony and perhaps foolish.

Announcing to others that one is controlling what one reveals to them frequently implies that personal knowledge is revealed only when the audience differs in some special way from the masses. Usually the specialty is his supposed trustworthiness. Another implication is that some subsequent revelation will indicate a change in the status of the recipient —from one of the mass to someone special (someone trusted, and someone who then knows what others do not).

The trustworthiness indicated by a revelation of what has been announced as reserved may be achieved by permitting some physical intimacy. The simple sequence of the game is: (a) announcing controlled disclosure, (b) the other permits sex, and (c) some revelation. Of course, in such a simple form the moves are crude and can be disdained by those with a delicate sense of the game.

Though a game sequence describes the action, except in the case of fast workers quite a bit of time may intervene between the announcement, sex, and the revelation. In the minds of the players the eventual revelation may be only hazily connected to the other steps. On the other hand, the announcement may be intended to produce sex, the sex may be intended to produce the revelation (a kind of James Bond seduction), and the revelation may be intended as a reward for the sex. Then again, given the entire absence of such intentions during the acts, should the incidents be referred to later, intention can be claimed for one or all.

An announced reluctance to discuss some particular issue can elicit a demand by the other that it be discussed. When the discussion entails the revelation of a secret, the one revealing may find himself more committed to the relationship and obviously obligated to involve himself further. Whether the story be trite or tragic (whether, indeed, they are able at such a time to distinguish between the two), having revealed what has been announced to be disclosable only to a select few, or one, the revelation imputes trust. Those who are trusted may receive, upon demand or otherwise, more basic kinds of gifts. In sum, by revealing or listening to a revelation once controlled disclosure has been announced a greater intimacy may be achieved.

When the recipient of information has encouraged its revelation there may be a more subtle effect as well. If an announcedly hesitant person is encouraged to divulge information, the recipient of that information may find it morally difficult to reject or disparage the other on the basis of it. To encourage someone to talk about himself when he has stated that he is hesitant to do so and then to reject him on the basis of what he says may be taken at the least as intolerance and, more likely, as hypocrisy. It is, at any rate, a violation of trust.

Properly speaking the information revealed in such a situation should be accepted with at least the demonstration of understanding. Though the recipient may find it distasteful enough to feel like disrupting their relationship, since the revelation was at his urging, he may think it more justifiable to wait for some other circumstance.

This normative demand for demonstrating tolerance and understanding increases whatever investment the recipient of a revelation already has in his relationship with the revealer. Demonstrating sentiments of acceptance, finding himself in the position of one who "understands," if he subsequently denies this understanding and demonstrates intolerance, he risks being made out a liar, a traitor, a hypocrite, or a fool.

To encourage disclosure is to promise tolerance and understanding. To disclose is to elicit investment from someone who has so promised.

An announcement of controlled disclosure that elicits such a promise produces the conditions under which a revelation can increase the investment of the recipient.

And, as all gamesters know, to induce tolerance and understanding is to evoke involvement.

Cooperative Ignorance

Sometimes both participants in a courtship (and in other relationships as well) cooperate in suppressing revelation—one not asking, the other not telling. When they believe that if concealed information were revealed it would have a negative effect on their relationship, the concealed past may best not become a fact to contend with in the present.

The reciprocity implicit in such an agreement often further strengthens the bond that they sense unites them. Those in the know can strategically instigate cooperative ignorance toward that end.

CONCLUSIONS

Courtships are, after all, commonplace events. But in spite of this players experience a heightened awareness of each other and of their affair. Although they do consist of publicly trivial and commonplace events, for those involved in one, a successful courtship is a very dramatic experience, accompanied by incredibly intense emotions.

Participation in courting is rewarding in its own right. It gives one a sense of heightened involvement in life and of drama often comparable to professional staged productions and great romantic movies. It transforms the mundane and lends to the ordinary at least the illusion of the unique. And if players come to think of each other as special and of their relationship as unique in terms of the drama and intensity it provides, it becomes particularly valuable and they have incentive for carrying it further. On the other hand, like Bogart and Bergman in *Casablanca*, sometimes it's best to have a glorious ending rather than an ordinary happiness.

Players can take the assumption that romantic scenes are generally pleasurable into account and produce events intended to increase each other's involvement in the affair. In fact, seduction applies to anything in the way of a show, and not only to sex. Romance is a broad category.

They take pains to insure that moments come off in a striking manner. Confessions are handled in this way. Situational paraphernalia are used to produce dramatic atmosphere. Restaurants, gardens, amusement parks, carnivals, theaters, cocktail lounges, canoes, and gondolas are put to use to produce drama. Ambiance is offered as a delight which puts the lovers in the mood. The various preparations and body paints ritually used by American women are also frequently viewed by those on the make as makeup for playing roles in personal theatrics. Even tragedy, as in *Room at the Top*, may be a move in the game.

e. e. cummings had an interesting idea which, to me, sums up the production of good times in courting:

> love is less always than to win
> less never than alive
> less bigger than the least begin
> less littler than forgive (16).

The good times last, so it seems, when no one wins the game; when they keep on playing it for each other.

Earlier in this essay I described some social problems theories, claiming their perspective sees social behavior in terms of evil. The analysis of courtship is a counterpoint to the social problems pathos. The emphasis has been on ways in which people create good times for each other. We could employ a social problems perspective to courtship and evaluate the tricks described here as nasty business. Inducement, after all, can be seen as the purposeful creation of a sense of anomie on the part of one participant by the other. Seduction can be considered the resolution of such anomie through the acceptance of an offered action which is sinful. This possibility reminds me of a quaint dilemma. Did the bundling board ward off evil, or enhance enticement? Both. Two different moods—two different sociologies!

NOTES

1. In this work I have thus far been supported for one-third of a summer and one-sixth of a semester for my studies of good times. I am grateful to the Center for Applied Social Science and the Graduate School of Boston University for their enlightened attitudes and generosity.

2. Howard S. Becker, *Outsiders*, Free Press, New York, 1963.

3. Alvin W. Gouldner, "The Sociologist as Partisan: Sociology and the Welfare State," *The American Sociologist*, 3, (2), 1968, pp. 103–116.

4. David Matza, *Delinquency and Drift*, John Wiley and Sons, New York, 1964.

5. Isaac Asimov, *Fantastic Voyage*, Bantam Books, New York, 1966.

6. Sebastian De Grazia, *Of Time, Work and Leisure*, Doubleday, Garden City, N.Y., 1964.

7. Plato, *The Republic*, translated by W. H. D. Rouse, in *Great Dialogues of Plato*, The New American Library, New York, 1956.

8. De Grazia, *op. cit.*, p. 332.

9. Søren Kierkegaard, *Either/Or*, Vol. 1, translated by David F. Swenson and Lillian M. Swenson, Anchor Books, Doubleday and Company, Garden City, N.Y., 1944.

10. Anonymous, *A Man with a Maid*, Tarus Publications, Wilmington, Del., 1969.

11. Erving Goffman, *Behavior in Public Places*, Free Press, New York, 1963.

12. Boone Hammond, "The Contest System in Lower Class Life", unpublished manuscript.

13. Alvin W. Gouldner, "The Norm of Reciprocity: A Preliminary Statement," *American Sociological Review*, 25, April 1960, pp. 161–178 and Ruth Leeds, "Altruism and the Norm of Giving," *Merrill-Palmer Quarterly*, 9, (3) July 1963, discuss, mostly in the abstract, giving and reciprocity as starting mechanisms in social interaction.

14. Leeds, *op. cit.*
15. Saul Bellow, *Mr. Sammler's Planet*, Viking Press, New York, 1970.
16. e. e. cummings, *50 Poems*, The Universal Library, Grosset and Dunlap, New York, 1940.

»»»»»»»»»»»»»»»»»»»»»»»»»»»«««««««««««««««««««««««««

The application of a phenomenological approach to the study of the everyday functioning of a large organization provides a different perspective on the presumably role-determined behavior of the members. The shifting and emergent character of even stable organizations becomes more apparent.

Yet Jehenson's study is largely conceptual and illustrative of how the social phenomenology of Schutz may be applied to research on the formal organization. More than any of the other applied studies in this book, this one approaches the task by first elaborating those concepts that may prove useful in research, showing by examples how they may be applied, and then developing new insights. Jehenson differs from Blumenstiel by first providing a comprehensive theoretical conceptual clarification. Where Manning and Fabrega are concerned with the content of the typifications members of a different society have regarding health and illness, Jehenson is instead attentive to the significance of alternative typificatory schemes for understanding how members of different professions, or lifeworlds within the same society, may interpret the same events. Thus perspectives in a life-world are seen to be "perceptive spheres" related to specialized training or perhaps subuniverses of social knowledge. As Berger and Luckmann would argue, the knowledge with which members operate in society, the epistemic community they share, is the foundation of the social world they construct.

A PHENOMENOLOGICAL APPROACH
TO THE STUDY OF THE
FORMAL ORGANIZATION

»»»»»»»»»»»»»»»»»»»»»»«««««««««««««««««««««««

Roger Jehenson

University of New Mexico

Organizational analysts frequently have been inclined to define the scope of their study as the investigation of specific and unique behaviors present when people act within organizational roles. This tendency to reduce the field of organizational theory to the study of "organizational behavior" has met with opposing reactions. An alternative preferred by social phenomenologists was recently suggested by Weick: "Rather than search for unique behaviors that occur within an organization and then build a theory about this uniqueness," he explains, "it seems more useful to build theories about the particular ways that enduring individual dispositions are expressed in an organizational setting and about the effects of this expression. (1). Indeed, for the social phenomenologist, the most characteristic and enduring individual disposition of human beings has to do with the fact that they live in a reality built out of their subjective interpretation, a "reality within the horizon of human interpretation and experience" (2).

The phenomenological approach to the study of a formal organization implies, then, that the attention of the researcher be focused not on specific organizational behavior but on the way organizational members interpret their own organizational world, which is nothing else than a special sphere of the individual's *Lebenswelt* or life-world. The phenomenological concept of life-world refers to the fact that in any real-life experience there is something that is pregiven, something that is there in advance, taken for granted, passively received by consciousness. This taken-for-granted world includes our cultural world and whatever prejudices and typical interpretations may derive from it (3). Acting as a member of an organization, therefore, does not differ essentially from acting as an individual, for "whether we happen to act alone or, cooperating with others, engage in common pursuits, the things and objects with which we are confronted as well as our plans and designs, finally the world as a whole, appear to us in the light of beliefs, opinions, conceptions, certainties, etc., that prevail in the community to which we belong" (4). Alfred Schutz has described an important characteristic of this experience as its organization into typical forms: "The individual's commonsense knowledge of the world is a system of constructs of its typicality" (5). And Natanson elaborates: "The typical is a deeply rooted feature of the very organization of experience into knowledge. From the very outset of the epistemological process, the world is constituted in typified form. The natural standpoint is a locus of typification" (6).

In this study, I would like to show how Schutz' social phenomenology can be applied to a formal organization, and how the theory of typification can be utilized to describe the cognitive prestructurization of organizational members' worlds. I shall show how this prestructurization is realized by typifications having their source either in the official organizational system or in the individual's own stock of knowledge at hand.

THE TYPIFICATIONS OF MAN IN THE NATURAL ATTITUDE

As a point of departure, a brief description of Schutz' view of the role of typifications in the social world experience will reiterate concepts already known to my readers but necessary if my practical application of them is to be demonstrated. These are: the distinctions between consociates and contemporaries; concrete personal types and abstract course-of-action types; the concept of the problem-relevance of the typification; the role of face-to-face interactions in the transformation of typifying schemes; and the social and cultural determination of the system of relevances and typifications. When examples are used to illustrate these processes, they will be taken from my field of observation, a psychiatric hospital.

The first point to be noted is that for Schutz the social world is from the outset experienced as intersubjective. As an actor on the social scene, I can recognize my fellow-man not as a "something," but as a "someone," a "someone like me." "I am already Thou-oriented from the moment that I recognize an entity which I directly experience as a fellow-man (as a Thou) attributing life and consciousness to him" (7). When the thou-orientation is reciprocal, that is, if each actor is thou-oriented toward the other, there is a face-to-face relationship, a relationship in which the partners are aware of each other and sympathetically participate in each other's lives for however short a time. This face-to-face relationship or relationship among *consociates* is thus experienced as a pure we-relationship concretized and actualized to a greater or lesser degree. Indeed, the face-to-face relationship, or the pure we-relationship, is a limiting concept, an "ideal limit." In real life, we do not experience the "pure existence" of others, we are not directed toward the pure being of another living and conscious human being, but we meet real people with their own personal characteristics and traits.

Most of the people with whom I relate, and everybody at times, are not my consociates, but my *contemporaries:* I am not involved in face-to-face relationships with them; I do not grasp them as unique individuals. My relationships with my contemporaries are characterized by the fact that I experience only their *typical* behavior, their *typical* pattern of motives and attitudes in increasing anonymity. The last point bears emphasis. In the face-to-face relationship of *consociates*, the partners share a community of space as well as a community of time. In this relationship the fellow-man is grasped as a unique individual in his unique biographical situation. In the relationship between *contemporaries*, on the other hand, the self of the partner is apprehended only by forming a construct of a typical way of behavior, a typical pattern of motives, and of attitudes of personality type.

These typifications depend on the actor's stock of knowledge at hand and his biographical situation. If the typifying scheme has been derived from firsthand direct experience of a fellow-man, we have what Schutz calls a "characterological (or subjective) personal type." A more anonymous and less concrete typifying scheme is the functional or "course-of-action type," which refers to contemporaries only with respect to their typical functions. It is clear that two organizational actors are not likely to have identical typifying schemes of the same co-worker. For example, the course-of-action type the director of a hospital has of a nurse may be so anonymous that it refers only to the behavior of "whoever" is acting in the way defined as typical by the construct. On the other hand, the chief nurse forms a more personal type of the same person.

Another point needs to be stressed at this time. Typification consists of the equalization of traits relevant to the particular purpose at hand for the sake of which the type has been formed; any individual differences not relevant to this purpose are disregarded. Because of the *problem-relevance* of the typification, different types of the same concrete individual can be formed, dependent on the situationally determined interest. For example, commenting on the performance of his clinical director after a conference, a psychiatrist perceives him as a "skillful diagnostician." After a meeting where the clinical director has presented drastic plans for the reorganization of the hospital, the same psychiatrist now typifies him as a "heartless computer." All social relationships with *contemporaries* are thus relationships with typified individuals to whom a certain role is assigned. The more anonymous the type, the more these individuals appear exclusively in the light of the functions they are expected to perform in typical ways.

Even in face-to-face relationships, I apprehend the other by means of typifying schemes. I apprehend him as a "man," a "Jew," a "psychiatrist," and so on. In these relationships, however, the other's course-of-action can be experienced in immediacy. His motives, insofar as they are manifest, are known immediately. His person, insofar as it is involved in the manifest action, is directly apprehended. For these reasons, the typifying scheme will show a high degree of concreteness. Moreover, the types used in face-to-face interaction are confronted with the other's subjectivity and, so to speak, tested. If they fail the test, that is, if the types are contradicted by the immediate experience, then they have to be modified. For example, I approach a senior psychiatrist with the type of an "austere, aloof scholar." After our face-to-face interaction, I leave him with the type of a "truly human person."

The typifying scheme may be transferred even in the case of "unfocused interaction" (8) in the absence of any verbal exchange. A case in point: while I am observing the clinical director's meeting with the director of the hospital, I see that the latter scrutinizes my reaction as he is about to make a policy statement. As a result of this simple gesture, my type of him as a "self-confident clinician executive" is modified, and I begin to form of him another type, that of a "self-conscious manager concerned about his administrative skills."

The process of typifying others so far described has its counterpart in a process of *self-typification*. I must typify myself, that is, assume a typical role and perform it in the way I assume my partner expects me to perform it. For instance, while asking the new director of the hospital for the authorization to do research in his institution, I had to conduct myself in the way the typical director expects the typical candidate-researcher to behave. My self-typification was naturally influenced by my own biographical situation (my age, my European culture, the feeling of being "legitimized" in the system where I had already conducted research for nine months, etc.). The director, on his part, typified me on the basis of an abstract functional type, seeing me as "a student who has to submit a detailed protocol of the research to him—the director—as if he were a supervisor." I could not accept his altercasting (9) of me as a "dependent student" any more than he was ready to validate the type I had of him as "a newcomer who would do well to realize that I had already been doing research in the hospital." Actually, the types we were having of each other did not pass the test of our face-to-face confrontation, and we were soon in the process of negotiating our respective typifying schemes. This example shows the importance of the problem-relevance of the type, that is, its reference to the particular purpose at hand for the sake of which it has been formed. It also shows how the system of relevances and typifications "transforms unique individual actions of unique human beings into typical functions of typical social roles, originating in typical motives aimed at bringing about typical ends" (10).

The last point to be emphasized is the *social and cultural determination* of the system of relevances and typifications. In order to "understand" another actor, that is, to interpret his actions from the point of view of the actor, I have to apply the system of typifying schemes accepted by the group to which both of us belong. In order to be understood by him, I have to avail myself of the same system of typification as a scheme of orientation for my future actions. An example will clarify this point. A "school" of psychiatric treatment is represented in the hospital by a ward-chief who considers that manic patients must be treated very "firmly." A patient whose behavior is inappropriate will be told before the entire community that "he behaves no better than an animal." In any other context this treatment would be considered brutal and cruel. The psychiatrists, however, who "understand" this behavior and accept this practice typify the behavior as "therapeutic."

A PHENOMENOLOGICAL VIEW OF THE FORMAL ORGANIZATION

In social interaction, the role of typification can be expected to vary according to the nature of the relationship. This can be concretely shown by a comparison of the different typifications at work in *face-to-face* or *concrete* societies in opposition to *abstract* societies (11).

In a face-to-face society where the relations consist of "concrete" meetings of the members, individual, person-to-person relations are all-important. The relationships between these consociates are characterized by the dominance of concrete personal types. The abstract society, on the other hand, is conceived by Popper as a society in which men practically never meet face-to-face. All business is conducted by individuals communicating by typed letters or by telegrams and going about in closed motor cars. This abstract society is characterized by the fact that it largely ignores persons and considers only their role or status. It is, in that sense, a depersonalized society in which relationships are mediated by anonymous course-of-action types. The question I would like to address now is: To which of these types do the social relationships found in formal organizations correspond? Recourse to the scientific literature on organizations, and to the second-order constructs used by social scientists in describing organizational processes, would probably not be of much help in answering this question. The theory of authority, for example, has been elaborated mainly by political philosophers and political scientists. Viewed from this perspective, the leader (the ruler) is rarely more than an abstract concept for the subordinate (the ruled). Even when both enter into a face-to-face relationship, it is a very transitory and short-lived one, and its formal character prevents the intrusion of any intersubjective manifestation. I submit that this is not the case when authority-relationships take place within an organizational context, especially in organizations staffed by professionals. In a psychiatric hospital, in particular, the incumbents of authority roles enter into frequent personal contacts with many of their subordinates. The dynamics of authority are considerably dependent on the changing meanings organizational actors impute to the acts of their superiors or of their subordinates in the transition from the relationship of "contemporaries" to the relationship of "consociates." This fact had actually been hinted at by Max Weber, who wrote: "Every social relationship which goes beyond the pursuit of immediate common ends, which hence lasts for long periods, involves relatively permanent social relationships between the persons, and these cannot be exclusively confined to the technically necessary activities" (12). This is, however, only one aspect of the picture. As many social scientists remind us, formal organizations, so far as they participate in the bureaucratic model, tend to discourage among their members the development of we-relationships. In the ideal case, the exercise of authority is seen as "wholly objective, impartial, impersonal, and disinterested" (13). The bureaucrat is expected to adopt this impersonal orientation with all the members of the organization, but it is especially required in authority relationships: "Impersonal detachment is designed to prevent the personal feelings of officials from distorting their rational judgment in carrying out their duties" (14). The fact that professional organizations are organized in work teams where members frequently meet does not seem sufficient to prevent them from being influenced by this principle. For example, in a psychiatric hospital the desire expressed by nurses to break the rule of impersonality in their relationships with the residents is seriously resisted by residents, who label this as the nurses' need for a time-wasting "therapeutic relationship." Even in organizations structured as primary groups, such as religious communities, the need to prevent the formation of we-relationships is present, as evidenced by the existence of a taboo prohibiting "particular friendships." This impersonality of organizational relationships first described by Max Weber has been explained by social scientists as a normatively regulated behavior, a functional prerequisite of impartial administration:

> Weber's emphasis on impersonality can be understood in the light of what it does to the organization, namely, it ensures and increases the reliability of response in the interpersonal behavior situation either between the personnel and the clientele or between the personnel themselves. In a large, complex organization in which constant turnover in transactions, personnel, and clientele is commonplace, the continuity and uniformity in policy and behavior need to be meticulously guarded (15).

The phenomenological theory of typification suggests another interpretation, for even if there is a norm of impersonal behavior that organizational members internalize in the course of their socialization, there is a more basic source of impersonality: the relationships are organized on the basis of a formally organized and functionally specific system of roles requiring only segmental involvement (16). This second type of impersonality is due to the substitution of the "agent" for the "person" (17) in the performance of organizational roles, and for this reason, the term "anonymity" seems to be more appropriate. The person is unique, irreplaceable, and is perceived only in a thou-orientation. This is precisely the pre-predicative experience in which I become aware of a fellow human being as a person.

The performance of an organizational role does not require the person, merely the agent. As Berger and Luckmann (18) point out, "The roles of secondary socialization carry a high degree of anonymity; that is, they are readily detached from their individual performers." The agent takes the role, and this means that the person is, so to speak, put in brackets, so that only the pure features of his role become relevant to the performance. This anonymity extends to the perception of those engaged in role-relationships with him (19). The "appropriate" behavior of staff members would thus correspond to what has been described as they-relationships. In the psychiatric hospital, for example, the staff member draws upon his stock of knowledge according to which there are people who are "typical" psychiatrists, nurses, social workers, and so on. He is not supposed to care about how they feel about being psychiatrists, nurses, social workers, that is to say how they experience their ongoing conduct in a *subjective* context of meaning. For him, their performance should stand basically in an *objective* context of meaning (20). The last point is essential, since it points to the fact that, in the social subsystem constituted by a formal organization, the assignment of meaning is not left to the discretion of the member. The organization presents him with a number of anonymous, functional typifying schemes that will help him orient his behavior toward the incumbents of other positions, especially hierarchical positions. These types are furnished to the newcomer in the organizational chart or the nomenclature of organizational titles. They underlie job descriptions, exposés of rights and duties attached to each organizational position, rules of conduct, customs, and so forth. By such standardization of the scheme of typifications, the organization attempts to establish a congruency between the typified scheme used by each actor as a scheme of orientation and that of his organizational fellow-men as a scheme of interpretation, with the expected result that the chances of success of human interaction in the organization will be increased. This standardization is supposed to promote the smooth flow of authority relationships required for the efficient functioning of the organization. When, for example, a hippie-like new resident enters the hospital, the staff is expected to typify him as a "psychiatrist in training" rather than as a "crazy, mixed-up kid." By the same token, the resident is encouraged to see himself not as a "rebel" but as a "responsible physician."

Actually, the organization is doing officially and systematically what each individual does daily when he constructs course-of-action types of *contemporaries*, imputing to the more or less anonymous actors a set of supposedly invariant motives that govern their action. An instance of such an interaction in an organizational context exemplifies how these processes are taken for granted. A director of a mental hospital calls a ward to require the direct admission of a patient. He takes for granted that this action will induce a typical sequence:

1. Anonymous nurses will perform certain typical actions (going to the admission office, preparing a room, etc.).

2. These actions are in proportion to certain typical motives (to conform to hierarchical injunctions, to insure good service) with the result that the state of affairs projected by the director is achieved.

3. A reciprocity of perspectives is also taken for granted: his construct of the nurse's course-of-action corresponds substantially to her own self-typification.

4. The nurse has a typified construct of her anonymous director: his behavior is based on typical and invariant motives (i.e. his call warrants that a room be immediately prepared for patient X).

In typifying himself, the director projects his action in the typical way a typical nurse expects a director to behave. The presumption is that the more institutionalized such a behavior pattern is—the more typified it is in an organizationally approved way by means of regulations, traditions, and so on—the greater is the chance that the director's own self-typifying behavior will bring about the result aimed at.

It is apparent that the personal types arrived at by referring such anonymous course-of-action types to such typical motives of the actor are themselves anonymous. The rationale for this relatively anonymous, and consequently more or less empty-of-content type proposed by the organization to its members is to be sought in the need experienced by the organization to impose an objective context of meaning.

The meaning of an action is different for the actor and for the partner involved with him in interaction. The reason is that only the actor knows the span of the project which determines the unit of his action. The only way to increase our understanding of another's action—and thus to increase the chances of success of our interaction—is to search for the meaning the action has for the actor. The "subjective interpretation of meaning" is possible merely by revealing the motives that determine a given course-of-action. On the other hand, all human actors are guided in their everyday life by varied motives. Their in-order-to motives are integrated into subjective motivational systems rooted in their biographical situation and organized into long-range life-projects (planning for their career in the organization, for their professional development, etc.). To obtain the coordination of the activities of its members, an organization has to reduce these variegated systems of motives to some common denominators: it presents the members with a set of "organizational goals." By asking its members to subordinate their in-order-to motives—while working—to the officially defined goals, the organization attempts *de facto* to substitute an *objective* context of meaning for the *subjective* configuration in which the individual actor discovers the meaning of his action (21).

The social world taken for granted in the organization is thus composed of anonymous actors following typical courses of action prompted by a set of invariant, typical motives. Such a system would remain unhindered in its functioning if the members could retain their reciprocal anonymity and interact only at the level of they-relationships (that of *contemporaries*). The functioning of the anonymous model presupposes the existence of a fairly well-institutionalized system of actions. Institutionalization is present when there is a reciprocal typification of habitualized actions by types of actors. In fact, however, all organizations are more or less removed from this ideal-typical situation. This is even more true in a young organization, or in an organization undergoing a process of reorganization, or in an organization staffed by professionals. Habitualized actions are not the norm, and many courses-of-action are new and tentative. The lack of habitualized actions makes it necessary for many situations to be defined anew. Therefore in most organizations different factors will call for the development of face-to-face relationships and the emergence of new typifying schemes.

Even when the ongoing actions that constitute the tasks of the organization are fairly well institutionalized, the functional types that regulate the life of the official organization are far from satisfying to the subjective needs of its members. The problem can be conceptualized, using the existential approach advocated by Tiryakian (22), in terms of the distinction between the ontological and the ontic levels of existence to which the *authentic* and inauthentic modes of comportment correspond. Authenticity, in this perspective, refers to "comportment of self carried out with an awareness of the ontological basis of others and in keeping with its own ontological structure." It implies that one views the self as *being*—a subject—rather than as *having*, and that one avoids manipulating other persons as one manipulates inanimate objects. Inauthentic behavior is a type of interpersonal relationship corresponding to Martin Buber's "I-it" relation—treating and perceiving persons as if they were objects, that is, submitting them to a process of objectification. Having inauthentic relationships with others is to relate with them only in terms of functional specificity. The anonymous types the organization presents its members are evidently conducive to objectified, inauthentic relationships. Since this system may function as an "existential defense mechanism" preserving the self from the necessity of facing up to others as subjects, it may be adopted with enthusiasm by some organization members for whom they serve as a shield separating them from their colleagues. The incumbents of authority roles will be especially tempted to use the system to avoid getting "entangled" with their subordinates. As a rule, the members will tend to resist the organization's attempt to impose a system of anonymous types and either change the official system or create an informal system where face-to-face relationships are entertained and are conducive to more authentic encounters.

Finally, in many organizations, the performance of *professional tasks* requires that the members enter into face-to-face relationships with each other. In a psychiatric hospital, for example, this entails the supervision of residents and other staff members by senior psychiatrists; the rounds where the treatment of the patients is organized; the meetings of the members with the leaders of their disciplines. In many cases these organization members had lost their anonymity even before entering the system. For instance, many psychiatrists entering the mental hospital have been in a former relationship of teacher-student or supervisor-supervisee in the department of psychiatry to which the hospital is attached, or have even been co-students during their medical training. By the same token, some nurses were roommates, and thus consociates for most of the time out of the hospital.

As a consequence of these past or present face-to-face relationships, the actual experience organizational members have of each other rarely maintains the characteristics of pure anonymity. The colleague, whether he be superior, subordinate, or peer, will be experienced as a consociate, as a contemporary who has been a consociate in the more or less recent past, or as a contemporary who though never encountered in a face-to-face manner is nevertheless known through the description of a consociate. Owing to these direct and indirect experiences which colleagues have of one another, the anonymous system of typifying schemes which the organization provides is supplemented by a multiplicity of more concrete types. The colleague is apprehended not only as the "director," but also as a "middle-aged man," a "Jew," a "manipulator," and so on.

This multiplicity of typifying schemes can be a source of dysfunctional ambiguity, however, as is well known in total institutions where a special effort is made through rigid mechanisms of segregation to prevent face-to-face relationships from corroding the official system of typifications. For example, in traditional religious orders, this is attested to by the existence of "categories" of members. Clerics are prevented from interacting with lay brothers, simple novices with professed novices, novices with priests. The members of each category are moreover dissuaded from communicating any knowledge they may have acquired about members of the other categories, unless it corroborates the official typification of "good religious." Even members who have been close friends before entering the religious order are invited to address each other by the impersonal appellation of "Sister" or "Brother" as if nothing remained of their former relationship.

Since organizational effort to eliminate face-to-face relationships is rarely successful, the members of formal organizations find that the official system of typifications can no longer explain their colleagues' courses of action satisfactorily. Since the scheme of interpretation which has stood the test so far does not allow the member to make sense of the new situation, he will have recourse to other typifying schemes likely to be conducive to a more acceptable interpretation. Phenomenologically, the process under consideration can be explained by recourse to Husserl's concept of *passive synthesis of recognition:* The perceiving subject superimposes the actual perception of a corporeal object with the recollection of previous perceptions of other corporeal objects having typically similar characteristics (shape, extension, color). Extending the application of this mechanism to the perception of concrete courses-of-action, we can say that in order to grasp the meaning of an action that has entered our perceptual field, we have to subsume it as to its typicality under the various typical prior experiences that constitute our actual stock of knowledge at hand. The ambiguity and indeterminateness of this process originates in the fact that only part of our total stock of knowledge appears relevant in the interpretation of an object, and that not all the characteristics of the perceived object itself are equally relevant for this interpretation: "certain particular moments of the object perceived obtain the character of major or minor interpretive relevance for the task of recognizing and interpreting the actually experienced segment of the world" (23).

It is important to note that the problem we are considering here is not one that could be satisfactorily solved by having recourse to attribution theory. As described by Jones and Davis, attribution theory is concerned with the processes by which a person-perceiver attributes intentions to a person-actor. The assumption is that "the person-perceiver's fundamental task is to interpret or infer the causal antecedents of action" (24). Moreover, as Argyris points out, "the actor is not conceived of as an equal partner, as an 'active' information giver, interpreter, or inferer of the causal antecedents of his behavior" (25). The problem we are studying implies different assumptions. When a partner in an organizational relationship interprets the action of a colleague, what is considered relevant by him is determined also by the response he has to give to the other's gesture. The perceiver, in this case, is also an actor and the interpretation he gives to his partner's action will also determine his own future reaction. The concept of "motivational relevance" has been proposed by Schutz to refer to the fact that a correct interpretation does not merely provide the perceiver with an explanation, but it gives him an opportunity to meet the situation effectively by an appropriate response. His interpretive decision will determine his decision on how to act. On the other hand, the actor whose gestures are interpreted also tries directly to influence the process of interpretation, since he knows it will determine the response of his partner. This characteristic of social interaction has been given special emphasis in symbolic interactionism. Blumer has given a brief, precise account of the processes that, according to G. H. Mead, take place in a symbolic interaction:

> Such things as requests, orders, commands, cues, and declarations are gestures that convey to the person who recognizes them an idea of the intention

and plan of forthcoming action of the individual who presents them. The person who responds organizes his response on the basis of what the gestures mean to him; the person who presents the gestures advances them as indications or signs of what he is planning to do as well as of what he wants the respondent to do or understand. Thus the gesture has meaning for both the person who makes it, and for the person to whom it is directed. When the gesture has the same meaning for both, the two parties understand each other (26).

Blumer makes clear that in this approach, the meaning of the gesture flows out along three lines:

It signifies what the person to whom it is directed is to do; it signifies what the person who is making the gesture plans to do; it signifies the joint action that is to arise by the articulation of the acts of both. If there is confusion or misunderstanding along any one of these three lines of meaning, communication is ineffective, interaction is impeded, and the formation of joint action is blocked (27).

It is not enough, however, for the partner to understand the meaning intended by the actor. He must also be willing and able to do what he is directed to do. If this condition is met, nothing will impede the normal course of the interaction as it is intended by the first actor. If, however, the partner considers as inappropriate the response he is expected to give, he will look for new interpretational elements that will give motivational relevance to his actual response. Whoever accepts the new interpretation will be able to respond to the new gesture (the first response) according to the expectations of its author. The absence of such agreement, however, will make the smooth flow of interaction among the actors impossible. Consequently, when the official system of types proposed to the members of an organization cannot be used by them as the basis for interpreting their colleagues' actions, a situation of crisis is introduced and another common basis of interpretation must be accepted.

It is important to point out that the selection of appropriate typifying schemes by the members of a group is not a process that takes place at the level of logical judgment. Rather, as Husserl's concept of "passive synthesis" indicates (28), it takes place at the level of pre-predicative constitution, that is, it is a "proto-logic" process (29). Moreover, the selection of an interpretive scheme, even though in opposition to the officially proposed system of typification, is frequently taken for granted. At the same time, the selection of interpretationally relevant material is conditioned by the biographically determined situation of the actors: In Schutz's words "the same life-world lends itself to a magic interpretation by primitive people, a theological one by the missionary, and a scientific one by the technologist" (30).

THE LIFE WORLD OF PSYCHIATRISTS: THE ROLE OF PSYCHIATRIC TYPIFICATIONS

I will now show how "the same life-world" lends itself to a psychiatric interpretation by psychiatrists. The concrete depictions that follow refer to a university-related psychiatric hospital which I shall call the State Mental Health Center (31). In the Center, the concrete courses-of-action pursued by various clinician-executives were based on divergent psychiatric ideologies, hence the psychiatrists were frequently unable or unwilling to interpret their colleagues' actions on the basis of the official definition of the organizational goals. Since I define the phenomenological approach as one that focuses on the way organizational members interpret their life-world, the following pages will show how in the absence of a satisfying official interpretation of their colleagues' courses-of-action the psychiatrists resort to psychiatric types. The expression "psychiatric types" will be used to refer to types borrowed from the psychiatric nomenclature, which are routinely used by psychiatric personnel to interpret the behavior of their peers, superiors, or subordinates.

A primary characteristic of psychiatric typification is that it is based on the diagnosis of a colleague. Turner has pointed out that an actor's reaction to a partner in a social interaction need not be based on the face value of the first actor's gesture, it can also be based on a *diagnostic interpretation*, "one that infers from the gesture something about the state of alter which is at variance with the face-value meaning of the gesture, and of which alter is assumed to be unaware" (32). In their interaction with patients, psychiatrists make constant use of diagnostic interpretations and have recourse to types which are directly borrowed from the stock of knowledge of the mental health professional. This procedure is not limited to their evaluation of patients. At the S.M.H.C., for example, recourse to diagnostic interpretation and psychiatric typification to explain the behavior of colleagues was a routine practice.

The following episode shows how Dr. Bloom, a psychiatrist and Director of the Center's First Division, interpreted the behavior of his subordinates by being especially aware of its irrational aspects, and by imputing irrational motivations rather than taking it at face value. When the reorganization of the Center's First Division required that one of the four existing facilities be closed in order to staff the new Evaluation and Brief Treatment Unit more adequately, Dr. Bloom decided to close the Day Hospital. In meetings with the staff of the Day Hospital, the Director justified his decision. He pointed out that there had been a consistent tendency in the meetings of the Division and of the Executive Committee of the Center to give the highest priority to the new unit (the Evaluation Unit), which was expected to give adequate evaluation and short treatment to some 4000 patients annually. The Day Hospital, on the other hand, had treated only 120 patients during the year, was not an innovative model, and did not give first-class training to the residents. Therefore it had the lowest priority in the Division and could be closed. In spite of Dr. Bloom's long explanations, the staff, and especially the psychiatric residents, were very angry about his decision. They insisted that the needs of the patients actually treated in the Day Hospital would not be taken care of after the suppression of that service.

Dr. Bloom's defense was to typify himself as a father reluctant to sacrifice his own child. He emphasized the fact that he himself had created the Day Hospital, had been its first chief of service, and personally felt that, "I do not want to be an infanticide." After a meeting where the residents had been particularly violent in expressing their feelings, I asked Dr. Bloom how he interpreted their aggressivity toward him. "It points," he explained, "to the kind of issues that I find extremely difficult to cope with in this organization, that is, the need to 'look for a powerful papa,' someone to pretend to keep things stable, to make things nice. What they are saying is: 'You are not a good father, you were just a very bad papa this year, and you put your efforts and energies elsewhere. That hurts, and is difficult to tolerate. And not only do you do that, but in fact even murder your children, or you raise up other children. And you had promised me I was your first born and chosen, and all the rest of that!' " (The projection involved in the use of diagnostic interpretations can be observed here. In fact, it was Dr. Bloom himself who introduced the theme of infanticide in his discussion with the residents.) Dr. Bloom continued, "I also think that the residents were caught up in their enormous ambivalence. I could have asked them: 'What is it that you wish to learn, and what sort of things do you think are important, what are the areas that you want to deal with?' I have the sense that many of the residents play games around what is important, that they have some ideas of all the knowledge they ought to obtain. Almost any attempt to teach them anything, or to open them up to new learning is frustrated. Ultimately, I think part of the anger is due to the facing up of the staff to what is real, instead of what the wished-for future is." The resistance manifested by the nurses and social workers in their hierarchical subordination to the psychiatrists was similarly diagnosed as inspired by an "irrational wish" on the former's part: "The dilemma," Dr. Bloom explained, "is the issue of autonomy, the wish not to hear that one is responsible to anybody else. There is the consistent wish to fantasy one's own autonomy." In actuality, the residents felt that they had legitimate reasons for opposing the closing of their unit. In their experience, the Day Hospital had been giving valuable service to a moderate number of patients. To close it was tantamount to denying the fact. However, between the "wish for a powerful papa" and the "wish for autonomy," Dr. Bloom's typifications left little room for interpreting both cases simply as oppositions to his authority or as legitimate grievances.

This recurrent "typification" of people and their behavior would be transmitted to other members and so perpetuated in the system. For example, following a reorganization of the First Division, the Day Hospital became a subdivision of the in-patient services under the general supervision of Dr. Hauser. At the weekly meeting of the head nurses of the Division, the nurses of the Day Hospital expressed their intention to keep the "Day Hospital's integrity," and therefore to meet separately to get organized, rather than meet with Dr. Hauser, whom they feared. To dissuade them from taking that course-of-action, the head nurse of the In-Patient Unit delivered a long monologue in which she transmitted to her colleagues the knowledge acquired during a long interaction with Dr. Peter Hauser:

> That may just be a fear of yours, honestly. You don't know what kind of negotiations are going on already, what specific thoughts Peter has, and he is going to be in a position of power. So I don't understand why you don't try to work it out together. Let me tell you one thing. Peter can be the most loyal, devoted, fantastic person you'll ever meet. However, he can also be a bastard, irrational, impulsive. And the one thing that I also know about Peter, and please believe me, I am telling you from my own experience, knowing how happy you can be in a relationship with him, and also how unhappy. He really has lots of ideas, and one of the biggest problems that I think enters into it is that he has so many ideas that he goes from this to that, and then another thing. They are all fine, they are all good ideas. However, what he zeroes in on is often . . . well, you don't always understand why he zeroes in on a particular thing that he zeroes in on, but if you are part of the discussion with him you can certainly influence what kind of zeroing in he does.

The head nurse of the Day Hospital proved she had understood when she said: "I think that what we have to do is accept the reality of Peter's personality, how he functions, how he is going to work and maneuver, and when we know this, establish a working relationship with him so that he can't push." Recurrent typifications were not limited to the staff. The psychiatrists were just as anxious to "collect" typical knowledge of their future collaborators. The head nurse of the in-patient service warned her colleagues of the Day Hospital: "Hauser asked about you yesterday. He is going to get to know about people pretty much. He probably knows things about you that you don't even know that he knows. It is unbelievable. He is a collector."

Ironically enough, psychiatrists verbally reject as totally inappropriate the use of psychiatric judgments or typifications of this kind in their relationships with colleagues: "It is extremely inappropriate," Dr. Bloom told me once, "to bring to bear the weight of your professional expertise in a situation where in fact you really have none." In fact, the existence of the unwritten norm: "You don't analyze, nor do you behave as a psychiatrist with the staff," was a source of considerable embarrassment for a clinician-executive caught in the very act of using his psychiatric skills to formulate a diagnosis about one of his subordinates. This was Dr. Bloom's reaction when I pointed out to him that he had publicly given a diagnostic interpretation of the behavior manifested by Dr. Samuel, chief of the Emergency Treatment Unit. Just after the announcement of his leaving for another university, Dr. Samuel had undertaken a number of long-term projects whose execution would stretch out well beyond the date set for his departure. Dr. Samuel presented this as the carrying out of designs of innovation. Dr. Bloom, on the other hand, interpreted it as an unconscious resistance to the facing up to a real situation, an "acting out." When I called his attention to the diagnosis made, Dr. Bloom tried to explain his remark away as a "nontechnical," at most, a "semitechnical" use of the psychiatric expression. Nevertheless, his explanations contradicted this statement, as he was himself forced to acknowledge. "What I mean," he told me, is "that he has trouble leaving and terminating, and he is pretending that he has not. Under the pretense that he has not, he is attempting to establish certain conditions for the Emergency Treatment Service that he cannot follow through. In that sense he is playing a game. When I said 'he is acting out,' I meant, at least for me, 'behaving destructively,' because he is making promises he cannot keep. To a degree, I guess, I was imputing motivation to it. The motivation imputed is: it relieves him of the necessity of dealing with his leaving and makes it easy for him to pretend until the very last minute that he stays."

PSYCHIATRIC TYPIFICATION AS A PROCESS OF ADAPTATION

It has been suggested that the human actor "enacts," rather than "reacts" to his environment: "Instead of adapting to a ready-made environment . . . actors themselves create the environment to which they adapt" (33). This enactment is not an automatic process, however, but depends rather on the way past experiences are attended to. As Schutz has shown, "the meaning of a lived experience undergoes modifications depending on the particular kind of attention the Ego gives to that lived experience" (34). The concept of motivational relevance emphasizes the fact that the kind of attention, the meaning, will be a function of the present interest of the

actor, that is, of the response he has to give *hic et nunc* (here and now).
The points I want to make here are:

1. An organizational actor is not a pure observer of himself or of others.

2. To discover the meaning of his own experience, that is, his "environment," he has to step outside the stream of experience and become an observer of himself.

3. The kind of attention he directs to his past experience in these conditions is never an "objective," "scientific" one but is determined by the problem he is faced with *hic et nunc*.

In an organization where the system of roles is completely institutionalized, the actors do not have the opportunity of choosing among different courses-of-action, and the process of attention has *in theory* no role in the determination of subsequent action. In the language of symbolic interaction: "As the context approaches one in which the behavior is completely prescribed and all misperformance is institutionally punished, the process of role-taking–role-making becomes increasingly an inconsequential part of the interaction that occurs" (35).

In an organization of professionals, however, the opposite should be true. The necessity to protect the rights of the professional as "the person who has the right to say what should be done and what is necessary to get it done" (36), entails the free selection of courses-of-action on the basis of the meaning given to lived experience. Yet even in this type of organization, the assignment of meaning is, in many cases, organizationally determined. Each member disposes of a number of anonymous, functional typifying schemes which "objectively" define the meaning of his colleagues' gestures. The organizational member takes for granted that his colleagues will see their daily interaction within the objective context of meaning determined by the official system. For example, when Dr. Rolf, Director of the Center's Out-Patient Service, invited the residents to attend a leadership meeting, the objective meaning of his invitation was clearly an injunction from their Director—hence the residents' presence was required. When half of them failed to show up at that meeting, Rolf immediately opted for a punitive course of action to force their compliance "should that happen again." Each would receive personal letters from Rolf; a report would be sent to the vice-chairman, with carbon copies to the Director of the Center and the Director of the Division; the residents would be put on probation for "insufficient performance." This interaction made sense in the context of meaning determined by the official system. When, on the other hand, half of the same group failed to show up at a party at Dr. Rolf's home for the staff of the O. P. Department, he was angry at their "rudeness." He could not, however, opt for punitive measures because the meaning of this "invitation" was not organizationally defined. The residents were free to see it, as they did, in three different ways: a courteous gesture on the part of a clinician-executive who was also a "nice fellow"; a leader's attempt to buy their compliance; and an obligation they could not bypass without exposing themselves to their "leader's" hostility.

The manifest meaning, then, that the organization invites the members to attend to in each other's gestures is not always satisfying. Two cases can be distinguished:

1. The response a member is expected to give on the basis of the official system appears incongruent, that is, evidently contradictory to the colleague's actual intention. In this case, the gesture manifested is interpreted as a false representation of the meaning actually intended by the actor, that is, one reinterprets the actor's gesture by disregarding its face value and adopting an *empathic* interpretation (37).

2. The response a member is expected to give on the basis of the official meaning is not only incongruent but also threatening to him, that is, self-destructive, and likely to put his own organizational fate in jeopardy. In this case, an empathic interpretation that merely acknowledges the aggressive intention of the colleague is not enough. It does not allow the threatened member to adapt satisfactorily to the situation. A response dictated by the covert meaning would make the antagonism between both partners public and any future collaboration extremely precarious.

In a hierarchical system, in particular, the consequences of a course-of-action resulting from the empathic interpretation would be extremely prejudicial to the functioning of authority relationships. A subordinate would find it difficult to avoid being seen as a rebel when responding to the aggressive intention of his superior. The superior would inevitably be perceived as an authoritarian tyrant if he tried to enforce his will under these circumstances. In order to elude this impasse, organization members may have recourse to another type of interpretation, one that takes place at the *diagnostic level*. By imputing to the partner an attitude of which he is supposedly unaware, one evades the self-destructive response called forth at the face value of the partner's gesture. At the same time, one justifies one's not responding to the covert meaning of the partner's gesture, since it is not intentional or deliberate. In particular, in a hierarchical system, a middle manager can present his own subordinates with diagnostic interpretations of senior managers' directives as a way to induce them (subordinates) to conform to his own expectations rather than to the senior manager's projects.

Diagnostic interpretations are not only used to evade complying with superiors' suggestions which could elicit self-destructive responses; they are also used to evade confrontation with a superior whose gesture, taken at its face value, constitutes a violation of one's own rights. The following episode illustrates the way a senior psychiatrist's intervention, which constituted an undercutting of Dr. Bloom, was justified by Bloom on the basis of diagnostic interpretation. Dr. Lamb, speaking with Dr. Rolf, Director of the Out-Patient Services of the First Division, and Miss Bart, chief social worker of the Division, told them he wanted to transfer to the First Division a social worker presently working at City Hospital. This gesture constituted a breach of the normal line of communication, since the transfer of the social worker should have been negotiated first between Dr. Lamb and Dr. Bloom. Rather than confront Dr. Lamb with the irregularity of this procedure, Dr. Bloom interpreted it as Dr. Lamb's problem, his "ambivalence" toward the social worker: "I think that one of the reasons the communication came to me in that way is so that I can say 'no,' and the people can get off the hook. You know, it is difficult to say no to Dr. Lamb. He knew that it would finally come to me. Lamb's motivation is very difficult to understand. He really perceives himself continually as being helpful. Unfortunately, my perception is that the help frequently means taking care of the inept." For Dr. Bloom, Dr. Lamb's ambivalence toward the social worker manifested itself in the fact that "At the same time he wants her, he also does not want her to have a job [in the system]. Since he is a kind person, he mixes the messages consistently, and he lets inept people think he cares about them a great deal, and he does, but he cares about them in a very different way." Moreover, the fact that Dr. Lamb spoke to Dr. Rolf, and not to Dr. Bloom, was also interpreted by the latter as a way to dissociate him (Bloom) from the problem. The blame of possible error would then fall on Rolf: "Lamb is still very ambivalent about Rolf, and if Rolf accepts Miss Y [the social worker], it is he, and not me. So it is Rolf's error, and I am protected. All of these crazy things, I think, enter into it."

The unwillingness to test psychiatric typifications for their validity is indicative of a defensive dimension that appears in many diagnostic interpretations. Such a defensive attitude inspired Dr. Lowry's interpretation of a predicament of the clinical executives at the second level of management. The senior leaders of the Department of Psychiatry, Dr. Lowry explained, had been unwilling to take upon themselves the responsibility for the failures and difficulties of the system. Rather than make themselves the objects of hostility and frustration, they had tended to deflect the hostility engendered by mismanagement on scapegoats, the clinician-executives working immediately under them, with the consequence that "We are blamed in a game that I call 'blaming the victim.' " Dr. Lowry's diagnosis was that an enormous need to be liked underlay the leaders' refusal to assume the responsibility of their office. They were therefore asking more junior people to take the burden of the hostility in exchange for the implicit promise that those who would be willing to take that burden would be identified as their favorite sons. Dr. Lowry realized that this privileged position of "favorite son" was precarious. It became necessary, after a period of time, for the top leaders to say of those who had accepted the role of scapegoats: "Really, they have generated far too much hostility. We now need to get rid of them." This interpretation can be seen as the denial of aggressive behavior directed toward Dr. Lowry. Dr. Lowry denied that the senior people wanted to force him out of the system and claimed that it was only their need to be liked that had indirectly contributed to their "focusing downward" of a hostility not directed at him personally.

A diagnostic interpretation, then, can serve as a defense, protecting the actor from responding to a colleague's aggressive intention. The mechanism can be described as a rejection of the empathic process involved in the attribution of an aggressive in-order-to motive to an adversary. It also involves the attempt to explain his gesture by reducing it to its because-motives. By denying that the aggression is intentional and deliberate, one can evade confronting it directly. In that sense, the attention given to the because-motives instead of the in-order-to motives of a colleague is dictated by the desire to react to his gesture without resorting to the aggressive response called forth by an empathic interpretation of his project (38). It should be added immediately that the diagnostic interpretation explains the other's behavior by focusing on his "irrational" or "unconscious" motives. The implication is that elements of his past that the other perpetuates in the present gesture are not those that would help him adequately define the situation. Rather they are deterministic forces which guide his conduct blindly and justify the rejection of his project on the grounds of its "irrationality."

An illustration will help explain this process. I had attracted Dr. Lowry's attention to a rumor circulating in the Center by which Dr. Greer, a senior official of the State charged with the supervision of mental health activities, wanted to "kill" the Center because it was out of his actual control. "This is quite possible," Dr. Lowry replied, "but I cannot make that inference. You are making inferences as to men's intentions. I don't think he is happy about the Center, because it is not under his control, and also because we are involved in certain programs which he does not agree with. To what extent Dr. Greer is out to kill the Center, I just don't know." Some time later, during the same interview, I asked Dr. Lowry if he thought Dr. Greer would take a more favorable attitude toward the Center if it would give more consideration to the need of the community:

I am not sure, because I am not sure how much it is an issue of policy, and how much it is the personal frustration of Dr. Greer because he feels he has been excluded. You see he has aspirations himself for academic status that he feels have been thwarted. And he did not want this institution to be a university-related institution. There is a long history that goes back many years. There is a paper by him in 19— called ". . . ." It is a good paper for the time, in which he contemplated a series of satellite hospitals related to the big State hospitals. . . . This Center was supposed to be the first satellite, but the State, the legislature, gave it to Eastern University.

There is a visible discrepancy between Dr. Lowry's reluctance to attribute a hostile intention to Dr. Greer and his readiness to find in Dr. Greer's past *because-motives* likely to explain his negative attitude toward the Center. An ethical explanation seems out of the question, for it is not more protective of Dr. Greer's reputation to insinuate that his official decisions are dictated by his personal frustration. By imputing Dr. Greer's hostile attitude toward the Center to his personal frustration, Dr. Lowry had defined the situation in such a way that he did not have to respond directly to this hostility. The "projects" Dr. Greer could elaborate under these "conditions" would all be inadequate since they would neglect the real situation (e.g., a change in policy) and would only perpetuate the alienated elements of Dr. Greer's own self. Consequently, the *because-motives* Dr. Lowry attributed to Dr. Greer can be summarized as follows:

1. Frustration arising from a feeling of being excluded from the management of the Center.
2. Frustration because of the Center's inability to realize his plans.
3. Frustration in his aspirations for academic status.

The parallelism between these motives and the reasons Dr. Lowry gives for his own frustration, in a lengthy interview, and his consequent decision to leave Eastern University is striking:

1. The feeling that he lacked control in the management of the Center because the Department did not give him sufficient formal power.
2. The impossibility of implementing his values in the Center.
3. Insufficient academic reward.

This parallelism can be compared to the "projection" that has been pointed out in Dr. Bloom's interpretation of the residents' anger. In each case the self-typification of the actor has influenced the *content* of the diagnostic interpretation he makes of his colleagues, that is, the choice of the psychiatric types he uses to typify their behavior. Dr. Bloom saw himself as an "infanticide," and attributed the residents' anger toward him to their typifying him in that way. Dr. Lowry saw himself as a "frustrated administrator," and attributed Dr. Greer's attitude toward the Center to a similar frustration, that is, to Greer's seeing himself as a man whose ambitions had been frustrated.

Dr. Bloom typifies himself as an "infanticide" against his will, as a way of insisting that such is the supremacy of his project of reorganization, that he is ready to accept being seen as an "infanticide" as the price to be paid. When he attributes this typification of himself as an "infanticide" to the residents, however, he describes it as wholly determining their conduct. They are only frustrated little boys who have been let down by a "bad papa." If their response to his project is dictated only by their perception of him as a "bad papa," their opposition can then be legitimately ignored.

Similarly, Dr. Lowry typifies himself as a "frustrated administrator." His reasons are valid enough to legitimize his project of leaving the Center. When he depicts Dr. Greer, however, as being frustrated, this typification takes on an entirely different importance. Dr. Lowry's project of leaving implies that he has a choice between different courses-of-action, and that he has explicitly rejected one of them, which is to remain in the position of a frustrated administrator. Dr. Greer, on the other hand, is presented as someone who is so determined by his frustration that even a change in policy could not alter his present course-of-action.

To recapitulate, then, interpreting Actor A's course-of-action on the basis of imputed irrational, or unconscious, motives, Actor B can avoid giving either a self-destructive response or a response that results in a direct confrontation. The diagnostic interpretation is obtained by reducing Actor A's action to some of its "conditions" and by ignoring his "project," that is, "the system of meaning in which action is viewed in its orientation to the future and therefore in its subjective meaning" (39). The response given on that basis by Actor B orients the interaction in the direction intended by him and makes it difficult for A to react adequately without giving up his project.

CONCLUSION

The phenomenological approach to social reality emphasizes the primary role subjective meaning plays in the interpretation of social action. In order to be able to perceive the subjective meanings an actor gives to his own or his partners' actions, the researcher has to abandon the perspective of an outside, detached observer and adopt the perspective of the actor himself. It should be pointed out that a paradox is involved here. While we define our approach as an exploration of the social from the standpoint of the subject, the naive actor does not perceive his action as the consequence of adherence to a standpoint but takes his action as being "natural." The concept of typifications of man in the "natural standpoint" refers precisely to the fact that mundane existence is structured by typifying schemes that are accepted without being questioned. These typifications are socially derived, being transmitted to the human actor through membership in a social group. It is, then, because they are taken for granted by the members of the group that they constitute what Scheler calls their relative natural conception of the world (40).

In this respect, formal organizations appear merely as a more structured type of social group. As long as organizational actors act as typical members, they tend to take the official system of typification for granted as well as the accompanying set of recipes that help them define their situation in an organizationally approved way. The emergence of other, nonorganizationally defined typifying schemes results from the breaking down of the taken-for-granted world when the actors enter into face-to-face relationships.

The description of interpretations elaborated by psychiatric personnel in a mental hospital has shown how the typifying schemes they use to make sense of their colleague's actions are borrowed from the specialized body of knowledge proper to their profession. As a result of this observation, I should like to emphasize two concluding remarks:

1. The first is concerned with the distinction between two orders of typifications or constructs. Social scientists influenced by Schutz' social phenomenology tend to make a clear distinction between first-order constructs or "existential types" used by human actors in their everyday life and second-order constructs or "constructed types" utilized by scientists (41). Whereas the first are naive and immanent to social life, the second are sophisticated and explicitly formulated in the theoretical apparatus of the science. As Schutz himself put it: "Typifications on the common sense level—in contradistinction to typifications made by the scientist and especially the social scientist—emerge in the everyday experience of the world as taken for granted without any formulation of judgments or of neat propositions with logical subjects and predicates. They belong, to use a phenomenological term, to prepredicative thinking" (42). The psychiatrists' use of psychiatric types in their interpretation of their own and their colleagues' behavior suggests that this distinction must not be pressed too far. The same typifying scheme that the psychiatrists create within the methodology of their discipline can be routinely used by them, within mundane existence. The significance of this "routinization" of scientific, technical typifications should not be underestimated. The scientist's specialized knowledge and techniques place within his reach, whether it be actual or potential, a region of the world that remains beyond the reach of those who do not share his skills and knowledge. In particular, it opens up for him a new "manipulatory sphere," a region of things he can manipulate and modify with the help of his specialized

techniques. More fundamentally, it creates for him a special "perceptive sphere," an area in which he has or can have direct perception because of his specialized training. The existence of this specific, profession-related world determines the scientist's system of interpretational relevances when he is acting as a scientist. It will also determine what the scientist considers as interpretationally relevant while attending to nonscientific business, that is, while acting as a member of a formal organization. This explains why psychiatrists are frequently unable to respect the norm of their profession and actually do behave as psychiatrists with their organizational colleagues, giving major interpretational relevance to the "irrational" or "unconscious" aspects of their colleagues' behavior.

2. The previously described process of routinization of the scientific system of typifications and relevances suggests one more conclusion. If the technical knowledge associated with a profession can become routinized to the extent that it influences the daily interaction among professionals working in an organizational context, then a new perspective could be open to the comparative study of formal organizations staffed by professionals.

The recourse to a phenomenological approach, with its commitment to the analysis of the meanings of action based on the typifications used by actors, would allow for differentiations much more radical than have formerly been made. By viewing the formal organization as a psychosocial reality built out of the human actors' subjective interpretations, and considering the typifying mode of awareness as constitutive of daily life, it would be possible to describe each type of professional organization as a *sui generis* reality whose specific characteristics are closely determined by the epistemic community to which its members are connected.

NOTES

1. Karl E. Weick, *The Social Psychology of Organizing*, Addison-Wesley, Reading, Mass., 1969, p. 26.

2. C. A. Van Peursen, "Life-World and Structures," in James M. Edie, Francis H. Parker, and Calvin O. Schrag, eds., *Patterns of the Life-World: Essays in Honor of John Wild*, Northwestern University Press, Evanston, Ill., 1970, pp. 139–153.

3. David Carr, "Husserl's Problematic Concept of the Life-World," *American Philosophical Quarterly*, 7, 1970, p. 338.

4. Aron Gurwitsch, *Studies in Phenomenology and Psychology*, Northwestern University Press, Evanston, Ill., 1966, p. 420.

5. Alfred Schutz, *Collected Papers*, Vol. I: *The Problem of Social Reality*,

edited and introduced by Maurice Natanson, Martinus Nijhoff, The Hague, 1962, p. 7.

6. Maurice Natanson, "The Phenomenology of Alfred Schutz," *Inquiry*, 9, 1966, p. 150.

7. Alfred Schutz, *The Phenomenology of the Social World*, translated by George Walsh and Frederick Lehnert, Northwestern University Press, Evanston, Ill., 1967, pp. 163–164. See also George Psathas and Fran Waksler, "Essential Features of Face-to-Face Interaction," this volume.

8. Erving Goffman, *Encounters*, Bobbs-Merrill, Indianapolis, Ind., 1961.

9. Eugene A. Weinstein and Paul Deutschberger, "Some Dimensions of Altercasting," *Sociometry*, 26, 1963, pp. 454–466.

10. Alfred Schutz, *Collected Papers*, Vol. II: *Studies in Social Theory*, edited and introduced by Arvid Brodersen, Martinus Nijhoff, The Hague, 1964, p. 237.

11. This distinction is borrowed from Karl Popper, *The Open Society and Its Enemies*, Princeton University Press, Princeton, N.J., 1950, pp. 170–171. Cf. also I. C. Jarvie, *The Revolution in Anthropology*, Routledge and Kegan Paul, London, 1964, p. 23.

12. Max Weber, *The Theory of Social and Economic Organizations*, translated by A. M. Henderson and Talcott Parsons, edited and with an introduction by Talcott Parsons, Oxford University Press, New York, 1947, p. 137.

13. Robert Bierstedt, "The Problem of Authority," in Monroe Berger, Theodore Abel, and Charles E. Page, eds., *Freedom and Control in Modern Society*, Van Nostrand, New York, 1954, p. 76.

14. Peter M. Blau and W. R. Scott, *Formal Organizations: A Comparative Approach*, Chandler, San Francisco, 1962, p. 33.

15. Narsi Patel and Jiri Kolaja, "Personal-Impersonal Dimension in Organizational Behavior: A Variation of the Weberian Model," *International Journal of Comparative Sociology*, 5, 1964, p. 73.

16. I owe the distinction between impersonality as a type of normatively regulated behavior and impersonality as "a consequence of that type of social differentiation which is characterized by the ascendance of formally organized and functionally specific sub-systems in society" to Renate Mayntz, "The Nature and Genesis of Impersonality: Some Results of a Study on the Doctor-Patient Relationship," *Social Research*, 37, 1970, p. 428. For the concept of segmental involvement, cf. the elaboration by Daniel Katz and Robert Kahn, *The Social Psychology of Organizations*, John Wiley and Sons, New York, 1956, of Floyd Allport's notion of "partial inclusion."

17. "We may distinguish between the person and the agent in role-taking. The person is the human being in his irreducible givenness, the agent is that being acting in accordance with the image and demands of his role. In cases where roles are institutionally patterned with great rigor and de-

tail, the agent shows itself most clearly. . . . The relationship between person and agent is not merely complementary. To the extent that the agent achieves dominance in the role-taking, to that extent the person is set aside or obscured. The fulfillment of pure agency may be called anonymity." Maurice Natanson, "Anonymity and Recognition: Toward an Ontology of Social Roles," in Walter von Baeyer and Richard M. Griffith, eds., *Conditio Humana: Erwin W. Straus on his 75th Birthday,* Springer-Verlag, New York, 1966, p. 259.

18. Peter L. Berger and Thomas Luckmann, *The Social Construction of Reality: A Treatise in the Sociology of Knowledge,* Anchor Books, Garden City, N.Y., 1967, p. 142.

19. "Much of our most highly integrated and efficient collective action must be presumed to occur within the framework provided by role systems. Whenever this is the case, individual participants are neither required nor permitted to let their perception of other people's intentions or preferences affect their behavior. Accuracy of social perception is largely irrelevant in such situations because it can have little effect upon individuals' behavior. Indeed, if it does affect individuals' behavior, it is likely to interfere with role enactment, and hence, to disrupt the behavior synthesis which is provided by the role system." Ivan Steiner, "Interpersonal Behavior as Influenced by Accuracy of Social Perception," *Psychological Review, 62,* 1955, pp. 273–274.

20. The *subjective meaning* is the meaning an action has for the actor, or the meaning a relation or situation has for the persons involved. The *objective meaning* is the meaning the same action, relation or situation has for anybody else. (Cf. Schutz, *Collected Papers,* Vol. II, *op. cit.,* p. 227.)

21. An objection can be raised at this point. The official goals of an organization define the organizational objectives as they are perceived by its leaders and, in that sense, are never entirely objective. As Katz and Kahn point out, "the stated purposes of an organization as given by its by-laws or in the reports of its leaders can be misleading. Such statements of objectives may idealize, rationalize, distort, omit, or even conceal some essential aspects of the functioning of the organization" (Katz and Kahn, *op. cit.,* p. 15). This does not contradict our thesis, however, for even if it is true, as Silverman suggests, that "organizational goals arise as symbols to legitimate the actions of certain actors in the eyes of others," it is nevertheless true that these goals are defined as the goals of the organization, thereby transcending the subjective motives of the individual members. David Silverman, *The Theory of Organizations: A Sociological Framework,* Basic Books, New York, 1971, p. 6.

22. Edward A. Tiryakian, "The Existential Self and the Person," in Chad Gordon and Kenneth J. Gergen, eds., *The Self in Social Interaction,* Vol. I: *Classic and Contemporary Perspectives,* John Wiley and Sons, New York, 1968, p. 77.

23. Alfred Schutz, *Reflections on the Problem of Relevance,* edited, anno-

tated, and with an introduction by Richard M. Zaner, Yale University Press, New Haven, 1970, p. 37.

24. Edward E. Jones and Keith E. David, "From Acts to Dispositions: The Attribution Process in Person Perception," in Leonard Berkowitz, ed., *Advances in Experimental Social Psychology*, Vol. 2, Academic Press, New York, 1965, p. 220.

25. Chris Argyris, "The Incompleteness of Social-Psychological Theory," *American Psychologist, 24*, 1969, p. 904.

26. Herbert Blumer, *Symbolic Interactionism: Perspective and Method*, Prentice-Hall, Englewood Cliffs, N.J., 1969, p. 9.

27. *Ibid.*, p. 9.

28. Robert Sokolowski, *The Formation of Husserl's Concept of Constitution*, Martinus Nijhoff, The Hague, 1964, p. 175.

29. Aron Gurwitsch, "Problems of the Life-World," in Maurice Natanson, ed., *Phenomenology and Social Reality: Essays in Memory of Alfred Schutz*, Martinus Nijhoff, The Hague, 1970, p. 59.

30. Alfred Schutz, *Collected Papers*, Vol. III: *Studies in Philosophical Phenomenology*, edited by I. Schutz, with an introduction by Aron Gurwitsch, Martinus Nijhoff, The Hague, 1966, p. 129.

31. All further reference to the psychiatric hospital will be written as "S.M.H.C." or simply "the Center." The term "Department" will refer to the Department of Psychiatry to which the Center is attached.

32. Ralph Turner, "The Self-Conception in Social Interaction," in Gordon and Gergen, *op. cit.*, p. 103.

33. Weick, *op. cit.*, p. 27.

34. Schutz, *The Phenomenology of the Social World, op. cit.*, p. 67.

35. Ralph Turner, "Role-Taking: Process Versus Conformity," in Arnold R. Rose, ed., *Human Behavior and Social Processes: An Interactionist Approach*, Houghton-Mifflin, Boston, 1962, p. 22. That this is only a theoretical or ideal-typical case is evidenced by Goffman's description of the processes of adaptation in "total institutions."

36. Rue Bucher and Joan Stelling, "Characteristics of Professional Organizations," *Journal of Health and Social Behavior, 10*, 1969, pp. 3–15.

37. Cf. Turner, "The Self-Conception in Social Interaction," *op. cit.*, p. 103. "Interpretation . . . in which the gesture is regarded as concealment or faulty representation of alter's actual feeling, can be called interpretation at the *empathic* level. In empathic interpretation, ego imputes an attitude or feeling to alter which is at variance with the face-value meaning of his gesture.

    An interpretation need not be correct to be empathic, and the feeling it imputes to alter may be favorably or unfavorably viewed. It merely imputes a disguised feeling to alter, but a feeling of which alter is assumed to be fully aware."

38. "When an agent vocalizes or imputes motives, he is not trying to *de-*

scribe his experienced social action. He is not merely stating 'reasons.' He is influencing others, and himself." C. Wright Mills, "Situated Actions and Vocabularies of Motive," *American Sociological Review, 5,* 1940, pp. 904–913.

39. Gibson Winter, *Elements for a Social Ethic: The Role of Social Science in Public Policy,* Macmillan, New York, 1966, pp. 147–148.

40. Cf. Schutz, *Collected Papers,* Vol. I, *op. cit.,* p. 348.

41. Cf. Edward Tiryakian, "Typologies," in David L. Sills, ed., *International Encyclopedia of Social Sciences,* Vol. 16, Macmillan and Free Press, New York, 1968, pp. 177–186, and John C. McKinney, "Sociological Theory and the Process of Typification," in John C. McKinney and Edward A. Tiryakian, eds., *Theoretical Sociology: Perspectives and Developments,* Appleton-Century-Crofts, New York, 1970, pp. 235–269.

42. Schutz, *Collected Papers,* Vol. II, *op. cit.,* p. 233.

» « «

*Manning and Fabrega provide a description of beliefs and practices in the
area of health and illness in order to get at the foundation or structure of
such beliefs—the body and the self. Clearly, the relation of body and
self is thrown into disjunction, one is "out of sorts," doesn't "feel well,"
when illness occurs. This fundamental alteration needs to be studied and
beliefs and practices concerning health and illness offer one source of insight into how objects (body and self) in their modes of appearing can affect the perceiving subject, the very person who is that same body and
self.*

    *The "new" ethnography in anthropology, ethnoscience, here is used
to uncover the structure of terms and meanings in one area of cultural
practices, health and illness. The relation of such an approach to that of
ethnomethodology and phenomenology is implicit without being elaborated. This is an applied study, then, drawing on several frameworks
among which is the phenomenological.*

THE EXPERIENCE OF SELF AND BODY:
HEALTH AND ILLNESS
IN THE CHIAPAS HIGHLANDS

» « «

Peter K. Manning
Horacio Fabrega, Jr.

Michigan State University

Social scientists and physicians share a general and fundamental concern in explaining human conduct. The principal locus of this concern, of course, differs. Social scientists' principal interest is in the organization of behavior; explanations derived primarily from the study of what we may term "normalized" activities are brought to bear on behavior that can be classified as deviant. Conversely, physicians regularly deal with what we may term deviant behavior, and from this seek generalizations about that which is normal or expectable in human conduct. Since human behavior necessarily involves the activation and expenditure of energy that can be traced to organs, systems, and ultimately cells and neurons, and, further-more, since only behavior of a socially meaningful sort is by definition the concern of *both* medicine and the social sciences, it is surprising that these disciplines do not have a broad framework that encompasses both biological and phenomenological aspects of behavior. This can be traced to reasons best understood with reference to historically developed paradigms within which the practitioners view, define, and solve their most significant "puzzles" (1).

Regardless of how understandable is the existence of the preferred analytic frameworks in social science and medicine, however, it is becoming clearer that many contemporary social problems persist largely because existing frameworks are unable to apprehend them in a systematic way. Current definitions of what is social and what is medical are simply too narrow and do not allow explanations of phenomena that are problematic to both social scientists and physicians. We start with the premise that there is a need for an analytic framework that can accommodate relationships between body and self which is deeply rooted in biology and in the social and cultural forms in which phenomenological experience is cast.

A central concept that could be used in the effort to construct such a synthetic framework is that associated with disease. A number of definitions of disease having broad intention have been offered (2). These definitions, however, do not give systematic attention to social aspects of behavior. Culturally oriented studies of medical problems offer, usually implicitly, other types of definitions of disease (3) which contrast with the traditional one employed in most epidemiological studies. No attempt has been made to integrate these, however. It is fair to say that thus far the concept of disease has not been sufficiently expanded to enable a satisfactory examination of human conduct (4).

A different way of developing a framework that can encompass the various factors that impinge on human behavior is to use the fixed and invariant properties of either body or mind as a basis for analyses. An imaginative approach suggested by Watson and Nelson (5) is based on certain biological "constants." They propose that the body orifices (e.g., mouth, ears, excretory openings) be used to anchor analyses of cultural forms and symbolizations of behaviors involved in body-environment transactions. The Watson-Nelson framework, however, is quite general. It does not make clear how phenomenological aspects of behavior are to be linked with these transactions, nor does it give clues to the manner in which situational contexts (within which transactions involving substances, behaviors, and orifices take place) are to be organized. We see, then, that there is a lack of and need for a framework that takes into account bodily states, feelings, and social aspects of human behavior. These separate factors that contribute to human experience must be accommodated in a systematic, logical framework.

Several desirable features of such a framework can be posited: (a) it must be based upon careful empirical investigation of social life; (b) it should be built inductively from ethnographical description and analysis attending to the variable nature of body-self connectedness; (c) it should be cross-cultural in scope; (d) it should take into account sociocultural and historical change and be able to suggest the effects and the directionality of these indicated changes; and (e) it should integrate the perspective in which the actor's social world is framed, what we can term a phenomenology of conduct, with known biological facts and theories.

In this chapter we intend to review conceptions about the body and conceptions about the self as we observed and studied these in the Chiapas highlands in Southeastern Mexico. The relationships that representatives of the various social groups see between the domains of body and self are brought into sharp relief when occurrences labeled illness or disease become evident. The study reviewed here attempted to analyze the behaviors and meanings associated with these occurrences. In contrast to other "medical" investigations that are concerned solely with quantifying aspects of disease distribution or with "exotic" or unusual features of native syndromes, or with explicating the cultural significance of medical beliefs and treatment practices, we study these themes in relation to how subjects interpreted their body and interruptions or alterations in its functions. The views held about the body, the factors that account for its state and functioning, and the social patterning of these concerns are the fundamental themes upon which are grafted the more formal taxonomies of illness and curing practices. Our analysis tries to provide a socially relevant and processual view of illness and medical care.

In explaining the material gathered in this investigation the lack of an analytic framework such as described earlier became apparent. Neither medicine nor social science seems to have developed a sufficiently broad framework that can accommodate biomedically significant actions in the context of socially meaningful activity. In addition to presenting ethnographic material about the illness-related social activities of residents of the highlands, we will present portions of a frame of reference that has proved helpful to us in our analysis and interpretation of the material. First, however, we would like to discuss why social scientists need to include reference to bodily activities and states in their analysis of behavior.

THE UNIVERSALITY OF THE BODY

One striking fact characterizing sociologists as fully acculturated, socialized, and competent members of their social worlds is that they share most of the assumptions about social life that are also shared by their fellows. Despite the "special knowledge" that may be derived from the use of their scientific perspective, the framework of presuppositions which shapes and forms their commonsense reality cannot be regarded as unique or even unusual. More specifically, social scientists, as socialized members of society, share a framework of presuppositions about "persons" that includes a view of the self as a product of social experience and interaction, but a self that can be said to be *disembodied*. The failure of phenomenological sociology to include in a systematic manner a concept of the body perpetuates commonsense notions and at the same time reflects little awareness of the limits of this view.

Salient among the assumptions made about the body by social scientists and others is what might be called *a radical equalization of the social significance of the human body*. That is, they have assumed that since the body is composed of universal features, it necessarily is experienced as such; furthermore, given this "universality," it need not be accounted for within any special system of propositions bearing on the explanation of human behavior. Put in more direct fashion, the attributes of the body equalize its social significance; any of its properties may be assumed to vary randomly and are therefore relatively unimportant in empirical analysis. Review of the literature discloses that sociologists have generally attended to the body only when its state or appearance has deviated significantly. Attention to the body under these conditions implies that under ordinary circumstances its characteristics can be taken for granted (6). The fact that people occupy space, possess senses (other than hearing and the capacity to speak), move, differ in physical attractiveness, and perceive and act upon fundamental bodily sensations and feelings (at all levels of "health") is usually not elaborated upon. This pattern of assumptions may in fact be as common among phenomenological and existential sociologists as among others. There is, as we noted earlier, very little systematic work in the social sciences which integrates in a satisfactory and empirically useful fashion the concepts of self and body.

Salient factors that lie behind this radical equalization and sociological neutralization of the body are the development of the scientific base of Western medicine (which is associated with profound empirical success) and the refinement of the germ theory of disease, which underlay its rapid growth and world-wide influence. Extraordinary discoveries in the biological and health sciences, and the consequent rapid growth and obvious effectiveness of the scientific institution in developed nations, are major forces in the public acceptance of biological metaphors for describing and understanding their bodies. It can be proposed that a vast majority of persons in industrialized nations when in medically defined situations implicitly view the body as a "biological machine" functioning as an integrated whole having highly specific parts and organs located and described with considerable accuracy. In this view, the body is seen as an object which is "attacked" by germs, which "battles" diseases, and which functions at differing levels of adequacy. It is assumed by definition to be a biologistic entity, to be "experienced" in a similar fashion, and to be capable, within limits, of more or less comparable levels of performance and function for members of the same age and sex cohorts. This paradigm, which attributes to the body universal features, has been accepted by social scientists and has, in turn, obstructed their vision. An uncritical, almost naive, acceptance of the medical scientists' conceptual scheme has been manifest, and this in turn has led to large-scale efforts to elaborate upon it and to apply it in various contexts.

It will be useful for the purposes of analysis to list a few tenets drawn from the biologistic view of the body:

1. The body can be partitioned internally into named organs, systems and functional relationships—liver, kidney, heart, nervous, muscular-skeletonal, and circulatory and other systems—each carrying out identifiable activities.

2. Unless external or internal causes intervene (germs, diseases), the body functions "normally." The body, unless a person is diseased and with minor variations involving age and sex, is comparably experienced from person to person, situation to situation, group to group, and culture to culture.

3. The senses are universal: everyone feels, sees, hears, touches, and tastes in comparable fashion.

4. Disease is a universal, cross-culturally invariant phenomenon.

5. Boundaries between self and body are nonproblematic, "logical," and empirically verifiable, as are boundaries between person and other, man and nature, man and the supernatural.

6. Death is a biological process that occurs when the body ceases to function.

7. The body should be seen by persons as a natural, objective, valuationally neutral entity.

This listing presupposes that the biological structures and functions and the resultant modifications that can be labeled as disease within a biological framework are themselves *universally experienced* as such, that is, the normal body (one without disease) for persons of similar age and sex is comparably experienced such that variations between persons, situations, groups, and even larger social units are of minor empirical significance.

The phenomenological experience of the body has not been adequately and systematically studied. Several types of inquiry stand out for attention, however. A variety of focused studies have examined cultural factors in the response to *pain* (7), the assumption being that fixed bodily states "produce" equivalent sensations which are merely "reacted to" differently. From these studies one may infer that cultural factors are certainly important, although the framework adopted does not clarify what aspects of pain are involved (or body sensation, or conception of disease) or how pain responses are systematically related to social activities. On the other hand, physiological studies of pain do not give attention to cultural factors, being content to explain variability using traditional psychiatric and psychological notions (8).

The body has been studied as a *cognitive map* whose external and internal "terrain" may be categorized and classified into taxonomic orders or hierarchies, and whose meanings (connotative and denotative) are acquired as a result of culturally structured experience (9). These findings suggest that the number and kinds of anatomical terms present within a particular phenomenological domain reflect in a very general way the salience of that domain to members of the group (10).

Knowledge about the body's functioning together with the experiential precipitates of significant past events involving the body will no doubt influence the role and importance that the body is given in general discourse and, more important, the nature of the reality that subjects attach to the body. Sensations and feelings that are linked to biologically altered states must be viewed as a function of the symbols and meanings that involve the body. If symbolic attributes of the body affect the experiences and sensations individuals have when the body is altered or stimulated, then the assumption that bodily states produce equivalent information is untenable and we cannot turn to neurophysiology in order to derive a framework or provide a common denominator that will unify our thinking about the body and self.

This conclusion does not appear to have influenced the analysis of the ethnomethodology of everyday situations. The study of the construction of social order in complex societies has proceeded on the implicit assumption that symbols associated with the body are more or less universally shared by members of the society. Furthermore, the framework of Western biology and its concepts of function, structure, and performance are believed to order and constrain abilities located in or derived from the human body. Acceptance of what are assumed to be "invariant and fundamental givens" within the biological paradigm has created a cultural blindness, which can be the source of errors in sociological analyses.

Minimal requirements for a social analysis of the body are an appreciation of the following factors: (a) the body moves through time and space, thereby altering the physical location from which the social world is viewed (11); (b) the body is the source of stimuli, both "external" and "internal," which in a fundamental sense are the raw data of action and choice; (c) body appearances pattern social choices (among the more obvious—marriage, courtship and dating, career and occupational success); (d) changes in body appearance affect the self-concept (e.g., the effects of stigmatic diseases, radical surgeries, alterations of face, amputations) (12); (e) the self is the means by which bodily states are monitored and regulated, while changes in bodily states in turn alter the self-concept (13); (f) body-image acts as a salient constraint on human action (e.g., obesity and some neurotic patterns are attributed to "distortions" in the body image) (14); (g) perceived connectedness of self and body, of being and doing, are problematic; alterations in their relationships can affect social conduct [Laing (15), for example, associates schizophrenia with a "disembodied view of self"; Matza has analyzed the social meanings of marijuana highs as they relate to altered mind-body states (16)]; (h) in all societies, people use agents (natural or artificial) to control, modify, and/or maintain desired body states: the degree of knowledge about these agents, their distribution within the society, shared understandings of their effects, and their perceived linkage to body changes appear to be variable from culture to culture (17); (i) systems of language terms referring to the body, its parts, functions, internal and external workings, what might be called ethnoanatomy and ethnophysiology, are culturally patterned. Insofar as language terms organize the physical body differently, they must be regarded as affecting in varying ways the perceptions and explanations of changes that are noticed. The number of terms in the vocabulary, their specificity, their accuracy in terms of the Western biomedical classification system and the degree of "intrusion" of these scientific terms into everyday discourse are all variable. We will return to this problem in the final section of the paper.

Lacking a satisfactory formal framework by which the body may be analytically viewed, it is difficult to organize parsimoniously and precisely observations and impressions obtained in field studies and to assert with certainty the nature of body conceptions in a given society. What is initially required, and is the task of this essay, is to specify and exemplify those dimensions of body-self relations that appear to be critical for understanding the phenomenology of the body. Such empirical data can also contribute to the understanding of how conceptions of self, body, and disease change as alterations in the structure of social relations in the process of social change occur.

Using carefully gathered ethnographic materials that describe the cultural patterning of body-self relationships, we will attempt to develop inductively a set of useful propositions regarding body-self relations. The following dimensions, which could also be used to organize the empirical data to be presented, are suggested as fundamental: (a) the posited nature of the *self*; (b) the posited nature of the *body*; (c) conceptions of the forms and types of *causes of alterations* of the body-self relationship, for example, disease; (d) assumptions about *treatment* and treatment options which are intended to either maintain, alter, or restore the body-self connectedness; (e) the place of the *emotions* or feelings in perceived body change and alterations in social conduct; (f) the importance attached to concepts such as *personality* or character (as patterns of emotions or the emotional tone of individuals) in perceptions of body changes and alterations in social relations (18).

RESEARCH SETTING AND METHOD

The research was conducted in San Cristobal de las Casas, a city of some 33,000 people in the highlands of Chiapas in Southeastern Mexico, and in two nearby Maya *municipios* (Tenejapa and Zinacantan) (19). San Cristobal is the commercial, social, and religious center for a hinterland containing about 175,000 Indians of Mayan descent. Within this region there are three principal ethnic groups. The dominant social groups are the *ladinos*, who are said to be of direct Spanish descent, and *mestizos*, or those of mixed Indian and Spanish descent. Members of these groups who are concentrated in San Cristobal and town centers speak fluent Spanish, wear Western clothing, and identify with the values and institutions of the Mexican government. Boundaries between the ladino and mestizo groups, however, are not clearly marked. When discussing these groups and their expectations we will refer to them as ladino-mestizos. The numerically dominant (outnumbering the ladino-mestizos by 6 or 7 to 1) but socially subordinate group is the heterogeneous *indigena* (i.e., Indian). *Indigenas* speak Mayan dialects (principally Tzotzil and Tzeltal); the 12 nearby "tribal" groups are distinguished by distinctive dress, language, and territory of residence (20).

San Cristobal is the largest city in a metropolitan hierarchy including adjacent villages, outlying towns, and isolated Indian hamlets, for which it serves important economic, religious, social, and political functions. It provides important services, goods, and access that makes regular visitation imperative for residents of the hinterland. Perhaps because there are four clinics, including a federally operated clinic for Mayans, as well as *curanderos*, midwives, witchcraft experts, and physicians (M.D.'s), San Cristobal is viewed as a medical center and is identified by residents of the area, both ladinos and *indigena*, as a source of help and support in time of crisis. San Cristobal and surrounding environs, even when compared with Mexico as a whole, are characterized by a very low standard of living. The Indian economy is a peasant type of subsistence agriculture based on corn, with quantities of beans, flowers, and squash and a few green vegetables and chili peppers also grown. Although small industries are common, there are no major industries in San Cristobal. The occupational structure is simple and is dominated by a few educated or professional people. Electricity is available, but the principal energy sources are men and animals. San Cristobal can be characterized on the basis of these facts as a preindustrial city (21), and its ecology also follows this pattern.

The most recent fieldwork was initiated in March-April 1972 (22). Using formal eliciting techniques, survey, and focused interviews, we observed and interviewed (a) *families* who have experienced illness episodes, probing for changes in behavioral expectations, help-seeking, and costs, (b) *curers*, including *curanderos*, witches, physicians, and midwives, and (c) knowledgeable *informants* living in the locales of interest.

The ethnoscience approach employed entails a careful attention to the rules and conventions that order or underlie the native categories which may be elicited or uncovered in systematic interviewing. Ethnoscientific approaches have primary utility, it would appear, in the study of collective, public, and concrete events, items, or situations such as kinship systems, fiestas, classes, or types of firewood or plants. The discovery of those hierarchial principles that provide an order for medically relevant knowledge, especially of illness episodes, is particularly complex because many episodes are not public (i.e., there are few noticeable or visible physical manifestations) and, at least in part, the units studied are not concrete. In other words, illness events are temporally bounded (not always present in given persons or social units), and they must be expressed (or "recalled") in subtle verbal formulas directed at capturing shifts in internal feelings as well as complex behavioral changes. As other ethnomedical studies have demonstrated, in folk settings medical vocabularies and accounts are placed within the context of moral and existential premises and belief systems. The elicited units can very often be vague and complex, are rarely mutually exclusive, and may be found to actually form "overlapping sets" rather than clear taxonomic hierarchies (23).

In the conceptual framework adopted here, medical terms are in part handled as linguistic labels. The segments of behavior denoted by such terms as "normal" and "sick," however, refer to aspects of an individual's continued adaptation to his environment. Although they are in many implicit ways acted upon as if they were continuous—as if one can "be" or have "both"—they are in an explicit sense often regarded as mutually exclusive. These highly abstract terms refer to clusters of behavior which in a given situation have relevance and validity given a known interactional context. Normal and sick can be seen as designations of a person's behavior by himself (a self-concept), or as designations by others, that is, as an imputed *identity*. These two, self-designation and other designation, may vary independently in given instances. These designations of identity may be viewed as the basis for a *role*—a set of expectations mobilized by an identity in a situation. Given these designations, the investigator must know how they are applied. In other words, how do people become differentiated and individuated over time by means of the categoric designations "well" or "sick"? The foregoing designations or labels come to be applied as part of an interactional process that is culturally structured. Culture in this context refers in part to such inferences from behavior as values, norms, attitudes, and "rules of thumb" or taken-for-granted assumptions.

There is need for careful research which isolates those *denotata* of given words that represent, as practical consequences, the necessary and sufficient conditions for invoking a vocabulary of changed bodily states (24). For example, we asked curers, both physicians and *curanderos*, to designate which items from a list of commonly used symptom terms (e.g., cough, headache, stomach pain) were associated with each of a series of folk illness terms (*colico, susto, detención*, etc.). The same matrix was presented in preliminary interviews to a panel of families. During a follow-up interview, a representative of the family unit was asked if a member had experienced an illness episode in the previous two weeks. If an episode had been experienced, the respondent was further asked what symptoms were associated with this self-defined problem, what interruptions took place in specified role spheres, and what actions were taken for resolution of the problem (e.g., going to a pharmacy for advice, seeking the aid of friends, physicians, clinics, or *curanderos*). In this research, then, the culturally based rules were inferred from the behavioral consequences associated with known linguistic pairings: symptoms, folk terms, and behaviors.

BODY AND SELF IN THREE SETTINGS

San Cristobal manifests the processes of cultural contact, conflict, and acculturation in a very visible, concrete, and everyday fashion. Before describing beliefs and practices related to body, self, and health and illness, we will briefly outline the characteristics of the medical care systems found in the area.

The services available in the city, including medical care, tend to be divided and duplicated along ethnic lines. *Medical care* may be defined as a set of one or more medical services administered to an individual during a period of relatively continuous contact with one or more providers of service in relation to a particular medical problem or situation (what is judged to be a medical problem obviously depends on culturally based definitions). A *medical care system* (MCS) is the organization or patterning of the way people of a selected group obtain medical care and discrete services from a set of persons with given training, facilities, and resources. Underlying this pattern is a constellation of beliefs, practices, and knowledge characterizing the clientele and a constellation characterizing the practitioners. Three analytically distinct medical care systems which we label as the Mayan, the Mestizo, and the Western system, exist in San Cristobal and can be outlined as follows:

Mayan. This is a MCS based upon a belief in sin and defalcation of moral responsibility as the cause of illness. The self and the body are only diffusely distinguished in social transactions and are considered continuous. As such, both are affected by illness and both constitute a generalized locus for intervention. Curing is accomplished by shamanistic part-time practitioners who mobilize generally available physical, social, moral, and supernatural resources in the curing process. Curers have no specialized knowledge and training which distinguishes them from nonpractitioners. Facilities and resources are limited. Ritual exchanges of food and other gifts remunerate the curer.

Mestizo. This is a MCS based upon belief in moral and social causation of illness, especially alterations in emotions and disruptions in social transactions and bodily states. The self and body are distinguished, continuous, and overlapping (e.g., some illnesses are said to affect certain organs or systems more than others) and closely and continuously linked. The body is seen as having a differential function and levels of activity, but nevertheless all alterations are linked with socially significant events. Changes in external social states and internal or bodily states are attended to. Part-time practitioners mobilize medicines (folk and manufactured), use ceremonies, and possess a degree of scientific or naturalistic knowledge for which they charge a fee. Other facilities and resources are limited.

Western. This is a MCS based upon belief in an empirically based scientific theory of causation, legitimated by a trust in scientific knowledge, training, and expertise bearing on the diagnosis, treatment, and care of illness. Curing is undertaken by a full-time, specially trained professional group, often salaried by a third-party organization or group, who possess a high degree of specialized knowledge and skill. Resources are relatively abundant and are present in the form of specialized and technically refined modes of treatment, instrumentation, analysis procedures, and complementary personnel.

All three systems may be utilized by persons in San Cristobal and environs in times of crisis and they may be simultaneously utilized if the resources of the person and/or the family permit it. A constellation of symptoms may be judged to represent one or more distinct medical problems. Thus at one point in time a person can become involved in one or more episodes of care, each of which corresponds to a different medical tradition.

In addition to their distinctive features, the systems contain similarities that also must be noted: the *charisma* of the curer enters all therapeutic transactions; the *environment* plays a part in views of illness causation in all three systems (a cold wind can cause a chill which may be the precondition for an illness); *pulsing* (taking the pulse inside the wrist or elbow of the person as a diagnostic tool) is found in all three, although its functions and purposes differ quite importantly; *medicines*, natural, patent, and what are considered "prescription drugs" in the United States are widely used and constitute important elements in all three. The populations using these systems share some dominant ideas, namely the interpretation of actions and behaviors within the traditional perspective drawn significantly from Mayan ideas.

There is an important constant in the two nonmodern systems to be discussed: the import of the "unseen." Chiapanecos believe that forces exist in the world that are dangerous, unpredictable, and uncontrollable. These mysterious forces exist in potential in virtually every situation or person. The evil forces in the world, as we shall see in the description of the Maya system, can be activated by witchcraft specialists. Although given men may vary in the point at which they act upon their feelings of hate and malevolence, these behaviors are always possible and may always be activated, and it is believed that any man (or person) is capable of hidden or covert revenge against another. It is agreed that even a good man may be forced to protect himself against others or may be unable to resolve an interpersonal conflict through other means. Witchcraft and witchcraft explanations thus inhere in the closed folk society where the limits of explanation for events are soon reached (there are few "accidents" in folk societies), and where the range of tolerance is very narrow.

Interpersonal conflict and its resolution remains central to the mestizo world view. Arising from diverse sources, and producing a number of results, conflict is the root of conceptions of health and illness. Envy, greed, fear, hate, shame, anger may trigger attributions of witchcraft and the search for supernatural assistance for resolution to the problem; or it may be seen immediately in the body of the person involved; or it may so corrode his interpersonal relationships that others may begin to question his health. These ideas can be quickly traced to Indian sources, which remain a repository and ultimate source of explanation for unexpected events. Mayan ideas represent the most enduring, general, and pervasive system of beliefs relevant to accounting for alterations in social relations (25).

Maya Traditional Medicine

The theory of disease that prevails among the Mayas of the Chiapas highlands can best be described as a *sociological* theory, although illness is nonetheless an event of significance to the individual (26). An instance of illness (in a parsimonious sense, a set of behaviors that are punctuated with pain, impaired bodily function, and/or inhibition and withdrawal) above all constitutes a socially constructed episode that involves the individual and all others who are implicated in the illness episode. An element in the patterning of an illness episode may be an individual's impaired functioning, but the significance of this element cannot be appreciated if it is not examined in the context of the symbols, actions, and social processes that combine to confer meaning upon the event.

Folk beliefs concerning *causation* or etiology (both in the ultimate and proximal sense), *susceptibility*, and *consequences* of illness as linked to conceptions of self and body are the most salient dimensions for understanding the context in which the interpersonal changes and readings of the intentions of others take place.

The centrality of the actions of the gods and their relationship to men in native explanations of the ultimate causes of illness is a theme revealed by careful investigation of Mayan religious beliefs (27). The direct actions of the gods, or altered personal conditions, controlled by the gods, such as one's *soul* or *spirit* and associated animal spirit (that which gives one strength and moral character), his *moral worth* (that which is inferred from one's commitment to religious obligations and the avoidance of sin) are in a sense the *ultimate sources* of illness (28).

The soul or spirit plays an important, if not crucial part in social life and is inexplicably intertwined with conceptions of health and illness. The Mayan's soul is composed of an inner and an outer or animal soul, and his relations to others are based in large part on his conception of or attribution of a degree of strength to their souls. A strong man has little to fear from others (gods or men), whereas a weak man without spiritual strength lives in fear, for he knows well the extent of his vulnerability. If guilt enters the person's thoughts, a strong man can lose his strength, while a cause that is just can provide strength to the weak and allow him to enlist the power of the gods. June Collier underscores these points:

A man who pictures himself with a strong inner soul and a jaguar animal spirit has little to fear. As long as he has committed no wrong (*Mulil*) he is invulnerable to punishment sent through the gods and constant vigilance can save him from the direct witchcraft of his enemies. But a man who doubts his soul lives in a very different world. He fears that the gods can be bribed to punish him even though he has done no wrong, and that witches can attack him in ways that he is not prepared for. Two contradictory beliefs thus run side by side through Zinacanteco culture. On the one hand, people will assert that the individual is always partly to blame for the evil that befalls him, while, on the other, there is the belief that the evil forces of the world are too great for the individual regardless of his soul strength (29).

The state of regulation of one's life, one's moral worth, and one's spirit, all of which relate to the ultimate source of all things—the gods—are reflected in various specific conditions and behaviors of the individual which may be seen as constituting the *proximal* factors causing illness. These more specific factors are witchcraft, and indications of moral failure, "sin," and emotional experiences we can gloss with the terms "resentment," "envy," and "jealousy."

The explanation of disease propensity and views of why illness strikes particular individuals and not others is not highly elaborate and can be described as truncated. On rare occasions naturalistic occurrences may be viewed as necessary and sufficient conditions for an illness. The influence of native classifications of types of naturalistic occurrences is not articulated. Illnesses that alter the face are viewed as punishment by the gods simply by definition and signify the personal failings of individuals as social beings. Two classes of actions can be conducive to illness: strong malevolence (usually associated with witchcraft) and weak malevolence. Two classes of men exist in the world, the strong and the weak. As the foregoing Collier quote suggested, strength is equated with survival and therefore is circular and somewhat tautological. That is, it is reasoned that those who are not sick must be strong, and the strong are those who have survived either sickness or the simple vicissitudes of the peasant life. The strength of malevolence is linked to notions of personal strength derived from the soul and is related to natural events or emotional upsets.

All illnesses are closely tied to interpersonal changes and readings of the intentions of others: illness can be said to represent a medium for expressing the state of relations between men and other men and between men and the gods (30). Gods express their anger through the attitudes toward oneself which a person reads in other men's feelings. Displeasure of the gods may be directed toward a person and be expressed as an illness. The recognition of illness and an attribution of cause is always problematic in any culture, but among Maya groups the principal authoritative judgment is made by a curer, although lay diagnosis is the first stage in illness recognition (31).

Curers are the principal available traditional means of dealing with illness after diagnosis. Their roles and traditional mandates require that they attempt to resolve or mediate socially defined "disequilibrium." The shaman does not deal exclusively with the mind or the body, nor does he act to resolve social conflicts associated with illness through the use of specialized skills derived from folk knowledge which one may analogically view as protopsychology, biology, or chemistry (32). Curing is not dependent upon nor does it involve detailed knowledge of the structure or function of the body; only the simplest of indicators, the temperature of the blood (which is read metaphorically and tautologically, rather than literally) is relevant. "The translation (by shamans) of the supernatural causes into physical symptoms is taken for granted, without reference to physiological explanations" (33). One may infer that the skills are above all those based upon detailed, concrete, commonsense knowledge of the social dynamics of the small *paraje*, waterhole group, or family with whom he is dealing. That is, the daily world of emotion, failure, and accident is his resource and provides a significant portion of the "technical" knowledge employed in diagnosis and treatment.

Most frequently, causes are ascribed by shamans and others to *failures*—sin or transgressions against the gods or other persons. Failures to meet obligations in religious/community service or in financial transactions are common. Violations of familial obligations, engendering the hate of others, or envying, fearing, or lusting after the possessions or life situations of others are secular sources of blame. Transgressions against the other-worldly code (wishes of the gods) are also seen as illness causes. These failures are not viewed as discrete, role-relevant, institutionally bounded failures but rather seem to refer to the attribution of a sense of generalized failure or moral indiscretion broadly and indefinitely related to religious and legal standards. In other words, like members of other folk societies, Mayans do not sharply discriminate the various modes of social control; rather, failure is judged in comparison to a broad and diffuse set of expectations for "the good man" (34).

What should be emphasized about an occurrence of illness, however, is the extent to which it provides a context or proximal stimuli for the acting out of a drama having important social implications and functions for the group. For illness is usually taken to represent (a) a sign that an individual has sinned and otherwise misbehaved and has been dutifully punished by the gods, or (b) an indication that a known or suspected antagonist or enemy has in fact plotted with the devil and witches to malevolently inflict harm on the person or family member who is ill. In the first instance, the illness itself constitutes the evidence needed by village elders that the sick person has misbehaved. As a result, either because of external prodding or because of a purely inward motivation, the sick individual and his family will make the necessary social, moral, and/or religious amends. These amends may involve mobilizing family, kin, neighbors, and friends for aid or for assistance in the form of participation in a curing ceremony, obtaining a curer, buying needed ritual items, or providing day-to-day care for the sick individual.

In the second instance, the occurrence of illness may stimulate two results. It may allow an individual to justifiably direct his aggression and hostility at the identified human agent believed to be responsible for the illness, in the form of witchcraft, violence, or personal insults. On the other hand, an occurrence of illness may actually constitute the necessary *evidence* that an act of malevolence has been perpetrated, in which case the afflicted person may report the illness as a criminal act in the same form that an assault complaint might be filed in this country to local civil authorities or to those in San Cristobal for appropriate decision and action. If the social friction involving the "assailants" is clear and easily documented, or if an individual "medical evaluation" by a shaman confirms the nature of the underlying illness, the suspected person will be reprimanded, physically punished, or placed in jail (35).

Mayans seem to lack a conception of the *self* which is internally located, autonomous, and separate from that of other "objects" (i.e., persons, things, dieties, animals). The person is seen as tied to his family, his land, and his activities; he is closely and invariably a member of a group, not a unique person. The concepts of self, personality, or mind, standing somehow separate from the concrete person and having the multiply layered and complex activities of ordering, monitoring, and controlling human actions, are not in evidence. Each person's animal spirit is capable of wandering, but it appears to be seen as a passive agent. It can be the object of injury and harm (which in turn is reflected personally), but it is not judged to be a controlling agent under the person's influence. Absent is the view that feelings are independent entities housed within the person which are capable of affecting choice and exerting influence on bodily concerns or human motivations, and which can exist as circumscribed reactions to interpersonal or impersonal occurrences. Instead, the prevailing view appears to be that pain, sadness, anger, happiness, envy, and so on, are concomitants of a person's experience of these reactions in types of situations and that these in turn channel the person in particular directions promoting similarly valued actions. We might describe the Mayan's view of self and person as equally "diffused" onto the family and group. Just as is the case with the body, the self (or "mind") appears reflected in and responsive to the transactions in which the person is implicated.

The body can be described as an unrefined, undifferentiated, and logically unarticulated "black box." Body parts, functions, and symptoms are perceived very generally; for example, virtually all illness seems to involve unhappiness, loss of appetite, and pain. The body, then, is a vehicle or receptacle for evil (when it intrudes), which crudely symbolizes the presence of "abnormality" (broadly and functionally construed within the sociocultural framework). Most illnesses are recognized by fairly simple indices. The body is not seen as capable of multiple-variable levels of functioning, indicated by reading of internal emotional or physiological changes, nor are events occurring outside the body differentiated from those occurring inside.

Maya medicine represents a continuing influence on the beliefs current in the highlands of Chiapas, including San Cristobal itself: it can be considered the context or *ground* against which subsequent or alternative systems must be viewed. The sociomoral theory of illness causation and therapy—the view that illness is a diffuse and general label for a wide range of disruptions in social expectations that make up the texture of everyday life—persists saliently in San Cristobal among Indians, mestizos, and ladinos. The Mayan view of the body as unsegmented and bound to others through highly determinant and multibonded transactions, and as a buffer for the shocks of everyday life, does undergo important modifications, as we shall show in the next section of this paper. Absence of a self-concept as a cybernetic governor of body and social changes does not indicate that Mayans do not reflect "psychosomatically" changes in their social relations. Rather, the body and the self do not possess logically independent status. Mayan cosmology, especially its principal tenet, the sociomoral nature of illness, remains a potent, if latent influence in mestizo medicine. However, in the mestizo system of medicine, the wholistic, undifferentiated nature of moral failure as a "cause" of illness, the associated integrated nature of social control (including legal, religious, and medical aspects), and the integrated simplistic body-self matrix are modified. As we shall see, these general areas become more differentiated.

Ladino-Mestizo Medicine

The content of the ladino-mestizo belief system is significant not only as a sociointerpersonal theory of conduct and illness but as a curative system ministering to the needs of a large number of persons in the region. Ladino-mestizo curers and their adherents utilize a mixture of naturalistic explanations and medicines (including patent medicines, herbs, and other natural remedies including injections) and supernatural beliefs and practices of curing (prayers, rituals). Located in the barrios around the edges of San Cristobal and in small towns of the hinterland, ladino-mestizo *curanderos* in many ways can be said to combine the two systems against which they compete and to which they accommodate in a dynamic fashion. A significant feature of change is the direct impact upon beliefs and practices of Western medicine through federally sponsored programs extending to even the most distant hamlets, in small ladino towns, and in San Cristobal itself (36). It would appear that in San Cristobal a very high proportion of the population, including even the most highly educated, utilizes the *curanderos* characteristic of the ladino-mestizo system, and in addition seeks aid from the medical clinics and private doctors located in the center of town. We shall see that what we term an integrated theory of disease is complemented by a view of interpersonal conduct, a phenomenological self, and an explanation for alterations in body states and feelings, all of which are contained in a complex verbal code. *Emotions*, or *sentidos*, provide the root metaphor in this theory, much as germs are the root metaphor of modern medicine. This concept is not explicitly developed in the Maya system. In order to systematically approach this subject, let us first review ladino-mestizo concepts of the body, the self, and personality prior to discussion of emotions.

Central to the understanding of disease among ladino-mestizos is the "illness propensity" of the person. These propensities are indicated by an interpretive framework that is quite unlike a Western medical system. Indications of physical and/or constitutional weakness together with excesses of the various sentiments that may either cause or weaken the body such that it is preconditioned to fall ill may be read in signs termed "mal agüero" (broken glass, animals seen at night, falls), suggestions of evil which others may emit (spitting, coughing, blowing, or intense looks), in dreams, or in interpersonal contacts with people of strong presence. The self, as we shall presently see, is believed to be continuous within the body is thus linked closely to changes in the personal environment, and these changes are in turn reflected in illness propensity and illness cause.

Ladino-mestizos judge an outbreak of illness to represent an overcoming of a person's strength, termed by them *consistencia*. This term designates various domains that appear to them conjoined as one entity. Thus the *naturaleza* of a person (roughly, inherited constitution) is at the basis of this strength. The physical, psychological, and moral health of the parents, particularly during the time of conception of the mother, and the wholesomeness of the pregnancy contribute to well-being of the fetus. A conception that occurred when the father was intoxicated or when the mother or father were tired and weakened, and a pregnancy characterized by little rest, sleep, and food and lack of emotional (and interpersonal) stability are factors weakening an individual's *naturaleza* and ultimately his capacity to withstand illness.

Features of a person's body and mind fall within the intention of the term *consistencia*. Bodies that are strong, resilient, constituted of good food, rest, exercise, and proper amounts of sexual vitality (specifically, amount and quality of seminal fluids) show high *consistencia*. Sexual energy or strength mainly refers to men, for women seem to be denied this feature of sexuality and are assumed to be virgins and to enter into intimate unions principally to satisfy the male's need. Excess sexual activity depletes the man and results in weakened sperm, just as insufficient activity may spoil the man's body and sperm and likewise contribute to a weakened fetus that will eventually have little capacity to withstand illness. A person's *caracter*, designating a mentalistic entity which can be translated or glossed as "personality," contributes importantly to good health by entering into a person's *consistencia*. Several key notions are held here. Intelligence, education, and ability to profit from previous experiences fortify the person since they contribute to level-headedness and cool rationality. These attributes enable the person to plan and deal effectively with life demands; during times of crisis these traits become more relevant since they allow the person to effectively discharge emotion and tension in a constructive way so that the mind and body are not harmed by excesses of emotion (see below).

One final feature of mind is relevant here. A person with a strong *consistencia* does not allow himself to become *sugestionado*. Here, ladino-mestizos appear to refer to preoccupations and worries of any sort. In a setting where persons are always potential targets of envy, anger, spiritistic influences, superstitions, and the interpersonal machinations of others, a strong person is one who withstands these influences, who does not allow them to gain a "hold on him." Thoughts, worries, and preoccupations that center on that which is potentially harmful can in fact take root in a person's mind and body and cause damage either directly or indirectly by weakening him. A clear mind that remains free of these suggestions is viewed as healthy and protective.

Observers of Latin American peasant life have noted the pervasiveness of the hot/cold dimension of life and observed that this dichotomy derives from a humoral balance notion that in practice is coupled with an allopathic theory of medicine emphasizing obtaining and maintaining bodily harmony (37). An extension of the balance notion intrinsic to the humoral theory of health and illness should be emphasized; that is, among ladino-mestizos the emotions themselves are seen as a reflection of the degree of balance obtaining in social relations, the degree of balance being reflected in the body's state, while the body's state can in turn disrupt or restore altered social patterns. Harmonious states are sought and maintained in what can be analytically partitioned as the psychological, social, and physiological domains. It is not difficult to demonstrate that arguments that assign alterations *exclusively* to one or the other of the foregoing domains are merely exercises in semantic or conceptual magic, unrelated to cognitive and emotive understandings of illness among ladino-mestizos in Tenejapa, for example. Informants explained to us that an angry encounter or argument between two men which is not consummated by a fight or resolved or mediated by others can rather quickly leave a residue of anger, spite, annoyance, and self-hatred. The explosive aspects of this type of encounter need to be underscored, for although fighting is itself expected and common, the open expression of anger is negatively sanctioned by gossip and active intervention. Pitt-Rivers (38) points out that people may fight, but avoidance of open antagonism is the first rule of conduct among ladino-mestizos in the highlands.

Anger is seen as producing impaired body functioning, pain, and physical harm, and it is in part indicated by the signs associated with the folk illness *colico* (stomach pain, vomiting of green bile, lack of appetite, pallid color in the face, and perhaps diarrhea). The excess of bile that is said to be produced by the anger may also (tautologically perhaps) be seen as the cause of the initial encounter. Alcoholic drink, herbal teas, and social support of friends and family are essential elements in restoring the body to a balanced state and in mediating the bile excess. In the same fashion, changes in interpersonal relations such as sympathy and empathy are revealed by the body and experienced by the interactants; they are not simply perceived during encounters. Socially supportive acts (offer of a drink, talk, touching) and underlying sentiments are seen by ladino-mestizos as directly converting (i.e., in a sociopsychological and bodily sense) previously felt pain or antagonisms into a sense of tranquility and well-being. (Psychosomatic notions of conversion have been pursued, it seems, primarily along the axis of how negative emotional tones are transformed or displaced on to bodily alterations without careful examination of the logically parallel process, found in our research, of elimination of pain and reconversion of harmony and well-being by the "infusion" of positive emotions and physical essences.)

Humoral theories of earlier origin thus continue to exercise influence in beliefs of illness susceptibility held in Latin cultures, although we are still gathering the necessary detailed knowledge of the degree to which the metaphor pervades and patterns not only the classification of foods, drinks, and illnesses but of social relationships themselves. The metaphor of balance and the avoidance, modification, and mediation of *excess* appears to apply to *natural events* affecting the body (a cold wind or cold water may cause illness or bring it on more quickly), *physical substances* such as food, drink, and medication, and the *products of social relationships* (bodily and mental states).

Among ladino-mestizos the *body* is viewed as a complex, functionally integrated, sacred unity. By the term "complex," we refer to the fact that the body is partitioned into broadly construed segments; for example, the *estomago* may be used to refer to the entire abdomen area below the chest cavity. Although some organs are named and associated with particular illnesses such as *dolor de higado, mal de riñones*, the organs themselves may be referred to generally as being in the middle of the body, or they may be incorrectly located (the "wrong" side of the body for the liver, etc.). However, organs are seen as functionally interrelated and mutually interdependent; changes in the functional capacity of organs are noted and attended to, as are changes in the systems in which they are thought to operate. Anatomical parts are named and seen as the locus of disease, for example, *mal de riñones, dolor de cabeza, dolor de hígado, pulmonía.* The level at which organs function is noted and monitored, and attempts are made to specifically alter the many uncomfortable states that are differentiated. Parts of the body are seen as aspects of a whole, each contributing to the status of the total. This integration is sought and considered ideal—terms such as *tranquilo* refer to a sense of well-being that includes mental ease as well as bodily comfort and satisfaction. The blood provides the most important unifying agent in the body as a multiplex set of systems and is the means by which homeostasis is achieved.

The self becomes more "complicated" in the social settings in which ladino-mestizo medicine dominates. If we follow the assumption that a person has as many selves as significant groups in which he interacts, we can easily understand the "expansion" of the self in the semiurban world in which mestizos and ladinos live. The range or scale of social relations in which a person may become implicated expands from the isolated villages to small pueblos, and expands markedly in ladino towns and cities. Institutions, occupational systems, and organizations are differentiated and role demands become more complex and must be hierarchically ranked and managed. Social conduct involves more audiences, contingent responses, and increased sets of options. This more elaborated scheme of social relations is reflected in a more elaborate and subtle etiology of illness, a larger number of illness terms in the lay vocabulary, and a more complex set of help-seeking options.

The ladino-mestizo sees the body and the mind as an interrelated continuum rather than a nonspecific "black box" or physical repository for externally based evil or punishment, as is the case among Mayans. In other words, self-conceptions exist, as does a protean notion of "personality types" as clusters of sentiments or propensities to act in particular ways that are somewhat consistent across situations. These orientations toward the social world, since they tend to represent the degree to which the person is susceptible to the consequences of interpersonal errors or excesses, are a component of the folk etiology of illness. The person who maintains strength and durability in his interpersonal style (whether or not it be a pleasant or admirable style) is seen as highly resistant to illness. These beliefs about character or personality are also linked to the outbreak of illness, the possibility for control or prevention of illness, and the specificity of illnesses.

A number of personality types or *caracteres* were elicited in the course of the research, and an association between illness and sentiments and between illness and "personality types" was revealed. This association shows what is meant by the emotional tone of a person. The idea of a personality as an individual possession, the person as possessing unique properties and having an overall sense of self that governs and constrains his conduct, emerges in this system and is logically inseparable from changes or alterations in conduct and appearance defined or labeled as illness, which in turn are seen as also having bodily or physical correlates. Feelings, in addition, are real, and differentiated. Numerous linguistic terms are commonly used to describe the changes in internal states. The person in this world-view is composed of bits of a puzzle, sometimes working together, sometimes out of harmony. He can master and control portions of his life by means of regular exercise, sex, food, and maintaining a good life, but he cannot predict when he will happen upon a large, goat-shaped animal at night (a possible witch in a transposed form), trip or fall and be frightened, be caught in a sudden blast of cold air, argue or fight with a neighbor, or suffer from the malevolence of others. This represents a crude list of the fearful, uncontrollable, irrational, aleatory features of peasant life.

We may illustrate the relations between these notions by examining *outbreaks of illness*. The first critical factor is the *resistencia* and *consistencia* of the afflicted person, including his physical constitution (as determined by his work history, habits, dietary intake, genetic endowment, etc.) and his personality or *caracter* (his emotional responsivity and tone, capacity for self-control, intelligence, education, etc.). The sum and balance of these determine his vulnerability, or propensity toward illness. The next factor is the interpersonal situation. A frightening occurrence or an embarrassing or shameful incident, for example, is a common cause of illness among women but rarely affect men, who are judged as more resistant along these emotional axes. Arguments and altercations, on the other hand, are equally pathogenic to the sexes. Unless resentments are discharged (by fighting, insulting, or acting out a plan of revenge, etc.) they will subsequently produce physical harm, including impaired bodily function, unconsciousness, and pain. Hostility is associated with the shortest "incubation period," and furthermore its effect is judged as rapid and direct. So are excitements and intensely satisfying or happy situations. Illness can appear in days or hours, and although they can be lethal they often are short-lasting episodes. Sadness and envy, on the other hand, produce illness gradually and insidiously; the components or manifestations of the illness, in addition, are general, diffuse, and less dramatic but longer-lasting and less easily removed.

The type of illness that develops as well as its gravity are a function of the constitution and character of the person and the evoking interpersonal situation. Analyses of the various emotions suggests that the degree of intensity bears a relation to the rapidity with which the emotion can bring on illness. Cleverness and intelligence are traits that modify the severity and duration insofar as they enable the person to discharge the emotion in a reasonably productive or adaptive way. A situation evoking anger or envy, for example, may in a labile person lead to violent acts of aggression and/or incapacitating pain and weakness; a more "dispassionate" person will be less physically and emotionally impaired and seek indirect means for the expression of his aggression. To the extent that his emotions are channeled at the offending party or situation, they are dissipated and lose their pathogenicity.

In this summary of ladino-mestizo medicine, we have seen the existence of a wholistic view of health and illness in which body (states, function, organs, and systems), interpersonal relationships, and sentiments or emotions are intimately interdigitated with behavioral changes associated with illness. An important implication of this theory of illness— illness as sociomorally and interpersonally construed—is quite simply that a person does not "get sick," "be sick," or "get well." First, a diseased body as established by a physician is neither necessary nor sufficient cause for attribution of the term illness or for adopting the "sick role." Illness can be seen more accurately in this setting and in the Maya cultures as a significant way to explain or rationalize human conduct. It is in effect the result of profound human concern with altered human relationships. Keeping bodily state independent or constant, we can say that the attribution of sickness is an effective, pervasive, socially sanctioned means of labeling changes in feeling, emotion, and perceived alterations in the quality and level of interpersonal transactions. Unlike complex societies, where altered body states are subsumed under a biologically derived vocabulary and are given more specialized, differentiated terms with more limited extension, sickness covers or glosses a wide range of events and changes.

Second, alterations effect and have an impact upon a network of persons who radiate outward from the person who is ill: family, kin, ritual kin, friends, and neighbors all share to some degree the impact and risk created by the illness. In a small town, during an occurrence of illness, neighbors may be asked to provide food, sugar, or salt, assume work tasks, or provide a loan to enable someone to travel to San Cristobal for material for a ritual cure. Thus, practically speaking, the risks of illness are broadly distributed across a number of people, each of whom takes rather diffuse responsibility for the welfare of the family. These persons, in turn, are closely tied to others also implicated in the network, their fellow kinsmen, neighbors, and friends (39).

Third, although the tasks that must be accomplished when illness occurs in a complex society or in a folk setting (i.e., provision and preparing of food, care of children, provision of daily care for the ill person) are parallel, the size of the group implicated in the restoration to health is much larger in the folk society. More specialized groups are implicated in the complex society, and their responsibility is professional and narrowly defined.

Fourth, cognitive, affective, social and moral disruptions in social relations (coded as illness) cannot be physically resolved by surgical intervention or by the use of drugs, nor can they be "psychologically" manipulated out of existence independently of altering the intrinsically relevant altered social patterns. Illness cannot therefore be privately resolved or cured, for it has social dimensions, nor can the experience of "treatment" itself be uniquely discrediting to the self since it involves the social network of the person who may be labeled as ill.

In a previous study, the striking characteristics that ladino-mestizos from the town of Tenejapa ascribed to what we would term psychotic disturbances were outlined (40). We observe that the causes of this type of illness are not judged as different from those of other types of illness. Furthermore, although ladino-mestizos may view the psychiatrically disturbed person as altered and changed in important ways during the time that he is ill (and this would include organismic changes), no stigma or other form of social discreditation (or differentiation) attaches to the person following recovery. Mental illness, in short, is not the occasion for morally censuring an individual—it is judged as an illness similar to others that can affect persons. The differential valuations that elsewhere are placed on afflictions of the mind as opposed to the body are thus not observed in ladino-mestizo communities. Related to this, we observe that many behavioral alterations that an outside observer may describe as psychiatric—depressive or paranoid reactions, antisocial outbursts, character disorders, and so on—are frequently also judged by ladino-mestizos as indications of illness, though the nature of this illness is not differentiated in any special manner. The illnesses, in other words, would not be described by them as essentially psychological or intrapsychic affairs, although their psychological (as well as social) extension would be acknowledged—the illnesses may even be called excessive envy or greed or sadness due to painful separations or the like.

The situational and interpersonal roots of these crises are included as indications of the illness state, but it is important that discussions with ladino-mestizos disclose that they consider the afflicted person or persons as also *physically* changed and ill—specific organs as well as their blood are described as altered and diseased. Psychiatric illness among ladino-mestizos of the Chiapas region has no unique and separate status. Attitudes and dispositions about its causes and attributes are continuous with those of other illnesses. The belief that it reflects dysfunction of only one type of system (mind versus body) is eschewed.

Fifth, no specialized vocabulary for the depiction of bodily feelings exists *apart* from terms that are applied to everyday interpersonal scenes and situations (shame, anger, disgust, embarrassment, envy) and persons (character types). Additionally, there is no specialized language of social relations derived from scientific bodies of thought such as psychoanalytic thought, or social sciences, analytic units, and conceptual schema which indirectly transform, mold, and shape interpersonal reality. There is a degree of connectedness between views of self, body, interpersonal social relations, and intrapersonal relations that is insured by the absence of specialized vocabularies.

Western Medicine

The propositions listed earlier describing the biological view of the body provide the root metaphor for the provision of medical care in the three federally sponsored medical clinics in San Cristobal and the offices of private physicians practicing in town. Studies of folk and Western medical systems have previously shown (41) that these premises contrast markedly with traditional or indigenous beliefs. Patterns of *competition* between systems, patient "*shopping around*" within and between curing systems, *exploitative* use (use of a curing system as a means of symbolizing ethnic or class loyalty rather than to obtain instrumental intervention or cure), and *encapsulation* or compartmentalization [seeking cures for one type of illness ("folk") within one system and cures for others within other systems (Indian curers, M.D.'s)] can be observed in the San Cristobal area (42). Although the three medical systems may be defined in the abstract, the conflict that must be considered is that which is experienced by the individual patient (and possibly his family) who undergoes the powerful socialization experience of receiving Western medical care in a clinic or office in San Cristobal. The organization of care, the occupation of the curer, the conceptions of health and illness, the nature of the diagnosis and treatment, the very essence of the patient's personal identity and body-image are both implicitly and explicitly questioned. The treatment experience creates and activates conflict between two sets (Indian and/or ladino-mestizo and Western medicine) of values, rules, and culturally rooted assumptions.

The degree of conflict experienced by Indian groups in their choice of medical aid and the rationalization of the meanings of that choice is less than that of the ladino or mestizo, who is attracted not only to "traditional" beliefs but who for symbolic and political reasons is attracted to national Mexican values and to rational scientific interpretations of events. From the perspective of culture contact and acculturation, ladino and Western medical values represent alternatives that have differential vectors for the groups involved. Moreover, shifts in the attractiveness of one or another are likely in this conflict context, and situational pressures and meanings are highly salient. Pitt-Rivers, in a perceptive paper on the ladinos of Chiapas, provides a suggestive hypothesis:

We might argue that simple traditional societies still live in ideological unity; but where cultures come into contact conflicting demands arise between which the individual is caught. He is no longer presented with the choice between conformity and deviation but rather with a choice of norms to which to conform. No longer a consistent whole, custom becomes fragmented into incomplete systems which offer the individual only rules that are disregarded and ideals that remain unattained (43).

Not only do the growing forces of nationalization and modernization fragment the indigenous belief systems, but the attractions and successes of Western medicine tend to undermine the legitimacy of both the Maya and ladino-mestizo systems. The inroads of Western medicine are complemented by the failures, which are to some degree endemic in the two folk systems, given their limited curative resources. Infant mortality and disease incidence and prevalence in the highlands are both high, as perceived by residents of the highlands and as shown in official health statistics for the region. Envy, fear, and distrust of the powers of the curer suffuse the curer-cured relationship and the limitations of crudely empirical folk approaches are commonly apparent.

The forces of "urbanization," "acculturation," and "education" can be specified in this context as bearing on the interpretation of the meanings of the specific encounters labeled as the dispensation of medical services. Western medicine, which symbolizes "progress" and disidentifies the user with "Indian" identities and a traditional style of life also provides a solution to many acute illness episodes, and it has been shown to be effective in public health campaigns in the highlands.

In the modern care systems of the city, the body is seen as an autonomous entity having an almost machinelike quality. This set of assumptions is established in interactions with physicians when they probe body openings and parts in order to examine or reveal body functioning. Instrumentation assists in these activities, separating even human touch from the process. Body parts, fluids, and emanation (sputum, feces, urine, sperm) are seen as discrete, detached, physical, independent units having no moral, sacred, personal, or unique meanings. They may in consequence be used to diagnose and treat impersonally defined illnesses.

The technology of modern medicine—its massive array of electronic instruments, plastic hearts, atomic probes, steel bones, plastic arteries and veins, battery-operated pacemakers, television-monitored patients in recovery and under the knife, sanitized hallways, and formalized billing—coalesces to create, dramatize, and symbolize the human being as an object for mere scientific curiosity, for mechanical alteration and control, as an object to be assessed according to economic formulas, or as a patient case number.

What assumes relevance in Western medicine are the person's complaints, signs, and symptoms indicating that he possesses an altered body, which bear on his condition as medically defined. His mode of relating to the world is reduced to those facts that are directly relevant to the scientific purposes at hand. The patient experiences a stripping away of identities to those bearing only on the medical history, and the language of the physician conveys this to the patient as an object, isolated from his self. All complaints become in this process "typical" instances of "typical disease." However, since patients do not experience altered bodies as "typical disease" (undetected diabetes or "invisible" cancer, parasitic infection), they often do not act in concert with physician expectations (44).

Emotional statements and meanings are avoided and/or minimized in the discussion of illness; the alterations in the self that occur in concert with or as a part of illness within the native conception are treated as intrusions into the diagnosis. The self as an entity is disvalued in the sense that the soul, the animal spirit, and the cosmological system in which the person has sacred status are disregarded as "primitive" or "irrational." The supernatural forces that are believed in other societies to tie man to other men and to his gods, those relationships which signify the very status of his being, are no longer acknowledged as real and are seen instead as impediments to "understanding the problem" the patient "has." In this same context, the consequences of a single encounter can lead to major modifications of the self and body of the person. This can be most dramatically illustrated by considering the consequences of the diagnosis of cancer involving facial surgery or radical amputation. Major changes in the body can now be generated by narrow, isolated transactions.

The system in which meanings are determinant is the impersonal and scientific world of medicine. The vocabularies of medicine are not shared: specialized terms are applied to bodily parts and functions—the previous intimate connection between self, body, and interpersonal language and transactions is severed—for example, red corpuscles now become the locus of illness and the target for medical intervention. All these features tend to sharply etch the boundaries of the two worlds in which the patient and the physician live—social distance is marked in every word, gesture, and symbol employed. Money payment is but the final distinction that places the treatment experience in an impersonal, distant, neutral, objectified context. (See Appendix for a summary statement of the nature of health, illness, self, and body in two settings.)

COMMENT

We have suggested the need to carefully examine the language systems by which members organize, structure, and label illness events. In a general sense, language allows the integration of social relations, self and body, and other social objects at the symbolic and behavioral level. In linguistic differences and changes, one sees modifications occurring in the concept of body from *sacred* to body as a *machinelike instrumentality*. Ladino-mestizo views, as outlined in the preceding section, contain a "sacred" conception of body which reinforces the symbolic ties of bodies to other bodies and strengthens a belief that bodies reflect both self-esteem and the attribution of positive qualities by others. In other words, the language of bodily reference and bodily imagery is projected outward into the world, establishing the meaningful boundaries of that world and setting the person apart from his significant social objects. The body serves as the center of a fundamental or natural classificatory system in folk societies (45). From the center of his world, man in the folk society constructs linguistically a symbolic universe that allows him to locate himself in a social world, attribute to it reality, give it substance and viability, and to array and symbolize social objects that are significant to him in terms that are both useful and familiar (46).

The language terms applied to the body are also found or replicated in a number of other social domains. Taking a note from Lévi-Strauss, Vogt notes that in Zinacantan (a municipio near San Cristobal in Chiapas) structural replication occurs: the same concepts are utilized to organize and make meaningful distinctive physical domains. Terms taking a significance from intimate familial usage such as "father" and "mother," "older" and "younger" brother are also applied to ritual relationships within the religious and associated cargo system. Most significant in this context is the pattern of structural and symbolic replication in the naming of house parts and mountains in Zinacantan:

. . . names for parts of the human body are replicated in the names for parts of houses and for parts of mountains. In the case of a Zinacanteco house, the walls are called "stomach," the corners are called "ears," and the roof is called the "head." The purpose of the new house dedication ceremony is to provide a soul for the house just as a human body is provided a soul by the Ancestral Gods. The same concepts are applied to mountains: the peak is a "head," the base are the "feet," and the sides of the mountain are called the "stomach." Some of the same terms are applied to fields and tables. The corners of a field are the "ears," as are the corners of a table. The top of a table is a "head" and its legs are its "feet" (47).

This same pattern of replication occurs among the Western Apache of North America. Anatomical terms can be elicited by the frame, "X, its parts, what are they called?," where X is the lexeme denoting the object whose anatomy is being investigated. The set that refers to "man" cannot

Table 1 Western Apache Anatomical Terms with Extended Meanings (48)

Apache Anatomical Terms	Anatomical Terms (re: man)	Extended Meanings (re: auto)
wos	shoulder	front fender(s)
g∂n	hand + arm	front wheel(s), tire(s)
dɔ	chin + jaw	front bumper
ke'	foot, feet	rearwheel(s), tire(s)
ni	face	area extending from top of windshield to bumper
ta	forehead	front portion of cab, or automobile top
čḭ	nose	hood
ɣ∂n	back	bed of truck
kai	hip + buttock	rear fender(s)
zɛ'	mouth	opening of pipe leading to gas tank
inda'	eye(s)	headlights
tsᴣs	vein(s)	electrical wiring
ɛbiyι'	entrails, guts	all machinery under hood
ȝιk	liver	battery
pιt	stomach	gas tank
ǰi	heart	distributor
ǰisolɛ	lung	radiator
čḭ	intestine(s)	radiator hose(s)
tikɔ	fat	grease

be considered semantically isomorphic with the terms for "horse," "bear," or "automobile," even though many of the same anatomical terms are present in all four (49). That is, depending on which set the term is in, it can have distinctive referents—when applied to man the term *Ke'* denotes "foot," when applied to the bear, "paw," when applied to horse, "hoof," and to the automobile, "tire." The argument of this paper is consistent with Basso's interpretation: Man provides the model for the extension of these terms. The meanings in the left column in Table 1 are glossed in the right column (it should be noted that a further table showed that the complete anatomical set of terms took the form of a three-level, part-whole taxonomy with man's body as cover term; the two subordinate but equal (covering about half the number of terms) terms being *ni* (face) and *ebiyi'* ("guts" or "entrails"). He concludes that "though the extended set contains only 19 terms, its taxonomic structure is identical to that of the anatomical set (50). The body provides the principal metaphor by which the automobile is encapsulated within a traditional system of meanings by which man maintains symbolic control over his universe of significant objects. Automobiles, like the body, are seen as being self-propelled but having the same structural properties as the body. By this metaphoric extension, man reinforces his belief in his capacity to control machines in the same fashion by which he exercises control over his own limbs.

In folk settings there is a degree of linkage between social order, self, and body that does not obtain in modern settings. Anomalies, uncertain events, and bodily alterations serve to mark violations of that order as well as to provide the stimulus for culturally occasioned remedial actions. Illness is among a class of events that symbolize the actor's perception of his malfunctioning, his desire for social support, and perhaps biological or physical changes (although the latter is not an axial consideration). In folk cultures the mind-body continuum and the intense, multiply determined quality of interpersonal relations insures that illness in some sense cannot be ascribed solely to a single person but must be seen in the context of the relevant social unit within which it occurs. Curing ceremonies can be seen in at least one sense as a mobilization of these interpersonal networks, and they cannot, as in modern societies, be seen as being directed solely toward rectifying either a disordered mind or a dysfunctional body.

Modern society, by contrast, is characterized by differentiated and striated social worlds, microcosms bounded by limited common experiences, definitions, symbols, and language. Within the larger social worlds considered sociologically as "institutional" are numerous more limited worlds circumscribed by such terms as "ethnic," "religious," or "occupational" worlds, and more limited microworlds of organizations, families, and other collective enterprises. Within these spheres meanings are provided by context, that is, by nonverbal understandings and tacit assumptions that provide the domain within which symbols assume a social significance. There is evidence that the range of possible meanings is becoming more diverse in modern society. It can be inferred that moral competition over meanings is also increasing. As the range of personal experience increases through mobility, education, media-exposure, and as the significance of tradition, ritual, and custom recedes, a new repetoire of symbolization grows apace. The existence of competing symbolic orders reduces the range of agreed upon standards, a "moral core" of rules and values. As a result, people are frequently cast into new situations where boundaries and outcomes are obscure or unknowable. A degree of *disconnectedness* between person and society and self and body becomes almost inevitable. The governing rule of modern society is *abstraction;* it provides a basis for establishing the rule of the group over the person and of the state over the group through the technological mechanism.

The escalation of the egalitarian spirit based on an abstract concern for equality, by making everyone a member only of the larger mass, makes everyone no one, everybody nobody. The increase in size in the society makes closeness to the realms of political decision making and power more problematic; simultaneously, these same forces increasingly impinge upon and alter the daily life of the person. Institutions, as they ramify in the extensiveness and intensiveness of their involvement in the lives of people (think of the enormous escalation in the power of the police, the welfare system, and the schools in the last five to ten years), can no longer command the loyalty of a growing minority of their participants. The machinations of large bureaucracies, distant, almost imaginary in their power, nevertheless deeply affect the lives of modern man in pervasive and subtle ways. In fact, the very subtlety of institutional influence, those influences that produce the "organization man," is a basis for an explanation for their insidious effects.

As institutions grow in power and authority, while simultaneously becoming less resilient and responsive to pressures and demands for change, the person sees them as receding into an inaccessible and distant social space which is thereby disconnected from his own immediate experiences and needs. The symbolic grids (language systems) found in urban societies, those patterns of meaning into which personal experience can be cast, tend to be more individualistic, discrete, variable, and situationally determined. Any member of modern society will immediately recognize that an explanation for events he encounters never fits a preestablished order, may in fact be set within any number of orders, or may strike him as absurd.

An explanation for changing conceptions of body and self can be drawn from the following general arguments:

1. The *vocabularies* available (moral universes and subuniverses as well as practically determined accommodations) are enormous—for ex-

ample, a moral language of sin, a legal language of social culpability, a biological language of physicalistic determinism; a psychoanalytic determinism; a psychoanalytic language of rehabilitation and justification; an everyday language of practical necessity; a computer-derived language of machinelike functioning of the mind and body.

2. Within each of these language subworlds disease terms exist (references to body changes) as do illness terms (socially defined alterations in functioning). These specialized vocabularies can be applied to mental, psychological, and physical or biological changes. They are often in conflict logically and in specific cases [cf. Szasz (51) on the conflict between legal and medical explanations for mental illness].

3. A number of new classification systems are emerging as a result of rapid social change, technological innovation, social and cultural mobility, and the diffusion of ideas through the mass media and acculturation.

4. Science continues to increase in acceptance as a rhetoric for the understanding and explanation of human behavior. Science, as an external, absolutistic system, is applied to the body, altering "private" meanings to public purposes, while the language of social science is growing as the preferred rhetoric of public affairs.

5. The vocabulary of self-description and the centrality of the self no longer dominate modern literature. In the first 50 years of this century perceptive critics such as Lionel Trilling saw the self-defined role of the modern novelist as limning the meanings and limits of the self; however, with time, these social boundaries became so blurred that many artists appeared to be almost entirely preoccupied with the *absence* of self in the modern experience (52). In the works of Robbe-Grillet, Sarraute, Pychon, Heller, and Bellow, for example, the person is overpowered by the forces described as surrounding and enmeshing him. The self is seen as a reflection, or as a refraction, as a mere juxtaposition of events; the person may be described in these works as existing as a function of what he sees. In the perceived absence of a vocabulary of naturalism, or a vocabulary of sensation and feeling, the void in language has been filled by the adaptation to human experience of technological language developed to describe, construct, repair, and destroy the machine.

Many sensitive observers have noted the erosion of the power of modern vocabularies to capture and to convey a set of recognizable and traditionally shared meanings. Daniel Bell sees trends in modern letters of an increased "mechanization of the vocabulary," as well as an increasing "rationality" and formality:

. . . the modern vocabulary is purely rational, with no referent other than itself—contained mathematical formulae. In modern cosmology (as in physics, and in the other sciences as well), pictures have gone, words have gone; what remains—apart from elegance, but the elegance of formal ingenuity—is abstract formulae. And underneath these formulae there is no law of nature as we knew it before, eternal, universal, immutable, and readily discernible. Underneath are uncertainty and the break-up of temporal and spatial sequence (53).

Some of the forces we have touched on are nothing less than synonymous with what we gloss with the term "mass society." They have displaced man as the center of his universe, an agent who sees the world unfolding with himself as *subject*, and they have substituted instead an *object* (54).

A theme of this paper is that one source of the apparently growing sense of a disembodied self, or a selfless body, is modern medicine. *In primitive society the body of man is the paradigm for the derivation of the parts and meanings of other significant objects; in modern society, man has adopted the language of the machine to describe his body.* This reversal, wherein man sees himself in terms of the external world rather than seeing the external world as a reflection of himself, is the representative formula for expressing the present situation of modern man (55). Even the development of psychosomatic medicine has reinforced the mind-body dichotomy insofar as it requires a posited dualism, with body and mind each capable of affecting the other. The psychiatric view of mental illness, as Szasz, Goffman, and Laing show, illustrates a disembodiment of the self.

In the case of "mental illness," there is little societal consensus concerning the nature, locus, and cause of the illness. There is, in addition, manifest disagreement within psychiatry itself on matters of etiology, diagnosis, and treatment. The techniques by which the disease is validated as "scientifically" real and applied to patients are objects of public and professional disagreement. There is little consensus between the patient and his significant others regarding the nature or definition of the illness. The physician is often called on to provide definitional clarity and to enter the struggle over meanings on one side or the other of the communication battle. The mandate of the physician to treat "biological" illness by "scientific" means seems now well established and legitimated: Society accepts in large measure the specific decisions he makes and applies to given persons. Given the *self-bound* nature of mental illness, however, it is not surprising that issues of diagnosis and validation are problematic.

Physicians as social controllers provide legitimate rationales for the alteration of social roles, have the legal power to allocate people into cure or constraint institutions, are sanctioned to enter into the daily lives of citizens, have access to drugs and other euphorics, and can make decisions about life and death. Physicians typically make their choice of the mode of social control they exercise on the basis of a *sample* of information they obtain from the patient's verbal reports, case history, or file if it is available, the reports of his family, and specialized tests they may wish to collect and analyze. In the case of a physical illness, physicians rely on a few rather well-developed techniques for eliciting the information needed for diagnosis and prognosis. They restrict attention or therapy almost exclusively to managing, treating, or curing the identified disease. Ethically, and in some ways legally, physicians must attend only to that aspect of a patient's behavior relevant to the cure. Other identities, and attributes, immorality, lapses in dress, demeanor, and the like, are theoretically excluded from relevance. Stated succinctly, in physical or biological *diseases* the segment of information used to make diagnoses and monitor treatment in a very real sense stands outside the patient, that is, it is drawn *from* him, perhaps constitutes a part of him, but *it is not him*. Physicians treating nonmental illness do not make moral judgments about *selves*.

When dealing with mental illness, on the other hand, the physician bases his diagnoses on information derived from the routines of everyday life. Because specific parsimonious diagnostic tests are lacking and he must deal primarily with reports made about everyday behaviors as data, his diagnostic information (expressed attitudes, beliefs, feelings, or signs and symptoms) should in principle approach a *comprehensive biography* of the patient. In practice, the record is likely to constitute but a small (and biased) portion or bounded segment of his social demeanor. The impossible mandate of the psychiatrist appears to be to delve into any and all aspects of the patient's life, public, private, past, present, and future. For without these data, it can be argued, the therapist might never discover that requisite bit of behavior, experience, or relationship that can become the *sine qua non* on which effective therapy can be based.

The social control of physical illness is based on a limited number of validating techniques, generally accepted as legitimate, and directly affects only a relatively small number of social relationships. The treatment relationship can provide a variety of sick roles which may serve to account to patient and others for changes in behavior and affect. The concept of mental illness, on the other hand, is the basis for invoking social control based on a diverse range of medical techniques and observational skills. This mode of control continues to be of questionable legitimacy in significant portions of the society. It tends to affect or rearrange a host of social relationships. It implies an attempt to control the person as he carries out his daily round of life; clearly, the focus of control efforts are the very behaviors he presents while engaged in routines of daily living.

Psychiatric illness not only represents in microcosm the *distance* that modern man feels from himself, but his distance from his body as well. In a setting such as San Cristobal, disease is so pervasive, so common, so much a part of everyday life that its incidence and effects cannot be uniquely stigmatizing to those who experience it. As a class of alterations in interpersonal relations, illness of all sorts must be socially dealt with and treated. Symptoms and their interpretations which we might label "mental illness" are logically nonexistent in the conceptual system of folk cultures. Treatment and recovery are not substantially different for "mental" as opposed to "physical" illnesses. A person in San Cristobal who has been treated for mental illness can be considered to have the status of the person in the United States who has recovered from pneumonia. Since in San Cristobal one's competence, integrity, rationality, and self are virtually always involved in an illness episode, no single class of illness can be uniquely discrediting. Diabetes and tuberculosis are discrediting in San Cristobal, and, like chronic illness in the United States, there is a high degree of probability that self-change will occur in a wide variety of episodes resulting in illness careers.

Since the label "disease" is attached to so many phenomena in San Cristobal, the *level of tolerance* is high in contrast to the situation described in studies of societal reaction to illness in modern societies. Although disease serves to rationalize and explain conduct in industrialized settings, the meanings of health and illness produced by practitioners of modern medicine are not uniformly accepted by all the groups or persons to which the label is applied (are "revolutionaries" "sick" or "mentally ill"?). Illness-relevant meanings and social roles tend to be controlled by physicians and have a level of specificity that is unknown in folk settings. In folk settings, the use of the illness label makes conduct understandable, is a consequence of human concerns, a way of labeling changes in feelings, emotions, and social relationships. If, as is the case in American society, "valid" (i.e., legitimated by relevant others) disease becomes attached almost exclusively to bodies that are malfunctional, disease that is thought of as socially derived (self-bound illness) is subject to great discreditation. Not only does this alteration of social response to the mentally ill person threaten the social being of that person, it casts doubt on the competence of those around him, those who conspire with him daily to maintain the human drama. In the face of the madman is seen the terror of humanity in disarray, especially the chaos of those intimate social scenes that affirm the *integrity* of the self and the body (56).

Social or people-oriented institutions can be considered to fail to the degree that they utilize linguistic mind/body paradigms that cast aside or deny the perceived *integrity* of the body and the *self*. The intrusion of science into the everyday life of man has devastated the previously strained cosmology of man in which everyday activities and social relations could not and were not divorced from the body and self as parts of a socioemotional puzzle.

APPENDIX: PROPOSITIONS BEARING ON HEALTH
AND ILLNESS IN TWO SETTINGS

The following propositions are advanced to suggest the nature of conceptions of self and body, illness and health, the character of health care systems, the curer-client relationship, tools, symbols, and setting of curing, and the occupational culture of curing in two different settings: (a) on the one hand a *personalistic* (e.g., the Mayan and the ladino-mestizo) system in which the relationships between people are seen in primary, intimate, face-to-face terms, where there is a high degree of value consensus, undifferentiated social roles and statuses, and a simple set of self-related concepts; (b) on the other hand a system in which persons are judged impersonally (Western medicine), on the basis of performance, where there are diminished face-to-face contacts, where associations tend to be formal and structured by organizations or rational rules, and where there is a low degree of value consensus and a highly differentiated social and cultural system (57). The self tends to be a situated self, varying by time, place, and the persons involved in the interaction. In this model *the self and body become increasingly thought of as separate and separable entities as change occurs from a simpler to a more complex social system.* Yet the problems of health and illness and the consequences and causes of illness can seemingly never be separated from an equation involving *external* relations (friendships, kinship ties, associations) and the *condition of the body* as perceived and defined (58).

Some important qualifications and limitations should be noted. First, the polar types may resemble broad stereotypes rather than accurate typifications of typifications. They outline specific domains to be investigated and present concepts requiring refinement and/or rejection on the basis of research. Second, the polarities are arrayed into clusters of relationships, permitting empirical types or subtypes to be delineated along the continuum. Third, the concepts tend to be "structural" rather than referring to those dimensions requiring detailed observation, coding, and analysis of behaviors or activities. Fourth, the concepts are based primarily upon research in Latin American settings, and the degree of fit between data and concept may be most precise in this cultural area.

Impersonal System   Personal System

A. Self and Body

1. The *body* and the *self* are seen as distinct entities, logically and socially.

1. The *body* and *self* are not seen as logically distinguishable entities: they form a continuum. Changes in one produces and cannot be separated from changes in the other.

2. Health or illness or "normal and sick" may be applied to either the body or the self in a logically consistent fashion.

2. Health and illness cannot be considered logically to be located exclusively in one *or* the other entity.

3. *Social relationships* tend to be partitioned, segmented, and situational, i.e., there are many selves and roles which are seen as discontinuous.

3. *Social relationships* tend to be nonpartitioned, diffuse, encompassing; i.e., there are fewer roles and selves and those that do exist are intimately linked.

4. Social relationships are relatively formal and impersonal and are evaluated without a consistent moral-judgmental framework.

4. Social relationships are less formal and more personal and are contained within a consistent moral framework which is legitimated by a higher, i.e., sacred, authority.

5. The body is described within a biological framework, i.e., everyday discourse about health concerns is heavily punctuated by the use of biological categories and explanations derived from scientific sources.

5. The body is not seen as an independent entity separated from interpersonal relations; everyday discourse is low in number of biological terms derived from scientific sources.

6. The body is understood as a complex biological machine.

6. The body is seen as a wholistic, integrated aspect of self and social relations which is vulnerable and may be easily affected by feelings, other people, natural forces, or spirits.

Impersonal System	Personal System
7. The body's structure and function are partitioned logically into specific parts and systems The levels of functions and interdependence are differentiated in a relatively precise manner.	7. Categories referring to the body are unrefined. The body as an anatomic and physiologic entity is only generally partitioned. A simple view of function, extension, and meaning of parts is held.
8. Health and restoration to health are perceived as dependent on and logically referring to the body as a physical entity or, alternatively, to the self as a mentalistic entity.	8. Health is equivalent to social equilibrium. In addition to having bodily correlates, restoration to health is seen as a product of (a) reequilibrated or more harmonious social relationships, (b) purging of emotional and spiritualistic forces, and/or (c) restoring equilibrium in socioritualistic bonds.
9. *Personality* is seen as a salient factor in interpersonal relationships—it is the means by which it is believed one shows a "consistent self," and it is conceptualized almost as a distinct entity that explains behavior.	9. *Personality* does not exist as a separate entity; all relationships are transactional and multibonded, and the guiding emotional tone and interpersonal style as revealed in these relationships is what is felt as characteristic of the individual.
10. *Character types* and personality styles are only minimally significant in the diagnosis and treatment of disease. Such labels as "moody," "insensitive," "silly" exist and are socially, not biologically, relevant.	10. *Character types* and self-presentation are intrinsic or isomorphic to the cause, type, diagnosis, and cure of disease.
11. *Disease* exists apart from the foregoing modes of self-presentation.	11. *Disease* cannot exist apart from these modes of self-presentation.

Impersonal System	Personal System
B. Conceptions of Health and Illness	
1. Although sometimes viewed as continuous, health and *illness* or disease are regarded as mutually exclusive.	1. *Illness* is a nonsegmentalized process punctuated by "key events" whose consequences are seen morally and interpersonally.
2. Disease is universal in form, progress, and content. It can be logically partitioned into stages, with beginnings and endpoints.	2. Illness to a significant extent is idiosyncratic in form, progress, and content. It can only be understood in the context of the social relations of the sick person.
3. The consequences of disease are seen intersystemically and organically.	3. The consequences of illness may be seen in virtually every facet of the person's transactions, activities, and concerns.
4. Disease and behavior are logically discrete.	4. Illness and behavior are linked, logically and empirically.
5. The clock and mechanical forces govern the progress of disease; the unfolding of disease is inexorable unless medical intervention is mobilized.	5. Spirits and evil forces and people govern the progress of illness. The unfolding of disease depends on the cause; these beliefs, in turn, determine the requisite options of intervention.
6. Specific identifiable causal processes are known to be based upon accumulated chemical and biological evidence.	6. Generalized categories of cause exist, but they lack technical bases and precise delimitation.
7. Almost all illnesses are caused naturalistically (biologically). Classification of illness is derived scientifically from type of system or tissue involved, from type of cause, and form.	7. Illness is caused by (a) spirits, (b) emotionally ladened transactions, (c) malevolent people, (d) natural forces, (e) "genetic" or constitutional weakness. Type of illness is determined by the source or cause.

Impersonal System	*Personal System*
8. *Mental illness* exists as a category of illness which affects the self.	8. *Mental illness* is one possible manifestation of processes causing other disturbances in the person's universe of bodily and sociomoral relationships. All illnesses affect the self and the body.

C. The Character of the Health Care System

1. *Help-seeking* is rationalized by scientific labels and explanations involving biological categories and terms.	1. *Help-seeking* is cloaked in moral symbols: patterns of help-seeking and sources of help are largely determined by perception of the locus of causation: evil forces, persons, naturalistic events, spirits, etc.
2. The aim of help-seeking is to restore bodily function.	2. Help-seeking actualizes the need to reestablish or reequilibrate physical, emotional, and social bonds, which are seen to some extent as fused.
3. Medical specialization is based on precisely defined knowledge, technique, and procedures, all of which are discontinuous from ordinary social processes.	3. Specialization of health care providers is based on types of *cause*, e.g., disease resulting from witchcraft can only effectively be treated by a witch; bodily malfunction can be treated by a herbalist. Rationales of these are continuous with ordinary social processes.
4. The risk a practitioner may incur as a result of accepting responsibility for treatment of an illness is *collectively* distributed by: a. Legal systems b. Professional associations	4. The risk a practitioner may incur as a result of accepting responsibility for treatment of an illness is individualized and *personal:* a. A person's "self" is his most significant posses-

Impersonal System

Personal System

c. Insurance
d. Referral systems (horizontal)
e. Specialization (vertical)
f. Collective"business"organizations, e.g., group practice, partnership, hospital.

sion and cannot be protected by formal means.
b. Legal controls on provision of health care are minimal or nonexistent.
c. No professional associations or collective means of distributing risk exist.
d. Little referral by curers, no interdigitated practice systems.

5. Referral is highly patterned and rationalized, differentiated (horizontally and vertically), and rule-oriented.

5. Referral is "unpatterned," i.e., personalized, idiosyncratic, localistic, and lay-dominated. It is nonhierarchical and undifferentiated.

6. Time is purchased in discrete units, it is contractually shared, and the clock governs the availability of physician; day is highly segmented, e.g., 15-minute time units, 8–10-hour day; 6-day week, 11-month year of practice.

6. Time is judged analogically, jointly owned and shared, and partitioned complexly, e.g., "moral" or "intersubjective" time, time since the event "causing" the illness, and clock time for appointments. The day is segmented into three or four units.

7. Treatment procedures are universal, formal, learned, impersonal, and are not altered significantly by time and place of the treatment nor by personality of physician.

7. Treatment procedures are personalized, idiosyncratic, based on the particulars of the transaction, and have an interpersonal basis.

D. Curer-Client Relationship

1. *Relationship* is highly patterned and based on formal, almost contractual role prescriptions:
a. Instrumental orientation
b. Universalistic
c. Neutralistic
d. Focused

1. *Relationship* is informal, diffuse, noncontractual, semicontinuous with everyday life.
a. Expressive orientation
b. Particularistic
c. Affectively loaded
d. Diffuse

Impersonal System	*Personal System*
2. Confidence or trust is to a considerable extent preestablished by formal means: titles, credentials, certification of legal right (license), membership in professional organizations.	2. Confidence or trust is transactional; it must be situationally legitimated by the self-presentations of both curer and patient. Trust varies as to time, place, person, day, and symbols used.
3. Self-presentation and body presentation are separated for all practical purposes, and the relationship is directed to either.	3. Body and self are seen as presented together, and relationship is directed to these but in the context of varied factors.
4. In most instances transactions tend to be limited to those intended to produce a change in the body, whereas the self is often secondary. Alternatively, if self is treated, body is considered unaffected and often left unattended.	4. Medically situated transactions always involve body and self in relation to others, i.e., they represent a microcosm of the "illness problem" itself. Therefore treatment and diagnosis tend to be wholistic and integrated. They affect human relationships and spiritual forces simultaneously.
5. The role of the *curer* is highly differentiated, segmented, professionalized: a. Full-time occupation b. Extensive formal training required c. Specialization is high d. Technical skill high e. Knowledge base is complex, extensive f. Political control over access to the profession is high	5. The role of *curer* is not differentiated: a. Part-time occupation b. Little or no formal training required c. Little specialization within curing occupations d. Technical skill is low e. Knowledge base limited f. Almost "open" access to curing role
6. Basis of power and authority over clientele is *science*.	6. Basis of power and authority over clientele is personal *charisma* as conveyed by repute, appearance, and curing performance.

Impersonal System	*Personal System*

7. Relationship is symbolized by distance, coolness, formal relations, use of abstract concepts (jargon).

7. Relationship is symbolized by closeness, shared meaning, warmth, informality, concreteness of reference (use of "everyday language").

8. Recruitment to curing role by choice, based on skill, performance, knowledge, and endowment.

8. Recruitment to curing role tends to be based on ascribed criteria (family associations); "personality" or natural qualities are also factors. Skill and knowledge are relatively unimportant.

9. Only for "mental illness" does curing process involve self-expressive, self-modifying components.

9. For all illnesses curing process involves symbolization of self and expression of a placement in sociomoral order.

E. Tools, Symbols and Settings of Curing

1. *Tools* and procedures are specialized, discontinuous from, and unavailable to the person in everyday life, e.g., otoscopes, X-rays, lab analysis techniques.

1. *Tools* and procedures are not specialized but are continuous with and available to the person in everyday/anyday life, e.g., candles, flowers, drink.

2. Tools and procedures aimed at revealing, probing, cutting a mechanical entity, i.e., the body.

2. Tools and procedures are intrinsic to social relations and are consistent with other symbolizations of social relations.

3. *Settings* are segregated, e.g., home-office.

3. *Settings* are multipurpose; curing setting is home, and also a religious place.

4. Treatment settings are rationally rule-governed. Specific staff with special roles used. Paperwork dominates procedures. Hierarchical and authoritative, i.e., a bureaucracy

4. Treatment settings are loci for diffuse, overlapping, multipurpose transactions; no special staff—other family members or relatives of curer help. No paperwork. Little or lim-

Impersonal System	*Personal System*
governs appointments, treatment, billing.	ited formal authority over staff: family structure is replicated in organization of treatment.
5. Curing resources are technological and scientific; economically purchased; manufactured and complex. Available in complex systems, e.g., hospitals.	5. Curing resources are proximal—many are available naturally. Some are purchased, others (drink, herbs) are handmade or grown. Simple and few specialized systems for obtaining needed curing resources.

ACKNOWLEDGMENTS

Peter K. Manning wishes to thank Elizabeth Clark and the staff at Na-Bolom, San Cristobal de las Casas, Chiapas, Mexico. This study was supported by NIMH grant MH 21430-01, 1 Roe MSM; a Biomedical Research Fund Grant from Michigan State University and a grant from the Office of International Programs, also at Michigan State University. The support of the Latin American Studies Center is also acknowledged.

NOTES

1. Thomas Kuhn, *The Structure of Scientific Revolutions*, University of Chicago Press, Chicago, 1966.

2. Compare George Engel, "A Unified Concept of Health and Disease," *Perspectives in Biology and Medicine, 3*, 1960, pp. 459–485; A. Howard and R. Scott, "A Proposed Framework for the Analysis of Stress in the Human Organism," *Behavioral Science, 10*, 1965, pp. 141–160; and H. G. Wolff, "A Concept of Disease in Man," *Psychosomatic Medicine, 24*, 1962, pp. 25–30.

3. Horacio Fabrega, Jr., "The Study of Disease in Relation to Culture," *Behavioral Science, 17*, 1972, pp. 183–203.

4. J. Cassel, "Social Science Theory as a Source of Hypotheses in Epidemiological Research," *American Journal of Public Health, 54*, 1964, pp. 1482–88; N. A. Scotch, "Socio-cultural Factors in the Epidemiology of Zulu Hypertension," *American Journal of Public Health, 53*, 1963, pp. 1205–1213.

5. James B. Watson and H. Nelson, "Body-environment Transactions: A Standard Model for Cross-cultural Analysis," *South West Journal of Anthropology, 23,* 1967, pp. 292–309.

6. See, for example, works in the sociology of deviance which implicitly and explicitly investigate problems in interactional competence derived from missing limbs, blindness, deafness, etc. Roger Barker, et al., *Adjustment to Physical Handicap and Illness,* SSRC, New York, 1953; Robert A. Scott, *The Making of Blind Men,* Russell Sage Foundation, New York, 1969; and Erving Goffman, *Stigma,* Prentice-Hall, Englewood Cliffs, N.J., 1963.

7. See the studies summarized in B. B. Wolff and S. Langley, "Cultural Factors and the Response to Pain: A Review," *American Anthropologist, 70,* 1968, pp. 494–501, and in R. Melzak, "The Perception of Pain," *Scientific American, 204,* 1961, pp. 41–49.

8. It should be emphasized, however, that the study of pain, involving such issues as its quality, its localization, its spread and reference, and its relationship to bodily events is far from being rigorously understood. Individuals who study the neurophysiology of emotion are frequently forced to rely on tautologies, in part because the mind-body dichotomy and our language demands it, in part because the bulk of the experimental subjects who furnish reports of pain are members of related cultural and language communities, and in part because of the obvious inability to capture precisely the essence of the sensation. The result is that there is no unambiguous manner of depicting pain and other bodily centered sensations, and thus one can expect to find much variability in the manner subjects report experiencing bodily changes.

9. Cf. G. Marsh and W. S. Laughlin, "Human Anatomical Knowledge among the Aleutian Islanders," *South West Journal of Anthropology, 12,* 1956, pp. 38–78; H. Miner, "Body Ritual among the Nacirema," *American Anthropologist, 58,* 1956, pp. 503–507; H. Landar and J. Casagrande, "Navaho Anatomical Reference," *Ethnology, 1,* 1962, pp. 370–373; K. Franklin, "Kewa Ethnolinguistic Concepts of Body Parts, *South West Journal of Anthropology, 19,* 1963, pp. 54–63; Watson and Nelson, *op. cit.;* and L. Stark, "The Lexical Structure of Quechua Body Parts," *Anthropological Linguistics, 11,* 1969, pp. 1–15. For a general argument, see Paul Schilder, *The Image and Appearance of the Human Body,* International Universities Press, New York, 1950; and P. K. Manning and H. Fabrega, Jr., "Self and Body" presented to third annual International Social Science in Medicine Conference, Elsinore, Denmark, 1972.

10. The methodological problems involved in these types of studies add an additional problem in interpreting the findings they present. The access that members of certain groups have to their bodies is a variable; such items as mirrors, specialized lights and probes (e.g., sigmoidiscope), the technology of modern surgery, and practices surrounding and explaining death all alter the degree of access to the interior of the body possible in a society and to selected members of that society. In addition, the mean-

ing and importance of some segments of the body varies and, indeed, may be taboo to the sight or touch.

11. H. Wapner and H. Werner, *The Body Percept*, Random House, New York, 1966.

12. Barker et al., *op. cit.*; Scott, *op. cit.*; Goffman, *op. cit.*

13. H. Fabrega, Jr., and P. K. Manning, "Health Maintenance among Peruvian Peasants," *Human Organization, 31*, Fall 1972, pp. 243–256.

14. H. Bruch, *The Importance of Overweight*, Norton, New York, 1957.

15. R. D. Laing, *The Divided Self*, Penguin Books, London, 1963.

16. D. Matza, *Becoming Deviant*, Prentice-Hall, Englewood Cliffs, N.J., 1969; P. Manning, review of David Matza, *Becoming Deviant*, in *Summation, 2*, December 1970, pp. 45–51.

17. Fabrega and Manning, *op. cit.*

18. The orienting framework of this paper is the philosophic-sociological phenomenology of Alfred Schutz, especially as elaborated and extended by Harold Garfinkel. Since the ideas suffuse our entire argument, rather than shoring up specific points within the argument, they are not traced to original sources. Readers who desire a general introduction to the phenomenological perspective should consult Alfred Schutz, *Collected Papers*, Vols. I, II, and III, Martinus Nijhoff, The Hague, 1962, 1964, 1966; Alfred Schutz, *The Phenomenology of the Social World*, translated by G. Walsh and F. Lehnert, Northwestern University Press, Evanston, Ill., 1967; Harold Garfinkel, *Studies in Ethnomethodology*, Prentice-Hall, Englewood Cliffs, N.J., 1967; Jack D. Douglas (ed.), *Understanding Everyday Life*, Aldine, Chicago, 1970; H. Peter Dreitzel, ed., *Recent Sociology No. 2*, Macmillan, New York, 1971; Peter K. Manning, "Existential Sociology," *Sociological Quarterly*, forthcoming, 1973.

19. For a general treatment of the Chiapas area, see Evon Z. Vogt, *Zinacantan: A Maya Community in the Highlands of Chiapas*, Harvard University Press, Cambridge, 1969; Frank Cancian, *Economics and Prestige in a Maya Community: The Religious Cargo System in Zinacantan*, Stanford University Press, Stanford, 1965, and by the same author, *Change and Uncertainty in a Peasant Economy: The Maya Corn Farmers of Zinacantan*, Stanford University Press, Stanford, 1972; B. Colby and P. Van den Berghe, "Ethnic Relations in Southeastern Mexico," *American Anthropologist, 63*, 1961, pp. 772–792, and P. Van den Berghe and B. Colby, "Ladino-Indian Relations in the Highlands of Chiapas, Mexico," *Social Forces, 40*, 1961, pp. 63–71; Rudolfo Stavenhagen, "Classes, Colonialism, and Acculturation: Essay on a System of Inter-Ethnic Relations in Meso-America," *Studies in Comparative Development*, Washington University, St. Louis, Mo., 1965; June Nash, *In the Eyes of the Ancestors*, Yale University Press, New Haven, 1970.

20. Genetically there are rather large variations in the ladino group, and as Colby and Van den Berghe, *op. cit.*, write, "the genetic continuum overlaps greatly the social class continuum." The characteristics that distin-

guish the groups are thus not exclusively genetic or biological, but are rather social and cultural (wealth, power, education, style of dress, etc.). A variety of social, economic, and political considerations associated with the city account for the fact that the transactions involving these two ethnic groups are typically between the ladino as the purveyor of the goods, services, or money, and the indigena as the deferential, subservient, recipient. These transactions link the indigenas with San Cristobal in a continuous symbolic and actual fashion which maintains the dominance of the ladino. The two groups, however, are not caste groups; passing from the Indian to the ladino group is difficult but possible; it is less likely that loss of status will occur from ladino to Indian. The class boundaries are nearly impermeable, the entrance to the small middle-class and a small elite is highly restricted. Status distinctions are clear and can be observed in speech, dress, and personal mannerisms. Critical in this class-ethnic system are the ways in which the external cues of status are translated in virtually all social interactions into asymmetrical transactions favoring the higher classes (mestizos and ladinos).

21. G. Sjoberg, *The Preindustrial City*, Free Press, New York, 1960.

22. Other field work has been undertaken by Fabrega in 1967 and 1969, some of the results of which have been reported in Fabrega and Metzger, "Psychiatric Illness in a Small Ladino Community," *Psychiatry*, *31*, November 1968, pp. 339–351; H. Fabrega, D. Metzger, and G. Williams, "Psychiatric Implications of Health and Illness in a Maya Indian Group," *Social Science and Medicine*, *3*, 1970, pp. 609–626; H. Fabrega, Jr., "Dynamics of Medical Practice in a Folk Community," *Milbank Memorial Fund Quarterly*, *48*, 1970, pp. 391–412; and H. Fabrega, Jr., and P. K. Manning, "The Activities of Beggars: Accommodations of Marginal Persons," unpublished paper, Michigan State University, 1972.

23. H. Fabrega, Jr., "Some Features of Zinacantecan Medical Knowledge," *Ethnology*, *9*, 1971, pp. 25–43.

24. For a discussion of the intentions and extensions of the term "disease," see H. Fabrega, Jr., "The Study of Disease in Relation to Culture," *op. cit.*

25. R. Adams and A. Rubel, "Sickness and Social Relations," in M. Nash, ed., *Handbook of Middle American Indians*, Vol. 6, University of Texas Press, Austin, 1967, pp. 333–355.

26. Cf. Adams and Rubel, *op. cit.*; Fabrega, Metzger, and Williams, *op. cit.*

27. See Fabrega, Metzger, and Williams, *op. cit.*; Vogt, *op. cit.*; and June Collier, "Zinacanteco Law," unpublished Ph. D. dissertation, Vanderbilt University, 1970. Our investigation included aspects of witchcraft belief and practice, a subject closely tied to broader religious beliefs and practices in Chiapas. See, in this context, A. Villa Rojas, "Kinship and Nagualism in a Tzeltal Community (Tenejapa)," *American Anthropologist*, *49*, 1947, pp. 578–587; June Nash, "Death as a Way of Life," *American Anthropologist*, *69*, 1967, pp. 455–470; Manning Nash, "Witchcraft as a Social Process," *American Indigena*, *20*, 1961; and Julian A. Pitt-Rivers,

"Spiritual Power in Central America: The Naguals of Chiapas," in Mary Douglas, ed., *Witchcraft Confessions and Accusations*, Tavistock, London, 1970, pp. 183–206.

28. To some degree, the explanation of illness is always tautological in Mayan and mestizo systems, for the usual causal sequence employed in Western science is reversed: Once an illness is identified it constitutes evidence that there must have been a social causal event necessary and sufficient to have created this state of disease. Ultimate control of events, i.e., the person's fate, is in the power of the gods and their actions are revealed in the world. Unexplained events are thus clearly by definition acts of the gods.

29. Collier, *op. cit.*, p. 103.

30. Daniel Silver, "Zinacanteco Shamanism," unpublished dissertation, Harvard University, 1966.

31. Zinacantecos believe that only a *H'ilol* (shaman) can detect with certainty the cause of the illness, e.g., read the action of witchcraft in the blood of the victim. However, since there are many available shamans, people can "shop" for a diagnosis that most agrees with their own assessment or diagnosis. Relevant dimensions other than cause by which Zinacantecos classify illness are (a) magnitude (small or large illness), (b) curability, (c) required number of curing personnel, (d) the state of the blood (hot versus cold), (e) the number of candles required in the curing ceremony, (f) the number of mountains to be visited during the ceremony, (g) applicability to age and sex groups, i.e., groups "at risk," (h) contagion, (i) fatality, (j) duration, (k) repetition, (l) recurrence in the world, (m) degrees of contagion (Silver, *op. cit.*, pp. 78–84, and D. Metzger and R. Williams, "Tenejapa Medicine I: The Curer," *South West Journal of Anthropology*, *19*, 1963, pp. 216–234.

32. Cf. Fabrega, "Some Features," *op. cit.*, and H. Fabrega, Jr. and D. Silver, "Some Social and Psychological Properties of Zinacanteco Shamans," *Behavioral Science*, *15*, 1970, pp. 471–486.

33. Silver, *op. cit.*, p. 66.

34. Francesca Cancian, unpublished manuscript on norms in Zinacantan, Stanford University, n.d.

35. Collier, *op. cit.*

36. Many writers consider the mestizo medicine system a transitional or "residual" set of ideas standing between the coherent Western rational system on the one hand and the rapidly eroding indigenous system of curing, a system composed of quackery, patent medicine, and exploitative manipulation of the Indian and lower-class mestizo clientele for money. However, this view of ladino-mestizo medicine is a rather vague and generalized stereotype which inadequately captures the range of curing activities that are encompassed by the ladino-mestizo urban *curandero* system. These views are expressed in Frank Miller, "Social Structure and Medical Change in a Mexican Indian Community," unpublished Ph.D.

thesis, Harvard University, 1960; Silver, *op. cit.;* and a critical note on these stereotypes is provided in Irwin Press, "The Urban Curandero," *American Anthropologist,* 73, June 1971, pp. 741–756.

37. The historic roots of these conceptions are to be found in the humoral theory, inherited from the Greeks and associated with Hippocrates. Humoral theory prevails in the folk medical systems of Latin America. Cf. A. Rubel, "Concepts of Disease in Mexican-American Culture," *American Anthropologist,* 62, 1960, pp. 1151–1173; R. L. Currier, "The Hot Cold Syndrome and Symbolic Balance in Mexican and Spanish-American Folk Medicine," *Ethnology,* 5, 1966, pp. 251–263; Adams and Rubel, *op. cit.;* J. Ingham, "On Mexican Folk Medicine," *American Anthropologist,* 72, 1970, pp. 76–87; and A. Harwood, "The Hot-Cold Theory of Disease," *Journal of the American Medical Association,* May 17, 1971, pp. 1153–1158. A useful historical review is found in George Fostor, "Relationships Between Spanish and Spanish-American Folk Medicine," *Journal of American Folklore,* 66, 1953, pp. 201–217. Originally introduced to Latin America in the sixteenth and seventeenth centuries and taught in medical schools established by the Spanish in Mexico and Peru, the ideas were spread by missionaries and subsequently diffused throughout Mexico and Central and South America. Harwood writes, "[the tenets of the humoral theory were embodied in and] spread by means of household medical references which were used throughout Spanish America by priests and others who provided European medical care to the indigenous and mestizo populations" (*op. cit.,* p. 1153). The four humors, according to this theory—blood, phlegm, yellow bile, and black bile— are normally in a state of equilibrium in the person's body. Natural adjustments are made to everyday events and changes in physical demands, but health is signified by a warm, moist body maintaining a balance among the four basic elements. In contrast, illness is believed to result from humoral imbalance said to be caused by an excess of one of the four, and reflected metaphorically in an excessively hot, cold, moist, or dry body. According to Harwood, "When the Hippocratic theory was incorporated into Latin American folk practice, the wet-dry dichotomy became insignificant as a basic for diagnostic and therapeutic decisions, and the hot-cold . . . dimension came to dominate the system" (*op. cit.,* p. 1153). There is a strong, culturally sanctioned emphasis upon the restoration of balance. Foods, drinks (teas, alcoholic beverages, etc.), herbs, and medicinal substances, themselves also classified into hot or cold categories, may be used to maintain health or to return the body to a previous healthful state. For example, cold illness (*mal viento*) may be alleviated by the use of drinks classified as hot such as alcohol.

38. J. A. Pitt-Rivers, "Words and Deeds: The Ladinos of Chiapas," *Man,* 2 (1), 1967, pp. 71–86.

39. This involvement of friends, neighbors and kin at every stage of illness, including death, is described in Fabrega and Metzger, *op. cit.*

40. *Ibid.*

41. For a summary of the most recent of these studies, see H. Fabrega, Jr., "Medical Anthropology," in B. J. Seigel, ed., *Biennial Review of Anthropology*, Stanford University Press, Stanford, 1971, pp. 167–229.

42. See Irwin Press, "Urban Illness: Physicians, Curers and Dual Use in Bogota," *Journal of Health and Social Behavior, 10*, 1969, pp. 209–218, and Press, *op. cit.*

43. Pitt-Rivers, "Words and Deeds," *op. cit.*, p. 71.

44. Joan Emerson, "Behavior in Private Places: Sustaining Definitions of Reality in Gynecological Examinations," Dreitzel, *op. cit.*, pp. 74–97; and James Henslin and M. Biggs, "Dramaturgical Desexualization: The Sociology of the Vaginal Exam," in James Henslin, ed., *Studies in the Sociology of Sex*, Appleton-Century-Crofts, New York, 1971, pp. 243–272; apparently both wish to document a dramatic instance of the impersonal approach which medicine has institutionalized by describing the management of the vaginal examination. In this case, they are drawing on the commonsense meanings that imply that sex and portions of the body directly involved (the "sex organs"), are personalized and sacred in this culture. It should be emphasized that traditionally and to an important degree at this point in modern societies, the body and its openings *still* maintain a phenomenological status as somewhat sacred objects. As these authors imply, the dramatization of the medical encounter requires consensus, cooperation between players, and an elaborate staging. As many physicians in San Cristobal sadly explained to us, the dramatic performance was regularly and routinely interrupted by a lack of patient cooperation in validating the scientific, impersonal approach. Patients openly question prescriptions, ignore advice, argue with doctors over the meaning of their problems, and continue to use other curers.

45. Mary Douglas, *Natural Symbols*, Pantheon Books, New York, 1971.

46. B. Berlin, D. E. Breedlove, and P. H. Raven, "Covert Categories and Folk Taxonomies," *American Anthropologist, 70*, 1968, pp. 290–299. Manning has discussed this general point in "Language, Meaning and Action," in Jack Douglas, ed., *Introductory Sociology: Situations and Structures*, Free Press, New York, 1973.

47. E. Z. Vogt, *The Zinacantecos: A Modern Mayan Way of Life*, Holt, Rinehart and Winston, New York, 1970, pp. 107–108.

48. Keith Basso, "Semantic Aspects of Linguistic Acculturation," *American Anthropologist, 69*, 1967, p. 472.

49. *Ibid.*

50. *Ibid.*, p. 473.

51. Thomas Szasz, *Law, Liberty and Psychiatry*, Macmillan, New York, 1966.

52. See W. Sypher, *Loss of the Self in Modern Literature and Art*, Vintage Press, New York, 1962; Charles I. Glicksberg, *The Self in Modern Literature*, Pennsylvania State University Press, University Park, 1963; and

Daniel Bell, "The Sensibilities of the Sixties," *Commentary*, *51*, June 1971, pp. 53–63.

53. Daniel Bell, "The Disjunction of Culture and Social Structure: Some Notes on the Meaning of Social Reality," *Daedalus*, *97*, Winter 1965, p. 219.

54. Manning has discussed the broader implications of these developments for sociology in a forthcoming paper, "Existential Sociology," *op. cit.*

55. Occasional comments from everyday conversations, especially slang, are illustrative of the application of machine language to personal action and intention:
    (a) A clock is the image of the heart (the old "ticker").
    (b) A spring is the image for emotional involvement or concern (I'm all "wound up").
    (c) A mechanical switch, the passive recipient of action, is the image for emotional excitement (I'm "turned on").
    (d) A fabricating or assembling process is the metaphor for sexual intercourse (we "made it" together).
    (e) The language of classic mechanics is applied to teaching and learning: teacher "outputs" and student "inputs"; and also to organizing a group of people for action: It's all "wired up."
    (f) The body is referred to as a "pleasure machine" or an "experience machine" in a variety of phrases, some derived from rocket technology: I can really "get off" on that, he really "took off."

56. See Goffman's discussion of the implications of the modern view of madness in "The Insanity of Place," in *Relations in Public*, Basic Books, New York, 1971, pp. 335–390.

57. A set of propositions designed to organize cross-cultural research on health and illness is presented in H. Fabrega, Jr., and P. K. Manning, "Disease, Illness and Deviant Careers," in R. A. Scott and J. D. Douglas, eds., *Theoretical Perspectives on Deviance*, Basic Books, New York, 1972, pp. 93–116.

58. Cf. June Nash, "The Logic of Behavior: Curing in a Maya Indian Town," *Human Organization*, *26*, 1967, pp. 132–140.

»»»»»»»»»»»»»»»»»»»»» «« «« «« «« «« «« «« «« «« «« ««

*The rich traditions of the two approaches Dallmayr examines, phenome-
nology and Marxism, have been linked in the works of many writers, but
the recent efforts by Enzo Paci provide, in Dallmayr's view, a significant
contribution. The changes in both phenomenology and Marxism as these
have developed historically would not make rapprochement necessarily
easy except that Husserl's later focus on the life-world and on intersubjective evidence is paralleled by developments in Marxism.*

*Clearly, these two major streams of critical thought have similarities
and convergences, but what a critical sociology will draw from each still
remains to be determined.*

*It is fitting that as Zaner's paper opened this book with its proposal
that phenomenology can be the critical foundation for the social sciences,
Dallmayr's should be the closing paper leading us to consider Marxism
and phenomenology as critical foundations.*

PHENOMENOLOGY AND MARXISM:
A SALUTE TO ENZO PACI

» « «

Fred R. Dallmayr

University of Georgia

A convergence of ills may justify resort to a battery of remedies or antidotes—provided the antidotes are mutually compatible and do not coalesce into a toxic compound. In our century, Marxism has been widely heralded as a basic remedy to the corrupting effects of a market economy geared to corporate profit and a technology obtuse to social concerns. However, as interpreted by communist hierarchies, Marxism itself has tended to be submerged in the dictates of industrial expansion and technological efficiency. Faced with this official interpretation, proponents of change have frequently sought to reinvigorate the salt of the dialectic by blending Marxism with newer philosophical perspectives; phenomenology and existentialism have served as preferred means to recapture the human dimension and purposive thrust of Marxism.

At a first glance, the attempted merger seems unlikely and ill-starred —given the Marxist focus on economic explanation and phenomenolo-

305

gy's preoccupation with intuitive understanding. Even where the two orientations are seen as broadly complementary rather than conflicting, their alliance is fraught with numerous hazards; a merger, for example, which simply superimposed apodictic intuition upon the self-assurance of a scientific determinism would accomplish little but the escalation of reciprocal defects. Recently, one of the milestone efforts in this domain has become available to English-speaking readers: Enzo Paci's *The Function of the Sciences and the Meaning of Man* (1). By exploring the humanist premises of Marxism and the social implications of a phenomenological analysis of experience, the study demonstrates the rich potential and stimulating vistas of a philosophical and practical reconciliation of the two perspectives. At the same time, however, the publication can be said to illustrate better than any other the inherent hazards of such an undertaking.

In large measure, the dilemmas of a phenomenological Marxism can be traced to latent ambiguities in both elements of the merger. As it seems to me (and as I shall try to argue in these pages), the alliance can be mutually beneficial only to the extent that both partners are able to assume a critical posture, a posture which, without lapsing into skeptical indifference, employs criticism not only as a weapon against opponents but as a means of self-scrutiny and self-reflection. On this score, however, the legacy of both orientations tends to be ambivalent.

In the case of Marxism, the basic thrust of the founders was undeniably critical in a comprehensive manner. All of Marx' writings involved an exposure of the congealed masks and ideological camouflages of existing social arrangements; such exposure, moreover, was intended as preparatory step to the broad-scale emancipation and critical self-awareness of all members of society (2). Yet this general outlook has been uneasily mixed with unexamined premises and assumptions—and this not only in the writings of Marx' successors. Marx' emphasis on labor and the development of productive forces has encouraged the streamlining of the dialectic into a synonym for industrial progress and technological evolution. Similarly, his observations on the relationship between infrastructures and superstructures, between material life and cognition, sometimes exhibit a doctrinaire flavor averse to further clarification; thus the statement that "the production of ideas, conceptions and consciousness is at first directly interwoven with the material activity and the material interaction of men" conceals the complex character of the nexus between thought and immediate experience. Also, the stress on the intimate linkage of theory and practice tends to short-circuit inquiry into the intricate liaison between knowledge and action, between exigencies of nature and standards of practical conduct. "It does not matter what this or that proletarian, or even the proletariat as a whole, *imagines* to be its goal at any particular moment," *The Holy Family* asserts. "What is important is what the proletariat is and what it must historically accomplish in accordance with its nature. Its goal and its historical action are irrevocably predetermined by its own life-situation" (3).

The legacy of phenomenology is hardly less ambivalent; moreover, the situation is aggravated by the diversity of definitions and interpretations. According to a recent student of this legacy, phenomenology should be conceived as a radically critical enterprise, as an effort to rekindle or reactivate the Socratic dialogue (4). This is definitely an attractive and, in the long run, very promising view. However, the question remains whether such a definition can be squared in every respect with the phenomenological movement as inaugurated by Husserl and whether it does not perhaps blur some distinguishing traits of this movement.

In the works of Husserl and most of his followers, one can hardly neglect the central role assigned to personal intuitive "evidence" as final criterion of true experience and valid cognition (5). Moreover, in Husserl's writings this stress on personal evidence was connected, at least during major phases of his work, with a monadic conception of consciousness—with the result that intersubjective relations tended to be seen as a series of analogous experiences and dialogical interaction as a synchronization of monologues. However, this is clearly only part of the story.

Husserl's turn to evidence and away from preconceived opinions was itself a decisive step in the direction of a critical reconstruction of philosophy. More important, his later focus on the life-world (*Lebenswelt*) disclosed the intersubjective matrix of personal experience and thus laid the groundwork for sustained mutual interrogation and critical dialogue. The implications of this focus are abundantly manifest in the *Crisis of the European Sciences* (and appended manuscripts). There, Husserl at one point describes genuine philosophy as "a new sort of praxis, that of the universal critique of all life and all life-goals, all cultural products and systems that have already arisen out of the life of man," a praxis whose aim is "to elevate mankind" and "transform it from the bottom up into a new humanity." In another passage, he directly reflects on the intersubjective dimension of individual cognition:

> Scientific propositions are formed by individual scientists and founded as scientific truths—but being and the verification of being are claims only as long as other scientists can put forth opposing reasons, and as long as these are inconfutable. This means that the realization of the cognitive purpose of the individual scientist is authentically scientific only if he has taken into account the universal horizon of co-scientists as real and possible coworkers (6).

The discussed vacillation has significantly conditioned past attempts to promote a rapprochement between Marxism and phenomenology. Paci's *Function of the Sciences* deserves attention because it epitomizes both the potential virtues and the intrinsic problems of this rapprochement. This paper is intended primarily as a critical salute to Paci—critical in the sense delineated by Husserl himself—presented in three main stages. In order to provide a context or foil for Paci's study, the paper initially sketches a synopsis or historical overview of prominent encounters or confrontations between the two theoretical orientations. Projected against this background, Paci's arguments are subsequently reviewed and their major strengths and weaknesses assessed. To round out the presentation, a final section compares his views briefly with various parallel endeavors in contemporary sociology and social thought.

ENCOUNTERS: FROM LUKÁCS TO HABERMAS

Paci's work is by no means the first example of a contact or liaison between Marxism and phenomenological inquiry. Actually, in large portion, his study takes the form of a sustained and occasionally critical commentary on the writings of philosophical precursors in this area. As he suggests, contacts between the two perspectives can be traced back to the early decades of this century, to the time of Husserl's first major publications. As one may recall, Marxism during this period experienced a striking revival of dialectical thinking—a revival which, nourished largely by the rediscovery of Hegelian sources, stood in stark contrast to the positivist and neo-Kantian interpretations of the preceding era.

There are important reasons that account for the mutual attractiveness or at least partial affinity of Marxist and phenomenological thought during this time. Both movements, it seems to me, were attempts to overcome the despair and relativistic confusion characteristic of the *fin-de-siècle* epoch and of a disintegrating liberalism. Reacting against positivist reductionism and compartmentalization of knowledge as well as against neo-Kantian antinomies, both perspectives sought to recover the unifying source of all knowledge and experience behind the dichotomies of nature and history, subject and object, external and internal, contingent and transcendental domains. In the case of phenomenology, this search led through a bracketing of received explanations and categories to the exploration of a substratum of intentional consciousness embedded in the lifeworld. Dialectical Marxism, in a similar manner, sought to restore the vision of a coherent totality or synthesis of experience buried under the disparate ruins of an objectified universe and arbitrary subjective impulses.

Among the pioneers pointing broadly in the direction of his own version of a phenomenological Marxism, Paci mentions Georg Lukács, but without specifying the character of the claimed relationship. Lukács' early contact or affinity with phenomenology has, of course, frequently been noted; the contact definitely preceded his affiliation with Marxism or with dialectical thinking in general. During his studies in Berlin and Heidelberg, he came under the influence of the dominant philosophical tendencies of the time—without, however, becoming the docile disciple of any school (7). Whatever fascination phenomenology held for Lukács seems to have derived chiefly from its concentration on metaempirical, ideal "essences." To a considerable extent, his early preoccupation with literary and esthetic questions was an expression of his passionate longing for a realm of absolute or pure experience transcending contingent reality and the confining splits of subjective and objective, normative and empirical dimensions. This longing was clearly evident in one of his first major writings, *The Soul and the Forms*, published in 1911. According to Lucien Goldmann, Lukács' thinking at the time stood at the crossroads of three philosophical currents: Southwest-German neo-Kantianism, Dilthey's historical hermeneutics, and Husserl's phenomenology. *The Soul and the Forms*, in Goldmann's view, constituted basically a merger of "two central notions of phenomenology and Dilthey's school: those of a *transtemporal essence* and of *Verstehen*" (8). The fusion of the two notions resulted in the concept of a transtemporal meaningful "form" designating an ideal structure accessible to pure understanding. At the same time, Lukács contracted the neo-Kantian juxtaposition of empirical world and absolute norms into a stark and uncompromising confrontation, a confrontation which, in the absence of mediations, was bound to culminate in a tragic vision of life. Thus, on the eve of the European conflagration, *The Soul and the Forms* expressed both the revolt and the inevitable failure of authentic existence in the midst of a corrupt and fragmented society.

His next work, *The Theory of the Novel*, written at the beginning of the war, showed a slight shift in perspective. While still clinging to the notion of transtemporal forms, Lukács now concentrated on the *entre-monde* between human aspirations and social environment; in contrast to the stark conflict peculiar to tragedy and the idyllic harmony characteristic of epic tales, the novel appeared as the medium portraying the tension and precarious interaction between authentic life and society, a tension intimating at least dimly the possibility of reconciliation. The acceptance of such a possibility implied a step in the direction of dialectical thinking and especially of a Hegelian phenomenology of experience—although the prospect of reconciliation was still relegated to a distant utopia. The outbreak of the Russian revolution in 1917 marked the beginning of Lukács' association with the communist movement.

A few years later he published one of his most brilliant, and also most controversial, books: *History and Class-Consciousness, Studies on*

Marxist Dialectics. The book lacked none of the uncompromising ardor and élan of his earlier writings. Written at the height of revolutionary ferment and expectations, *History and Class-Consciousness* boldly aimed to unravel the meaning of human development by focusing on the progressive transparency of social antagonisms and their impending *dénouement* in a classless society. To be sure, the turn to dialectical thought entailed an important change in vocabulary and philosophical conceptualization: instead of the previous stress on transtemporal essences, the study focused on the evolving synthesis of historical experience, on the total fabric of meaning emerging out of dispersed and possibly opposed fragments. In semi-Hegelian fashion, history was seen as the alternation of estrangement and self-discovery. Capitalist society signified a growing objectification of human relations, with the laboring class suffering the highest degree of estrangement due to its transformation into a commodity on the market. Yet the worker was not only a victim but also an avenger and possible redeemer: by becoming conscious of its condition, the proletariat was destined to abolish exploitation and usher in a new era permitting free and authentic existence to all members of society.

History and Class-Consciousness remains one of the most remarkable documents of the period; in a philosophical sense, its virtues are many and continue to provide yardsticks for Marxist thought. One of the chief assets of the study was the delineation of a dialectical Marxism. By reviving an almost forgotten dialectical legacy, the book overcame both positivist and subjectivist distortions of the past; in the words of Goldmann: "Lukács' outlook restored to Marxism its internal coherence and swept aside with one stroke all the imputed 'dualisms,' 'inconsistencies,' 'confusions,' and 'philosophical inadequacies' " (9). Equally significant was the stress on estrangement and alienation—aspects that were soon to become major themes in existentialist literature. For present purposes a central value of the study resided in its incipient critical posture, in the author's repeated emphasis that Marxism should be viewed as method and key to further inquiry rather than as compendium of fixed propositions (10). Unfortunately, statements to this effect remained undeveloped and were counteracted by the bold venture to gain absolute or total comprehension. At least in this respect, the book's outlook was subterraneously linked both with Lukács' previous writings and with the thrust of phenomenological inquiry. Just as phenomenology was characterized by a "leap into evidence," by the claim of an intuitive grasp of essences, *History and Class-Consciousness* can be said to betray a "leap into synthesis," a plunge into the full meaning of historical experience.

Although understandable and valuable as a reaction against positivist fragmentation, the leap in both cases had the effect of discouraging critical inquiry into crucial mediations and linkages. Despite his portrayal of

Marxism as a method, Lukács described the nucleus of this method as the focus on the total fabric of history—a fabric which seemed accessible to immediate inspection without requiring the patient labor of intersubjective interrogation and corroboration. Contrary to the author's intention, historical development thus appeared subject to a predictive calculation only partially different from positivist determinism. In the same manner, the contraction of the dialectic prevented investigation of the nexus between theory and praxis. To the extent that the proletariat was presented as both the object and the subject or sovereign agent of social change, revolution and emancipation seemed the direct result of social exploitation and practical conduct immediately deducible from observed conditions (11).

As is well known, *History and Class-Consciousness* suffered a peculiar fate: Eclipsed and bypassed by political developments, it was soon repudiated not only by official communist circles but also by its author. Whether for tactical or philosophical reasons, Lukács soon moved from his early concerns into almost the opposite direction, toward a moderate realism or objectivism which seems difficult to reconcile with dialectics and definitely incompatible with phenomenological inquiry. In his writings published during his Moscow years and the immediate postwar period, he actually adopted a vehemently hostile attitude toward phenomenology and existentialism—a posture that may in part have been a reaction against some of his own early leanings. In *Existentialism or Marxism?*, phenomenological and existentialist thought was portrayed as manifestation of the progressive disintegration of bourgeois culture during the "phase of imperialism"; both movements, Lukács claimed, were based on the method of subjective intuition and thus entirely at odds with rational inquiry—an inquiry whose relationship to, or distinction from, scientific objectivism was unfortunately not clarified.

In *The Destruction of Reason*, the attack on intuition was expanded into a broad overview of the decline and degeneration of German philosophy from Schelling to Hitler's time. Phenomenology and existentialism were treated as appendices or special types of an irrational "life philosophy"; as in the previous essay, the phenomenological reliance on "bracketing" or *epoché* was castigated as a subjectivist maneuver to elude the question of objective social reality (12). More recently, in a treatise completed shortly before his death, Lukács slightly relaxed his categorical opposition. His *Ontology of Social Life* draws very heavily on the work of Nicolai Hartmann, a thinker who was at least partially influenced by phenomenology. Like Hartmann, the study accepts, within limits, the legitimacy of a plurality of individual concerns and subjective perspectives; however, all such perspectives are ultimately rooted and combined in a complex hierarchy of reality independent of human awareness (13).

Not all of Lukács' friends and followers share his hesitations and scruples with regard to phenomenology. Not long ago, one of his students explored the affinities between Marxism and phenomenological inquiry, through the medium of a friendly, imaginary dialogue between a number of participants, including a Lukácsian thinker and a phenomenologist whose views closely resemble Paci's (14). The topic of phenomenology and existentialism is treated with little suspicion, and sometimes with moderate sympathy, also by other East-European writers today, especially by members of the so-called *Praxis*-group. Gajo Petrović, a Yugoslav philosopher and leading member of the group, observed less than a decade ago that "the contemporary philosophy of existentialism is concerned with humanistic problems about which the young Marx wrote but which were neglected by Marxists afterwards. Its conception of man is, on the whole, different from the Marxist one, but on some points they come near each other" (15). A Marxist perspective at least partially reminiscent of Husserl's phenomenology has been developed by the Czech philosopher Karel Kosík. In his *Dialectic of the Concrete*, Kosík distinguished between the dimension of phenomenal appearances, comprising unexamined objects and ideological opinions, and the basic structure of reality or the concrete essence of the "things themselves." In contrast to phenomenological formulations, however, appearances and essence were seen as intimately linked and the piercing of "pseudo-concreteness" was to be accomplished not through a return to pure intuition but through the method of dialectical thinking—a method which, moreover, was seen as chiefly a critical enterprise (16).

The mentioning of the *Praxis*-group evokes the memory of an earlier reformulation of Marxist thought: Antonio Gramsci's "philosophy of praxis." A brief consideration of this precedent is indicated in this context, since Paci understandably devotes considerable attention to the founders of Italian Marxism, Gramsci and Antonio Labriola. Both writers are notable for their reactivation of a dialectical and nonpositivist conception. Their outlook, in this respect, parallels closely that expressed in Lukács' *History and Class-Consciousness;* their relationship to phenomenology, however, is considerably more indirect and tangential. Both Labriola and Gramsci objected strenuously to the reduction of Marxism to a naive naturalism or objectivism; valid cognition, in their view, depended not merely on the reflection of objects in passive minds but on the purposive interchange between man and the world (17). Historical development, above all, could not be conceived as the mechanical operation and unfolding of natural laws; rather, social innovation presupposed the active intervention and praxis of the proletariat. On all these points their writings exhibited the same promise, as well as the same shortcomings, as Lukács' early position. Yet, as it seems to me, there are at least a few aspects where Gramsci's arguments point beyond these confines. Valid cognition, he noted, was not simply the result of isolated observation or insight, but the fruit of universal consultation and confirmation. What Marx called the "structure" or "infrastructure" of society was a set of given and taken-for-granted factors that effectively conditioned human aspirations. Dialectical thinking, from this perspective, was the movement from an opaque evidence over speculative interpretation to full comprehension (18).

The relationship between structure and superstructure, thought and matter, also was a central preoccupation of the French or French-speaking school of existential phenomenology during subsequent decades—a school comprised of Sartre, Merleau-Ponty, and, at least for a brief time, the Vietnamese theorist Tran Duc Thao, whose interest in Husserl seems to have resided primarily in the distinction between appearances and essence. In an essay of 1946 entitled "Marxism and Phenomenology," Tran Duc Thao reformulated the Marxist nexus of infrastructure and superstructure in terms of the opposition between a basic layer of experience and awareness—revealed through bracketing—and the realm of opinions and institutional objectifications. Husserl's fascination, however, seems to have waned quickly, for a few years later the same author tried to demonstrate the inferiority of intuitive inspection to the method of dialectical materialism with its stress on labor as source of human values; at least in part, the change derived from disenchantment with the nonapodictic implications of Husserl's turn to the life-world (19).

Despite obvious parallels, Sartre's intellectual development deviates in many respects from that of the Vietnamese philosopher: the attempt to reconcile Marxism and phenomenology constitutes a late rather than a preliminary phase in his thinking; moreover, his interpretation both of Marxism and of existential phenomenology acquired increasingly critical and self-critical connotations. Until the end of World War II, Sartre's writings reflected a purely phenomenological outlook devoid of Marxist overtones, an outlook combining the teachings of Husserl and Heidegger together with some Hegelian vocabulary. His major studies of the period, including *Being and Nothingness*, further radicalized the pure inspection of essences by purging consciousness of any concrete or subjective traces —an operation that transformed phenomenology into a stark dichotomy between awareness and the world of things or, in Hegel's language, between the domains of the "for-itself" and the "in-itself." In contrast to the dialectic of synthesis elaborated by the young Lukács, Sartre thus developed a dialectic of antithesis and negation. Both the plunge into synthesis and the reliance on absolute freedom and negation, however, produced the same result: the neglect of intersubjective mediations.

During the postwar period Sartre slowly sought to repair the breach between human awareness and the world that characterized his earlier works. This search led him to a more attentive examination of dialectical thinking in general and of Marxism in particular. An important step along this road was his essay "Materialism and Revolution," published in 1946. In this essay, Sartre defined Marxism essentially as a philosophy of praxis and revolutionary action, while relegating both materialism and idealism to the status of contemplative or metaphysical doctrines; in doing so, he boldly cut through the entangled knot of structure-superstructure relations, opening the way for a fresh reexamination of the issue. Despite the boldness of formulation, however, the essay still bore the imprint of earlier arguments and doctrinaire assumptions: Largely identified with labor and completely absorbing theoretical reflection, revolutionary praxis was depicted as an act of total transcendence and self-realization on the part of the proletariat (20).

Some ten years later, Sartre made another move toward a rejuvenation of Marxism. The opening section of his *Question of Method* affirmed not merely the possibility but the urgency of a combination of Marxism and existential phenomenology. Although Marxism was recognized as the dominant and unsurpassed "philosophy" of our age, superior to other trends or "ideologies," existentialism (at least its nonreactionary variety) was portrayed as a vital corrective in view of the stagnation of official Marxist thought. While "living Marxism," Sartre complained, was "heuristic" and its concepts exploratory "keys" or "interpretive schemata," official doctrine had degenerated into ritual: "The totalizing investigation has given way to a scholasticism of the totality. The heuristic principle —'to search for the whole in its parts'—has become the terrorist practice of 'liquidating the particularity.' " Since existentialism "reaffirmed the reality of men" and focused on "experience in order to discover there concrete syntheses," it could serve as an antidote to Marxist sclerosis (21).

Unfortunately, Sartre's subsequent writings did not quite live up to the promise contained in these statements. The remaining part of *Question of Method* was devoted to the methodological implications of dialectical thinking, in particular to the elaboration of a "progressive-regressive" method linking phenomenological description with theory and scientific analysis with synthetic comprehension. In 1960, the *Question* was attached as preface to Sartre's most ambitious theoretical undertaking, the *Critique of Dialectical Reason*. However, the title does not entirely match the content (at least of the portion published so far); starting from a primordial level of material needs and deriving the genesis of society from human labor and the struggle with scarcity, the study constitutes more a sociological application of the previously sketched method than an effort of dialectical self-scrutiny. The goal adumbrated by Sartre was pursued with greater perseverance and, perhaps, greater circumspection by

Maurice Merleau-Ponty—although his early death prevented a full development of his thoughts. Actually, his writings frequently tended to anticipate Sartrean themes. Relying strongly on Husserl's life-world studies, Merleau-Ponty's early investigations of human behavior and perception completely avoided the antinomies of Sartre's dialectic of negation; by reconciling Husserl with the intricate pattern of Hegelian phenomenology, they pointed the way toward dialectical thinking and, ultimately, toward Marxism. Well in advance of Sartre's formulation, the *Phenomenology of Perception* depicted Marxism as a philosophy of human praxis—but without identifying praxis narrowly with labor or with a total act of transcendence. Over a decade before the *Question of Method*, the essays collected in *Sense and Non-Sense* delineated a merger of Marxism and existential phenomenology.

By focusing on praxis, Merleau-Ponty suggested, Marxism bypassed both materialism and idealism as abstract doctrines; but the same focus could also be described as existential—provided existence was seen as "the movement through which man is in the world and involves himself in a physical and social situation which then becomes his point of view on the world." Existence, moreover, denoted not merely a general species or an elusive collectivity, but concrete human experience. To this extent, existentialism corroborated the critical and nondogmatic thrust inherent in Marxist thought from the beginning. "A philosophy," he observed, "which renounces absolute spirit as history's motive force, which makes history walk on its own feet and which admits no other reason in things than that revealed by their meeting and interaction, could not affirm *a priori* man's possibility for wholeness, postulate a final synthesis resolving all contradictions or assert its inevitable realization" (22).

The implications of these lines emerged more clearly ten years later, in a study which reviewed the developments of dialectical thinking in our century. Starting from Max Weber, whose outlook fully revealed the tensions of traditional liberalism, Merleau-Ponty credited Lukács with the formulation of a genuinely dialectical perspective—a perspective, moreover, which in large measure remained tentative and self-critical. Yet, infected by the revolutionary ebullience of the period and the trust in a ready-made proletariat, Lukács' work in important respects tended to encourage a visionary short-cut: "the revolution appeared as the *climax* in which reality and values, subject and object, opinion and discipline, individual and totality, present and future were destined to converge instead of being in conflict." Overtaken by political events, this vision soon disintegrated; Lenin's *Materialism and Empiriocriticism* marked the decline of dialectical thought and the return to dogmatic self-assurance. Since that time, Marxism constituted at best a coerced synthesis, concealing the survival of unresolved antinomies; stripped of crucial mediations the dialectic was identified either with a crude objectivism absorbing human praxis, or with a blind activism or voluntarism shunning reflection.

The task ahead, Merleau-Ponty suggested, was the cautious reconstruction of dialectical thought, a reconstruction which, instead of mutilating opposing elements, would permit scrutiny of their complex relationships. Among the themes requiring renewed attention were the linkages between thought and action, philosophy and practical life. Without lapsing into either a dialectic of synthesis or a dialectic of negation and total freedom, such an investigation would restore Marxism as a "questioning philosophy of history"; more important, it would revive its capacity of self-criticism, presenting it as a perspective "open even to those who challenge it and acquiring legitimacy precisely by facing such challenge" (23). Merleau-Ponty died while he was working at a comprehensive philosophical enterprise: an inquiry into the meaning of truth and its origins in opaque experience. In contradistinction to transcendental reflection, as well as to the dialectic of negation and the intuition of essences, the study portrayed philosophy as continuous interrogation—a quest that could not be exhausted "because the existing world exists in the interrogative mode" (24).

Merleau-Ponty's life-work remained a torso; but his inquiry has not been abandoned. As it seems to me, traces of his argument can be found in another brand of contemporary Marxism: the so-called Frankfurt School, committed to the elaboration of a "critical theory." Paci completely bypasses this school—not without reason, for the attitude of Frankfurt theorists toward phenomenology has largely been hostile. This attitude, however, has not precluded encounters of both an obvious and a subterranean kind. An overt and direct liaison can be found in the early writings of Herbert Marcuse—most of which, it is true, predate his affiliation with the Frankfurt group. A brief consideration of this encounter seems justified mainly because of certain affinities with Paci's work.

As a student in Berlin and Freiburg, Marcuse came under the influence of Husserl, Heidegger, and also Lukács; but whereas Lukács moved quickly from essences to dialectical synthesis, Marcuse tried to achieve a theoretical merger. In an essay of 1928 entitled "Contributions to a Phenomenology of Historical Materialism," Heideggerian phenomenology was presented as philosophical corroboration of Marxist aspirations. The nucleus of Marxism was seen in revolutionary praxis—in the "historical possibility of radical action which is to bring about necessarily a new reality that makes possible the total man." Action of this kind was termed necessary, for "every act lacking this specific character of necessity is not radical and need not happen"; it was also endowed with an overriding finality, "the determinate realization of human essence." The first concern of praxis, in the Marxist view, was with the "material needs required for self-preservation"; society developed in accordance with the different modes of production used to meet material needs. Division of labor made class antagonism the driving historical force: once conscious of its situation, "the chosen class matures to become the agency for historical action." All these Marxist notions were able to receive a solid theoretical grounding in phenomenology, especially in Heidegger's existential categories.

According to existential analysis, man was initially "thrown" into a world of ready-made concepts and social arrangements; but moved by "care" for the purpose of life, he was able to overcome this bondage and to realize his "essence" or "authentic existence." This realization occurred in a historical context, in the mode of "historicity"—"the decisive point in Heidegger's phenomenology"; moreover, steps in this direction were conditioned by basic existential "needs," including the need of production and reproduction. Yet, while providing a theoretical foundation, Heidegger's analysis remained abstract and elusive, refusing to proceed from general categories to the examination of concrete historical experience. In order to achieve a comprehensive perspective and to join general insight with concreteness, therefore, phenomenology had to be merged with dialectical materialism: "The phenomenological analysis of universal historicity becomes a theory of revolution only when it penetrates concrete historical conditions" (25).

After a few years of additional experimentation, Marcuse discarded the phenomenological focus in favor of other formulations—although one can plausibly argue that the quest for essences and apodictic insight was continued in later writings under different guises (e.g., the guise of Freudian instincts). Other members of the Frankfurt group never shared or condoned Marcuse's early infatuation. Theodor Adorno—together with Max Horkheimer a founder of the school—wrote a lengthy treatise denouncing Husserl's intuitionism as subjective speculation; on another occasion he harshly castigated Heidegger's verbal obscurities (26).

The same critical posture pervades the writings of Jürgen Habermas, the leading younger representative of the group. In his *Theory and Praxis*, which appeared in 1963, Habermas portrayed both phenomenological and existential interpretations of Marxism as essentially speculative or intuitionist distortions. Subsequent publications reiterated and reinforced this judgment. Thus, in an essay of 1965, Husserl's *Crisis* was singled out as an attempt to revive a purely contemplative outlook oblivious of its practical underpinnings (27). Yet, despite these critical strictures, I think it is possible to discover some subterranean linkages with the intentions of both Husserl and Merleau-Ponty. As it seems to me, Habermas' formulation of a basic framework of interests underlying cognitive efforts is not entirely at odds with Husserl's notion of the life-world. In *Knowl-*

edge and Interest of 1968, cognitive endeavors were depicted as rooted in a "life context," a context conditioning the character and the validation of knowledge claims. One should note, however, some important features of the postulated framework. First, cognitive interests as defined by Habermas are not merely endowments of a transcendental consciousness; rather, they are both the premises and the product of a concrete historical learning process. Also, interests of this type should not be conceived as private impulses but as parameters guiding the inquiries of an intersubjective "community of investigators." Finally, instead of denoting a uniform structure of needs, the framework is differentiated into a variety of basic orientations, especially those of work and interaction. Recently Habermas further refined his conception of the cognitive framework and of the linkage between thought and experience by stressing critical "discourse" as the medium of intersubjective interrogation and verification; reminiscent of Husserl's method of "bracketing," such interrogation is designed to loosen the grip of habits and unexamined opinions (28).

PACI'S FUNCTION OF THE SCIENCES

Viewed against the background of the sketched story of encounters, Paci's arguments in *The Function of the Sciences* assume distinct contours and accents. As the story suggests, the merger of Marxism and phenomenology can produce different, even sharply divergent, results. The admixture of phenomenological insights can help in reactivating Marxism as an open theoretical and practical venture; it can also corroborate or reinforce ideological self-sufficiency. Easily the most ambitious example of the genre in contemporary philosophy, Paci's work tends to reveal the entire range of implications (29). The overriding impression left by his study, however, is the immense suggestiveness and fertility of the life-world focus; conceived as a realm of concrete pretheoretical experience, the life-world poses a definite challenge to doctrinaire enclosure. Over long stretches, *The Function of the Sciences* offers a running commentary on Husserl's *Crisis* and his elaborations of the *Lebenswelt* as a counterpoise to scientific objectivism. According to Paci, these elaborations unmistakably point in the direction of dialectical materialism—but without reaching this goal. Both the *Crisis* and Marx' analysis of the capitalist economy, he argues, are critical efforts designed to rescue human experience from reification and estrangement. Once the life-world is interpreted as incorporating the level of basic needs and of material production, phenomenology and Marxism are destined to converge.

The study abounds with statements testifying to the critical and open-ended character of phenomenological inquiry. As a search for the meaning of experience, phenomenology is an incessant pursuit; since events are always embedded in a broader fabric with elusive boundaries or horizons, their interpretation has to be constantly renewed. Although partial elements are pregnant with universal significance, Paci notes, "this universal horizon is never given in its totality"; consequently, "if phenomenology is an ontology, it is not so in a dogmatic or metaphysical sense." Although inquiry has to start from the "evidence" available to individuals, the context surrounding such evidence extends in all directions, with the result that "the task of phenomenology is both temporally and historically infinite." Given the task of constant renewal, it is clear that phenomenological findings have to be amenable to challenge and correction. In Paci's words: "Verification must always be perfected, rectified, and corrected. The life-world does not leap once and for all from *doxa* to science." Seen from this perspective, phenomenology cannot be satisfied with momentary intuitions or spontaneous convictions; rather, infected by systematic doubt, it recaptures the intentions of the Socratic dialogue. "Philosophy," we read, "is the human activity in which life resumes the journey toward truth by continuously returning to its own origin and by becoming transformed in the horizon of truth, i.e., by always reconstituting being into intentional meaning" (30).

The journey toward truth, moreover, is not a solitary adventure, just as the discovery of meaning cannot be confined to private speculation. Experience is predicated on interaction and the decoding of meaning thus involves the confluence and interchange of outlooks. The world, Paci writes, "is a unity of horizons that I must constantly experience and relate in an open perspective. The representation of the world is a synthesis that is always in process, a unification that is always making and correcting itself in the explication of the movements of my body and other bodies, in the constant attempt to reach a unity of the world." In the terminology of Husserl and Leibniz, the world may be viewed as composed of monadic units and dispersed fragments; but "the transformation and perfection of the world presuppose intermonadic life and reciprocal agreement between the monads." Interchange of perspectives and reciprocal agreement, to be sure, cannot simply be presupposed or taken for granted. On the contrary, human relations at present are characterized—as they have been in much of the past—by incomprehension, antagonism, and manipulation. Intersubjective agreement and consensus thus is not so much an actual condition as an ideal standard of conduct; but "it is an ideal immanent in the structure of the world." Ultimately the postulate of a universal community transcends even the boundaries of a given generation and assumes a broadly historical connotation: "The 'unity of spiritual life' is the intentional-historical meaning which is maintained in the totality of human persons, in tradition and renewal and in the relation between the living and the dead. This totality is the totality of real men who in their dialectic tend toward an open meaningful synthesis, toward the meaning of truth that dialectically develops in the clashes and encounters of men and cultures" (31).

This conception of phenomenology has definite implications for social theory and practice, and especially for Marxism. Although the vision of a universal community may never be fully attainable, social relations are poised in this direction and cannot be abandoned to relativistic apathy; by the same token, however, the purpose of social life cannot simply be divorced from actual human conduct and experience. The goal, Paci notes, "is not *any* indifferent end"; rather, it involves "action for the realization of a rational society which overcomes war and exploitations, along with 'naturalism,' fetishism and slavery. This is the *horizon of truth*, although it is not the horizon of a philosophy understood as ideology or as a purely formal dialectic. It is the horizon of truth of a philosophy that is based on what men actually experience as they experience it and within the limits in which they experience it." A social theory incorporating this outlook is bound to assume a critical posture, a posture encouraging self-scrutiny. By rejecting both indifference and dogma, Marxism is able to regain its original momentum: "Each man contains the principle of truth; yet no man can ever be the truth: this would be idolatry. Critical Marxism could rediscover its own secret religious tone as the overcoming of every idolatry and as the movement of liberation from every type of alienation." As long as Marxism is treated simply as another type of scientism or objectivism, it falls short of its significance; while not rejecting technology in a romantic manner, Marxist praxis cannot be reduced to the mere application of scientific formulas. Once it is recognized that, contrary to the assertions of classical economists or social Darwinists, society is not simply governed by naturalistic laws or by a crude "struggle for survival," social theory has to return to the human foundations of prevailing structural arrangements. The abandonment of objectivism, however, cannot mean indulgence in unprincipled speculation; rather, it demands a constant "critique of what is only illusory and apparent. In a rigorous sense, it demands the critique of ideology" (32).

In all these statements, it seems to me, the promise of a phenomenological Marxism is compellingly evident. Unfortunately, however, the statements are scattered and dispersed over the bulk of a lengthy argument that tends to be pervaded by a different tenor—a tenor more inspirational than Socratic in character. The two perspectives or styles of presentation, to be sure, are not neatly segregated; occasionally they merge in one and the same passage—but without effacing underlying fissures. Instead of stressing the need for patient exploration and consultation, many portions of the study present phenomenology—and Marxist phenomenology in particular—as an act of revelation, as a sudden glimpse underneath the covers of phenomenal appearances. The reality revealed in this manner is usually described as the dimension of the "pre-categorial" or pretheoretical life-world—a life-world seen from the angle of an experiencing subject who is both concrete and "transcendental," and which is directly endowed with a basic finality or teleology. As one will note, the hidden dimension is a somewhat complex scenery, and it may be well to examine its component elements in detail.

Probably the most recurrent and most emphatically expounded theme of the study is the stress on the subject as source of all insight and on the "return to subjectivity" as phenomenology's basic goal. "Phenomenology," the opening section proclaims, "wants to return his 'subjectivity' to man. It wants to return man to himself, freeing him from every fetishism, from the mask behind which humanity has been hidden or 'veiled.' " Somewhat later Husserl's work is described as a "founded philosophy that returns to apodictic subjectivity which is, as such, serious and rigorous." Paci does not tire to explicate the significance of this starting point. "The crisis," he writes, "is the forgetting of the origins, the human roots, the human subject, and the precategorial genesis." The implications for social, and especially Marxist, thought are correspondingly evident: "The center of the whole problem is, and remains, the return to subjectivity. We have alienation when social relations do not allow this return" (33). Assertions to this effect seem plausible enough as reaction against reification and exploitation and as reaffirmation of man's relevance as a thinking and experiencing subject. Complications arise quickly, however, when subjectivity is meant to serve as theoretical cornerstone and as foundation of a "first philosophy." That this is Paci's ambition can hardly be doubted. At one point, it is true, he seems to suggest that "the first person" is simply "a *fact*, a reality which cannot be altered by any theory or argument"; but he soon proceeds beyond the factual level. Phenomenology, he asserts, is "the only precategorial philosophy," adding that "as first philosophy," it is "a science of subjects and not objects." It seems clear, however, that, on a theoretical level, "subjectivity" immediately presupposes, and cannot be conceived without, the counterterm "objectivity" and that both can claim equal status.

Paci might counter that his argument aims not at the conceptual but at the preconceptual level of experience. In fact, he writes at one point that "the word 'subject' [is] but a category" and that one must return instead to the "original subject, i.e., the ego in flesh and blood." One wonders, of course, how the latter can be described and, more generally, how a first philosophy is possible without articulation. The quandary, in any case, remains: Either the argument operates on a theoretical level, in which case subjectivity evokes objectivity as its partner; or it is meant to be "precategorial"—in which case the emphatic use of the term seems arbitrary or puzzling (34).

A more serious dilemma deriving from the stress on subjectivity is the proximity to traditional idealism—a perspective according to which the "outside" world is either the result of a mental construction or the manifestation of an ideal core. Numerous statements seem to point in this direction. In several passages the subject is portrayed as an "internal" agent or consciousness contrasted to outside conditions. "If we depart from the 'internal' subject and analyze his operations," Paci contends at one time, "we find everything." Dialectical Marxism, we read in another context, is oriented "toward a maximum of the internal and a minimum of the external," that is, toward a "minimization of dependence" and a "maximization of the autonomy of each subject." To this may be added the notion that "the phenomenological subject is a conscious and therefore free subject," whereas unconsciousness characterizes the "external material world." More important are statements suggesting a far-ranging potency or creativity of the subject. "Philosophy, science, culture, and institutions are all human products," we are told; "they should not be extraneous objects turned against men. We are the subjects of historicity, the persons who create culture and function in the totality: the personal functioning mankind." On other occasions, man's creative role is expressed in even more dramatic language. A "transcendental" or philosophically radical attitude, Paci indicates, cannot simply accept the world "as already done and accomplished"; rather, rigorous reflection requires "taking a dialectical, revolutionary position on the intentional level." Phenomenological bracketing thus acquires a practical connotation: "The transcendental *epoché* is a total transformation" (35).

Paci, to be sure, is quick to reject any idealistic implications of his argument. Man's internality, we are given to understand, does not really contrast with outside conditions, and human creativity has to be understood at most in a figurative sense. "Man is internal while the world is external," he writes. "However, the internal man is within the external world, while the external world is within the internal man." As a result, one can say that "man is both internal and external." By returning to the subject, Paci adds later, "I discover in myself and in others the ways in which the external is given to me: Each one of us contains the external." In a similar manner, the stress on creativity is corrected by the reminder: "If we think about what Husserl says, we readily understand that consciousness discovers that it does not posit the world. Contrary to traditional idealism, consciousness discovers precisely that the world is pregiven." It may very well be that Paci with these assertions obviates the danger of subjective idealism; but at what price? While the merger of the external and the internal evokes the legacy of an absolute synthesis, the nexus of creativity and discovery seems to be predicated on the assumption of an ideal core, a hidden finality contracting theory and practice. The latter assumption is by no means fortuitous.

In trying to avoid idealist subjectivism and at the same time a naive realism according to which the mind simply mirrors an objective world, Paci is led to embrace the notion of a dynamic essence, which, although discoverable, is not ready-made but awaits implementation through human involvement. This conception permits Paci to write passages in which action and receptivity are intimately linked. Thus the preceding reference to Husserl is followed by these comments: "We live in order to overcome the already constituted world, to direct ourselves toward a new world that we can conceive and whose realization we can seek to effect. Here the interest has changed, since it is no longer concerned with the given world but with a world evolving from it by means of reflection" —a reflection aiming "toward a teleological and intentional meaning." From this perspective, Paci adds, "the world no longer interests us for what it is, but for the meaning it can have and for the meaning we can give to it and realize" (36).

The linkage of action and reflection is hardly conceivable without the other feature: the merger of subject and the world. This fusion— the notion that "each one of us contains the external"—is reiterated in many variations. Thus, at one point, Paci affirms that "subjectivity is the *entire world* to the extent that it is subjective, intentional activity." In even bolder terms, another passage refers to "the total subject who contains the world—even that world he does not knowingly contain and the past that he ignores." This view has immediate relevance for intersubjective relations; even if restricted to the "subjective, intentional" domain, the "world" contained by the individual would seem to comprise his fellow-men. Paci tends to be explicit on this point. The study speaks of "the structures of intersubjectivity which inhere in every individual subject, in every monad" and of "the internal immanence of society in individuals." In a later section, Paci elaborates on the aspect in greater detail. "The problem of the 'constitution of the other' by the subject," he states, "is the phenomenological history of the individual in relation to other individuals and the inherence of 'society' in the individual. In fact, the individual finds others within himself even if he becomes an absolute solipsist." Actually, he continues, the individual has no choice but to start from "the *solus ipse* of solipsism"; by bracketing all external factors, including society and state, the individual "truly finds the others and society within himself." Social life, it is true, is not simply deduced or extracted from individual awareness; repeatedly Paci stresses the importance of "coupling" or intermonadic contact. Such contact, however, tends to be presented either as an "immanence of monads and individuals in one another" or as the reciprocal discovery of affinity through "empathy" (37); what is missing is an actual confrontation or struggle with strangeness. As it seems to me, Paci's comments on this issue tend to fall short of Husserl's own insights, especially his endeavors in *Cartesian Meditations* to conceive a relationship between ego and others which would not efface their otherness. Most important, his view evades the task of interaction: on the premise of reciprocal immanence or affinity, social agreement does not seem to presuppose the arduous labor of intersubjective questioning and correction.

The conception of a subject-object convergence, however, extends beyond the social domain. Paci does not ignore the limits of conscious intentionality. "Matter," he acknowledges, "is given to me as matter in its impenetrability, opacity, passivity, and resistance. It provokes me, conditions me, and makes me experience what has not been done by me: being as such (*Sosein*) or matters of fact." Yet, even on this level, the gulf does not seem insurmountable, for he adds that "*Sosein* can be reduced to a lived modality. It is reducible to an *Erlebnis* that can be characterized as the *Erlebnis* of passivity of the hardness of things." Thus matter can be integrated into the life-world, the opaque into conscious experience. "The 'unconscious,'" Paci notes, "appears as the external material world and as the otherness not yet consciously constituted in my *Umwelt*." However, when viewed in the context of the life-world, "we become aware of the fact that even external and material nature is internal to the extent that it is life experienced by transcendental subjectivity." Man, in Paci's view, is able to incorporate matter chiefly through the medium of his body, which is anchored in inorganic nature and unconscious causality. Although the "phenomenological subject" has to be viewed as alert and aware, "it would not be conscious without its animated body: its soul or psyche and its organic body which is rooted in causality." By virtue of his body, he repeatedly stresses, man becomes the "point of insertion and encounter (*Umschlagpunkt*) of the internal and of the external," a notion he finds reflected in the "admirable phenomenological and Marxian concept of the nature which is *in me* as man's inorganic body." The vision of man's linkage with nature inspires Paci occasionally with rhapsodic formulations, reminiscent of the idealist philosophy of identity. Geological nature, he observes at one point, "has preceded me and continues to permeate me as if the planet Earth and the entire universe were the inorganic body of my individual, concrete, and transcendental ego. It permeates me as my material, organic, and animated individuality: as the body of intersubjective humanity, animals, plants, and the very minerals as material bodies. Inert matter is mine but I am also inert matter, the inert universe" (38).

A vision of this kind, it would seem, cannot readily be reconciled with dialectical thought: Where subject and object are reversible, a crucial dialectical tension appears suspended. Paci's comments on the topic are correspondingly elusive. The dialectic, he writes, "is the inclusion of the totality in the part, of the infinite in the finite, and of truth in individuality"; at the same time it is "the identification of the part and the whole, of actuality and rationality, and of individuality and totality." To be sure, inclusion and identification do not adequately convey the meaning of the dialectic as a process and Paci is fully aware of this circumstance. In trying to render his conception dynamic, however, he tends to present dialectical movement simply as a process of progressive revelation, as a struggle to remove the cloak of objectification from a hidden, purposive reality. Phenomenological dialectic, we learn, is "a dialectic of the hidden and the revealed," a dialectic "which unravels and persists." Discovery of the hidden occurs through a dual negation: the rejection of the negative veil of appearances. In Paci's words, phenomenological reflection "is a human operation of negating that negation which is appearance." While appearance "operates by negating and alienating man," *epoché* or the act of bracketing must "prevent these forms from once again becoming prejudicial." By collapsing or cutting through mediation, bracketing thus emerges as gateway to essential meaning and social transformation, the dialectic of negation as the harbinger of synthesis. "In the dialectic," we read, "we must bring about a *radical revolution* wherein each man and humanity deal with their own negativity while attempting to negate it (negation of the negation). In this revolution, quantitative operations must be transformed into qualitative ones. They must allow a qualitative change; they must permit a change of life's meanings and goals so that, ultimately, the paradoxes and contradictions become functions of a totalizing and constructive synthesis." Not surprisingly, the proletariat is invoked somewhat later as the chief motor of the dialectic, as the agency performing the dual negation: "It is insofar as it is not; and it is not insofar as it is."

What, in Paci's opinion, is crucial in dialectical thought, properly understood, is the dismantling of apparent objectivity in favor of authentic experience. "The fundamental point," he avows, "is the insertion of the dialectic into subjectivity and the penetration of subjectivity as a causal element into every dialectical modality." Such a view, he maintains, is entirely congruent with the outlook of the founders of Marxism: "Dialectical modalities such as those presented as laws by Engels must necessarily begin with subjectivity, both as a point of departure and as living and operating presence." Taking his cues from Engels, Paci even speculates on the notion of a "dialectic of nature." By relying on life-world experience and the role of subjectivity, he claims to be able to clarify its significance; but his comments on the issue are at best puzzling. Orthodox proponents of the notion, in any case, would hardly appreciate his endeavors when learning that such a dialectic "must be constituted by us" and must necessarily begin "with us" (39). According to Paci, the focus on subjectivity also provides a reliable demarcation line between Hegelianism and genuine Marxist thought. As he tries to show, Hegel's dialectic—despite its pioneering value—was marred by overconceptualization, by an excessive indulgence in abstract categories; ultimately, this excess derived from a neglect of subjective life and of the method of bracketing. Hegel's philosophy, he says, "is a dialectic of abstract concepts, ideas, and constructions that have occluded their genesis in the precategorial world and in subjective and intersubjective operations." What is missing in Hegelian idealism "is precisely the subjective and precategorial point of departure;" in other words, "what Hegel lacked was the *epoché:* the first reflective dialectical operation of the subject living in the world." As he adds, this is a criticism that can be directed against Hegel's entire system, "as has already been done by the Left Hegelians" (40).

There are other reminders of Left Hegelianism in Paci's argument. A chief example is the intimate juncture of transcendental reflection with empirical contingency; one of the traits peculiar of the Hegelian Left was the assignment of absolute functions to empirical agents. "The transcendental reduction," he writes, "allows us to find what Husserl indicates as absolute subjectivity." However, the same reduction also reveals a "concrete living presence"; its aim thus is not an "abstract transcendental ego separated from the ego which we are or separated from that concrete world in which we have always been living." An "extreme" type of bracketing involves "reduction to an 'absolute' subjectivity," yet—since "subjectivity without the world contains it"—what emerges is not emptiness but a "new world" which is "to be found in subjectivity itself and is intentionally constituted by it." At other points Paci expresses himself even more succinctly. "The transcendental ego," he asserts, "is each one of us in his concreteness as a human being in flesh and blood"; by the same token, absolute subjectivity is "simultaneously the concrete ego" (41). Of course, Paci does not simply identify transcendental and mundane levels without further elaboration. However, as in the case of the dialectic, his elaboration takes the form of a two-layer theory according to which the mundane subject is merely a camouflage covering authentic man. Phenomenology, in his view, clears the way to a "transcendental foundation," provided the mundane is bracketed: "Objectivism and factuality are masks behind which man is hidden and fetishized. Therefore, the transcendental foundation requires the transcendental reduction to pure subjectivity, that is, to transcendental subjectivity." Properly performed, the transcendental reduction leads to "a subjectivity which is not mythological," to a "life oriented toward truth, the life which I somehow always live behind my masks"; once man "in the name of reason rejects his mask," he is able to discover "his own truth" and "his proper authentic nature." One may recall in this context what Merleau-Ponty wrote in 1960: "Man is hidden, well hidden, and this time we must make no mistake about it: this does not mean that he is there beneath a mask, ready to appear. Alienation is not simply privation of what was our own by natural right; and to bring it to an end, it will not suffice to steal what has been stolen, to give us back our due" (42).

As presented by Paci, the relationship between substance and mask is the basic key to historical development; although not presently accomplished, their convergence is the driving motor of mankind's teleology. In his words: "Our most secret nature, what we actually are in the most profound sense, first and foremost, is also the rational ideal, the teleological end and the final goal." Within man, he affirms, "there is a latent humanity—and here we interpret Husserl in a radical sense—a humanity which has not yet been born but which can be born if man so desires, if man assumes the responsibility for becoming what he can become." History, from this perspective, appears as "the progressive self-revelation and self-realization of what is hidden; and what is hidden is the authentic original man: both his meaning and his *telos*." While at present we do not yet live "according to our true life and therefore do not live according to reason" but rather "in a sort of pre-existence," our duty is "to realize our existence in history, to come really into being in history." By bringing to light and rendering manifest what has been concealed or latent from the beginning, teleological development links the past with the future. Historiography in its true sense, Paci comments, is "a process of continually bringing back to life," a persistent "rediscovery of the hidden historical meaning"; in this manner, "the historical-genetic origin becomes the goal: beginning and goal meet one another in a circle." This circle, however, is not merely pointless repetition; rather, it is an effort to resurrect and implement purpose in life, a constant "renewal in the present of the past for the future, of the *Lebenswelt* for the *telos*." In terms of human involvement, the renewal implies the investment of "will, decision, interest and praxis": the "return to subjectivity" is also a "return to action" entailing an "actual commitment directed toward a finality" (43).

The difficulty in these passages lies not in the general vision of a goal—which is bold and captivating—but rather in its formulation, and especially in the portrayal of history as teleological revelation. Such a portrayal tends to bypass or shortchange the complexity of meaning in concrete situations. Above all, the perspective implies a contraction of theory and practice, reflection and action—or, at least, it fails to elaborate sufficiently on their relationships. Paci emphatically insists on their intimate nexus; thus he finds the genuine character of Marxism in the aspect that "the historical and the scientific meanings of truth coincide." One may wonder, however, how a coincidence of this type can escape the lure of scientism and, in particular, how it can resolve the quandaries attached to the juncture of norms and observation (44). More important, the notion of an immanent finality or *telos* in history tends to favor a posture of apodictic certainty, while dampening the taste for intersubjective discourse. Despite the recognition that mankind's goal is an "infinite task" which "is never completely realized," many statements in the study suggest that practical standards are the direct result of individual reflection. The transcendental reduction or *epoché*, we read, "has a moral aspect which, by freeing us from the mundane, must allow us to rediscover the 'natural' direction of the will toward the good and the evidence of the will 'pointed toward the ultimate meaning of determinate being.'" Transferred to the concrete political domain, the reduction has distinct implications—especially if coupled with a negative dialectic, the notion that "in the negation of the negation" the essence "becomes consciousness, will, and praxis." The apodictic character of these implications is reinforced when praxis is seen as rooted in, and basically conditioned by, material needs—needs which are universal and thus hardly amenable to dispute. "The proletariat fights and must fight for all, that is, for the *telos* and meaning of human history," Paci notes; in this case, "the subject, or groups of subjects, know and will according to a universal aim" (45).

The apodictic thrust of Paci's political outlook is predicated on, and supported by an important feature of early phenomenology: the notion of intuitive evidence as criterion of truth. Evidence, he writes, means experience and presence "in the first person." Although limited and finite, it is "the pledge and the proof that man can bring to light what is latent within himself, what he has hidden, what is not yet human, what is not rationally or philosophically grounded. For the philosopher who wants to constitute humanity and ground it upon philosophy, evidence is therefore the starting point, the beginning." Whatever can be experienced, he adds, "can be experienced directly through intuition"; the life-world in particular allows "an evident, convincing, and original experience in the first person." As universal science, phenomenology treats existential life "as the original source of verification and as the basis of truth." The basic principle of phenomenological inquiry is, in fact, "that it is always possible to depart from a presence, from actual evidence (an *Erfüllung*)." Paci realizes, of course, that individual evidence is restricted and that there is the possibility of deception and error in judgment. However, such error seems to be chiefly a failure of reflection and, as such, subject to the dialectic of substance and appearance. While surrounded by a penumbra like a source of light, evidence "must have a nucleus of certainty: it must be a basic revelation. Even though it is finite, it must be apodictic." The doubting ego "that has not yet reflected and recognized that it thinks while doubting" always "precedes the ego which is certain of its doubt- ing"; thus "even while doubting, the preceding ego contains certainty."

At some points, especially when reporting on Husserl's notion of a community of investigators, the study seems to open up the prospect of corrective interaction; yet Paci's comments usually point back to the premises of reciprocal immanence and self-revelation. Phenomenological philosophy, he writes, is "rigorous because of its beginning anew and be- cause of its continuous return to the factual and transcendental apodictic- ity of the human subject." On this level, "each man can discover in each part, beginning from himself and his own apodicticity, the meaning of the whole"; departing from the evidence in the first person, "he discovers in the universal correlation the possibility of knowing all that his evidence implies" (46).

The effects of this phenomenological starting point reverberate in many other facets of the study, not all of which can be mentioned in this context. One example is the formulation of the "precategorial" life-world: occasionally there is the suggestion of an apodictic knowledge on this level serving as groundwork for specialized inquiries. As a rule, the study is quite explicit in portraying the life-world as a domain of relative opin- ion or *doxa*—at least from the vantage point of immediate experience. The *Lebenswelt*, we read, conceived as "relative and prescientific life is the subjective world of the *doxa*." Paci, however, is by no means content with opinion, seeking instead grounded knowledge. Rigorous scrutiny, he notes, is required "insofar as the *Lebenswelt* needs techniques, theoretical praxis, and elaborations of teleological theories"; phenomenological brack- eting must even "allow for a subjective science of the *Lebenswelt*." We may bypass here the question how a theoretical elaboration of a precon- ceptual domain is possible. As Paci repeatedly insists, a "science" of the life-world is not the investigation of a chimerical "thing-in-itself," but rather the search for the meaning and intentional purpose of life, a mean- ing inherent in practical conduct: "The science of the life-world is essen- tially praxis precisely because it is the science of the precategorial and of the operations performed and being performed by the subjects" (47). Pas- sages of this kind, however, do not entirely banish the dilemmas endemic in the theory-praxis nexus. In his effort to show the cognitive potential of practical life, Paci is led to structural considerations. Without becoming an "objectified" discipline, he affirms, "the science of the *Lebenswelt* dis- covers a general structure," that is, a configuration of the "typical" and "invariable forms" of life. The task of phenomenology is to capture the life-world in its "essential forms" and in its "necessary and essential struc- ture"; although life experience may be subjective, "its structures are not relative," but rather provide the nucleus for a phenomenological "ontology." At some points, the vision of a structural ontology acquires distinct connotations of a dual or two-layer reality, with the life-world providing the ideal forms of concrete phenomena. Despite his aversion against a naive realism, Paci's argument at these points tends to lend involuntary support to a "mirror" or correspondence theory of knowledge (48).

The bent toward a more apodictic than critical outlook is also illustrated in Paci's comments on the various writers discussed in the study. Although painstaking and thorough, the commentary on the *Crisis* at important junctures tends to be obtuse to Husserl's subdued and careful formulations. This tendency has already been noted in regard to the concept of an investigating community, but examples could be multiplied. Usually, Paci's elaborations in such instances imply a de-emphasis of mutual correction in favor of experiential evidence and individual reflection (49). Marx similarly undergoes occasional simplification. Thus, citing his statement of 1843 that "in the investigation of political conditions one is too easily tempted to overlook the objective nature of the relationships and to explain everything from the will of the persons acting," Paci concludes that its thrust does not affect "the person but only the person separated from the situation"; again, Marx' later stress on the precedence of economic categories—such as wage-labor or capital—over supposedly concrete initiatives is interpreted to mean that "the original concreteness from which Marx in fact departs, is the subjects."

Similar impressions can be gleaned from passages dealing with more recent Marxists or neo-Marxists. Lukács is commended primarily for his adherence to a dialectic of synthesis, with its insistence on dual negation and the movement toward totality under the aegis of the proletariat. Synthesis and emphasis on proletarian action are also the chief merits of Labriola and Gramsci; while Labriola is noteworthy primarily for his merger of subject and object, theory and praxis, Gramsci is singled out for his practical philosophy and for showing that "the humanly objective is grounded by the historically subjective, that is, by the universally subjective." By and large, Paci praises Sartre's endeavors—including his move toward an existentialist Marxism—but is slightly suspicious of his *Critique*, finding it insufficiently strict in terms of a departure from subjective evidence: Only phenomenology, he observes, can offer "a rigorous and consequential foundation to Sartre's position." Criticism is heaped more lavishly on Merleau-Ponty, but basically for the same reason. Repeatedly, Merleau-Ponty is taken to task for favoring an abstract and ambivalent symbiosis of idealism and realism—a charge which finds little or no support in his writings; but the real complaint is readily apparent and involves another "ambiguity": a deficiency of apodictic firmness (50).

CONTEMPORARY SOCIOLOGY AND SOCIAL THOUGHT

As is well known, social science in Western countries is presently in a state of considerable ferment, a ferment characterized by the weakening of positivist predominance and the search for alternative methods and theoretical vistas. Increasingly, contemporary sociology and social thought are beginning to reflect the imprint of both phenomenological and neo-Marxist perspectives. While, in regard to phenomenology, the legacy of Alfred Schutz is exerting a growing influence, Marxist impulses are evident in the emergence of a "dialectical" or "critical" sociology with its emphasis on stratification, conflict, and social change. So far, however, sustained encounters between phenomenology and Marxism are infrequent; some of the pioneering works in the contemporary endeavor of reorientation do not indicate such a possibility.

Although informed and elaborate on Marxist trends in sociology, Norman Birnbaum's *Toward a Critical Sociology* makes only perfunctory reference to phenomenology as a quest for a trans-social human essence and authenticity. Similarly, Alvin Gouldner's *The Coming Crisis of Western Sociology* contains a sympathetic account of Marxist tendencies, but only an offhand allusion to Schutz during the discussion of one specialized type of inquiry; although reminiscent of phenomenological *Verstehen* and imbued with a Marxist concern for praxis, his "reflexive sociology" does not involve an articulate merger of the two perspectives (51). Yet there are signs that the situation is changing—in no small measure due to the impact of Paci and kindred thinkers. Actually, phenomenological Marxism is not an entirely novel venture in Western social science. For several decades, the French sociologist Georges Gurvitch has experimented with such an alliance and his works have received a fair share of scholarly tribute and critical scrutiny (52). For present purposes, I shall limit myself to more recent endeavors and briefly review the work of two American writers. The two examples, it seems to me, vividly illustrate the significance of phenomenological Marxism for social theory and sociological research, while at the same time disclosing instructive differences of accent and formulation.

The first example is Paul Piccone, one of the translators of *The Function of the Sciences* and chief editor of a social theory journal whose title, *Telos*, suggests its Husserlian inspiration. As translator and attentive student of the philosopher, Piccone to a large extent shares the ambivalence of Paci's outlook—including the bent toward apodicticity. The similarities in perspective are clearly revealed in the Introduction to the *Function*, which he coauthored with his fellow translator. The essay is strongly critical of "orthodox" Marxism, depicted as an abstract, objectified doctrine and as tool of manipulation in the hands of a ruling bureaucracy. The affinity between Marx and Husserl is seen precisely in their common struggle against objectivism and reification, with Husserl focusing on developments within the "European sciences." From this perspective, "capital, science, and Marxism are three different products of the *same* sociohistorical process of capitalist development." Analogous to the crisis of the sciences and capitalism, Marxist orthodoxy involves "essentially the separation of subject (workers) and object (their objective consciousness: Marxism), with the subsequent reification of the object to the level of an objective science." In his *Crisis*, Husserl had definitely pierced the cloak of scientific objectivity, laying bare the underpinnings of human knowledge: "The *leitmotiv* of Husserl's work is the return to the subject as the *real foundation*. Meanings are constantly referred to the human operations that constitute them." By returning to the subject—and to the life-world as its habitat—phenomenology boldly surpasses abstract philosophical systems and "categorial" schemes: "The life-world is fundamental to any philosophy that seeks to avoid naive realism or idealism and give an adequate analysis of knowledge." In contrast to realism, in particular, phenomenology insists that concepts "cannot be mechanically *derived* from the object, but must be constituted in terms of a *telos* that furnishes a precategorial criterion" of relevance and validity.

Although compelling in its domain, however, Husserl's phenomenology according to the authors is incomplete: His account of scientific developments ends abruptly at the point where he attempts to articulate the broader "roots of the crisis." At this point, Marxism can offer assistance by penetrating into the material infrastructure of social life. Husserl's analysis, it is true, "turns to the precategorial world as the world of human operations," but here "the world of materiality becomes central." Together with Paci, the authors consider "need" as "the precategorial foundation upon which everything else depends." Need, they write, is "determining. The life-world is the world of needs and of their satisfaction by means of labor." Thus Marxism is able to supplement phenomenology by integrating the question of scientific knowledge into a general social perspective: "A developed phenomenology coheres with Marxism as a dialectical account of how men make themselves and their institutions in the laboring process"; in fact, "phenomenology as a whole can already be found *within* Marxism as a necessary and essential moment of the whole structure, and the crisis of the sciences can be seen as a *special* case of the capitalist crisis."

While being supplemented and corroborated, phenomenology in turn offers a vital impulse destined to reactivate a stagnant Marxism. This impulse consists in the renewed focus on the crucial role of subjective experience: "What is needed is the development of a new subjective philosophy which, unlike the objectivistic systems developed since the Renaissance, would lay major stress on the subject, the life-world, and the all-important *telos*." In emphasizing the role of the subject, the authors occasionally seem willing to strain phenomenological vocabulary. Despite Paci's repeated avowal that "to constitute does not mean to create"—and despite the "determining" character of needs—they observe that "pseudo-rationalism camouflaged as 'scientific neutrality' is divorced from the creating subject who originally constitutes it" (53).

Many of Piccone's writings have been published in *Telos*. The mixture of criticism and apodicticity is strongly evident in a recent essay entitled "Phenomenological Marxism." The essay contains a vehement indictment of Marxist orthodoxy and an urgent plea for the adoption of a "critical" Marxist outlook. Reduced to an instrument of Soviet policy, Piccone writes, "orthodox Marxism as a theory has become an empty shell held together by dogmatic slogans—so empty that only the cynicism of its supporters can prevent it from being discarded as an intellectual aberration." The transformation of Marxism into an "ideological fossil," in his view, was not merely a vice of the Stalinist period, but continues to characterize official Soviet doctrine from Khrushchev's reversed "personality cult" to Brezhnev's "computerized Stalinism." Controlled by the party hierarchy and treated as unchallengeable dogma, orthodoxy has a philosophically and culturally stifling and even lethal effect: "All philosophy and culture is immediately reduced to the level of a weapon committed to fighting battles in which the sides are predetermined by the objective requirements of Soviet policy—which means, purely and simply, their destruction as philosophy and culture" and their degeneration into "apologetics."

This decay, Piccone adds, is not merely a fortuitous accident, but the expression of a deep-seated crisis involving the progressive reification of industrial society and the "disintegration of the working class as a revolutionary political force"; consequently, "any attempt at a critical Marxism today must start out in contraposition to the orthodoxy." In order to meet and overcome the crisis, "radical theory" must attempt "to rescue Marxism from the dogmatic stranglehold" by "developing a new critical Marxism." Such an effort implies, above all, a reexamination of the traditional conceptual arsenal: A Marxism "adequate to today's realities must start out by reconstituting first and foremost the notion of class and, specifically, of working class, in order to both capture and explain the myriad of phenomena that senile 'orthodox' Marxism cannot." Likewise, the relationship between structure and superstructure must be reinterpreted in such a manner that structure is no longer defined in a narrow economic sense as linked with "the physical means of production," but broadly as a "socio-economic situation which determines one's life style" and "the quality of life." If this is done, then revolution can be conceived primarily "as a qualitative change in this everyday life whereby today's fragmented and robotized workers would become subjects consciously (politically) engaged in concretely determining their destiny" (54).

As the essay emphasizes, phenomenology can significantly help in this critical endeavor by elucidating the crisis both of industrial society and of Marxist theory; in fact, "phenomenological Marxism is precisely the theoretical self-consciousness of the crisis of Marxism and an attempt to explain and overcome it." Phenomenology's contribution can be found mainly in Husserl's later writings; according to Piccone, "certain notions developed by the later Husserl can become extremely useful in the reconstitution of Marxism" by providing "fundamental categories of analysis which can adequately deal with the present socio-historical realities." Husserl's analysis of science in the *Crisis* revealed "the failure of this science to actually change reality by occluding it with its categories and thus checkmating man as the historical agent to the level of a mere passive object operating among similar objects." Basically, this analysis meant the recovery of the source of knowledge in preconceptual experience: "Phenomenology, critically understood, is the tracing back of all mediations to the human operations that constituted them." On a broader scale, the impulse of genuine Marxism points in a similar direction. "The difference between Marxist and bourgeois philosophy," Piccone notes, "does not concern the metaphysical quandary whether consciousness precedes matter or vice versa: on the contrary, the difference is between a dynamic, creative philosophy which explains man's making of himself by making the object and contemplative philosophies which contrapose an abstract subject to an abstract object, both equally inert." From this vantage point, the concerns of Marxism and phenomenology can be seen to be intimately meshed: "Phenomenological Marxism can be preliminarily described as that approach which constantly reduces all theoretical constructs—including Marxism—to their living context in order to guarantee the adequacy of the concept not only to the object it claims to apprehend, but also to the goals it seeks to attain. In fact, its point of departure is precisely the rejection of the theory of reflection so dear to 'orthodox' Marxists."

So far, the argument in its general outline appears clearly motivated by a critical intent, by the endeavor to reconcile "a relevant phenomenology and a non-dogmatic Marxism." However, Piccone's further elaborations raise serious doubts about the thrust of the proposed merger. These doubts emerge when one reads that Marxist philosophy, bent on changing rather than reflecting the world, "not only reconstitutes the world physically but conceptually as well" and that the basis of this reconstitution resides in class position—even though the term is redefined to mean a broad amalgam of underprivileged groups. Husserl's analysis is said to be congruent with this outlook because of its aim "to uncover the transcendental subjectivity which generated these concepts and which is constantly repressed in *mundane* experience." The theme, to be sure, was not fully developed in the *Crisis;* however, once it is realized that the "human operations to which phenomenology reduces all mediations" are historically and socially conditioned, "phenomenological analysis unavoidably ends up in Marxism as the class-analysis that explains the different kinds of consciousness in terms of class position (a result of social sedimentation) and labor (the teleological activity which allows the class engaged in it the *true* consciousness of its situation and the possibility of changing the world by means of the mediations that it itself creates)."

Regarding the question of validity, Piccone at this point resolutely endorses the phenomenological notion of the apodictic evidence of intentionality. "True consciousness," he writes, refers "simply to a consciousness that expresses the objective interests of the subjects possessing it; it is *true* because it is constituted by the subjects that have it." The same rule of evidence applies to all domains of knowledge and cultural experience. "The relation between concept and object," he continues, "is not one of reflection or symmetry, but one of adequacy"; consequently, "the criterion of truth cannot be correspondence between concept and object, but must be between the concept and its fulfillment of the goal for which it was originally devised." Since a concept cannot reflect reality, "it must be created"; but given the infinite number of possible concepts, the standard determining adequacy "is always a function of a social situation with its own needs and problems. In other words, the process of concept formation should not be seen as at all different from the process of commodity production; both processes are teleological and based on labor. Thus, it is possible to talk about all knowledge, including science, as class-determined" (55).

These passages conjure up a series of quandaries. If all knowledge is class-based and all science "class-science," then this statement is subject to the same standard and becomes a victim of the same relativity. More important, one may wonder whether, on these premises, philosophy and culture are not bound to be transformed into "weapons" in the class struggle and thus be reduced to "apologetics"—a result that was previously deplored. Piccone is eloquent in depicting the practical implications of phenomenological Marxism and of the reliance on primary evidence. Just as Marx "materialized" Hegel, he observes, "Marxism must 'materialize' Husserl by interpreting the base as the *Lebenswelt* and the worker as *transcendental subjectivity*"; only in this manner "is it possible to vindicate the need for revolution and the quest for a qualitatively different way of life." From the perspective of a revitalized Marxism, "revolution is necessitated not only by the exploitation and starvation of the proletariat, nor by cultural deprivation, but, more importantly, by its dehumanization whereby under capitalism men (both the capitalists and the proletarians) are limited to *mundane* experience." The proletarian, he explains, "ends up as the revolutionary agency not because of any inner superiority or higher moral character, but because in having to work he is always forced into the role of a *transcendental* subject who not only *mundanely* transposes pre-given categories into a pre-given reality, but also transforms that pre-given reality." While being treated as an object, the worker through his labor transcends and molds objective conditions; but this rift cannot endure: "Revolution is necessitated by the need to be an openly transcendental subject, that is, really human." Several questions arise again in this context. Does the portrayal of revolutionary praxis as "transcendental" constitution and creativity not transform phenomenological Marxism into the kind of ambitious "voluntarism" which is elsewhere denounced as the "construct of alienated intellectuals"? If revolution, on the other hand, is seen as implementation of objective interests and a latent teleology, is the rule of evidence not subtly changed into a "correspondence" of practical outcome and life-world conditions (56)?

As in Paci's case, some of the accents of Piccone's outlook are revealed in his comments on other writers. Lukács is credited for his effort to overcome the positivist scientism which dominated Marxism at the turn of the century—although *History and Class-Consciousness* is criticized for resorting to a ready-made but irrelevant conceptual arsenal (57). One also finds a sympathetic appraisal of Gramsci's contributions, including his stress on proletarian praxis and on the subject-object nexus. Strong endorsement is given to the early writings of Tran Duc Thao, especially his attempt to reformulate the structure-superstructure relation in terms of a dialectic of essence and appearance. Largely for the same reason, Kosík's *Dialectic of the Concrete* is singled out as "the high point" of the Marxist reawakening in Eastern Europe and as representing "a phenomenological Marxism of a quality unreached since Marx and Lukács' early work." By contrast, comments on Marcuse and the French phenomenologists tend to be much less favorable—a fact that may be connected with Piconne's somewhat summary dismissal of existentialism as a form of bourgeois decadence and escapism. Marcuse's Heideggerian Marxism is attacked for being a haphazard undertaking and, above all, for not penetrating sufficiently to Husserl's transcendental subjectivity; beset by "insuperable intrinsic difficulties," his "forced synthesis" of phenomenology and Marxism was "bound to fail from the very beginning." Sartre's work is dismissed as unreliable—but mainly for political rather than theoretical reasons, especially his "long history of flirting with the French Communist Party." Merleau-Ponty receives the least favorable treatment. In contrast to Marcuse's "forced" merger, his "philosophy of ambiguity" according to the author was a piecemeal amalgam which was "neither an exclusively phenomenological nor an exclusively Marxist perspective, but a phenomenology that paved the way for structuralism and a tamed Marxism that gave way to social democracy" (58).

Particularly relevant for present purposes are Piccone's observations on some key sociological theorists. In discussing Husserl's account of the life-world, he takes Alfred Schutz to task for inappropriately identifying this domain with the mundane or "commonsense" world and for bypassing the transcendental reduction. Such a treatment, he notes, "ends up by occluding precisely that crucial dialectic which makes the notion fruitful and relevant. The *Lebenswelt* does include the empirical and the common-sense world, but it also encompasses much more." Although ordinarily one may take features of the life-world for granted, "the *Lebenswelt* is also the domain in which concepts are invented and historical projects are formulated." Although it may be true that "most experience is of the mundane type," the "crucial point" is that "this mundane experience is parasitic on the original constitutive experience" (59). Even more severe strictures are leveled at Georges Gurvitch for his attempt to introduce a "dialectical realism" or "dialectical hyperempiricism" into sociology. By expelling reflection and intentionality, Piccone notes, Gurvitch's attempt shipwrecks on the "rocks of empiricism" and cannot "transcend the reified structure of the given, thus failing the acid-test of any meaningful dialectic." While the dialectic, properly understood, "draws its strength and dynamism from its ability to deal with teleology," which is "introduced by the omnipresence of subjectivity," the suppression of teleology in the name of realism "amounts to the attainment of a spurious objectivity which is scientifically trivial and socially useless." Rejecting "all a priori principles," the "empiricist dialectic" focuses "on the given in its phenomenal and reified form," with the result that "no radical change is either conceivable or required" (60).

The second example is John O'Neill, a sociologist and social theorist primarily (but not exclusively) known as a translator and interpreter of Merleau-Ponty (61). Apart from their impressive stylistic flavor, O'Neill's writings are marked by their sensitivity for the nuances and intricate texture of concrete experience—and by a certain weariness with sudden ruptures and transcendental vistas. These qualities—and perhaps limitations—are clearly evident in a recently published collection of his essays entitled *Sociology as a Skin Trade*. As the author notes in his introductory remarks, his "thinking represents a blend of Marxism with phenomenological concerns about language, embodiment, and intersubjectivity"; while his understanding of Marxism is indebted to recent French

exegesis, including Jean Hyppolite, in phenomenology "the principal influences have been Maurice Merleau-Ponty and Alfred Schutz." There
are many meeting points between his outlook and preceding discussions.
Together with Piccone (and Paci), O'Neill laments and denounces scientific objectivism and the sway of technology. Many of his essays, he states
in the opening section, seek to question "the restrictive code of objectivist
science" and to demonstrate that "the basic norm of liberal capitalism is
contained in the pattern of scientific and technological rationality which
legitimates a corporate agenda of the over-privatization of all social resources, including individual knowledge and conduct." To a considerable
extent, the interpretation of sociology as a "skin trade" is a reaction
against the discipline's excessive concern with "scientism, value-neutralism
and professional sociologism." In its scramble to gain professional status,
"sociology has uncritically assumed all the trappings of science," lodging
itself "in the bureaucratic organizations which are the institutional expression of the process of rationalization that has made the fortune of modern
science and technology." In contrast to this sterilized self-enclosure, the
author stresses the need of working with people and sharing their experiences: "Working with people creates a bewildering variety of practices
which I shall call skin trades. . . . In my view sociology is a symbiotic
science. Its promise is to give back to the people what it takes from
them" (62).

 O'Neill's criticism of scientific objectivism extends also to a positivist
conception of Marxism—a conception which, in part, can be traced
back to Marx himself. In his later writings, O'Neill notes, Marx "allowed
the theory of historical materialism to harden into the form of a theory of
economic, perhaps technological epiphenomenalism," thus giving it the
cast of "an alienated (estranged) ideology of which he himself had been
an early critic." Together with Piccone, he also favors a reexamination of
Marxian concepts in the light of contemporary experience; for the "forms
of power arising from the industrial and political system and their interrelations with the social class and stratification patterns of a given society"
are matters for "empirical not logical" determination. In opposition to an
objectified perspective, O'Neill stresses the human thrust of Marxist
thought. Genuine Marxism, he contends, is neither a simple materialism
nor idealism, and certainly not based on a correspondence theory of
knowledge but rather an expression of practical concerns. At least in his
early writings, Marx "rejected classical objectivist epistemology and
sketched a phenomenology of a world-view based upon the creativeness
of authentic personality"; this position, according to the author, is "the
only positive path to the formation of a nonestranged world-view, in
which the cultural world is considered a human project and human existence as an *Ecstasis*, as Heidegger, for example, has considered it." The

stress on human purpose, to be sure, does not imply a leap into spiritualism. Like Paci, O'Neill insists on the bodily dimension of human experience—although his arguments hardly dispel the riddles surrounding the notion of embodiment. Actually, the focus on skin trades also reflects a preoccupation with the bodily aspects of human contacts, with the operation of social life conceived as a "body-politic" (63).

Affinities and convergences of this type, however, do not entirely efface significant—perhaps more weighty—differences of accent. Such differences emerge already from the choice of mentors and the tone of citations. O'Neill's sympathies for Merleau-Ponty and Schutz have already been mentioned. At one point, he even admits, in regard to phenomenology, an "underlying attachment to Hegel rather than Husserl"—a confession which is amply supported by his frequent reliance on the *Phenomenology of Mind* in many portions of the study (64). As a previously quoted passage indicates, his attitude toward Heidegger tends to be favorable, if reserved; generally speaking, his comments on existentialism, although fluctuating, never approximate Piccone's vehemence. In his concern with embodiment and especially with the "libidinal" qualities of social relations one readily detects the imprint of Marcuse's *Eros and Civilization*. By themselves inconclusive, these differences of intellectual parentage and affiliation are matched by divergences of substantive outlook. In a subtle manner, Hegel's influence is noticeable in O'Neill's conception of the dialectic which, by comparison with the Husserlian return to subjectivity, tends to accord a somewhat more prominent status to the "object-pole," viewing the world and society as a result of the interchange "between intentionality and an irreducible ontological difference"; for, "if consciousness did not encounter the resistance of things and others, it could only know things perceptually and others by analogy and it would have no organic or social life." This view of the dialectic goes hand in hand with a more ready acceptance of objectification or externalization —as distinguished from alienation or estrangement—as a process indispensable for the manifestation of human purpose. "The process of externalization," he writes, "is the natural expression of the kind of being man is. Marx does not lament the external world, for it is the precondition of all human effort, the means to human expression." While from the perspective of Hegel and Marx, alienation or estrangement occurs only when social institutions "fail to achieve purposes which the participants intended," their position was "quite clearly that the necessity of objectifying man's natural capacities is not at all problematic" (65).

More important and telling than his view of objectification is O'Neill's stress on the crucial role of intersubjective relations. As he points out in his opening remarks, one of his central complaints against scientific objectivism is its contribution to "repressive communication," to the stifling of intersubjective contacts and understanding. Easily the most attractive and intriguing passages of the study reflect the endeavor to counter this plight. "The error in modern communication and information theory," he states, "is that it overlooks the rhetorical vehicle of speech, reading, and writing. It does this because in turn it lacks any conception of the intention to institute solidarity and a just social order in the relations between the partners to human speech." Human action, he adds, "is essentially the unfolding of a cultural space and its historical dimensions, so that in a strict sense we never accomplish anything except as a collective and historical project. For the individual action involves, therefore, a constant dialogue with others, a recovery of the past and the projection of breaks which are never entirely successful" (66). In his attack on repressive communication, O'Neill claims to find an ally not only in Hegel's *Phenomenology*, with its emphasis on the struggle for recognition, but also in Marx. Despite previous reservations concerning the character of Marx' later works, the concluding portion of the study presents communicative interaction and the concern for moral recognition as cornerstones of Marxist thought, overshadowing economic considerations (67). At this point, the author goes beyond Piccone in defending a broad interpretation of structure-superstructure relations in such a manner that the base refers generally to "human production which is *as such* rational and moral," while economics becomes "in fact a subculture within the total social culture." From this vantage point, material needs and the instrumental satisfaction of needs appear as a relatively subordinate aspect within the overall cultural matrix. By the same token, social life and development are no longer rigidly guided by economic class position or other structural factors, as alleged by a crude Marxism or a narrow sociology of knowledge. Such a claim, the author affirms, has in practice "brutalized political awareness," instead of making "for a moderation of political argument" (68).

The preceding passages are indicative of the nondoctrinaire thrust of the essays; but the author is more explicit in other contexts. In discussing the process of objectification, O'Neill describes "sociological anarchism" as "the dangerous possibility which derives from understanding alienation as a phenomenon resulting purely and simply from the institutional organization (externalization) of human behavior." At another point he defends intersubjective discourse against "certain highly subjectivist and solipsistic postures as well as political ideologies which invade classrooms and conferences and threaten to turn the modern mind into an armed camp—a result which, as Camus has remarked, would separate us from the Greeks." In reviewing Gouldner's proposal for a "reflexive sociology," O'Neill finds the formulation overly ambitious, "a quest for transcendence rejecting the conventional sociological celebration, embracing action and responsibility." For his own part, he asserts, "there can never be any question of the transcendence of sociology: it is given with my relation to the world and others around me without flight beyond this touch or talk. Socially, our universals lie between heaven and earth, in the toss of the clown, not on the tightrope of pompous metaphysical generalities but in the face-evident relations between myself, others, and the world around me." The social life-world, in his view, is anything but a chaos or a restless adventure. Rather, "in the ordinary course of life we take others at face-value and expect to be sustained" in the same manner: "There is a commonsense experience of the world and society as that which precedes us and survives us in which the simple sense of tradition and posterity is cultivated." The essay on Gouldner carefully shields contemporary ethnomethodology against sociological perspectives which depict concrete reality as a flimsy veil of appearances masking a realm of freedom and unlimited possibilities. "The possibilitarian," he notes, "is potentially a crackbrain, a dreamer, a fool, and a god who like Musil's man without qualities risks the possibilities of reality in the reality of possibility. But we cannot be above society or outside of it *and* part of it by means of a simple schizophrenic copulation or momentary inspiration" (69).

Probably, the author's intent is best revealed in his attempt to formulate an alternative version of reflexive or critical sociology. In contrast to Gouldner's "defiantly romantic" posture, O'Neill stresses the need for a "limited reflexivity" and for a more careful attention to social institutions. "Social science knowledge," he writes, "needs to be grounded in a limited but authentic reflexivity through which it recognizes its ties to individual values and community interests, notwithstanding its attempts to avoid bias and ideology." To accomplish this aim, reflection must be seen not only as embedded in social life but as itself endowed with an institutional dimension. By viewing "reflexivity as institution rather than as transcendental constitution," we gain a vantage point which, "instead of resting upon a transcendental subjectivity, is given in a field of presence and coexistence which situates reflexivity and truth as sedimentation and search." Far from being an *a priori* basis, reflexivity from this perspective appears as "a task which we take up in order to achieve self-improvisation, as well as the acquisition of a tradition or style of thought which is the recovery of original auspices opened in the past." The notion of "critique" which emerges from these considerations is "one which is grounded in a contextual environment which lies open horizontally to the corpus of social science knowledge rather than through any transcendental reflection." In contrast to Husserl and much of past philosophy, O'Neill maintains that "universality and truth" are not "an intrinsic property of the idea," but rather "an acquisition continuously established and reestablished in a community and tradition of knowledge called for and responded to by individuals in specific historical situations." As a corollary, the targets of human awareness are not abstractions, but "cultural objects"—"the vestiges of embodied beings" who "have opened up for us the hearth of culture and institutions which it is our first duty to tender." The critical act, in any case, implies a "declaration of membership in a continuing philosophical, literary, or scientific community"; the severance of these ties "would be the consequence of an absolute knowledge and ultimate nihilism." So understood, criticism is "close to Camus' conception of rebellion and order under the sun. Criticism reflects an aspiration to order under the auspices of the things that are present and of our fellow men, under a limit which is reflexively the recognition of solidarity and a rule of memory as an antidote to revolutionary absurdity" (70).

Although impressive as a corrective to militancy, O'Neill's antidote unfortunately is not free of hazards and questionable side-effects. While shunning the temptation of apodicticity, his argument—at points—risks muffling or compressing critical discourse from the opposite direction. The appeal to a "cosmic order," for example, hardly encourages a clarification of practical standards of conduct in relation to contemplation. More important, the stress on commonsense opinion occasionally tends to submerge knowledge entirely in social and historical contingency. Human speech or discourse, he notes at one point, "has no absolute goal of rational clarification, of disbelief, and rejection of prejudice," but "seeks just as well acceptance, or the understanding of what was already our belief, our native prejudice. This is the circle of language in which we dwell—the hermeneutic circle—which is not broken even when all come to understand our motives, our past experience." Although language, in Heidegger's terms, may be the "house" of man, it is not simply a dark cell, but endowed with luminous transparency. Human understanding, it seems to me, is not merely an indifferent mélange of knowledge and ignorance, a conglomeration of "clarification" and "prejudice"; nor does the "multiplicity" of meanings necessarily entail "a babel of tongues." Human cognition may be circular in the sense that an effort to understand always presupposes some prior understanding; but this does not mean that understanding cannot grow and that there is no hope of discriminating between levels of insight, between truth and falsehood. The "hermeneutic circle" in this sense is not so much a hopeless cycle as a porous spiral pointing beyond itself (71). By stressing the opacity of concrete experience O'Neill's perspective occasionally approximates (but does not merge with) Gurvitch's "empirical dialectic." When moving in this direction his presentation, in my view, is not entirely faithful to the legacy of Merleau-Ponty, who wrote: "What we propose here, and oppose to the search for the essence, is not the return to the immediate, the coincidence, the effective fusion with the existent" which "would nullify our questions and even reprehend our language" (72). Sociology, against this background, cannot entirely be identified with a "skin trade"—at least as long as color of skin is a powerful barrier in human discourse.

» » » » » « « « « «

The present paper has traversed a broad terrain: After presenting a condensed historical retrospective it delineated the contours of Paci's work, in order finally to compare his perspective with recent developments in sociology and social thought. However, the question animating these various explorations has been the same from the beginning: What is the character of phenomenology and of its relationship to Marxism? Now, at the end, we find that this question is far from resolved. Actually, we encountered a variety of responses and interpretations which do not seem readily compatible; but perhaps the situation is not hopeless. As the historical overview indicated, phenomenology during our century has tended to move from absolute evidence to a more subdued and critical posture open to intersubjective scrutiny and reciprocal correction; a similar development can be detected in neo-Marxist thought. These trends may furnish a direction signal for our question; they definitely provide a connecting link between the examined writers. Paci's study is replete with passages affirming the need for open-ended inquiry and the continued reexamination of convictions; however, this thrust tends to be blurred and sidetracked by his reliance on apodictic evidence. Both Piccone and O'Neill are committed to a critical Marxism and invoke the assistance of phenomenology in formulating this outlook; but both ultimately stop short of their goal, by retreating either into intuitive certainty or commonsense belief. In every instance, the incongruity seems to derive from the role assigned to phenomenology and from its somewhat indiscriminate fusion with Marxist thought. As it appears to me, there are hazards both in equating phenomenology with an apodictic "first philosophy" and in limiting it to conjecture without appeal. Perhaps, as long as it is tied to intuitive evidence, phenomenology cannot really be expected to be self-critical in a comprehensive and Socratic sense—although it can certainly be critical by insisting on the constant renewal of intuitive insight and by being aware of its own limitations.

Such a result need not be damaging to phenomenology, nor should it imply a disparagement of its significance for human thought. If knowledge and wisdom are to be neither an esoteric privilege nor a memorized formula, learning has to proceed on the basis of evidence gained "in the first person," of what makes sense to the individual involved. In an age weary of philosopher-kings, when mankind seems intent on coming of age, truth has to be the result of personal acquisition, of the slow transformation of habits and idiosyncracies—just as standards of conduct are not moral unless freely adopted. What the suggested view does entail, however, is the need to reconsider the relationship of phenomenology to Marxism or to any perspective laying claim to philosophical relevance and validity. The various formulations of this relationship encountered in the preceding pages do not appear to me entirely adequate or persuasive. Least acceptable seems to me the notion—one not actually asserted but merely intimated in some passages—that phenomenology and Marxism might complement each other by focusing respectively on subjective and objective dimensions. Such a division of labor would entirely prevent genuine contact; if spheres of concern were so rigidly segregated, no amount of surgery could transplant ingredients of one perspective into the other. Equally unconvincing, in my estimate, is Sartre's differentiation between "philosophy" and "ideology." If, as he insists, a primary task of existential phenomenology is to recover the critical impulse in Marxism, I do not see how this endeavor can be termed "ideological" while the label of "philosophy" is accorded to a stagnant orthodoxy. Another suggestion contained in Sartre's argument is that the distinction between phenomenology and Marxism might follow the demarcation line between singular experience and general propositions; however, as far as I can see, any type of knowledge involves some relationship of particulars and universals. A related view—suggested by Paci and elaborated more fully by Piccone—holds that phenomenology concentrates on a special problem, the function of the sciences, to which Marxism offers the more general solution. On these premises the relationship emerges as a territorial dispute whose settlement hinges on the accident of prior occupation. The situation is not improved if—as in the case of the early Marcuse—roles are reversed and existential phenomenology is depicted as general philosophy and Marxism as concrete application.

Perhaps the notion of a critical learning process can assist us at this point. What I wish to suggest for consideration is the possibility that phenomenology and Marxist theory might be related like "philology" and "philosophy," as these terms were used by Giambattista Vico. In his *New Science*, Vico delineates the respective preoccupations as follows: "Philosophy contemplates reason, whence comes knowledge of the true; philology observes that of which human choice is author, whence comes consciousness of the certain. In its second part this axiom comprises among philologians all the grammarians, historians, and critics who concern themselves with the study of the languages and deeds of people." This same axiom, he continues, "shows the partial failure both of the philosophers who did not test their reasoning by appeal to the authority of the philologians, and likewise of the philologians in not taking care to give their authority the sanction of truth by appeal to the reasoning of the philosophers." A resort to these terms should not seem far-fetched from a Marxist perspective. At least one leading Marxist in our century has invoked Vico's distinction as a vital key to the understanding of social life. "If the concept of structure is approached speculatively," Gramsci wrote, "it certainly becomes a 'hidden god.' Therefore, it should not be conceived speculatively but historically, as the whole fabric of social relations in which real men move and operate, as the whole of objective conditions which can and must be studied with the methods of 'philology' and not of speculation, as something 'certain' that may also be 'true' but which must first of all be studied in its 'certainty' in order to be studied as 'truth' " (73).

Actually, the combination of philology and philosophy may be not only compatible with but crucial and indispensable to Marxism. This would be so if we accept Merleau-Ponty's suggestion that Marxism is peculiarly lodged at the threshold of truth: "The mood of Lukács and, we believe, of Marxism as a whole is the conviction to be not in the possession but on the threshold of truth—a truth which is at the same time very close, being adumbrated by the entire past and the entire present, and in the infinite distance of a future waiting to be implemented" (74).

NOTES

1. Enzo Paci, *The Function of the Sciences and the Meaning of Man*, translated with introduction by James E. Hansen and Paul Piccone, Northwestern University Press, Evanston, Ill., 1972; originally published as *Funzione delle Scienze e Significato dell' Uomo*, Il Saggiatore, Milano, 1963.

2. In the words of one observer: "It has seldom been remarked that nearly all of Marx's theoretical works were called, or subtitled, 'A Critique. . . .' " See Dick Howard, "On Marx's Critical Theory," *Telos*, No. 6, Fall 1970, p. 224.

3. See *Karl Marx: Selected Writings in Sociology and Social Philosophy*, edited by T. B. Bottomore and Maximilien Rubel, McGraw-Hill, New York, 1964, pp. 74 (from *German Ideology*) and 232–233 (from *The Holy Family*). For an extensive review of the doctrinaire elements in Marxist thought compare Dietrich Böhler, *Metakritik der Marxschen Ideologiekritik*, Suhrkamp Verlag, Frankfurt-Main, 1971.

4. "Phenomenological philosophy," Richard M. Zaner writes, "is most accurately conceived as criticism now firmly established on its own sound foundations." Critical inquiry in this sense, he adds, "is the rigorous sci-

ence of presuppositions: of beginnings, origins, or foundations. It is this reflexive character of critical dialogue, grounded both in the things being examined and in the dialogic responsibility to others mutually engaged in the quest, which uniquely characterizes the discipline of criticism." See *The Way of Phenomenology: Criticism as a Philosophical Discipline*, Pegasus, New York, 1970, pp. xii, 207, and his paper in this book.

5. In the words of Dorian Cairns: "No opinion is to be accepted as philosophical knowledge unless it is seen to be adequately established by observation of what is seen as itself given 'in person.' Any belief seen to be incompatible with what is seen to be itself given is to be rejected." See "An Approach to Phenomenology," in Marvin Farber, ed., *Philosophical Essays in Memory of Edmund Husserl*, Greenwood Press, New York, 1968, p. 4.

6. Edmund Husserl, *The Crisis of European Sciences and Transcendental Phenomenology*, translated with introduction by David Carr, Northwestern University Press, Evanston, Ill., 1970, p. 283; also *Die Krisis der europäischen Wissenschaften und die transzendentale Phänomenologie*, edited by Walter Biemel, Martinus Nijhoff, The Hague, 1962, pp. 506–507.

7. Compare Andrew Arato, "Lukács' Path to Marxism," *Telos*, No. 7, Spring 1971, pp. 128–136; also G. H. R. Parkinson, "Introduction," in *Georg Lukács: The Man, His Work and His Ideas*, Vintage Books, New York, 1970, pp. 1–33. For Lukács' own account of his intellectual development see, e.g., "Mein Weg zu Marx" (1933) with "Postscriptum" (1957) in Georg Lukács, *Schriften zur Ideologie und Politik*, edited by Peter Ludz, Luchterhand, Neuwied, 1967, pp. 323–329, 646–657; and his Preface to *Geschichte und Klassenbewusstsein*, *Werke*, Vol. 2, Luchterhand, Neuwied, 1968, pp. 11–41.

8. This merger, Goldmann adds, implied both a progressive and regressive step on the part of Lukács: progressive in that he subjected Dilthey's intuition to rigorous phenomenological description; regressive in that he abandoned historical experience for Husserl's inspection of transtemporal essence. See "Zu Georg Lukács: Die Theorie des Romans," in Lucien Goldmann, *Dialektische Untersuchungen*, Luchterhand, Neuwied, 1966, pp. 287–289.

9. See "Gibt es eine marxistische Soziologie?," *ibid.*, p. 229.

10. "Assuming, though not conceding," he writes, "that recent research had clearly proved as substantively incorrect each and every individual assertion of Marx, a serious 'orthodox' Marxist could acknowledge all these new findings without hesitation and reject all of Marx's particular theses —without having to abandon for a moment his Marxist orthodoxy. Orthodox Marxism, thus, does not mean the blind acceptance of the results of Marx's inquiry, nor a 'belief' in this or that thesis, nor the interpretation of a 'holy' text. Orthodoxy in regard to Marxism refers exclusively to *method*." See Lukács, *Geschichte und Klassenbewusstsein*, *op. cit.*, p. 171.

11. The concrete political consequences of the above defects are noted in these comments: "As soon as Lukács (following Marx) posits a *universal* class, an absolute class (the essence of society), he is in trouble in so far as he fails to ground this (ideal) class in the particular, concrete lives whose actual consciousness and intersubjective experiences, as well as praxis, (potentially) comprehend it. Once the carrier of proletarian true consciousness becomes the party, the danger becomes even greater; and when the party announces its monopoly on true class-consciousness, the dialectic of equivocation turns into its opposite, reification: the subject-object of history becomes the object of a false subject, the historical falsity of which was announced by each peasant murdered by Stalin in the name of socialist 'reason.' " See James Miller, "Marxism and Subjectivity: Remarks on Georg Lukács and Existential Phenomenology," *Telos*, No. 6, Fall 1970, pp. 179–180.

12. In both writings, Husserl is depicted as chiefly or exclusively concerned with "formal-logical" problems; however, his method is said to be entirely congruent with subsequent elaborations by other phenomenologists and existentialists (especially Scheler and Heidegger). See Georg Lukács, *Existentialisme ou Marxisme?*, Editions Nagel, Paris, 1948, pp. 57, 74–84; *Die Zerstörung der Vernunft*, 1st ed., 1954; 2nd ed., *Werke*, Vol. 9, Luchterhand, Neuwied, 1960, pp. 16, 378–379, 415–458, 722–723.

13. Georg Lukács, *Ontologie des gesellschaftlichen Seins*, *Werke*, Vols. 13–14, Luchterhand, Neuwied, 1973. To some extent, the treatise still corroborates Maurice Merleau-Ponty's judgment: "Lukács' story is that of a philosopher who believed it possible to encompass realism within the dialectic and the thing itself in the thought of the thing. The blade eventually wears through the sheath, and ultimately neither the philosopher nor the ruling power remains satisfied." See "Pravda," in *Die Abenteuer der Dialektik*, Suhrkamp, Frankfurt-Main, 1968, p. 88. (For a translation of the essay see *Telos*, No. 7, Spring 1971, pp. 112–121, at p. 121).

14. Mihály Vajda, "Marxism, Existentialism, Phenomenology: A Dialogue," *Telos*, No. 7, Spring 1971, pp. 3–29. The participants in the discussion are Louis, an orthodox Marxist-Leninist; Andras, a flexible Marxist close to Lukács' position but open to other perspectives; Pietro, a Husserlian phenomenologist; and Erich, a somewhat cynical and individualistic existentialist (strongly influenced by Heidegger). The dialogue is full of revealing exchanges and suggestive observations.

15. Gajo Petrović, *Marx in the Mid-Twentieth Century*, Anchor Books, Garden City, 1967, p. 17. Compare also Gajo Petrović, ed., *Revolutionäre Praxis: Yugoslavischer Marxismus der Gegenwart*, Rombach, Freiburg, 1969.

16. "Dialectic means critical thinking which aims to grasp 'the thing itself' and queries systematically how such grasping of reality is possible." See Karel Kosík, *Die Dialektik des Konkreten*, Suhrkamp, Frankfurt-Main, p. 15, and p. 16, note 5 (for a specific reference to Husserl's phenomenology).

Compare also "Introduction to Karel Kosík," *Telos*, No. 2, Fall 1968, pp. 19–20.

17. In Gramsci's words: "The concept of 'objective' in metaphysical materialism seems to mean an objectivity which exists even without man. . . . We know reality only in relation to man, and since man is historically evolving, knowledge and reality are a becoming; and even objectivity is a becoming." Antonio Gramsci, *Il Materialismo Storico e la Filosofia di Benedetto Croce*, Einaudi, Turin, 1948, pp. 142–143. Compare also Antonio Labriola, *Essays on the Materialist Conception of History*, translated by Charles H. Kerr, 1903; 2nd printing, Monthly Review Press, New York, 1966.

18. Compare on these points Andrea Calzolari, "Structure and Superstructure in Gramsci," *Telos*, No. 3, Spring 1969, pp. 33–42.

19. See Tran Duc Thao, "Marxisme et Phénoménologie," *La Revue internationale*, No. 2, 1946; also *Phénoménologie et Matérialisme dialectique*, Minh-Tân, Paris, 1951. For a review of these studies and some of his later writings compare Silvia Federici, "Viet Cong Philosophy: Tran Duc Thao," *Telos*, No. 6, Fall 1970, pp. 104–117; also Guido D. Neri, *Prassi e conoscenza*, Feltrinelli, Milan, 1966, pp. 149–163.

20. Jean-Paul Sartre, "Materialism and Revolution," in William Barret and Henry D. Aiken, eds., *Philosophy in the Twentieth Century*, Vol. 2, Random House, New York, 1962, pp. 387–429. The doctrinaire features were corroborated in the domain of practical politics by Sartre's strong endorsement at the time of the policies of the Communist Party.

21. See Jean-Paul Sartre, "Marxism and Existentialism," in *Search for a Method*, translated by Hazel E. Barnes, Alfred Knopf, New York, 1963, pp. 26–30. Sartre's formulation of an existentialist Marxism has given rise to a large bulk of both supportive and critical literature. Compare, e.g., Raymond Aron, *Marxism and the Existentialists*, Simon and Schuster, New York, 1970; George Novack, ed., *Existentialism versus Marxism: Conflicting Views on Humanism*, Delta Books, New York, 1966; Walter Odajnyk, *Marxism and Existentialism*, Anchor Books, Garden City, 1965; Arthur Lessing, "Marxist Existentialism," *Review of Metaphysics*, Vol. 20, 1967, pp. 461–482.

22. At another point he added: "This concrete thinking, which Marx calls 'critique' to distinguish it from speculative philosophy, is what others propound under the name of 'existential philosophy.'" See Maurice Merleau-Ponty, *Sense and Non-Sense*, translated by Hubert L. and Patricia A. Dreyfus, Northwestern University Press, Evanston, Ill., 1964, pp. 72, 79–81, 133. Compare also his critical comments on Communist policies ("For the Sake of Truth," pp. 153–171); and his differentiation between Husserl's "oldest formulas: the philosophy of essences, philosophy as a strict or absolute science, consciousness as a transcendental and constituting activity" and some more recent accents: "the point of departure as a 'dialectical situation,' philosophy as 'infinite mediation or dialogue'" (pp. 134–135).

23. Maurice Merleau-Ponty, *Die Abenteuer der Dialektik, op. cit.*, pp. 11, 38, 70–71, 249, 273, 279–280. For the relationship between philosophy and politics compare also his comments written in 1960: "One thing that is certain at the outset is that there has been a political mania among philosophers which has not produced good politics or good philosophy. . . . Instead of combining their virtues, philosophy and politics exchanged their vices: practice became tricky and thought superstitious." See Introduction to *Signs*, translated by Richard C. McCleary, Northwestern University Press, Evanston, Ill., 1964, p. 6.

24. Maurice Merleau-Ponty, *The Visible and the Invisible*, edited by Claude Lefort, translated by Alphonso Lingis, Northwestern University Press, Evanston, Ill., 1968, p. 103.

25. Herbert Marcuse, "Contributions to a Phenomenology of Historical Materialism," *Telos*, No. 4, Fall 1969, pp. 5–11, 14–16, 21–22, 26, 29–30, 33. (The essay appeared first under the title "Beiträge zu einer Phänomenologie des historischen Materialismus" in *Philosophische Hefte*, No. 1, July 1928, pp. 45–68.) While stressing the validity of universal historical principles, Marcuse acknowledged the "ambiguity" of historical details due to the "multiplicity of meanings" inherent in concrete contexts. For this concession he is taken to task by Mitchell Franklin in "The Irony of the Beautiful Soul of Marcuse," *Telos*, No. 6, Fall 1970, pp. 3–35. For a review of "Contributions" together with related writings of the early Marcuse see Alfred Schmidt, "Existential-Ontologie und historischer Materialismus bei Herbert Marcuse," in Jürgen Habermas, ed., *Antworten auf Herbert Marcuse*, Suhrkamp, Frankfurt-Main, 1968, pp. 17–49.

26. Theodor W. Adorno, *Zur Metakritik der Erkenntnistheorie*, Kohlhammer, Stuttgart, 1956; *Jargon der Eigentlichkeit*, Suhrkamp, Frankfurt-Main, 1964. For later references of Marcuse to phenomenology compare, e.g., "The Concept of Essence" (1936) in *Negations: Essays in Critical Theory*, Beacon Press, Boston, 1969, pp. 43–87 (where he criticized the phenomenological inspection of essences as purely receptive and contemplative, but without abandoning the apodictic thrust); also *One-Dimensional Man*, Beacon Press, Boston, 1964, pp. 162–166; and "On Science and Phenomenology," in Robert S. Cohen and Marx W. Wartofsky, eds., *Boston Studies in the Philosophy of Science*, Vol. 2, Humanities Press, New York, 1965, pp. 279–290.

27. Jürgen Habermas, *Theorie und Praxis*, Luchterhand, Neuwied, 1963, pp. 299–306, 329–335; "Erkenntnis und Interesse" (1965), in *Technik und Wissenschaft als "Ideologie"*, Suhrkamp, Frankfurt-Main, 1968, pp. 146–168. For a critique of phenomenological applications in social science (Alfred Schutz, Aaron Cicourel, Harold Garfinkel, Erving Goffman) see "Zur Logik der Sozialwissenschaften" (1967), in *Zur Logik der Sozialwissenschaften; Materialien*, Suhrkamp, Frankfurt-Main, 1970, pp. 188–220.

28. See Jürgen Habermas, *Erkenntnis und Interesse*, Suhrkamp, Frankfurt-

Main, 1968, pp. 239–244; translated under the title *Knowledge and Human Interests* by Jeremy J. Shapiro, Beacon Press, Boston, 1971, pp. 194–198; also Einleitung to *Theorie und Praxis*, 4th rev. ed., Suhrkamp, Frankfurt-Main, 1971, pp. 9–47; and "Vorbereitende Bemerkungen zu einer Theorie der kommunikativen Kompetenz," in Jürgen Habermas and Niklas Luhmann, *Theorie der Gesellschaft oder Sozialtechnologie — Was leistet die Systemforschung?*, Suhrkamp, Frankfurt-Main, 1971, pp. 101–141.

29. A professor of philosophy at the University of Milan, Paci is the leading member of a circle of "Left Husserlians" or phenomenological Marxists in Italy. Among his other works compare *Tempo e Relazione*, Taylor, Turin, 1954; *Dall' Esistenzialismo al Relazionismo*, G. d'Anna, Messina-Florence, 1957; *Tempo e Verità nella Fenomenologia di Husserl*, Laterza, Bari, 1961. For a perspective similar to his see Pier Aldo Rovatti, "A Phenomenological Analysis of Marxism: The Return to the Subject and to the Dialectic of the Totality," *Telos*, No. 5, Spring 1970, pp. 160–173.

30. At another point Paci observes: "Essentially, since truth as the meaningful direction of being can never be possessed, intentionality is infinite and its goal unreachable. The goal has always been, is, and always will be present as a demand in the world; but it is not the world. It is the meaning of truth that is inexhaustible in the world. The inexhaustible demand is such that the movement is perennial and the becoming immortal." See *Function of the Sciences, op. cit.*, pp. 59–60, 71, 78, 202–203, 251.

31. *Ibid.*, pp. 81, 187, 230.

32. *Ibid.*, pp. 318, 345, 443. Compare also the statement (p. 360): "It is certainly not technological and scientific success that differentiates socialism from neo-capitalism. If the problem is only practical and technological, and praxis itself is reduced to technology in both the socialist and the capitalist camp, it becomes increasingly difficult to distinguish the neo-capitalism that proclaims the abundance of goods as its goal from the empirico-pragmatic Marxism which merely seeks to replicate the same abundance."

33. "In the phenomenological sense," Paci adds, "beginning from the subject means beginning from that nucleus of truth which, although minimal, the subject contains precisely because he is a subject who departs from the evidence of what he directly experiences in the first person." Turning to Marxism he notes: "By returning to the subject and his operations, I can discover that appearances are abstractions that have become real and have transformed workers into abstractions, while actually the worker is the concrete man. . . . Therefore, the original concreteness from which Marx in fact departs, is the subject." See *ibid.*, pp. 6, 240, 340, 346, 352, 415.

34. The arbitrary character of the reliance on "subjectivity" can be gleaned from the following statement: "The ego as a man— as a real man of

flesh and blood who contains the world and yet constitutes it, and who contains the past and yet founds it, the individual ego born from intersubjectivity and yet constitutive of intersubjectivity—this ego is the real precategorial foundation of phenomenology." The same impression can be gained from the critique of the dualism between objective and subjective reality as a "construction" which phenomenology should overcome. See *ibid.*, pp. 129, 221, 235, 262, 284, 347.

35. *Ibid.*, pp. 66–67, 172, 216, 295, 297, 352.

36. Compare also these statements: "The true being of the world is its progressive self-revelation as truth, as phenomenon. Phenomenology discovers that *the world has being insofar as it has a meaning*, to the extent that the truth inhering in it is discovered and becomes the aim and intentional meaning of human life. . . . Since being is meaning, the being of the world is constituted in subjectivity. Transcendental consciousness (subjectivity), as the being of the world that is constituted in consciousness, is not the acceptance of the pregiven being (which is not true being). Rather it is the active constitution of meaning: forming subjectivity." See *ibid.*, pp. 63–64, 68–69, 131, 353.

37. *Ibid.*, pp. 35, 85, 91–93, 96, 253, 334–336.

38. If this is so, he adds, then "inert matter is *subjective* in its own way. Materialism is not a substantialism extraneous to the subject: I am the world, the whole world." For a more subdued and plausible formulation compare his comment that, in Marxism, "matter and structure are vindicated in order to negate the dualism imposed by bourgeois society which divides the *soul* from the *body*, the *res cogitans* from the *res extensa*, just as the feudal world reduced the serf to pure *res extensa*, reserving the soul to the *otium* of the lord. The aim of Marxist materialism is to vindicate the whole man, the concrete monad, or simply, *man*, if we do not thereby reduce him naturalistically, as Feuerbach does." See *ibid.*, pp. 132, 161, 172, 175, 218–219, 294–295, 398.

39. Easily one of the most puzzling comments of the study reads: "Therefore, in terms of a coherent Marxism, the dialectic of nature must be non-naturalistic and it must not be a dialectic of history." See *ibid.*, pp. 72, 106, 279, 290–291, 299, 301, 318, 336, 367, 444.

40. "The problems of Hegelianism and the Hegelian Left," he notes at another point, "live their hidden and unrecognized life within the turbulent elaboration of Husserlian phenomenology." *Ibid.*, pp. 248, 281–283. Compare also his essay, "Anthropology, Dialectics, and Phenomenology in Hegel," *Radical America*, Vol. 4, September-October, 1971, pp. 33–53.

41. "To be so, in flesh and blood," he notes, "is to be transcendental, like all other egos. . . . Thus, it is clear that when I speak of the transcendental ego in the Husserlian sense I am speaking of my singularity in the first person." He also acknowledges the Fichtean overtones of this view: "Fichte's individual ego contains transcendental self-consciousness." Paci, *Function of the Sciences, op. cit.*, pp. 21, 34, 93–95, 100, 140.

42. See Merleau-Ponty, *Signs, op. cit.,* p. 33; Paci, *Function of the Sciences, op. cit.,* pp. 6, 8, 10. Compare also Paci's statement (p. 435): "Capital is the abstract first person who acts as if he were concrete against man's authentic and unmasked experience of himself, others, and the world in the first person."

43. *Ibid.,* pp. 6–7, 28, 44. The above, it is true, should be compared with the statement: "This does not mean that the final meaning is there, or that it is innate in man, and that, as such, it tries to express itself as much as possible" (p. 269).

44. *Ibid.,* p. 373. As Goldmann indicates, the concept of an immanent, evolutionary teleology was strongly cherished both by Social Darwinists and Darwinian Marxists; Goldmann, *Dialektische Untersuchungen, op. cit.,* p. 219. Apart from the vision of a scientific history, Merleau-Ponty points to the opposite alternative of permanent unrest, deriving from the incongruence between internal impulse and external conditions; see Merleau-Ponty, *Abenteuer der Dialektik, op. cit.,* p. 267.

45. "What is reasserted," he adds elsewhere, "is the fact that the species and mankind's *telos* lives in the individual. Furthermore the individual can negate the negation of the life of the species through revolutionary praxis." Paci's statements on these issues, it is true, are by no means unequivocal. Thus, in regard to concrete political involvement he writes at one point: "Given all these modalities, my actions can very well result in something I did not want, or at any rate, result in something very different from what I intended. Here we rediscover the theme of ambiguity." On class struggle through dialectical negation he comments: "How this inversion is going to take place cannot be defined a priori, nor can it be left to an abstract revolutionary will or to a revolution for the sake of revolution. Furthermore, the model of one inversion cannot be applied to another situation, except for the gravest situations which are common to all men." See *ibid.,* pp. 36–37, 264, 271, 296, 327, 330, 397, 438; also pp. 182, 289–290, 353–355 (on needs).

46. Compare also the statement: "The criterion of truth becomes the precategorial and subjective foundation which can clarify in the diverse philosophies the way in which the foundation has been pursued and forgotten, ignored and prepared, investigated or occluded, and negated or distorted in theoretical or intellectualistic constructions." *Ibid.,* pp. 8, 53–54, 107–108, 238–239, 242, 321, 348.

47. As he adds: "Here, *science* has a *new* meaning. It is no longer the verification of an objectivity in itself. Rather, it is the consciousness of praxis, its intentional direction, the positive meaning of truth, and the effort of actualizing this meaning in the *epoché* of the mundane, i.e., in the *epoché* of a truth coinciding with the given." See *ibid.,* pp. 47, 52, 75, 282, 381, 445.

48. Compare, e.g., the statement: "The surveyor who uses idealized figures to measure the field that has now become an exact figure, or that has been

divided into exact figures, already exists in the *Lebenswelt* and in its spatio-temporal causal nexuses. These nexuses are given to him before the idealization as figures which are not yet exact but susceptible to idealization. The field is not exactly divided into perfect squares. By surveying and measuring its surfaces, I perform the operations that lead me to squares that 'correspond' to the field." See *ibid.*, 58–59. 96–98, 209, 417; and for comments on the correspondence theory, including Lenin's formulations, pp. 332–333.

49. Thus the previous quote referring to the "evidence of the will" is part of a comment on Husserl's statement (in *Krisis*, pp. 485–486): "Every purpose, in particular that which intentionally implies a multiplicity of mediations, requires a recurring consideration, a recurrence as a renewal." See Paci, *Function of the Sciences, op. cit.*, pp. 232–233, 235–238, 243–244, 264–265, 276–278.

50. For the comments on Marx see *ibid.*, pp. 371–372, 381, 407–409, 413–415; on Lukács pp. 331–333, 336–340; on Labriola and Gramsci pp. 305–316, 342; on Sartre pp. 297, 347–370; on Merleau-Ponty pp. 251–252, 283, 325–326, 328–329, 346.

51. Norman Birnbaum, *Toward a Critical Sociology*, Oxford University Press, New York, 1971, pp. 94–129, 234, 367–392; Alvin W. Gouldner, *The Coming Crisis of Western Sociology*, Basic Books, New York, 1970, pp. 157–163, 390, 481–512.

52. See, e.g., Georges Gurvitch, *Dialectique et sociologie*, Flammarion, Paris, 1962; *The Spectrum of Social Time*, Reidel, Dordrecht, 1964; also Phillip Bosserman, *Dialectical Sociology, An Analysis of the Sociology of Georges Gurvitch*, Sargent, Boston, 1968; Marcel Rioux, "Critical versus Aseptic Sociology," *Berkeley Journal of Sociology*, *15*, 1970, pp. 33–47.

53. See Paci, *Function of the Sciences, op. cit.*, pp. XIX–XXVII ("Translators' Introduction" by James E. Hansen and Paul Piccone); also p. 454.

54. As he adds: "If oppression is first and foremost a function of sex, race, etc., and only after considerable Marxist theoretical mediation becomes a function of the proletarianization process produced by the bourgeois mode of production, then it does not make much sense to retain the old class analysis, which is mediated, but it becomes necessary to scrap the entire approach." See Paul Piccone, "Phenomenological Marxism," *Telos*, No. 9, Fall 1971, pp. 3–6, 23, 27, 29.

55. Compare also the statement: "Far from being a passive process, perception itself is a form of labor: the very process of perception exhibits the structure of labor. It involves the preconceptual apprehension of reality, the sorting out of concepts needed to abstract certain crucial features of that reality, and the conceptualizing of these features of reality deemed relevant, i.e., determined as essential in relation to some *telos* itself given to us as need in the *Lebenswelt*." *Ibid.*, pp. 6, 12–13, 15–17, 24–25, 30–31. For the relationship of consciousness and labor see also Paul Pic-

cone, "The Problem of Consciousness," *Telos*, No. 5, Spring 1970, pp. 178–187.

56. Piccone, "Phenomenological Marxism," *op. cit.*, pp. 19, 23–26. Similar arguments can be found in another article by Piccone entitled "Reading the Crisis," *Telos*, No. 8, Summer 1971, pp. 121–129. Regarding the proposal for a coalition of underprivileged groups—coupled, however, with the plea for a flexible strategy—compare also his "Students' Protest, Class-Structure, and Ideology," *Telos*, No. 3, Spring 1969, pp. 106–122.

57. "In reaction to the mechanistic Marxism of the Second International," he writes, Lukács "sought to dialectically articulate a dynamic Marxism free of the metaphysical shackles of scientism and positivism. He did this by vindicating the Hegelian heritage of Marxism and uncompromisingly approaching every problem in terms of totality. His whole effort, however, was fundamentally vitiated by objective idealism, since it did not deal with the concrete realities of the time but instead substituted for them a set of highly articulate categories lifted out *tout court* from Marx's works." See Piccone, "Phenomenological Marxism," *op. cit.*, p. 8; compare also his "Lukács' *History and Class-Consciousness* Half a Century Later," *Telos*, No. 4, Fall 1969, pp. 95–112.

58. Piccone, "Phenomenological Marxism," *op. cit.*, pp. 4, 10–11, 14–15. At one point (p. 12, n. 24) the essay suggests that the difference between Sartre and Husserl is one between an egocentric and an intersubjective outlook; but the intersubjective character is not fully explicated. In another context existentialism is described as "a pessimistic expression of cultural bankruptcy which tells the European petty bourgeois to accept his *Angst* as a state of being and which seeks to eternalize the bankruptcy as an unsurpassable, uneliminable metaphysical dimension"; see Piccone, "Reading the Crisis," *op. cit.*, p. 123. In regard to Marcuse compare also Paul Piccone and Alex Delfini, "Marcuse's Heideggerian Marxism," *Telos*, No. 6, Fall 1970, pp. 36–46.

59. Piccone, "Phenomenological Marxism," *op. cit.*, p. 25. The reference is to Alfred Schutz, *Collected Papers*, Vol. 1, edited by Maurice Natanson, Martinus Nijhoff, The Hague, 1962.

60. See Paul Piccone, "Dialectical Logic Today," *Telos*, No. 2, Fall 1968, pp. 45, 65–66.

61. Compare John O'Neill, *Perception, Expression, and History: The Social Phenomenology of Maurice Merleau-Ponty*, Northwestern University Press, Evanston, Ill., 1970; among his translations see Maurice Merleau-Ponty, *Themes from the Lectures at the Collège de France, 1952–1960*, Northwestern University Press, Evanston, Ill., 1970, and *Humanism and Terror: An Essay on the Communist Problem*, Beacon Press, Boston, 1969.

62. There are overtones of class antagonism in the focus on skin trades: "The vast symbiosis of social life is naturally represented as a body in which

the spiritual functions are relieved for prayer and thought through the excremental services of the lower orders. In this scheme of things, the skin trades have been traditionally low-caste, their services being required in order to keep the higher castes free from bodily impurities and thus holy." See John O'Neill, *Sociology as a Skin Trade, Essays Towards a Reflexive Sociology*, Harper & Row, New York, 1972, pp. xi, 5–8.

63. As he writes: "In calling sociology a skin trade I want to restore its symbiotic connections with the body-politic and to situate it in relation to the exchange of organic needs and the utopian celebration of libidinal community which surpasses all understanding." *Ibid.*, pp. 10, 116–117, 119, 120–121, 129.

64. "It is this Hegelian legacy," he observes, "which is the treasure of Marxist critical theory. I hold Hegel in this regard for the reason that it was he who took over Hobbes's vision of man's bodily organization and its competitive felicity and built its capacities of reason, fear, and speech into a covenant with the whole of humanity and not just a convenient article of peace in an essentially unstable social order." *Ibid.*, pp. 238, 261.

65. Contrary to the widespread allegation that Hegel collapsed objectification and alienation, O'Neill maintains that Hegel and Marx were in accord in the differentiation of the two processes; see *ibid.*, pp. 77, 118, 128–131, 156–159, 161, 168. For differences between Hegel and Marx compare pp. 114–115, 193–194.

66. What tends to be overlooked, he notes at another point, is "that the claim to truth is a call to the freedom of the other and is inseparable from its dialogic constitution. That is why we read and think and talk and argue—not endlessly but because of the inexhaustible depth and variety of human culture to which we are always latecomers." *Ibid.*, pp. xxi, 232, 234, 262.

67. On this basis, he criticizes Habermas for presenting communicative interaction as a supplementary dimension to instrumental labor—but without disclosing where and how Marx explicated the dimension sufficiently in both an epistemological and a practical sense. See *ibid.*, pp. 243, 247, 249, 259.

68. *Ibid.*, pp. 118, 160, 162, 226, 243.

69. More generally, he detects "a naive dogmatism underlying the liberal social science conception of understanding which still draws upon the rationalist tradition of Enlightenment unmasking. But there is nothing behind the face of a man who speaks, beyond what else he has to say or how he keeps his silences." In regard to ethnomethodology compare this comment: "So far from putting commonsense knowledge of social structures up for grabs, Garfinkel's experiments are intended to show that our mundane experience of the self and its definition of the situation is given to us through the same set of typifications, role-conceptions, and course-of-action patterns which are the convenience of anyone." See *ibid.*, pp. 132, 173–175, 217–219, 222, 236.

70. *Ibid.*, pp. 224, 226, 230–234.

71. O'Neill himself seems to suggest such a view when he writes that "there is no privileged standpoint from which either Marx himself or ourselves as interpreters could see or fail to see what he had in mind, except as the production of its sense within this same hermeneutic circle and the conjuncture of meaning and facticity which makes it impossible for us to foreclose upon its sense." *Ibid.*, pp. 236, 239, 254, 262. On the question to what extent hermeneutics is self-enclosed or self-sufficient compare Jürgen Habermas, "Der Universalitätsanspruch der Hermeneutik," in Karl-Otto Apel et al., *Hermeneutik und Ideologiekritik*, Suhrkamp, Frankfurt-Main, 1971, pp. 120–159; also Hans-Georg Gadamer, "Rhetorik, Hermeneutik und Ideologiekritik," *ibid.*, pp. 57–82.

72. *The Visible and the Invisible*, pp. 121–122. Compare also his *In Praise of Philosophy*, translated with preface by John Wild and James M. Edie, Northwestern University Press, Evanston, Ill., 1963, pp. 3–5, 58–64.

73. Giambattista Vico, *The New Science*, Book 1, Section 2, Axiom X, Anchor Books, Garden City, 1961, p. 21; Gramsci, *Il Materialismo Storico, op. cit.*, p. 191.

74. Merleau-Ponty, *Die Abenteuer der Dialektik, op. cit.*, p. 66.

INDEX

Abel, Theodore, 244n
Academy, 201; and good times, 201-202
Academic sociology, 26, 29
Accounts, 115-116
Acculturation, 260
Act, delinquent, 195-196; deviant, 164; and generalized other, 95; and interaction, 172-178; interpretation, 170; patterned, 12; and project of action, 172; reciprocal, 144
Action, by actor, 6-7; features of, 168, 172-173; intended, 171; in interaction, 159-161; interpretation, 230; and meaning, 3, 227, 230; rational, 80; recipe of, 38; and spontaneity, 196; understanding, 223
Actor, constitution of, 171-172; experience of, 14; features of, 163, 168-170, 171-172; model of, 163; perspective of, 6, 107, 116, 118, 160, 182n
Adams, R., 297n
Administrator, 240, 241
Adolescents, 81, 82, 84, 202
Adorno, Theodor, 317, 349n
Adult, 82, 83, 84
Affecting-the-other, 160, 161, 172-173, 177, 178, 179
Affluence, 81
Agee, J., 34
Aggression, 266
Aiken, Henry D., 348n
Alcohol, 207, 270; alcoholism, 191
Alienation, 40, 73, 84, 94, 98, 101, 310, 320, 321, 327, 339-340; unalienated, 84
Allen, Woody, 202
Allport, Floyd, 244n
Alston, W., 155n
Altercasting, 223
Alter ego, general thesis of, 37, 38, 52, 120
Alternation, 105n
Ambience, 213
America, 2, 77, 136; American society, 285; way of life, 76
American Sociological Association, 43, 47, 48
Angst, 120
Anomie, 78, 192, 202, 203, 214; and conformity, 192; and evil, 197; and good times, 197,

214; and individual, 101; and membership, 195; and mood, 197; resolution of, 192
Anomie theory of deviance, 188, 192-193; of Durkheim, 192-193; of Merton, 192-193
Anomic man, 197
Anomic suicide, 78
Anonymity, in formal organization, 226-229, 236-237
Anschauung, 145
Anthropologists, cultural, 58n, 75; radical, 58n
Anthropology, 102, 249; philosophical, 54, 103
Antinomies, neo-Kantian, 308; sociological, 91-103
Appearances, phenomenology of, 127, 139, 145-148
Approach, and courtship, 206-208
Apriories, of presentation, 102; of symbiosis, 98, 102; of typification, 102
Arato, Andrew, 346n
Argyris, Chris, 230, 246n
Aristotle, 30, 201
Arms race, 51
Aron, Raymond, 348n
Art, 51
Asimov, Isaac, 214n
Asleep, 53, 57n
Assumptions, bracketing of, 14-15; challenge to, 86n; commonsense, 11; cultural, 62; disturbance of, 175; explication of, 11; of everyday, 14, 89; in interaction, 175-176; taken for granted, 175; thematic, 73
Astrology, 83
Astronomy, 111, 112
Attitude, 5, 98, 209, 221
Attribution theory, 230
Auslegen, 33
Austin, John L., 130, 133, 134, 137, 138, 148
Authenticity, 119, 228
Authority, diagnostic interpretation of, 232-235, 238-241; relation, 224, 228; awareness, of body, 171; and courtship, 213; mutual, 172, 178, 182n; of other, 165, 172, 179

Background, features, 169; horizon, 143; knowledge, 169; understanding, 11

357